D0866204

Georgia Democrats, the Civil Rights Movement,
and the Shaping of the New South

UNIVERSITY PRESS OF FLORIDA

Florida A&M University, Tallahassee
Florida Atlantic University, Boca Raton
Florida Gulf Coast University, Ft. Myers
Florida International University, Miami
Florida State University, Tallahassee
New College of Florida, Sarasota
University of Central Florida, Orlando
University of Florida, Gainesville
University of North Florida, Jacksonville
University of South Florida, Tampa
University of West Florida, Pensacola

Georgia Democrats,

the Civil Rights Movement,

and the Shaping of

the New South

TIM S. R. BOYD

University Press of Florida

Gainesville · Tallahassee · Tampa · Boca Raton

Pensacola · Orlando · Miami · Jacksonville · Ft. Myers · Sarasota

Library of Congress Cataloging-in-Publication Data
Boyd, Tim S. R.
Georgia Democrats, the civil rights movement, and the shaping of the new south
/ Tim S. R. Boyd.
p. cm.
Includes bibliographical references and index.
ISBN 978-0-8130-3765-3 (alk. paper)
1. Georgia—Politics and government—1951– 2. Democratic Party (Ga.)—
History—20th century. 3. African Americans—Civil rights—Georgia—History—
20th century. 4. Civil rights movements—Georgia—History—20th century.
5. Georgia—Race relations—History—20th century. I. Title.
F291.2.B694   2012
975.8'043—dc23
2011037504

The University Press of Florida is the scholarly publishing agency for the State
University System of Florida, comprising Florida A&M University, Florida
Atlantic University, Florida Gulf Coast University, Florida International
University, Florida State University, New College of Florida, University of Central
Florida, University of Florida, University of North Florida, University of South
Florida, and University of West Florida.

University Press of Florida
15 Northwest 15th Street
Gainesville, FL 32611-2079
http://www.upf.com

To the members of "Team Delta" from March 2007—
for an unforgettable firsthand experience of the continuing triumphs
and traumas of life in the twenty-first-century South.

Contents

Figures

Abbreviations

ABC	American Broadcasting Corporation
ADA	Americans for Democratic Action
AFL, CIO, AFL-CIO	American Federation of Labor, Congress of Industrial Organizations (the two organizations merged in 1955)
ANVL	Atlanta Negro Voters League
DFC	Democrats for Callaway
DLC	Democratic Leadership Council
DNC	Democratic National Committee
GDF	Georgia Democratic Forum
GLWV	Georgia League of Women Voters
GOP	"Grand Old Party"/Republican Party
HOPE	Help Our Public Education
HUAC	House Un-American Activities Committee
IRS	Internal Revenue Service
KKK	Ku Klux Klan
MASE	Metropolitan Association for Segregated Education
MFDP	Mississippi Freedom Democratic Party
MFPE	Minimum Foundation for Public Education
NAACP	National Association for the Advancement of Colored People
NBC	National Broadcasting Corporation
SCLC	Southern Christian Leadership Conference
WIG	Write-In Georgia

Acknowledgments

This book would never have been started and could not have been completed had it not been for the generous financial support provided by Vanderbilt University and the Robert Penn Warren Center for the Humanities. The importance of this support, however, was secondary to that which I received from so many on Vanderbilt's faculty. In particular, I am grateful to Devin Fergus, for sound, cautionary, and helpful advice, as well as several lengthy and engrossing conversations about race, politics, and life in America. I also owe a sizeable debt to David Carlton for passing on to me his infectious love of the South and for constantly encouraging me to expand and develop this project in new directions. To Gary Gerstle, John Geer, and Tom Schwartz, I am thankful for all their input and guidance over the years of research—it was invaluable.

In the years I have spent revising and refining my research to put together this book, I have been fortunate enough to get expert and helpful criticisms and suggestions from several distinguished scholars. I would especially like to thank Matthew Lassiter at the University of Michigan and David Chappell at the University of Oklahoma for taking the time to read and comment on drafts of several of the chapters that follow. Their input has unquestionably strengthened this book, although of course, I alone am responsible for the remaining shortcomings.

I am furthermore grateful to all those who have provided me with assistance on my various research trips across the South over these past six years. In particular, I thank the staff at the Richard Russell Library in Athens, Georgia; Cliff Kuhn at Georgia State University in Atlanta; Allen Fisher at the Lyndon B. Johnson Library in Austin, Texas; and Mel Steely for his help and hospitality during my visit to the University of West Georgia in Carrollton. I am also deeply appreciative of the advice and suggestions given to me by Kevin Kruse at Princeton, who helped me locate a great deal of material and put me in touch with several of the above archivists and whose own work on southern and American political culture is a wonderful example of how history should be written. The editorial staff at the University Press of Florida—in particular Eli Bortz and Meredith Babb—have also been supportive, encouraging, and invaluable in helping this book come together. I could not have asked for more.

I also owe thanks to the many friends and colleagues who provided invaluable intellectual and emotional support ever since I arrived in Nashville and who have helped shape the arguments that follow. In particular, LeeAnn Reynolds, Pete Kuryla, Bob Hutton, Clare Austin, Debi Back, and Steven Miller have contributed immensely to the successful completion of this project, and I will always be grateful to them for everything they have done for me.

Finally, it is unlikely that I would have had the commitment necessary to even start this project were it not for the love of learning and intellectual curiosity that I have been fortunate enough to receive from my family. My interest in American history can be traced back to sitting down on Sunday evenings as an eleven-year-old to watch Ken Burns' documentary on the Civil War with my parents. My subsequent certification as a lifelong history nerd was confirmed by my delight when they gave me James McPherson's *Battle Cry of Freedom* as a Christmas present that same year. There is no question that they generated in me a passion for history that has yet to die down, and for that alone, I will forever be thankful.

Introduction

"Out of the Shadows"

To those who say that this civil rights program is an infringement on states' rights, I say this: that the time has arrived in America for the Democratic Party to get out of the shadows of states' rights and walk forthrightly into the bright sunshine of human rights.

Hubert Humphrey, Democratic mayor of Minneapolis, 1948

Given Lyndon Johnson's proclivities for seeing dark conspiracies all around him, one would expect his regular predictions of impending disaster to be treated with a certain amount of skepticism. For the most part, this is indeed how Johnson's utterances have been treated by historians. For example, few if any scholars believe that Robert Kennedy actually spent his every waking moment directing global events in such a way as to undermine the Johnson presidency, even if Johnson himself seemed regularly to believe this was the case. It is therefore somewhat surprising that Johnson's reported comment to an aide after signing the 1964 Civil Rights Act that "I think we [just] delivered the South to the Republican Party for your lifetime and mine" has become so widely accepted as the shrewd, if fatalistic, assessment of the impact of desegregation on southern politics.[1] As far as current conventional wisdom is concerned, Johnson's prediction of a solidly Republican South has been internalized to such a degree that it did not seem at all remarkable when 2004 Democratic presidential candidate John Kerry responded to an inquiry about why he was not campaigning in Dixie with the rhetorical question, "Why would a Democrat go South?"[2]

In the particular case of the Civil Rights Act, Johnson's penchant for seeing the worst-case scenario has most likely been excused because his comment serves as a neat, quotable summary of the dominant interpretation of post-1945 southern politics, which sees the contemporary South as having been primarily shaped by the white backlash to the civil rights movement. Ever since the 1968 election signaled the end of the

Democrats' dominance of national politics, this "white backlash narrative" has been the most frequently offered explanation for the partisan and ideological turnover that occurred in both the South and the nation.[3] In several of the best and most recent works on the South, the continuing centrality of this narrative remains evident. For example, Kevin Kruse's *White Flight*, a compelling account of white resistance to racial change in Atlanta, concludes that "the rise of southern Republicanism . . . was largely due to the white backlash against the [1964] Civil Rights Act."[4] Likewise, Jason Sokol, in his rich and detailed analysis of white southerners' reactions to civil rights, *There Goes My Everything*, also comes to the view that "as much as anything else, [the rise of southern Republicanism] was the legacy of the Civil Rights Act."[5]

The dominance of this "white backlash" interpretation has also manifested itself in discussions over how the civil rights movement impacted the Democratic Party. While scholars and political commentators may disagree over whether identifying itself with "black interests" through its support of civil rights legislation was a self-inflicted wound or a necessary and noble sacrifice for the Democratic Party to make, all emphasize the negative impact such a move had on the party's electoral fortunes, especially in the South. The largely unchallenged acceptance of this view was evident in discussions of the 2008 presidential election, even among well-informed Democratic strategists and sympathizers celebrating the more competitive showing by Barack Obama in the South. On ABC's *This Week with George Stephanopoulos*, Donna Brazile, senior Democratic strategist and former presidential campaign manager for Al Gore (and a southerner), cited Lyndon Johnson's quote about the Civil Rights Act as an explanation for why Democrats had to wait so long to be competitive again in the region.[6] The Democratic-leaning pollsters who ran the Web site fivethirtyeight.com—and whose accurate electoral projections throughout 2008 revealed their sophisticated understanding of voting trends—also attributed contemporary Democratic weakness in the South to the fact that "Democrats are still seen as the party that tried to let black people vote in the 60s, and that ruffled a lot of feathers."[7] Another highly regarded observer, NBC's chief White House correspondent Chuck Todd, wrote a state-by-state postelection analysis in which the Republicanism of various southern states was described "as a result of Democratic support for civil rights legislation."[8] As such, while Ronald Radosh may be somewhat more apocalyptic in his language than most, his assessment that "the civil rights movement launched the Democratic Party on a trajectory that ended in disaster" is really only a more strongly worded version of an otherwise generally accepted consensus.[9]

This perception that the Democratic Party collapsed in the South following its association with the civil rights movement has had far-reaching consequences for our view of the contemporary South in particular and modern American politics in general. The South has become tagged as a pathologically conservative region unable to transcend the burden of its racial divisions; as a result, the much-heralded "New South" that emerged after the end of Jim Crow did not result in a liberalization of southern politics as many had hoped. Instead, it represented little more than a politer version of the massive resistance of the White Citizens' Councils. This sense that the New South was a betrayal of the postwar potential for a liberal South is hinted at in the titles of several works on the 1940s and 1950s, such as Patricia Sullivan's *Days of Hope* and Pete Daniels' *Lost Revolutions*.[10] Glenn Feldman recently expressed this view in more explicit terms, when he charged the South with having failed to take advantage of its opportunity for a liberal political culture because of its compulsive addiction to a reactionary "politics of emotion."[11] Feldman argued that this form of politics allowed conservative Republicans to prey on people's racial and cultural fears in order to induce the southern white population into "unwittingly" supporting a self-defeating agenda of "economic conservatism."[12]

Given the nature and timing of the Republican dominance of late-twentieth-century American politics, it is easy to see why this composite view of a racially charged southern conservatism as the driving force behind the GOP's rise is so popular. Since Lyndon Johnson signed the landmark civil rights legislation of 1964 and 1965, Jimmy Carter is the only Democrat to have won a majority of southern electoral college votes in a presidential election. This was a dramatic turnaround indeed for a region that as recently as the 1940s had been considered "solidly Democratic."[13] In addition, an extensive cast of southerners, including Strom Thurmond, Jesse Helms, David Duke, Newt Gingrich, and Trent Lott, have risen to prominence in the Republican Party on the back of political rhetoric that has frequently relied on thinly veiled appeals to white racial fears. When one further considers the critical role of these southern Republicans in their party's majorities in Congress from 1995 to 2007, and the dependence of President George W. Bush on white southern support for his electoral victories in 2000 and 2004, the white backlash narrative offers itself as a highly tempting explanatory framework for the contemporary partisan divide.

Despite its appeal, however, the white backlash narrative provides an incomplete and frequently inaccurate account of the origins and nature of modern southern politics. My intention in this book is to provide an alternative narrative that posits a different framework for understanding the political culture of the New South. This alternative narrative presents the encounter between southern Democrats and the civil rights movement as a more complex and ambiguous dynamic than the white backlash narrative suggests. In particular, rather than seeing this encounter as the cause of a political catastrophe for the southern Democrats, it should instead be seen as the driving force behind the creation of a New South that was largely shaped by southern Democrats—specifically, by those Democrats who supported racial accommodation and acceptance of desegregation, and who had spent thirty years challenging and eventually supplanting the "Solid South" Democratic leadership that was committed to maintaining segregation and disfranchisement.[14] It was these "New South Democrats," rather than Republicans riding the white backlash, who were most significant in determining the political landscape of the South in the post–Jim Crow era.

Equally, the New South that emerged in the 1970s, while far from being a liberal utopia, was not as shallow or reactionary a creation as some of its critics have suggested.[15] The dominant views on racial politics and the role of government espoused by New South Democrats represented a sharp and decidedly progressive shift from the attitudes in the region prior to the 1960s.[16] While politics during the Solid South was based on keeping race in the forefront of people's consciousness, the dominant approach in the New South was to avoid discussing racially divisive issues as much as possible. As for the role of government, while previous generations of southern politicians had sought to keep the state's intervention in socioeconomic matters to a minimum, New South Democrats (and some Republicans) preferred to use government as a means of generating and regulating economic growth. The once pervasive southern reluctance to spend government money on social programs—particularly education—was also sharply diminished.

To argue that the actual nature of the New South was more progressive than it is sometimes given credit for is not to claim that it was actually a misunderstood triumph of southern liberalism. Rather, it is to echo Matthew Lassiter's recent argument about the suburban culture of the Sun Belt; namely, that the New South represented a "middle path" between the liberalism some may have hoped for and the "caste framework" of politics during the Jim Crow era.[17] Stressing the importance of progressive southern Democrats in the creation of the New South is in fact extending Lassiter's framework for the development of southern suburbs to the partisan sphere of southern politics.

The critical role played by Democrats in shaping the New South is in turn a sign that reports of the party's demise in the South at the hands of the white backlash have been greatly exaggerated. In this regard, I am building on the work of several political scientists, most notably Byron Shafer and Richard Johnston, who have already significantly challenged the white backlash explanation for southern partisan change using extensive quantitative analysis. In doing so, they have also highlighted the impact the political changes caused by the civil rights movement had on continued Democratic *strength* in the New South, pointedly noting that this strength is evident in the hard data of electoral returns, even if it does not coincide with the preference of observers to focus on "headline events" out of a desire for more dramatic explanations of partisan change.[18]

Furthermore, in order to understand the way in which southern Democrats were able to adjust to the political challenge of the civil rights movement, the focus must be on developments within the party at the state and local levels. This is necessary in order to fully understand both the gradual, evolutionary nature of the emergence of New South politics as well as the centrality of subnational politics for the transition of southern Democrats from defenders of Jim Crow to spokespersons for a desegregated racial order. Laying out the narrative in this way is in contrast to much of the existing literature on the history of the Democratic Party, which has generally focused either on southern Democrats *after* the 1960s, implying a sharp break with what came before, or has prioritized the actions of the *national* party leadership as decisive in the decision to reach an accommodation with the civil rights movement.[19] Works dealing with postwar southern Democrats at the state and local levels have been few and far between; the most notable exception is Kari Frederickson's *The Dixiecrat Revolt*, which provides a thorough overview of Democratic politics in the southern states during the 1940s.[20]

Lastly, the New South Democrats also played a critical role in shaping national politics through their influence on two central developments in the evolution of the national Democratic Party in the postwar years. The first was the ending of the sectional rift over race that simmered, and occasionally erupted, within the party for thirty years after World War II. Central to this intraparty reconciliation was the convergence of the racial views espoused by New South Democrats and those espoused by the majority of Democrats in the national party. While this convergence was uncoordinated, it was not coincidental. After all, it was not just southern liberals who had to decide how to respond to the pressure for racial change after 1945: it was a decision facing liberals everywhere. It is therefore not surprising that the responses that progressive southern Democrats formulated to address questions of race bore a strong resemblance to the responses adopted by progressive and liberal Democrats in other parts of the country. By the 1970s, Democrats in the South and elsewhere found common cause in the need to build interracial coalitions by accommodating to desegregation while seeking to downplay race as a politically divisive issue. As a result, southern Democrats were no longer seen as a "problem" within the party because of their obsession with white supremacy. This in turn removed the disqualification that had previously prevented southerners from being considered as viable presidential candidates, a development of no small significance given the failure of any nonsouthern Democrat to win the presidency from 1960 to 2008.

The second way in which New South Democrats played an important role in national politics was, ironically, by taking sides in the new intraparty tension that replaced the one over race. Beginning in the late 1960s, New South Democrats overwhelming aligned themselves with the so-called New Democrats who were concerned that their party was being defined by cultural permissiveness, a dovish foreign policy, and a reputation for fiscal profligacy. New Democrats blamed this image for the back-to-back defeats in the presidential elections of 1968 and 1972, a view that resonated with many prominent southerners including, perhaps most significantly, Jimmy Carter. As such, New South Democrats were a crucial factor in the dispute within the national party over whether to adopt "liberal" or "centrist" positions on cultural, economic, and foreign policy issues. As Bruce Miroff has recently argued, this dispute remains crucial to understanding the "identity" of today's Democratic Party.[21] The heavy representation of southern Democrats among such groups as the fiscally conservative "Blue Dog Democrats" and the Democratic Leadership Council (DLC) from the 1980s onward speaks to the southern influence in this internal party debate, an influence that was symbolized most powerfully by the presidential election victories in 1992 and 1996 of Bill Clinton, a former governor of Arkansas and head of the DLC.

In short, the alternative narrative to the white backlash that I present in this book can be summarized as follows: the civil rights movement did not destroy the Democratic Party in the South; rather, the ability of New South Democrats to adjust to it at the regional level allowed them to take the lead in shaping a more progressive political culture for the South. This process of accommodation with the civil rights movement was primarily driven by Democrats at the local and state levels. Furthermore, it was a long-term process born in the 1940s, not a sudden change in response to the 1960s, and it was critical to enabling southern Democrats first to rejoin, and subsequently to reshape the identity of, the national party.

By contrast, the white backlash, far from helping Republicans take control of the South, proved to be a highly unreliable political force. The pursuit of the "backlash vote," while occasionally successful, was less a help than a hindrance to the GOP, especially in terms of winning consistent support from its natural base of high-income suburban voters. As it happened, Lyndon Johnson once speculated that this would become a problem for the Republican Party, although in this instance his prediction has not received as much attention or notoriety as his commentary on the likely effects of the Civil Rights Act. And yet it was an equally valid projection of subsequent political developments in the South.

Johnson made his prediction during a telephone conversation in July 1965 with Martin Luther King Jr. over the most appropriate strategy for securing congressional passage of the Voting Rights Act. Johnson warned King that Republican support for the act would be harder to come by than people thought, but that this determination on their part to capture the support of racially conservative whites would ultimately prove detrimental to the GOP. Johnson told King that the Republicans' commitment to seeking support from the white backlash was so inflexible that whenever they were presented with the chance to win over some black voters, they would "blow it," which meant that they were missing out on the chance to elect some "good men" in "suburban districts and in cities." In fact, Johnson concluded, the shortsighted decision to write off the black vote (a sure sign, the president believed, that the Republicans "haven't got that much sense") was central to explaining why the GOP was in the process of "disintegrating."[22]

As it turned out, expecting the Republican Party to "disintegrate" was no more realistic than fearing that Democratic support for civil rights would produce several "lifetimes" of Republican dominance in the South. Nonetheless, Johnson's prediction to King is significantly closer to what subsequently happened in the South after federally mandated desegregation than his reported comment on signing the Civil Rights Act: thanks to a combination of embracing racial accommodation and the decision by many Republicans to pursue too zealously the white backlash, New South Democrats became the most influential group in southern politics and played the leading role in shaping the political landscape of the post–Jim Crow South.

The Postwar Roots of the New South Democrats

In the spring of 1971, *Time* magazine dedicated an issue to a study of five youthful and telegenic men who had been elected governors of various southern states in 1970. The cover story focused on Jimmy Carter of Georgia, but there were also profiles of fellow Democrats John West of South Carolina, Reuben Askew of Florida, and Dale Bumpers of Arkansas, along with Republican Linwood Holton of Virginia. These men were presented as evidence that a New South had arrived, and that it represented a dramatic departure from what had come before. Indeed, from the cover story ("Dixie Whistles a Different Tune") to the article headlines inside the issue ("New Day A'Coming in the South," "Four Men for the New Season"), the novelty of this new generation of southerners was the central theme of *Time*'s coverage.[23] While it was noted that each of the five held economic views that were noticeably more progressive than people might expect for southern governors, there was no doubt that it was their positions on race that *Time* considered the most compelling evidence for the "different tune" being heard throughout the South. Carter in particular was singled out and praised for telling Georgians "quite frankly" during his inaugural address in January 1971 that "the time for racial discrimination is over."[24]

Time's analysis of Carter and his fellow New South governors captured a good deal of what made their elections so significant. The absence of race-baiting from the 1970 campaigns, the open appeals for black support, and the disavowal of massive resistance to desegregation both before and after the elections represented an important sea change in southern political culture. Equally, the relative youth and similar generational experience of all five men lent credence to the notion that a changing of the guard was taking place. Nonetheless, *Time* left out a fair amount of context that was crucial to understanding the arrival of New South politicians, especially New South Democrats. As such, the piece created a misleading impression of how Carter and the others had risen to prominence. Specifically, by focusing so heavily on the "newness" of their political and racial views, *Time* suggested these had developed only relatively recently and were a clean break with southern politics to that point. In fact, the New South governors represented not so much something "new" as they did the culmination of a thirty-year struggle for control of the political agenda in the South. Their story actually begins in the 1940s, not the 1970s. This was particularly true for their racial views. Carter's rejection of racial discrimination in his inaugural was without question a dramatic political moment. However, it was less a radical new departure in southern racial rhetoric than it was the logical culmination of efforts by a previous generation of southern Democrats to accommodate to the postwar pressures for racial change.

The attempts to reach this accommodation had taken place against the backdrop of a bifactional split among southern Democrats in the postwar years. The political predecessors of the New South Democrats had coalesced around a program in the 1940s that sought to achieve a prosperous South by modernizing the region's economy and reforming its political system. These Democrats further believed the South must invest heavily in education so as to overcome its underdeveloped and backward status relative to the nation as a whole. Collectively, these policies would remove from the South the moniker of "the nation's number one economic problem" bestowed on it by the 1938 *Report on Economic Conditions in the South*. Democrats who subscribed to this position drew their inspiration from what they interpreted as the successes of a more activist government during the Roosevelt administration in first alleviating the Great Depression and then enabling the country to triumph in World War II. These Democrats were accordingly determined to align the southern state parties in support of the national party's core economic principles and to implement those policies within the South. In light of their support for the New Deal agenda and presidential candidates of the national party, and their opponents' general hostility to both, they became known as "Loyalists."[25]

The Loyalists' factional opponents within the southern Democratic parties were known as "Regulars." In 1944, a group of anti-Roosevelt Democrats from Texas had gone to the Democratic National Convention as the "Texas Regulars," and in the postwar years the term was commonly used to describe southern Democrats hostile to the policies of the national party leadership. Regulars' dislike of the national party encompassed a broad range of issues, reaching back to the struggles over Prohibition at the national conventions during the 1920s. The tension had intensified with the advent of the New Deal, which offended both the economic and racial sensibilities of many southern Democrats, but it did not reach its zenith until after President Truman made support for civil rights a key part of his 1948 reelection campaign. Regulars were primarily concerned with maintaining the racial order and limiting government intervention on socioeconomic questions—the two principles around which they had organized the southern one-party system in the 1890s. As far as Regular Democrats were concerned, seeking to enlarge the role of government and thereby overturning the South's socioeconomic structure posed a direct threat to the maintenance of white supremacy. Therefore both Loyalists and the national party had to be opposed.

Through their dominance of most state Democratic organizations in the South during the 1940s, the Regulars represented the biggest immediate obstacle to Loyalist Democrats and their hopes of a modernized New South. As big an obstacle as the Regulars were, however, they at least presented a straightforward political problem—an opposition that needed to be overcome. The other obstacles that Loyalists faced were in many ways more complex to address, insofar as they often came in the form of potential allies who were simultaneously potential problems. Chief among them was the civil rights movement. Like the Loyalists, civil rights activists wanted to reform southern society and build a New South. Additionally, many black southerners were strongly in favor of the New Deal and supported a more activist government. Unlike the Loyalists, however, civil rights activists prioritized reform of the racial order—something that the vast majority of Loyalists either did not support or had little interest in addressing directly. Even Loyalists sympathetic to calls for desegregation worried that expressing support for it would scuttle any hope of winning political office. As such, a politically mobilized black community offered the prospect of support for much of the Loyalist agenda, but also the potential to undermine Loyalist support among white voters if their agenda was seen as advocating black interests.

The national Democratic Party presented a similar dilemma. Loyalists were comfortable extolling the virtues of many of the New Deal's achievements, especially those associated with economic modernization such as the Tennessee Valley Authority. They also feared many of these programs would be scaled back or discontinued if conservative Republicans returned to power in Washington. Loyalists therefore had an incentive to work for the election of Democratic administrations and congressional majorities. However, as the national party moved toward an increasingly firm position in favor of civil rights, it became electorally risky to associate too closely with it in the South. Loyalists therefore had to find a way to maintain their ties to the national party without being seen as favoring its position on civil rights.

Finally, even though the Republican Party appeared only distantly on the horizon in most of the South during the 1940s, the GOP also presented Loyalists with a dilemma. While Republicans would have been the opposition party in any normal political system, the South's one-party system was anything but normal. As a result, Republicans and Loyalists often found themselves occupying common ground. Both favored a systematic overhaul of the southern political system, which they each considered to be outdated, inequitable, and corrupt. Both also drew on demographically similar parts of the South for their support—in particular, high-income white suburban voters and urban voters of all races—and so had a shared interest in eliminating the prorural biases built into southern politics. On the other hand, the mutual desire for ending the Solid South did not mean a shared set of priorities for what the New South should look like. Republicans advocated a more conservative economic agenda than Loyalists were willing to support. When and on what issues to make common cause against Regular Democrats, and when to oppose each other, was therefore a persistent concern for Loyalists and Republicans alike from the 1940s onward.

The Politics of Color Blindness

The various dilemmas that other Democrats, the civil rights movement, and southern Republicans provided for Loyalists were simultaneously distinct and yet interrelated. Any change in strategy in dealing with one would inevitably have ramifications for dealing with the others. One theme in particular, however, ran through the Loyalist relationship with each of them: race. Civil rights groups insisted on Loyalists not actively resisting racial change as the minimum price for black electoral support. Loyalty to the national Democratic Party would similarly require keeping a distance from the massive resistance movement against desegregation. An additional incentive to avoid embracing massive resistance was Loyalists' own belief that the obsession with defending white supremacy was the most visible sign of the backwardness of southern politics. On the other hand, refusing to resist racial change to the utmost would be used by Regulars, and later by some Republicans, to portray Loyalists as too closely associated with black voters. This had the potential to drive white voters away from Loyalist candidates. Finding a politically viable position on race that could navigate between these potential pitfalls was therefore the single most important goal for Loyalists to achieve. There was a considerable irony in this: an issue that Loyalists had little interest in talking about and that was often peripheral to their overall priorities was the one that would be most crucial to their larger prospects for success.

Finding a viable position on race was no easy task. There was no perfect option available. No matter what position Loyalists adopted, they risked losing support from either black or white voters. In the absence of a perfect solution, the strategy that proved most effective was to advocate an approach that can be termed "progressive color blindness." The use of "color-blind" rhetoric as a political strategy to limit the use of affirmative action, busing for racial balance, and government-led efforts at residential integration has been well documented.[26] The color blindness that has received the bulk of scholarly attention thus far, however, has been "conservative color blindness." It is important to qualify it as such, because color-blind rhetoric can in fact be used to advance policy positions from across the ideological spectrum. Its flexibility in this regard stems from the fact that while it is based on a universal and very straightforward premise—that a person's racial status ought to accord him or her no privileges or disadvantages in society—the interpretations of that premise can lead to entirely contradictory policy positions. For example, one could argue in color-blind terms that affirmative action is necessary to overcome the structural disadvantages that minority racial groups still face in American society; alternatively, one could use color-blind rhetoric to argue that affirmative action should be opposed as it grants privileges to people from minority racial groups.

While conservative color blindness is therefore an important feature of contemporary discussions of race, it would be misleading to assume that it was the only form of color-blind ideology worth paying attention to; in particular, focusing on conservative color blindness alone risks overlooking the progressive form of color blindness that Loyalist Democrats were able to use as a means to reshape the politics of the postwar South.

The range of ideologies that can draw on color-blind rhetoric to advance their political agenda is such that there is reason to be hesitant before placing its various uses into neatly defined ideological blocs. Whatever labels are used to categorize color-blind rhetoric, there is likely to be some overlap in attitudes at the edges of each group. Likewise, within each category there will likely be varying degrees of emphasis that could be considered subcategories in themselves. With these provisos and caveats in mind, however, there are at least three iterations of color blindness—classical, conservative, and progressive—that are distinct enough to be useful categories of analysis. The key differences between them are their initial motivations, their ultimate goals, and the standard of proof they set for considering a given phenomenon to be the product of racial discrimination.

"Classical color blindness" was the basis for the arguments advanced by the National Association for the Advancement of Colored People (NAACP) and other civil rights groups to challenge the constitutionality of segregation during the early part of the twentieth century. Classical color blindness is markedly different from the other two variations, because it is used to seek out and highlight examples of racial discrimination in order to do something about them. By contrast, advocates of both conservative and progressive color blindness are more interested in limiting discussion of race as a social or political issue. In other words, while these latter two versions of color blindness will speak out against racial discrimination where it has clearly occurred, and even take action against it, they do so in a reactive rather than a proactive manner. While classical color blindness was advocated by those who wanted to grapple with the fundamental problems caused by racial divisions in society, conservative color blindness and progressive color blindness were both a means of shifting attention away from these divisions. They were developed as a response to the pressure for civil rights and not from a desire to grant them. As a result, it is not surprising that these two more recent versions of color blindness, both of which claim to be loyal to the legacy of the civil rights movement, should often be viewed with such suspicion by those who were actually part of that movement.

Nonetheless, while adherents of conservative and progressive color blindness are resistant to the idea of aggressively pursuing racial equality through structural change in the way civil rights groups might want, their reasons for doing so are very different. The core belief of conservative color blindness is that the reason public policy and the law ought not to show favor to any race is that to do so would be a violation of individual rights. Conservative color blindness opposes affirmative action as "reverse racism" and is most often articulated as a defense against proposals that would give an advantage to nonwhites over whites. The standard social narrative of conservative color blindness is that whereas America suffered from institutionalized racial discrimination in the past, this has since been dismantled. While pockets of racism may linger on in the private sphere, to eradicate them by using government compulsion would be to risk punishing innocent whites for the sins of others.[27] Furthermore, as this racism is taking place in the private sphere, it is something that must be solved by changing the hearts and minds of individuals, and not through an act of government.

To support this outlook, advocates of conservative color blindness are keen to link their ideas to the vision outlined by Martin Luther King Jr. in his "I have a dream" speech. In particular, they cite the passage where King advocates judging people by "the content of their character" and not by "the color of their skin" as an argument against affirmative action.[28] This is a highly problematic claim, as many of King's public statements on affirmative action suggest that he favored this and other efforts by the government to tackle structural inequality.[29] Indeed, the "conservative color-blind" interpretation of King represents a profound narrowing of his overall beliefs, ignoring as it does his criticisms of the effect of capitalism on poverty, racism, and war. By reducing his overall critique of society to the "I have a dream" speech, King's philosophy becomes simply a more rhetorically elegant version of "can't we all just get along?" It remains true that some of King's speeches would appeal to a conservative color-blind mind-set, but it is hard to believe he would have been satisfied with the idea that the government ought to simply stay out of racial questions and wait for the hearts and minds of the citizenry to be cleansed of racism. Partly due to their attempt to co-opt King, and in part because of their reluctance to address issues of structural racial inequality, supporters of conservative color blindness have variously been accused of living in "racial denial," seeking to "redeem white supremacy," or deluding themselves with an ideology of "suburban [racial] innocence."[30]

The level of analysis and criticism that conservative color blindness has received is indicative of the dominant contemporary view that "color-blind" politics is something practiced predominantly by the Right. Ironically, however, this has also contributed to very little attention being paid to progressive color blindness, which has played at least as significant a role in shaping how race and the civil rights movement are viewed in twenty-first-century America. Like its conservative counterpart, progressive color blindness is based on the "classical" premise of equal treatment for all individuals. The motivation behind progressive color blindness, however, is fundamentally different. From a conservative standpoint, dwelling on race is problematic because it encourages a false sense of entitlement in people who then push for special treatment based on their racial status. For progressives, by contrast, dwelling on race encourages people to act politically according to an emotional bond with their racial group, instead of making decisions based on their broader socioeconomic needs. In other words, to progressives, race is used by cynical politicians—black and white—to distract voters from their true interests and so is best suppressed as a political issue.[31]

Another feature that distinguished progressive color blindness from its conservative counterpart was the subversive aspect of the former, at least at the time it originated.[32] Whereas conservative color blindness was generally adopted from the late 1960s onward, often by people who had once fervently supported the institution of segregation, progressive color blindness grew out of opposition to such fervent support for Jim Crow and disfranchisement in the 1940s. Progressive color blindness reflected a belief that for too long southern politicians had race-baited their way to office by preying on the prejudices of ordinary white southerners to convince them to oppose socioeconomic change of any sort. Progressive color blindness did not generally involve an active argument that segregation should be ended. Instead, it made the claim that segregation might be expendable when it conflicted with other, more important issues.

As well as enabling Loyalists to claim that they were not actually supporting civil rights while simultaneously arguing against endless resistance to all racial change, progressive color blindness also contained two additional benefits within the context of southern politics. The first was that by emphasizing the need for collective socioeconomic progress, Loyalists could defend maintaining contacts with "respectable" black leaders in the state for the purpose of achieving that progress. After all, the rhetoric and beliefs of progressive color blindness were economically inclusive, even though they were not integrationist as such. So long as a given policy could be framed as benefiting blacks *along with* whites (and did not involve social integration between the two), interracial cooperation in achieving it was politically viable.

As a further consequence of this, Loyalists were able to benefit electorally from the growth in the number of black voters, who saw them as less hostile to black progress than the Regulars. Of course, this also required a delicate balancing act, as it was, at least in the 1940s, political suicide in a southern election to *openly* appeal for black support at the polls. Loyalists and black political organizations accordingly found more surreptitious means of electoral cooperation. By the 1960s and 1970s, it would become even more advantageous for Loyalist Democrats to establish strong ties with black voters, given the reemergence of the southern Republican Party. As black voters were both growing in number and were supportive of the Loyalists' and national Democrats' outlook on socioeconomic matters, they were valuable in countering Republican challenges to the Loyalist agenda at the ballot box. This concurrently reinforced the need to reach an accommodation with the civil rights movement so as to be able to attract black voter support against the GOP.[33]

The second benefit that progressive color blindness provided for Loyalist Democrats was that while they believed they could not advocate desegregation ahead of time, they did feel able to justify accommodation to it once it had become a fait accompli. By never vowing all-out resistance, it was possible for advocates of progressive color blindness to adjust to desegregation by framing it as a price worth paying for the larger goal of economic prosperity. Furthermore, progressive color blindness allowed for the subsequent celebration, or at least positive defense, of racial change. As such, by the 1970s progressive color blindness as practiced by Jimmy Carter and other New South Democrats could openly praise the end of Jim Crow as representing a critical *contribution* to southern progress using the same underlying logic as the Loyalists of the 1940s, even if the latter group could never have made such positive statements about desegregation.

As well as containing several potential political benefits, however, progressive color blindness also shared with conservative color blindness the tendency to narrow the legacy of the civil rights movement to the absence of racial discrimination rather than the achievement of full racial equality. In doing so, progressive color blindness also contributed to the modern perception of Martin Luther King Jr. as a historical figure concerned only with the pursuit of civic equality and not structural change. This was powerfully evident during the at-times surreal debate on the floor of the U.S. Senate in 1983 over the creation of a federal holiday honoring King's birthday. As Jesse Helms spoke out against the holiday by reading several of King's more politically controversial statements out loud on the floor of the Senate, he was roundly denounced by Democratic senators Edward Kennedy and Daniel Patrick Moynihan for smearing King's memory. Of course, Helms was also trotting out old innuendos about King's association with Communism and distorting the context of several of King's comments, but it was nonetheless apparent that King's beliefs were evidently more provocative than his ostensible supporters in the two major parties were willing to admit. Rather than face up to this, advocates of progressive and conservative color blindness stood together and argued for the de-radicalized version of King that dominates the public consciousness of his memory to this day.[34]

The inability of progressive color blindness to come to grips with more radical approaches to reducing racial inequality proved a consistent liability for white Democrats in the New South in addressing the needs of their black constituency. By being willing to address black concerns yet not wanting to focus on them, supporters of progressive color blindness found themselves caught between the conservative argument that black concerns were an attempt to enforce group rights at the expense of individual ones and the "classical" one that race remained a central fault line in American society. Despite its limitations, however, progressive color blindness proved itself to be a distinct and powerful force in the reshaping of southern politics after 1945.

"Marching through Georgia": From Solid South to New South

The basic process by which the Loyalist Democrats of the 1940s laid the foundations for the rise of the New South Democrats in the 1970s was common to all eleven states of the former Confederacy. Across the South, the state Democratic parties split into Regular and Loyalist factions; across the South, Democrats in both factions had to engage the civil rights movement, the national party leadership, and the Republican Party; and across the South, the outcome of these engagements resulted in New South Democrats holding the balance of power in regional politics. Nonetheless, despite these similarities, the precise nature and timing of this overall political transformation was different in each of the southern states. In Tennessee, it had taken place by the end of the 1950s. In Mississippi, it did not occur in full until 1980. Different political systems and priorities, different demographics, different economic structures, individual political leaders, and state-specific contingent events were all responsible for a collective regional experience unfolding in distinctive ways within each state.

Such similarities in kind but differences in degree present a difficult choice in how to present the overall story. Both a regionwide analysis and a single-state case study have disadvantages. Trying to incorporate the entire South runs the risk of producing an unwieldy narrative and oversimplifying the complex nuances of what happened in each state. Focusing only on a case study of a single state runs the risk of neglecting the regional nature of what took place. Nonetheless, the advantages of the single-state approach outweigh those of the regional overview, and its shortcomings are easier to minimize. Using a single state means it is possible to better compare the continuity in personnel, issues, and electoral coalitions that existed during the postwar years. A regionwide survey would produce so many of each that detailing them all would be prohibitive in a book of this length. Furthermore, as each state is a self-contained political system, it provides a central focus for the various political groupings within it. It is therefore easier to demonstrate the effect of the interaction between political parties, the civil rights movement, and other interest groups in a single state where they are all seeking influence within the same political structure than it is to analyze such interactions across eleven mostly independent structures.

Given these considerations, this book focuses on the events that took place in a single state: Georgia. In order not to lose sight of the regional trends that Georgia was part of, developments elsewhere will be regularly referred to, but they will be in the background of the narrative. The decision to focus on Georgia is based on it being both an excellent representative of the transformation taking place across the South as a whole as well as events there being an exceptionally important part of that transformation. This is not to claim that at every stage of the process events in Georgia were always the most important for understanding what was happening in the South, nor is it to suggest that there were not individual people in other states who were just as significant as those who were active in Georgia. Still, taking the thirty years after World War II as a whole, Georgia was consistently a bellwether state for what was taking place politically across the South.

While it was one of five states that made up the more rural, racially conservative Deep South, Georgia was the closest of the five to the more urban, racially moderate "Rim South" states in its political behavior.[35] On the cusp between these two subregions, Georgia's position at the center of southern political trends was evident at several critical moments in the postwar period. In 1948, Georgia was the only Deep South state not to have its Democratic Party taken over by supporters of the third-party "Dixiecrat" campaign of J. Strom Thurmond; however, it also gave the highest level of support to Thurmond of the seven southern states that voted for President Truman that year. In 1964, Georgia joined the rest of the Deep South in voting Republican—an electoral first—but did so by the smallest margin. Similarly, of the four Deep South states that backed George Wallace's independent candidacy in 1968, Georgia gave Wallace the smallest plurality. Time and again, Georgia occupied the middle ground of southern electoral trends. Prior to the New Deal, a popular saying in presidential contests was "as goes Maine, so goes the nation." In the postwar years, one could equally have said of regional voting trends, "as goes Georgia, so goes the South."

The central position that Georgia occupied in the southern body politic was also manifested in the way the state's leadership reacted to the civil rights movement. Georgia had powerful "Solid South" constituencies that favored massive resistance to civil rights and an electoral system that gave these constituencies disproportionate influence in shaping state policy.

On the other hand, thanks to the economic power and demographic growth of Atlanta and its suburbs, Georgia also contained influential advocates eager to focus on economic prosperity rather than racial resistance. Finely balanced between these two core constituencies, Georgia found itself caught between the devotees of absolute, often violent resistance who dictated the response of, say, Mississippi and the supporters of gradualist, if reluctant, accommodation who shaped the response of Tennessee. As a result, while Mississippi and Tennessee often represented the respective extremes of the postwar South's transformation, Georgia can be seen as a "Goldilocks" state. To put it another way, in comparative terms with the other southern states, the rise to power of the New South Democrats in Georgia was neither the fastest nor the slowest; it was neither the most painful nor the most painless; and they faced neither the easiest nor the toughest hurdles to overcome. In short, if the encounter between Democrats and the civil rights movement in Mississippi was "too hot" to be representative of the entire South, and the encounter in Tennessee was "too cool," then the manner in which it happened in Georgia was "just right."

A final reason for singling Georgia out for special consideration is the disproportionate contribution made by Georgians to the national debate over civil rights, the South, and the Democratic Party. As the home state of Richard Russell, Herman Talmadge, and Lester Maddox, Georgia claimed some of the leading figures of the attempt to resist the civil rights movement and to maintain Regular control of the Democratic Party. On the opposite side of the debate over desegregation, Georgia was a base for several central figures of the movement for racial equality, such as Martin Luther King Jr., Julian Bond, and John Lewis, along with less well known but also important activists such as Grace Towns Hamilton of the Urban League and Austin ("A. T.") Walden of the Georgia NAACP. The state also produced many of the leading challengers to the Regular leadership of the Democratic Party in the South—people such as Ellis G. Arnall, Helen Douglas Mankin, Carl Sanders, and Charles Weltner—all of whom played a critical role from the 1940s onward in making it possible for a politician like Jimmy Carter to rise to prominence in the state and the nation. Finally, as Carter is arguably the ultimate symbol of the significance of the New South Democrats for national politics, the fact that he was a product of Georgia's political transformation is a further sign that what transpired there had particularly significant regional and national implications.

"Out of the Shadows"

The 1948 Democratic National Convention in Philadelphia set the tone for the debate that would take place within the Democratic Party in the South and across the nation for the next thirty years. The debate revolved around two key dilemmas: first, what the party's response to the civil rights movement would be; and second, what the role of the South within the party would be. In 1948, these dilemmas dominated the convention. Allies of President Truman wanted to put the national party on record as supporting racial equality under the law so as to follow up on the president's own civil rights proposals of earlier in the year. Truman faced a delicate judgment call in his reelection bid that year that would soon become familiar to southern Democrats as well: the need to appeal to black support in order to defeat the Republicans without driving away white support in the process. Truman hoped that a moderately pro–civil rights plank—one that was nonetheless more assertive than anything the party had offered in the past—would strike the right balance.

Once Truman's intentions became clear, all eyes turned to the South. In the run-up to the national convention, a group of southern Regulars had organized a convention of their own in which they vowed to walk out in Philadelphia if the party acquiesced to Truman's nomination or a pro–civil rights plank. At the same time, Truman was also facing pressure from another wing of the party that wanted a more strongly worded endorsement of civil rights. Organized around the recently formed Americans for Democratic Action (ADA), these ardently pro–civil rights Democrats represented a form of "Cold War liberalism" that combined a belief in using government to expand equal rights with support for an assertive, anti-Soviet foreign policy. In Philadelphia, they found an eloquent and able spokesman in future vice president Hubert H. Humphrey, then a candidate for the U.S. Senate in Minnesota.

Humphrey's speech to the delegates on behalf of a strong civil rights plank was the pivotal moment at the convention. In an oration filled with passion and dramatic rhetoric, Humphrey directly addressed the threatened walkout by the southern Regulars who were already talking of themselves as "States' Rights Democrats." In his peroration, Humphrey argued that support for civil rights was a moral imperative as well as a political one and called on his party to step "out of the shadows of states' rights and into the bright sunshine of human rights." In the aftermath of Humphrey's speech, the convention adopted a stronger version of the civil rights plank than even Truman, let alone the southern Regulars, had wanted. A partial southern walkout followed, led by Regulars from Mississippi, Alabama, and South Carolina, who then convened in Birmingham, Alabama, a few weeks later to nominate Governors Thurmond of South Carolina and Fielding Wright of Mississippi as candidates on an anti–civil rights platform that became known as the "Dixiecrat" ticket. Thus began a quadrennial series of disputes at national conventions between southern Regulars and the national party leadership that would go on until 1976.

For the southern Loyalists watching this unfold, Humphrey's speech and the Dixiecrat walkout represented their worst nightmare. Having hoped to marginalize the role of race in southern political culture in order to reorientate the region around a politics of prosperity and economic modernization, the convention fight of 1948 had just made that task infinitely more difficult by explicitly placing race at the center of the political debate. What was more, Loyalists had just had the political space they hoped to operate in cut out from under them. The ideal Loyalist scenario would have been a Truman nomination along with a tepid endorsement of racial equality that could have been presented to southern voters as a toothless platitude they did not need to worry about. Instead, Loyalists now had on one side a national party platform that directly endorsed civil rights, and, on the other, a third-party campaign that vowed to resist it. Neither was an appealing option for Loyalists to align themselves with. Both the "bright sunshine" that Humphrey was inviting southern Democrats to step into by endorsing civil rights and the "shadows" of states' rights that the Dixiecrats were seeking to keep the South a part of were equally undesirable choices.

And yet for all the Loyalist discomfort over the events in Philadelphia, there was actually considerable common ground between them and Humphrey; certainly there was far more than between Loyalists and the Dixiecrats. On issues other than race, the similarities were already clear. Loyalists shared Humphrey's support for the New Deal and his faith in the abilities of an activist government to achieve economic growth. These attitudes were diametrically opposed to the Dixiecrat position. On foreign policy, there was a shared skepticism of the conciliatory approach to the Soviets proposed by former vice president Henry Wallace and a shared belief in the need for a tough line against Communism. Their shared perspective on these matters foreshadowed the manner in which New South

Democrats and Humphrey found themselves allied against the more dovish, anti–Vietnam War Democrats who challenged them over the direction of the national party during the 1970s.

Most significant, though, even on the question of civil rights, Humphrey and the Loyalists were not as dissimilar as each might have thought in 1948. Like Humphrey, the Loyalists agreed that cries of "states' rights" were keeping the South in the "shadows," although Loyalists would have argued that this was more of concern because it prevented economic, rather than racial, progress. Nonetheless, Loyalists would soon realize that to create the New South they wanted they would have to convince the white southern electorate to relegate racial concerns to a secondary status in their political consciousness. Over time, the only way to do this was to move "out of the shadows" and reach an accommodation with the civil rights movement and desegregation in just such a way as Humphrey might have imagined during his speech. In this sense, then, it did not matter that the motives that Loyalist Democrats eventually had for stepping "out of the shadows" were not those that Humphrey had envisaged in his 1948 speech. What was far more significant was that Loyalists took this step at all. In doing so, they not only transformed politics and race relations in the South, but reshaped the Democratic Party in the process. The New South could not have been created without them.

1

Competing Visions for Postwar Georgia

1946

A Revolution is coming . . . we can affect its character, we cannot alter its inevitability.

U.S. senator Robert F. Kennedy (D-NY), 1966

Judging by the results of the 1946 congressional elections in the South, the region had come through the twin cataclysms of the Great Depression and World War II with its political order still largely intact. While the balance of power elsewhere in the nation had been entirely recalibrated by the social and economic upheavals of the 1930s and 1940s, voters in the eleven former Confederate states were still voting the same way as they had been since the one-party "Solid South" came into being half a century earlier. The most obvious sign of this was the continued stranglehold on electoral office that the Democratic Party held in the region. As of January 1947, Democrats controlled 103 out of the 105 southern seats in the U.S. House of Representatives, all of the southern U.S. Senate seats, and the governorship in all eleven southern states. In his 1944 reelection campaign, Franklin Roosevelt had secured around 75 percent of the vote in the South, even as he was running twenty points below that in the rest of the nation. The Solid South was apparently in rude health, and it was therefore entirely understandable that Clark Clifford, an aide to President Truman, should come to the conclusion that as far as the 1948 presidential election was concerned, the South would still be "solidly Democratic."[1]

As understandable as Clifford's assessment was, in reality the political unity of the South that emerged from the war was more apparent than real. Within barely six months of his prediction being made, the third-party presidential campaign launched in opposition to Truman by disgruntled southern "Dixiecrats" would make Clifford seem hopelessly optimistic. The Dixiecrats' campaign made the true state of southern politics abundantly clear: not only did it reveal that there was a deep split within the southern Democratic Party, but it also showed that despite the seeming continuity in electoral outcomes, there were multiple economic and political divisions within the region. Over the course of the following decades, these divisions would split the Solid South wide open.

That it took another twenty years for the last vestiges of the Solid South to collapse has obscured just how weakened it was by 1946. Historians and political scientists—especially those who favor the white backlash narrative—have mostly focused on the 1960s as the critical decade in the transformation of southern politics.[2] This focus on the 1960s has in turn generally been accompanied by an emphasis on the centrality of federal civil rights legislation to the emergence of two-party politics in the South, as in Earl Black's assessment that the civil rights laws of 1964–1965 "finally de-stabilized the traditional one-party system."[3] It is indisputable that the 1960s in general, and the civil rights laws in particular, had a major impact on the *type* of two-party politics that would emerge to replace the Solid South. It is, however, not the case that the 1960s *caused* two-party politics to emerge: in that regard, the 1940s were far more important.

That it took time for the burgeoning political divisions of the postwar years to make their impact felt, or that the formal arrival of two-party competition in every southern state was not apparent until the late 1960s, does not alter the fact that by the 1940s it was already as close to inevitable as history can ever get that the Solid South was going to collapse. The apparently rapid pace of political change in the South during the 1960s was therefore largely the product of myriad social and economic developments that were already well under way by the end of World War II, rather than simply the result of the Civil Rights and Voting Rights acts. Historian Jack Kirby makes a similar argument with regard to the apparent speed of the demise of traditional southern agriculture during the same period. In fact, substitute the one-party system for the state of agriculture, and Kirby's conclusion serves just as well for describing the demise of the Solid South: "change merely seemed sudden during the 1950s and 1960s, when foundations, long before undermined, collapsed."[4]

The primary cause of this collapse was straightforward enough: by the end of the war, the Solid South contained an electorate with interests too diverse for the one-party system to represent. Expressed in more theoretical terms, the Solid South was becoming ever less able to achieve that which political scientist Joseph LaPalombara has described as the critical precondition for a party system to endure: "the accommodation of counter-elites."[5] In LaPombara's framework, the dominant elite(s) in a party system must be able to adjust to the demands being put forward by those challenging them for control of the political agenda, otherwise the system will collapse. In the context of the Solid South, the Regulars were the dominant elite. They were the group that benefited the most from the one-party system and had the greatest interest in maintaining it after 1945, yet their task was made far more challenging precisely because they wanted to maintain one-party politics. A two- or multiparty system, such as existed in most of the rest of the United States and Western Europe in the 1940s, has more options for accommodating counter-elites than was the case for the Solid South. In a multiparty system, when a section of one party's base or leadership becomes disenchanted with the status quo (that is, it becomes a counter-elite), it will either switch parties and thereby alter the balance of power, or it will form a new political organization (often a new party). Alternatively, if a new group not aligned with any party gains political popularity, it might also form a party of its own, or eventually become incorporated into one of the existing parties. This process has been observed time and again in U.S. history.[6]

In each case, a multiparty system has every chance of "accommodating" the counter-elites. The Democratic leadership in the Solid South did not have the same flexibility. Counter-elites could not be allowed to form new parties. Regular Democrats therefore had only two options for responding to counter-elites: either incorporate their demands into the party's agenda or suppress them. The first of these was possible only if the counter-elites' demands did not directly conflict with the dominant elite's agenda; the second option was only viable as long as the suppression was not so egregious that it violated the national conception of democracy and prompted outside intervention in southern affairs. The ideal scenario was therefore for the Regular Democrats to limit the possibility of counter-elites even appearing in the first place.

From the 1890s until the end of World War II, Regular Democrats had managed to do this very successfully. Indeed, from its inception, the Solid South had been premised on marginalizing counter-elites who threatened white, conservative rule. During the 1890s, this meant excluding African Americans and Republicans, and neutralizing the Populist Party's insurgency. This was achieved by disfranchisement of black voters and the Jim Crow laws, by de-legitimizing the GOP on the grounds of it being the party of Reconstruction and "race-mixing," and by embracing the Populists' rhetoric of anti-elitism and victimhood while abandoning their earlier emphasis on interracial cooperation. The common theme tying these three things together was the Regulars' unrelenting emphasis on the primacy of white supremacy within southern political culture.[7]

In addition to these political features of Regular dominance, the Solid South was also able to endure thanks to two additional factors. First, Regulars benefited from the level of economic, cultural, and demographic homogeneity that existed in the white South during the late nineteenth and early twentieth centuries. Far more agricultural, far less urban, and with less religious or ethnic diversity than the rest of the nation, the economic and social basis of the South's politically active population helped create a greater unity of interests in southern political culture than existed in the rest of the United States. Such relative unity of interests already served as a critical prop in preserving Regular Democratic hegemony by reducing the need for a second political party. To further capitalize on it, Regulars instituted political structures that gave disproportionate electoral weight to rural areas and minimized the potentially disruptive political influence of the more diverse populations in southern cities. Finally, the disfranchisement measures that targeted black voters also had the effect of truncating the poor white electorate, thereby further restricting the scope for political competition.

Regular Democrats also benefited from the lack of interest outside the South in intervening to prevent the exclusion of African Americans or Republicans from southern politics. The Solid South coincided with the "nadir" of race relations, during which antiblack feelings and a belief in social Darwinism were so high throughout the nation that very few white people objected to the demotion of southern blacks to second-class citizenship.[8] It also coincided with a period of Republican dominance of national politics, which meant that the GOP had little motive to compete for southern support, and in fact was able to benefit politically from portraying the Democrats as an exclusively "southern" party.

Each of these various features of the Solid South was essential to its survival. So long as they remained in place, the region was a virtual political fortress for the Democratic Party. However, the one-party system's dependence on so many factors for its survival—some structural, some political, some external—also emphasized how artificial a political entity it was. If any of these props were removed, it would generate serious pressure for political change. Prior to the 1930s there had not been any pressure on the system serious enough to threaten to undermine it. The onset of the Great Depression and then World War II changed all that. While it is not possible to isolate one single moment or development that deserves the title "most critical factor" in weakening the foundations of the one-party system, all the serious contenders for that title were set in motion during the 1930s and 1940s. A more urbanized population, a more diverse economy with an ever more mechanized agricultural sector, a federal government more actively involved in the socioeconomic structure of the nation, and the removal of some of the barriers to political participation that Regular Democrats had depended on for their electoral monopoly all combined to create a political climate by the end of the war that was ripe for the emergence of powerful counter-elites who had a very different vision for the postwar South than did the Regulars and were unlikely to be easily accommodated within the existing party system.

Disentangling the exact role each of these developments had in creating this climate is also not always possible, as many of them had overlapping and reinforcing effects. Between them, however, they made it ever more unlikely that a single political party or faction would be capable of representing the increasingly diverse political needs of the American South. Nowhere was this better illustrated than the change undergone by the southern economy during and after the enactment of the New Deal. In the early twentieth century, it was still possible to speak of the South as a regionally isolated economy (even without resorting to the term "colonial," which has been more controversial). The region's agricultural and industrial leaders were, until the 1920s, largely in agreement that the desired economic priorities for the South should be to keep wages low and to keep the federal government out.[9] On the eve of the Great Depression, the South's leaders had been remarkably successful (or lucky) in achieving these priorities. Wages in the South were well below the national average and, with the exception of Virginia and North Carolina, were actually lower relative to northern wages in 1929 than they had been in 1899. Similarly, federal intervention in the southern economy at the time of the Wall Street crash was all but nonexistent.[10]

With the arrival of the New Deal, this unity of interest in regard to economic policy began to unravel. World War II accelerated this process, and by 1950 the old economic policy priorities of the Solid South had become outdated. A full discussion of all the nuances in this process is beyond the scope of this book, and in any case has been thoroughly addressed by economic and social historians.[11] Suffice it to say, however, that although the South had not been economically monolithic even in the 1920s, there is no question that economic diversification and mechanization accelerated sharply during the 1930s, fundamentally altering the structure of the southern economy. New Deal legislation designed to sustain crop prices broke the back of the tenant-farming system that had underpinned southern agriculture by encouraging landowners to consolidate their holdings and drive their tenants off the land. In addition, helped by New Deal funds for capital development, the 1930s saw southern agriculture become ever less labor-intensive. As mechanization gathered pace, southern farms became more reliant on capital than ever before, which required a different economic outlook from the days when sharecropping was the norm.[12]

Southern industry was similarly affected, becoming both a larger part of the region's economy and simultaneously more diverse. In the 1930s, in an urgent search for new investments, several southern states authorized subsidies and local bond issues to attract new manufacturing.[13] At first, many of the new plants opening in the South, which could draw on the now-displaced agricultural workforce, were similar to the low-skill, low-wage industries with which the region had long been associated. In the years after 1945, however, this changed, as new and more capital-intensive, high-skill industries began to grow in the South. Around one-third of all the factories opened in the South from 1945 to 1955 that employed more than twenty-five workers were in these "new" industries, including transportation, chemicals, and heavy machinery plants.[14]

The southern workforce was not only increasingly employed in new jobs; they were also living in urban areas to a much greater degree by the postwar years. In 1920, areas defined by the U.S. Census as "urban" accounted for just 25.2 percent of the old Confederacy's population. By 1960, this was up to 53.1 percent. Of the total increase in the southern population during those forty years from 25 million to 43.5 million, only 1.5 million came through additional rural residents, compared to nearly 17 million new urban ones.[15] The rise of suburbia after the 1950s would only further reduce the share of the South's population that lived in rural areas.[16]

This overall combination of demographic changes and economic diversification in both agriculture and industry served to demolish what historian Gavin Wright has described as the "economic underpinnings" of southern regional isolation.[17] Those southern leaders who wanted to continue moving their region toward economic modernization and diversification realized that doing so would require a far greater level of interaction with the national economy than had existed prior to the Great Depression. Simultaneously, southern political and economic leaders found that their choices and prospects were being affected by the change in the federal government's attitude to economic intervention after 1933.

The increased activism of the federal government would have impacted southern politics even if it had merely shored up rather than helped transform the southern economy. As LaPalombara has noted, when government starts to take an active role in "economic and social-welfare spheres," it encourages political elites to become more competitive and makes the rise of new political parties more likely.[18] This occurs quite simply because there are more resources over which to compete. Once the federal government began to make money available in these "spheres," a process that accelerated even more with the onset of World War II, it was politically difficult to turn it down (at the very least, there would likely be divisions over whether to turn it down). In short, as long as the federal government was providing no money, there was no opportunity to disagree over how not to spend it. With money available, however, there would inevitably be political disagreements over whether to take it, or how it should be spent—disagreements that would be difficult to contain within a one-party system.

The weakening of several of the political structures that Regulars had established to ensure their electoral hegemony also put pressure on the Solid South. A new drive for political reform in the 1940s began to prize open some of the barriers to political participation that propped up one-party politics. In many cases, this demand for change came from within the South, often in response to demands from the new political constituencies created by the socioeconomic upheaval of the previous decade. For example, the poll tax, initially introduced to restrict the size of the electorate (especially the black electorate), was increasingly seen as an unfair and outdated burden on low-income white voters. Southern governors as ideologically different as Georgia's Ellis G. Arnall and South Carolina's Strom Thurmond took steps to remove the poll tax from their state's voter registration requirements during the 1940s.

In other cases, outside forces intervened, most significantly the 1944 Supreme Court decision *Smith v. Allwright*, which outlawed the racially exclusive Democratic primary in Texas.[19] As the federal courts extended the ruling to make it universal, the NAACP launched a drive to register black voters. From just 5 percent of southern blacks being registered in 1940, the number increased to 20 percent in 1952. This regional figure masked significant variation between states; the share of black voters in Mississippi lagged at only 6 percent as late as 1960, a time when the registration rate for black voters in Tennessee had topped 60 percent.[20] Such variation notwithstanding, however, there was no doubt that as the number of black voters grew, the chances of survival for a one-party system primarily devoted to defending white supremacy fell.[21]

The scale of the inroads made into the Solid South's political barriers by the mid-1940s should not be exaggerated. While economic and demographic change was fairly advanced by this stage, significant barriers to political participation still remained. These barriers to voting included an array of literacy tests, interpretive tests, the need to prove "good moral character," and residency requirements. Nonetheless, there were some significant breaches in the Solid South's walls by the early postwar years, which was reflected by the increasing level of voter participation in southern elections. Calculating turnout in nonpresidential elections in the South at this time is haphazard at best, as so many state and local offices went uncontested. However, looking at presidential elections, the trend is clear. In 1944, voter turnout averaged 22.9 percent across the South compared to a national rate of 53 percent. By 1952, southern turnout had risen to 35 percent. Although this was still below the national rate, it was rising at twice the rate of turnout across the nation. Southern voter participation was clearly increasing sharply, a development that both represented and reinforced the pressure for increased political competition. That the breach in the barriers against black enfranchisement was at most only partial by this stage does not detract from this point, not only because it proved impossible to ever roll back these gains by African Americans but also because a rise in turnout even among white voters would inexorably lead to greater political competition.

Finally, as well as the structural changes that they produced in the South, the Great Depression and the war also resulted in changes in southern political culture that had far-reaching consequences. Collectively, they changed the way that southerners—white and black—thought about politics. For the most part, these changes were deeply ambiguous. Southerners reacted in very different ways to the same phenomena. For example, in the case of the New Deal, many black southerners and some white southerners saw its policies as having saved the region from the Depression and thought they provided a blueprint for ending the South's chronic poverty and economic backwardness. Other southern whites were alarmed at the control over the economy and race relations that the New Deal was giving the federal government and saw it as a threat. Such an ambiguous response actually served to further undermine the prospects for political consensus in the South. Already in the 1930s there were fierce contests taking place in southern primaries between candidates who opposed or favored the New Deal. The intensity of these contests would only increase after 1945.

The experience of World War II had similarly significant ramifications for southern politics. Unlike the case of the New Deal, the ambiguity of the southern response to the war was not the result of debating whether it had been a "good thing." It was all but universally believed that the fight for victory over Germany and Japan had been just and worthwhile. Rather, the ambiguity arose from the differing interpretations of what the war was for and how its legacy should be realized in postwar politics. While the nuances within southerners' different opinions about "what the war meant" are almost infinite, historian Jennifer Brooks has laid out a useful framework for understanding the broad thrusts of these opinions. In her study of war veterans in Georgia, Brooks details the interpretations of the war as seen by four kinds of southerner: white reactionaries who interpreted their wartime experience as justifying a fierce defense of the traditional social order in the South; white "good government" supporters who saw the war as a fight for modern, clean, democratic government; liberal white veterans who saw the war as legitimizing an effort to improve the lives of ordinary white and black southerners through unionization and interracial cooperation; and black veterans who embraced the logic of the "double V" campaign and returned to Georgia determined to fight for their rights at home.

While Brooks's study specifically addresses the views of actual veterans, her categories serve equally well for understanding how the war impacted the political thinking of southerners who experienced only the home front. As with the New Deal, sharply contrasting views about what a collective experience meant for the future of southern politics set the stage for a sustained challenge to the existing political order. Combined with the structural change that it produced, the war's impact on southern political culture was a direct cause of greater political competition. Brooks captures these twin aspects of the war's impact on postwar politics nicely in her assessment that it "put economic, social, racial, and political relations in flux, generating a political instability that permeated the postwar era at every level." The result of this flux was "the most significant electoral challenges many of [Georgia's] mossbacked incumbents had ever faced."[22]

Such was the true state of southern politics that was masked by the apparent uniformity suggested by the results of the 1946 congressional elections. Collectively, the social, economic, political, and cultural changes in southern life during the 1930s and 1940s had loosened the Solid South from its moorings. By 1946, conditions in the South were such that a change in the party system was unavoidable. At this stage, it was far from clear what the outcome of this change would be. Determining that would be the chief occupation of the Regulars and their challengers over the coming decades. In Georgia, as was the case in most of the South, the most serious of those challengers in 1946 were dissidents within the Georgia Democratic Party and the civil rights movement. Within a few years, the national Democratic Party would join the fray. Not long after that, Republicanism would reappear in the state as a political force to be reckoned with. Each of these groups had its own vision for what postwar Georgia should look like, and the conflicts between these visions shaped the political system that replaced the Solid South. All of these groups had the capacity to shape postwar change, but none of them had the power to undo the transformative forces unleashed during the 1930s and 1940s that made change unavoidable. In short, as of 1946, Georgians, regardless of their differing political beliefs, were in exactly the position that Robert Kennedy described America as being in twenty years later. All knew that change was coming, and while none were in a position to prevent it, all hoped that they might yet have a decisive impact on shaping its character.

Progress, Without Change: The Regular Agenda in Postwar Georgia

In his study of contemporary North Carolina politics, Paul Luebke divides elite opinion in the state into two worldviews: "traditionalists" and "modernizers."[23] Although Luebke primarily deploys his categories to discuss events in North Carolina in the 1980s and beyond, his descriptions of each group's characteristics are also a useful framework for understanding the divide within the Georgia Democratic Party from the 1940s onward.

Luebke's description of the characteristics of traditionalism in southern politics fits the Regular outlook perfectly. Leaders of the Regular faction in Georgia did indeed feel "threatened by change and growth." This did not mean that they were opposed to economic growth or industrialization per se, and they certainly were not opposed to the existence of wealth as evidenced by the close ties between many Regular politicians and business leaders. However, in line with traditionalist priorities, Regular Democrats favored "economic growth that could reinforce the established social order"[24]—in other words, growth that would maintain the "traditional" characteristics of the pre–New Deal southern economy: low-wage, low-skill industrial and agricultural labor. Labor unions, especially the Congress of Industrial Organizations (CIO), were to be discouraged and, ideally, kept out of the workplace altogether.

Regulars were similarly hostile to government spending, especially on social welfare. They subscribed to the skepticism typical among traditionalists that government spending would not be able to "solve social and economic problems."[25] In fact, Regulars often went farther than this: they were of the view that the "problems" advocates of government intervention wanted to address were best left unsolved. The number one priority for Regulars in this regard was white supremacy. While hesitant to embrace most forms of change, few Regulars were so hidebound in their outlook that they expected the status quo to be maintained in every respect. However, on the question of race relations, the line was to be held at almost any price.

As central as segregation was to the Regulars' view of the world, their traditionalism extended beyond race to include broader cultural issues. In general, this reflected the affinity of Regular Democrats for the patriarchal values of what Numan Bartley has termed the "county seats" that served as the base for the Regular Democratic faction in 1946.[26] Always partial toward invoking fundamentalist Christianity in public and zealously anti-Communist, Regulars were hostile not just to the civil rights movement but also to feminists, secularists, hippies, gay rights advocates, and other "countercultural" movements of the postwar years.

During the 1930s and 1940s, the Regulars' champion in Georgia was Eugene ("Gene") Talmadge. Elected as commissioner of agriculture in 1926, then reelected to that position twice more, Talmadge first ran for governor in 1932. Successfully elected, he went on to win three further gubernatorial contests and dominated Georgia politics like no other individual during the 1930s. Scathingly critical of the New Deal, Talmadge tried to persuade others to join him in launching an anti-Roosevelt slate of electors in 1936 and ran against U.S. senator and New Deal supporter Richard Russell during the 1936 primaries. In both of these campaigns, Talmadge was unsuccessful. Federal political campaigns were not his strong suit, though his twin defeats there were also a sign of how controversial an individual he was. In terms of statewide office, though, he was defeated only once in a career spanning twenty years. During that time, politics in Georgia operated as a contest between those who loved Talmadge and those who loathed him. In his 1949 state-by-state study of southern politics, V. O. Key Jr. identified only two factions in Georgia during the 1930s: "Talmadge" and "anti-Talmadge."[27]

A sampling of Talmadge's rhetoric demonstrates the manner in which Regular Democrats used traditionalist appeals to win electoral support. He declared that there were only four things that patriotic Americans cared about: "white supremacy, states' rights, Jeffersonian democracy and old time religion." To Talmadge, the New Deal was flawed not just from an economic standpoint but also because it threatened all manner of southern racial and sexual mores. The public works programs it funded, for instance, created the horrifying possibility that "a negro" might receive 40 cents an hour working on the side of a road "in country communities where white women and girls pick cotton right beside [them]." Talmadge's hostility toward blacks only marginally exceeded his hostility toward unions, which he suspected of Communism. On one notorious occasion during the 1930s, he rounded up striking workers, put them behind barbed wire, and read extracts from *Mein Kampf* to them. Such was his mastery of the tenets of traditionalism that on another occasion during his final gubernatorial campaign in 1946, Talmadge managed to touch on almost every social and cultural trope of the Regular worldview in a single sentence. In a peroration to his standard campaign speech, Talmadge told his audience what he was against "social equality, alien influences, [and] Moscow Harlem zoot-suiters who would go into Atlanta's First Baptist Church and try to sit down right there alongside a white lady."[28]

By 1946, some of Talmadge's more colorful behavior and campaign style were becoming a little outdated even to other Regulars, but his basic beliefs remained at the core of the Regular agenda. Defending the color line was still the absolute priority. Beyond that, it was vital to maintain the political structure that had suppressed the emergence of counter-elites.

Within Georgia, this meant preserving the malapportionment of the state legislature and the county-unit system. The county-unit system was a method of allocating political power within the state that all but removed Georgia's cities from electoral influence. The system had been formally adopted in 1917 as the means for determining winners in primary elections, but it had already been in de facto operation before then. It built on the distribution of seats in the General Assembly, the state's bicameral legislative body, which allocated representation on a per county rather than a per capita basis. As of 1945, Georgia's 8 largest counties sent three representatives to the Georgia House; the next 30 largest counties sent two; and the smallest 131 counties each sent one. In the state senate, counties were grouped into three, and each set of three elected a state senator. The only exceptions were Fulton County (Atlanta), which was entitled to its own senator, and the two counties comprising Savannah and its suburbs, which also elected one senator. The result was that Georgia's half-dozen largest cities, which already provided nearly a third of the state's voters by the time of the 1948 presidential election, held only 8 percent of the seats in Georgia's House of Representatives and around 5 percent of the seats in the Georgia Senate.[29]

The county-unit system extended this pro-rural bias by allocating to each county a certain number of "unit votes" in the Democratic primary equal to twice the number of representatives it had in the lower house of the General Assembly.[30] Whichever candidate in the primary won the most votes in a given county would receive that county's unit votes. With a total of 410 unit votes available, the winning candidate needed at least 206 of these to gain the Democratic nomination. It did not matter who had won the most votes statewide; whoever won the majority of the unit votes was declared the nominee. This overrepresentation of small-town and rural areas gave a significant political advantage to Regular candidates, as it was these parts of Georgia that were most supportive of racial and cultural traditionalism.

In order to further ensure against the return of African Americans to political influence in the state, Regulars were also determined to do more than just defend the existing segregation and disfranchisement laws. Specifically, they set themselves up for a fight along three fronts. In the first place, they supported measures designed to cripple the civil rights movement in the state, especially its flagship institution—the NAACP. Second, Regulars vowed to combat any efforts by the federal courts to bring about racial change in Georgia. Whether it was the existence of the whites-only primary, school segregation, or interstate transportation, Regular leaders promised to disregard, subvert, or overturn the court's orders. In 1946, Talmadge illustrated this attitude when, in response to a court ruling against segregation in interstate travel, he pledged to stop all buses coming into Georgia at the state line, have the passengers disembark, and then resegregate any who were sitting in interracial groups.[31] Finally, Regulars intended to prevent the national Democratic Party from supporting or enforcing civil rights—if necessary by denying its presidential candidates the southern support that Regulars believed they could not do without.

Overall, owing to their incumbency, their built-in structural political advantages, and the fact that a large majority of those who were able to take part in Georgia's elections favored racial and cultural traditionalism, the Regulars emerged from the war as the most powerful group in state politics. For the short term, they held most of the cards. For the long term, however, they were in a far more tenuous position. As the group most interested in preserving the existing order at a time when the pressure to reform that order was gathering strength and momentum, the Regulars were in a position akin to that of King Canute commanding the tides not to come in: like the king, they were the most powerful political figures in the land, but there were still some forces beyond their control. Just as Canute could not hold the tide at bay, neither could Regular Democrats simply decree that southern society remain static.

The debate over how to resolve the tension between resisting change but being unable to stop it entirely lay at the heart of the main divide within the Regular faction. This divide was between pragmatists and purists. Pragmatists hoped to preserve as much of the traditional order as possible, but were concerned that inflexible resistance to any form of change risked giving away everything. In other words, if it was possible to preserve 95 percent of the way things were by acceding to a change in the other 5 percent, pragmatists were willing to make that deal. They would do so only when pushed, to be sure, but ultimately they believed this was a more sensible political choice than attempting to fight for 100 percent and instead losing it all.

A good example of a Regular pragmatist was James S. Peters, the Georgia state Democratic chairman from 1944 to 1954 and an influential adviser to senior figures in the party. Peters was well aware that change was coming to southern politics, but believed it could be strictly controlled as long as Regular Democrats updated their image a little. After what they had experienced in the Depression and the war, Peters believed voters would no longer be satisfied with rhetorical assaults on blacks, the federal government, northern business, and the Republican Party. Regulars would have to show they had more to offer than that. As Peters put it in an interview with the *Macon Telegraph* in 1954, the minimum wage, federal programs, farm benefits, and the transition from agriculture toward industrialism had all "affected the thinking of the southern voter" and cut "gullies in the political top-soil that Democrats had [trod] on so long unchallenged."[32]

To address this changed reality, Peters stressed to Regular candidates that they needed to convince voters they could manage the economy and provide good schools in order to maintain the necessary electoral support to resist civil rights. In the summer of 1953, Peters wrote to outgoing governor Herman Talmadge, Gene's son, that a positive reputation for economic management was vital for any Regular candidate hoping to win the 1954 gubernatorial primary. Only when sound economic credentials had been established would it be possible to focus on defending "segregation and the county unit system."[33] When Georgia faced its moment of crisis over whether to close the public schools rather than allow even a handful of black students to attend, Peters again advocated a pragmatic approach, warning that if the schools were not kept open once all legal remedies to avoid desegregation had been exhausted, the result would be the defeat of Regular candidates. Better to let a handful of black students attend a few schools in Atlanta than risk the election of a candidate committed to more comprehensive desegregation.[34]

Peters's views reflected the general position pragmatic Regulars took on the question of desegregation. To use a military metaphor, pragmatists were willing to resist fully and for as long as possible, but once the other side threatened to encircle them, they thought it was better to withdraw to the next line of defense rather than risk giving up their whole army. As well as Peters, other important Regular Democratic leaders in the postwar years who were also pragmatists included governors Herman Talmadge (1948–1955) and S. Ernest Vandiver (1959–1963). As both of these men proved in their gubernatorial campaigns and administrations, being a pragmatist did not mean shying away from deploying incendiary racial rhetoric for electoral gain. That was common to all Regulars. But it did mean holding the view that the ground rules of Georgia politics had changed fundamentally, and recognizing that this might require making compromises in order to stay in office. Peters summed up this underlying feeling in a letter to U.S. representative John J. Flynt in 1960, in which he warned that "you are going to have to deal with such minority groups" as those willing to countenance desegregated education. Politics in the state was changing, and soon more and more groups, including "negroes and catholics," were going to become more influential and needed to be acknowledged as such, "and you men and women are going to have to recognize this fact."[35]

In contrast to Peters, Regular purists believed that even with all the changes that had taken place since the 1930s, an absolute defense of the racial status quo was both possible and desirable, no matter what the cost. Gene Talmadge had been the patron saint of those subscribing to this view. After his death in 1946, leadership of the purist group devolved to others, including former Speaker of the Georgia House Roy V. Harris; constitutional lawyer and member of the State Democratic Executive Committee Charles J. Bloch; and S. Marvin Griffin, who served as governor of Georgia from 1955 to 1959. Of the three, Bloch was the one to express the purists' belief in the most flamboyant terms. As a delegate supporting the breakaway Dixiecrats at the 1948 Democratic National Convention, he had invoked William Jennings Bryan in explaining his stance by declaring, "You shall not crucify the South on a cross of civil rights!"[36] In defending the county-unit system, Bloch did not even pretend to believe that it was democratic. In fact, he did quite the opposite; he celebrated its nondemocratic rules as both vital to the preservation of white supremacy and perfectly constitutional. As for those who disagreed with this view, Bloch told one audience, "I defy them to point out to you the word 'democracy' in the Constitution of the U.S.!"[37]

As far as both Bloch and Harris were concerned, compromising on desegregation even to the smallest degree was unthinkable. In response to suggestions in the press that white Georgians may not want an all-out fight for segregation if it meant closing their schools, Bloch angrily responded that "our Georgia people are not in any mood for any compromise on this subject. I believe that 99% of them would rather fight and wholly lose than to compromise even one percent."[38] Harris, as head of the States' Rights Council that was formed after the *Brown* decision, circulated a pamphlet arguing that interposition and school closures were perfectly viable options and were a price worth paying to preserve segregation.[39]

The absolutism of the purists should not be mistaken for a lack of political skill. Bloch was a highly respected constitutional lawyer who was regularly employed by the state in cases involving segregation law and the county-unit system. Harris was reputed to be the most sophisticated political observer in the state, with a network of contacts in almost every county that allowed him to correctly predict the outcome of most statewide contests weeks before polling day. Even his opponents respected Harris's political skill. A 1947 profile of Georgia politics written as an indictment of Harris's policy agenda nonetheless concluded that he was the most "conspicuous and most expert" political kingmaker in the state.[40] It was precisely this combination of devotion to their cause and political skills that made the purists a force to be reckoned with.

The tension between pragmatists and purists in the Regular faction was already evident by 1946. It was clearest in the generational differences between Gene and Herman Talmadge over just how to run the gubernatorial campaign for that year's primary. At that stage, however, the tension had not yet developed into the public, open split in Regular opinion that would be visible by 1960. It is also important not to overstate the ideological differences between the two groups. It was not that they disagreed over the desirability of the basic Regular agenda; their disagreements were only ever over how far to go in defending that agenda, and when or whether to give a little ground in order to stay in power.

Regardless of their differences on this issue, in 1946, and for close to two decades more, all Regular leaders were in agreement that their position was strongest when race was central to the political debate in Georgia. As such, whether it was directly opposing desegregation or voting rights, or opposing government intervention in the economy, or opposing changes to the antidemocratic features of the state's political structure, Regular Democrats invariably sought to frame their arguments in terms of the threat such polices posed to the racial order. So long as they were able to convince Georgia's electorate that race must be their number one concern, their status as the most powerful group in state politics would likely remain intact.

A Modernized New South: The Loyalist Agenda in Postwar Georgia

The Regulars' effectiveness in using appeals to racial and cultural traditionalism as a way to limit political and economic reform in Georgia was the chief reason that their opponents within the Democratic Party wanted to marginalize race as a political issue. This became a central goal of the Loyalist faction of the party, which embraced the economic activism of the Roosevelt administration and wanted to emulate this activism in post-war Georgia. Their "loyalty" was therefore to the national Democratic Party as an institution and the legacy of the New Deal as a political inspiration. As far as Loyalists were concerned, the New Deal had enabled the southern economy to turn the corner during the Depression, and they believed that an extension of the basic philosophy behind the New Deal to the South would, in turn, create a New South.

The Loyalist vision of what that New South would be like is not easily placed on a conventional ideological spectrum. The difficulty in doing so is perhaps the biggest reason for not framing the Regular-Loyalist divide as a straightforward conservative-liberal one. Simply put, while virtually all white southern liberals were Loyalists, most Loyalists were not liberals—at least not in the way the term has been understood for postwar America. While Loyalists in general espoused ideas that were more liberal than those favored by Regulars, and while Loyalists were more receptive than Regulars to the demands of interest groups who favored liberalizing economic, social, or racial policy in the South—such as labor unions, civil rights activists, or women's rights groups—they still frequently took antiliberal positions. Loyalists were often strong supporters of regressive taxation and close, corporatist relationships between business leaders and government. Labor unions were tolerated, but generally not welcomed. Adjustments in the racial or social order were accepted, but rarely advocated. Government activism was desirable to promote education, but not to redistribute wealth. Overall, most Loyalists had more in common with the Progressives of the early 1900s than with the liberals of the 1960s.

As such, it is more helpful to see the New South envisaged by Loyalists as being based on a desire for a "modernized" South. According to Luebke's framework, at its heart the modernists' belief was that the South's problems were a result of its economic backwardness. As a result, the modernizers' priority was to find ways to generate economic growth. Loyalists believed in the economic maxim that a "rising tide lifts all boats," or, to put it in Luebke's words, "by promoting growth, modernizers [envisioned] prosperity for all through an expanded economic pie."[41] In other words, the region's social and political problems were really economic problems; solve the latter, and the former would disappear as a consequence.

Drawing on this general belief, the Loyalists' agenda for a modernized New South centered around three policy priorities. One was political reform. Loyalists saw election mechanisms such as the county-unit system, the malapportionment of the General Assembly, and the endemic corruption for which southern elections were notorious as both antidemocratic and antimodern. In line with the Progressive advocates of government reform fifty years earlier, Loyalists believed in making politics more "rational," which to them meant basing it on majority rule (or at least white majority rule). A second priority was an activist government dedicated to promoting economic growth. Loyalists wanted to use the state government to bring new investment to the state, ideally in high-skill, high-wage industries. In essence, they wanted to build on and continue the industrialization and mechanization of the southern economy that had been set in motion during the 1930s. Loyalists hoped that this would "liberate" the southern economy from its decades-long stagnation.

The third policy priority for Loyalists was education. The focus on education served a dual purpose: as a means of creating a workforce that would prove attractive to modern industrial employers but also as a mechanism for bringing about economic opportunity. In this sense, Loyalists tapped into a long-standing American belief—that education was the "silver bullet" to end inequality of opportunity in U.S. society. Each of these three priorities was connected to the other two; as such, it would not be accurate to describe them in terms of a hierarchy of goals. They were intended to reinforce each other, and all three were critical to the Loyalists' hopes for an industrialized, prosperous, educated, and modernized New South.

Loyalists did not advocate dramatic changes to the traditional social order, but, crucially for their ability to respond to the civil rights movement, they placed "no special value on existing social relations."[42] In other words, if political reform, economic growth, and educational expansion could be achieved within the existing social order, then all well and good; if they required an alteration in the existing social order, however, then growth and education were to be given priority. In an echo of Lincoln's 1862 views on the Union and slavery, if Loyalists could promote economic growth without abandoning segregation, they would do it; if they could only promote it by agreeing to desegregation, they would do it; and if they could promote it by keeping segregation in some areas and abandoning it in others, they would do that also. This is not to deny the presence

of some in the Loyalist faction who genuinely wanted to reform southern race relations, but in 1946, with the exception of antilynching movements, they were a distinct minority. Most Loyalists preferred to ignore
race altogether.

Within the Loyalist faction, there were also two main groups, which it
is most helpful to think of as mainstream Loyalists and liberal Loyalists.
Mainstream Loyalists were by far the more numerous of the two. They
supported the three principal policy aims of political reform, government
activism, and public education, but had little interest in pursuing changes
in the social order beyond the bare minimum required to achieve these
goals. They embraced the "good government–progressive" ideology that
Jennifer Brooks identified in her study of veterans in postwar Georgia.
Mainstream Loyalists were concerned with economic expansion. Social
or racial justice was generally a secondary consideration, if it was considered at all. Accordingly, the political and social system embraced by
Regular Democrats was not objectionable because it denied people their
individual rights, but rather because it stifled economic growth. Brooks
captures this view in her description of "good government" veterans' critique of existing southern politics: "Conservative local regimes were objectionable not because they routinely denied civic and economic rights
to black southerners and workers. Rather, their habits of electoral fraud,
civic intimidation and political corruption impeded creating programs
of industrial recruitment and economic development that these veterans
believed to be the foundations of real progress."[43]

Mainstream Loyalists were also likely to be culturally traditionalist
by inclination. They were uneasy about labor unions and skeptical toward the civil rights movement, primarily because they saw both unrest
in the workplace and debates over desegregation as potentially disruptive to economic growth. Significant individuals who can be considered
mainstream Loyalists in the postwar years include James V. Carmichael,
Talmadge's chief rival in the 1946 gubernatorial primary; Melvyn ("M.
E.") Thompson, interim governor of Georgia from 1947 to 1948; as well
as George T. Smith and Carl Sanders, Speaker of the Georgia House and
governor from 1963 to 1967, respectively.

The more liberal minority within the Loyalist faction agreed with all
the policy positions of mainstream Loyalists, but wanted to push further
and actively pursue social and economic reform. For some, this involved
advocating more interracial cooperation or even a removal of some of the

laws that caused black disfranchisement. For an even smaller number, it involved a direct critique of segregation itself. Others wanted to change the way labor relations operated in Georgia by improving working conditions and promoting the growth of labor unions.[44] Future U.S. representative James MacKay and his fellow World War II veteran Calvin Kytle produced a study of the state's political culture in 1947 entitled *Who Runs Georgia?* which set out just such an agenda.[45] For Loyalists like MacKay and Kytle, their political role model was Ellis Arnall, governor of Georgia from 1943 to 1947. The combination of political, economic, and social reform that Arnall advocated both during his administration and in his unsuccessful comeback effort in 1966 was exactly what these more liberal Loyalists wanted to pursue.

The differences between these two groups of Loyalists were generally ones of degree, not of kind. To say that mainstream Loyalists did not prioritize social justice or improved race relations does not mean they were necessarily opposed to these things occurring. Similarly, the fact that more liberal Loyalists wanted to reform the social and racial order did not mean they were ignorant of how unpopular or politically risky advocating such reform might be. Ultimately, however, both types of Loyalists agreed on the need for a postwar New South that required a different set of polices from those advocated by Regular Democrats.

Collectively, Loyalists hoped their vision of a New South would be realized by establishing a virtuous circle of self-sustaining progress. Political reform would both eliminate corruption and "drain the swamp" of demagogues, so that a man like Gene Talmadge would not be able to win statewide office. This in turn would allow government to focus on doing more to encourage economic growth, including attracting business and promoting education to produce a more skilled workforce. Economic growth and a more educated population would in turn further weaken the appeals of demagogues as people learned to let go of their fears and focus on more rational political concerns. This would result in a lessening of racial tensions and bring about a more peaceful (if potentially still segregated) racial order. Black Georgians themselves would benefit not just from a reduction in white hostility but also from the universal gain of all citizens from the new prosperity and opportunities. In sum, the result would be a more rational and harmonious political culture in which figures such as Gene Talmadge would be nothing more than historical curiosities.

As hopeful as Loyalists were that their vision for a New South might come to pass, they were also keenly aware that racial strife contained the potential to derail it. As far as Loyalists were concerned, whatever their personal view on segregation, an obsession with race was politically unhealthy. It was a sign of irrationality and, Loyalists believed, produced destructive behavior that would harm black and white southerners' prospects for mutual progress. Avoiding anything that might stir up racial feelings was therefore a top priority, and Loyalists justified doing so in terms that implied racism was chiefly a phenomenon present only among uneducated, poor whites. David L. Chappell has described the rationalization behind this attitude as a belief among white southern moderates that "if we disrupt race relations . . . then rednecks, egged on by demagogues, will react violently, and that will only harm the Negro in long run."[46] If the concern over harm to the economy was added to this summary, it would encapsulate the Loyalist fear over what would happen if race remained central to southern politics.

In light of this, the appeal of addressing racial issues through the use of progressive color blindness is obvious. As focusing on race was irrational, and as progress was intended to be universal, it was in the best interests of whites *and* blacks not to dwell on their racial differences. Instead, all voters should recognize their shared interest in a modernized economy, political reform, and greater educational opportunities. Progressive color blindness allowed Loyalists to affirm the principle of universal citizenship, but without taking proactive steps to achieve it. It gave them the flexibility both to distance themselves from the "racial agitation" of the civil rights movement and also to refuse to condone extralegal or violent resistance to racial change. Progressive color blindness was also a message Loyalists could use to seek support from the growing number of black voters in Georgia.

The two best expressions of the Loyalists' overall agenda in 1940s Georgia can be found in what are effectively two manifestos for the Loyalist cause: Kytle and MacKay's *Who Runs Georgia?* and outgoing governor Ellis Arnall's 1946 roadmap for his vision of a New South, *The Shore Dimly Seen.*[47] As the title of his book suggested, Arnall was aware that Georgia was undergoing a major political transition and also that this transition was by no means complete.[48] The book laid out the path that Arnall believed Georgia ought to take in order to reach "the shore." Arnall argued that economic backwardness was at the root of the South's relative poverty and its social problems.[49] To remedy this would require pursuing policies that would extend economic opportunity to those most victimized by the existing structure, and this in turn would require a change of attitude in regard to the role of the state government.

Specifically, Arnall argued it required state governments to take a proactive role in pursuing economic prosperity and evince a willingness to work with the federal government in the process. Arnall criticized those who resisted federal attempts to address socioeconomic problems in the name of states' rights by accusing the states of having wanted to "shirk responsibility" for taking care of those problems themselves.[50] This desire for greater government activism did not, in Arnall's view, represent a fundamental critique of capitalism: rather, it was necessary in his eyes in order to protect the values of "free enterprise" against unscrupulous and monopolistic (and generally nonsouthern) corporations. As he put it, free enterprise and economic prosperity could only be secured by "government cooperation at every level, and careful planning," for "the truth is that more planning is necessary under a free economy than under a planned economy."[51]

Arnall argued that expanding education must be at the heart of this "planning." Not only would it help to give people the tools to compete for high-skill, high-wage industrial and manufacturing jobs, but it would also serve to lessen the ability of Regular Democrats to win elections by appealing to prejudice. Greater education would produce a more knowledgeable and progressive electorate less prone to demagogic appeals, which explained to Arnall why Regular Democrats were so hostile to spending more on public education. After all, he argued, "reading and writing are the enemies that [the demagogue] fears the most."[52] Arnall therefore called for major increases in spending on education and advocated federal-state cooperation in raising the necessary funds.[53]

In some other areas of the economy, Arnall was more liberal than most of his fellow Loyalists. He argued that greater protection should be provided for labor unions, as "collective bargaining is the device that can produce the greatest democracy in the American industrial system."[54] Additionally, he advocated universal job-insurance programs and health benefits for sick workers and their families.[55] Nonetheless, there is no mistaking in Arnall's rhetoric the common Loyalist view of the New Deal as an inspiration. This was nowhere more apparent than in the Rooseveltian tone of Arnall's overall vision for the nation: "I want an America in which the son of any citizen can become President or a millionaire; but I want an America in which possession of wealth equates no possession of power, and in which hunger and fear have been eliminated."[56]

This vision, once achieved, would leave behind not only a prosperous South but also a South no longer obsessed with the "negro problem." In line with the principles of progressive color blindness, Arnall acknowledged that blacks did perhaps suffer more than most, but he believed that at its heart "the problem of the Negro in the South is a problem of economics."[57] Healing the racial divisions in southern society therefore did not require addressing race per se: rather, it required providing a collective economic uplift for *all* southerners. To Arnall, racism was a symptom of economic backwardness and ignorance encouraged by unscrupulous Regular Democrats to consolidate their own power. This did not mean that Arnall advocated desegregation, but rather he found distasteful the exploitation of racial animosities that Gene Talmadge thrived on: "[Racial prejudice] does not arise from any dislike for the Negro, but from a dislike for all mankind. It comes of a desire for power and wealth at the expense of other men, and from cowardice that understands it is easier to rob a blind man than one who can see and less dangerous to slap the face of a man whose hands are tied."[58]

During their interviews of Georgia politicians conducted the following year, Kytle and MacKay echoed Arnall's prescriptions for what should happen to southern politics, although they were somewhat less optimistic than the governor about the prospects for success. Throughout their book, Kytle and MacKay described in a fatalistic tone the ways in which various corporate lobby groups had blocked the General Assembly from raising the necessary taxes to improve the educational system. They further noted that in 1947, the General Assembly had passed four tax bills, none of which provided extra revenue, but all of which gave tax breaks to Georgia corporations.[59] As additional evidence of the regressive outlook of those favored corporations, Kytle and MacKay pointed to the manner in which comprehensive anti-union measures were adopted by the state after lobbying from those corporate leaders who stood to benefit most from such laws.[60] As far as the two young veterans were concerned, this was entirely the opposite of what Georgia needed. Instead, like Arnall, they advocated more education, more government, and political reform.

Kytle and MacKay also shared Arnall's dim view of how race was used by Regular Democrats. In discussing the 1946 gubernatorial primary, they concluded that "fear ran the campaign that elected Eugene Talmadge . . . the fear of change."[61] In their eyes, Talmadge's racially charged rhetoric mixed with an antimodern agenda threatened to undermine both economic growth and social stability. Rather than stir up racial divisions, Kytle and MacKay argued race should be discussed in a way that drew on the principles of progressive color blindness. They frequently stressed mutual interest and universal gain between racial groups, as in their concluding call that in order to advance the cause of economic justice and democracy in the South, "one must first accept the principle that in a political democracy *there are no Negroes and no whites*, only citizens."[62] To be sure, it was a strikingly different tone from anything a Regular Democrat might have said. And yet, as was generally the case with progressive color blindness during the 1940s, the *principle* of mutual interest between the races was stressed repeatedly, but proposals for *achieving* racial equality other than through promoting economic growth were hardly ever to be found.

Overall, both the rise of the Loyalist faction and the belief in modernization that informed their vision for a New South were a sign of the changes the 1930s and 1940s had produced in Georgia. Having seen the New Deal in action, and having witnessed the acceleration of urbanization, diversification, and mechanization in the region's economy that followed it, white southerners who wanted these trends to continue viewed the Regulars as standing in their way. They hoped to create a society that was the polar opposite of the benighted South depicted in *Tobacco Road* and usher in an era of politics that no longer "revolved around the status of the Negro."[63]

Raising "the Status of the Negro": The Civil Rights Movement in Postwar Georgia

Trying to capture the full range of ideas, personalities, and agendas of multiple politicians by dividing them into just two factions is a difficult enough undertaking; trying to capture the full range of ideas, personalities, and agendas of something as complex as the campaign for black equality in the twentieth century by distilling it into a single entity—the civil rights movement—is even more problematic. Whereas the King-focused "Montgomery to Memphis" narrative of the civil rights movement once reigned supreme, a generation of scholarship has since described a more intricate and varied series of civil rights movements in all regions of the country and often stretching back fifty years or more from the end of World War II. Determining when the civil rights movement started, or who could claim to represent it or lead it at any given time, remains one of the liveliest areas of scholarly debate. In terms of understanding the impact of campaigns for black voting rights and desegregation on postwar Georgia politics, however, these debates are interesting, but not central; clearly "civil rights" as a political issue was near the top of the state's agenda for at least thirty years after 1945, but as it is the reaction of the politicians and the political parties that is the focus here, the history of the civil rights movement itself is not as critical a concern.

Nonetheless, a basic definition of how the term "civil rights movement" is being interpreted during the subsequent chapters is necessary. Accordingly, throughout this book, the civil rights movement is defined as the political and social mobilization of black Georgians to gain equal access to political, social, and economic rights from which they were formally excluded. The primary goals of civil rights activists were desegregation and voting rights, with a secondary goal of expanding black representation in positions of political power. These goals were complementary: a gain in one would not detract from gains in the other; instead, gains in one would likely lead to additional gains in the other. A wide range of civil rights activities fall within this definition, including sit-ins, voter registration drives, lawsuits to equalize facilities, and lobbying for the appointment of black public officials.

In this form, the civil rights movement in Georgia began to coalesce after 1942 into the form it would take in the postwar years. This does not mean that before 1942 there was nothing—far from it; rather, it means that beginning in 1942 there was a decisive shift in the organizational structure and scale of activities of Georgia's black community. In 1942, the Reverend Mark Gilbert rechartered the NAACP in Savannah, thereby setting in motion a revitalization of the statewide organization and creating a structure through which pressure on the state's white political leadership could be sustained and coordinated. For the next thirty years, the civil rights movement in Georgia evidenced a strategic unity of purpose, defined by the twin pursuits of desegregation and political power. Following Gilbert's rechartering of the NAACP in Savannah, black leaders and activists tried to create their own virtuous circle, whereby increased black voter registration would serve as a bargaining chip to persuade white politicians to accept changes in the racial order with the ultimate goal of desegregation.

Such changes in the racial order would in turn allow black political influence to increase.

Similarly, during that same period, differences between Georgia's civil rights activists were defined by consistent and familiar tensions. Along the way, those same leaders and activists disagreed—often vehemently—over how best to pursue this overall agenda. They differed over the appropriate targets, strategies, and leaders, and when and how to compromise. There were tensions over class, gender, and region, as well as over partisan preferences and simple personality clashes. Underlying it all, though, no one disagreed that the ultimate goals were an end to Jim Crow and a greater black political influence in the state.

In the early 1970s, the nature of black politics in Georgia changed once more, as the twin goals of desegregation and political power began sometimes to conflict with each other. For instance, during the 1973 dispute over busing policy and suburban annexation in Atlanta, some civil rights groups called for reversing white flight and busing black children to suburban schools to integrate them, while others countered that this would dilute black political influence within Atlanta and would deprive black parents of control over their children's education. Just as the end of Jim Crow and the arrival of black voting reshaped the party system in the South, so, too, did it reshape black political activism. The broad consensus that had existed since the 1940s was gone.[64]

The importance of the postwar consensus on ultimate goals was critical to smoothing over the disagreements among black leaders in Georgia. According to Jacob Henderson, Atlanta's director of federal housing projects since 1941 and a mediating figure within the city's black elite, it was only this agreement on basic aims that kept the civil rights groups working together. Indeed, Henderson recounted needing all his patience to smooth over the fractious political relations between black leaders in Atlanta to persuade them to join forces in a citywide voter registration drive. Despite the partisan and tactical disagreements he encountered, Henderson succeeded when "everybody finally agreed that . . . the important thing was how we can use [black voting] power to get response and influence in the white political arena." Furthermore, once "blacks began to see what the power, what the vote could do," it was no longer difficult to persuade black leaders to work together to maximize it.[65]

The effect this had on white politicians was as predictable as it was significant. The presence of a large group of previously ignored voters represented a tempting proposition for any candidate. At the very least, it created a powerful incentive to listen to black leaders. In areas where black registration was particularly high, it could soften the hostility of even committed segregationists. Robert Flanagan, the executive director of the Atlanta NAACP in the 1940s, noted that even Herman Talmadge changed his attitude as black voting strength increased. According to Flanagan, Talmadge's reaction was not unusual: "this is what the vote did [for blacks] throughout the South because a lot of white politicians told me, says, 'I'll tell you the truth. I would do something for you, but y'all are not on the books.'"[66]

Flanagan also observed this firsthand in the gradual development of an alliance between black voters in Atlanta and Mayor William B. Hartsfield. Although Hartsfield was a confirmed ally of Governor Arnall and Loyalist in his political sympathies, as late as 1944 he was still suggesting in letters to the House Un-American Affairs Committee (HUAC) that the NAACP should be investigated as a subversive organization. In his 1945 reelection campaign, Hartsfield showed no interest in courting black votes and reiterated his desire not to tamper with segregation. Over the following few years, however, black registration in Atlanta dramatically increased. By the 1949 campaign, Hartsfield was courting support from black voters— support that turned out to be crucial in securing his reelection. Thereafter, Hartsfield began appointing black police officers and other public officials, and also meeting regularly with black political leaders. By 1951, he was personally welcoming the NAACP to Atlanta for its annual convention.[67] To be sure, race relations in Atlanta remained a divisive political issue, and Hartsfield remained a lukewarm ally as far as many civil rights leaders were concerned, but there was also no doubt that increased black voter registration had reshaped city politics.

The process by which civil rights activists were able to leverage black political strength into persuading Loyalists such as Hartsfield to seek the support of black voters by acquiescing in a degree of racial change was repeated time and again in Georgia during the postwar years. Step by step they were able to pressure, persuade, or cajole Loyalists (and even some of the more pragmatic Regulars) to make concessions. This does not mean it was a teleological process that simply "naturally" happened—it took patience, commitment, and skill by black leaders and activists. The fact that it was ultimately so effective, however, reflected a key insight that civil rights leaders had into the psyche of the white South: namely, as David

Chappell has put it, that "southern white resistance, if determined and vicious, was surmountable because its very determination and viciousness imposed too high a cost on southern society."[68]

Nonetheless, surmounting the resistance still required a mass movement and the institutions to mobilize it that black Georgians simply did not possess at the start of World War II. A generation earlier, Georgia had several functioning civil rights organizations, but by the end of the Depression many of them, including the state NAACP, had atrophied. Individual acts of resistance were still present, but nothing on the scale of resistance and mobilization that would be required to mount a serious challenge to Jim Crow.[69] The catalyst for such a mobilization came with Rev. Gilbert's arrival in Savannah. Having reestablished the NAACP as a significant force in city politics, Gilbert turned to reestablishing it as a statewide presence by organizing a meeting between its extant branches in the state. To this end, he was able to tap into like-minded black leadership in other Georgia towns and cities. William Randall Sr. in Macon, Dr. Thomas Brewer in Columbus, and J. M. Atkinson in Brunswick had already taken steps to organize civil rights activity in their cities by 1942, and their actions dovetailed with Gilbert's ambitions. All of these men, and many others who took part in the organizational efforts of the 1940s, became influential figures in the civil rights movement over the next several decades.[70]

Along with this renewed sense of activism around the state, the civil rights movement in Georgia was able to draw on the established cadre of black leadership in Atlanta. Even in the 1930s, with organized black protest at a low ebb throughout the state, Atlanta's black community had been sufficiently organized to defeat a 1938 bond issue that would have provided funds for white schools only.[71] Prominent black leaders in Atlanta included A. T. Walden, an attorney and the most powerful black Democrat in the city; John Wesley Dobbs, a postmaster, Republican leader, and grandfather of future Atlanta mayor Maynard Jackson; Ruby Blackburn, a former beautician turned community organizer who presided over the largest black voter organization in the city; John H. Calhoun, Dobbs's assistant and fellow Republican activist; and Grace Towns Hamilton, the executive director of Atlanta's chapter of the National Urban League. Given its size, economic importance, reputation for racial moderation, and central status in Georgia's politics, Atlanta always produced a disproportionate share of Georgia's civil rights leaders. Paradoxically, however, leaders from Atlanta were often more conservative and reactive than those from elsewhere.

By 1946, thanks to the collective efforts of these leaders and activists across the state, NAACP membership was more than tenfold what it had been in 1940, and black voter registration was up to 125,000—around 20 percent of the state's adult black population. This was well in advance of registration in neighboring Deep South states.[72] Also in 1946, a lawsuit instigated by Thomas Brewer on behalf of Primus King that sought to have the federal courts strike down the white primary in Georgia was successful. The *King v. Chapman* ruling officially opened up the Democratic primary to black voters in Georgia for the first time. This gave additional impetus to the registration efforts, with Atlanta alone registering 18,000 black voters in the fifty or so days between the *King* ruling and the last day for registering.[73] The results of elections across the state in 1946 would showcase the potent but complex impact of black voting on Georgia's politics. On the one hand, it proved a vital base of support for Loyalists in ousting Regular incumbents in several cities; on the other hand, the presence of black voters was also used by Regulars as a way to appeal to white voters not to support Loyalist candidates.

The potential influence that increased voting strength gave to black leaders also created some difficult choices for civil rights leaders. While all agreed that rising influence was a good thing, there was considerable disagreement about how such influence ought to be deployed. Having identified the split in white opinion over how far to go in preserving white supremacy, should civil rights activists push for direct confrontation or gradual suasion? Should they engage in a war of maneuver, whereby electoral support was offered to white candidates willing to support incremental racial change, or should black leaders seek a decisive confrontation with the segregated system in the hope of achieving more radical, comprehensive change?

Many of the established leaders in Atlanta favored the first of these two strategies. No one favored it more than A. T. Walden. By 1946, Walden had already been active in black politics for several decades. Born in 1885, Walden became one of the most prominent black lawyers in the state. In 1932, he had set up citizenship schools for black voters as head of the Atlanta NAACP, and for the rest of his life he was an integral part of the black political leadership in Georgia. Walden's view was that the best way to bring blacks into the mainstream of political life in Georgia was to seek alliances with Loyalist Democrats. As far as Walden was concerned, blacks could not operate as effectively if they tried to stay outside the system. A Democrat because of his support for the New Deal, Walden envisioned a New South where blacks and Loyalists would be in control of the Georgia Democratic Party. To achieve this, Walden believed that he could not push for civil rights too assertively, as this would make it impossible for Loyalists to reach compromises with him; yet he could also not afford to push too little, as then Loyalists might not offer compromises at all.

Ben Brown, a leader of the 1960 and 1961 student protests in Atlanta that were the very opposite of Walden's preferred form of engagement, described Walden's approach as being premised on keeping things "cool" with the city establishment in exchange for a limited quid pro quo. Despite Brown's rejection of this approach when it came to his decision to join the protests (and Walden's own criticism of those protests), he nonetheless described Walden as an inspirational figure.[74] Brown's positive view of Walden was not always shared by other civil rights activists, many of whom saw "the Colonel" (as Walden was known) as too cautious and conservative. On one occasion, Ruby Hurley, the NAACP's southeastern regional director, asked for Walden to be removed from handling civil rights cases in the state because of his gradualist approach.[75] Yet Walden's beliefs appealed to just as many as they angered, especially to his fellow leaders on Auburn Avenue, the center of black middle-class leadership in Atlanta. Indeed, so many of the Auburn Avenue elite shared Walden's outlook that this gradualist approach became known as the "Auburn Avenue Strategy."

In contrast to the mixture of respect and frustration that he received from the black community, Walden was frequently lionized by Loyalist Democrats. They appreciated his willingness to hold back from pushing for immediate desegregation and valued his ability to get out the black vote on their behalf. This made Walden just the sort of civil rights leader with whom Loyalists wanted to be dealing. Osgood Williams, a state legislator and campaign adviser to a slew of Loyalist candidates, accordingly interpreted Walden's gradualism as a sign that he "understood the cold, bloody, political reality" and was willing to make whatever compromises it took "to win." As a result, Williams believed, "what influence the black community had in a political way" by 1946 was due to Walden.[76]

An even more glowing tribute to Walden appeared in the *Atlanta Constitution* upon the Colonel's death in July 1965. The *Constitution* was essentially the Loyalists' house journal, and its editor, Eugene Patterson, wrote a personal eulogy to Walden in which he referred to him as "the old man, my friend." Patterson described Walden as having commanded, "often alone," the "formative years, the hard and dangerous years, of an historic revolution." Such was Walden's greatness, Patterson thought, that he was "perhaps the southern negro's greatest soldier manning the gap of history between Booker T. Washington and Martin Luther King."[77]

That Walden was so well thought of by white Loyalist leaders was a source of great influence for him but also fueled the suspicions of others in the civil rights movement that Walden was keeping things too "cool." The chief alternative to Walden's approach was to pursue direct-action protests aimed at comprehensive racial change. In the 1940s, this alternative approach was practiced by Mark Gilbert and his allies in Savannah. Gilbert wanted more black voters, but he also wanted a mass movement that involved multiple organizations pushing for change on multiple fronts. Gilbert was particularly keen that there should be organizations for young people. Under his direction, the NAACP Youth Council in Savannah became the largest such organization in the nation.[78]

Unlike Walden, Gilbert was perfectly happy to rely on confrontation, or at least threats of it, to force the pace of change in Savannah. Others followed his lead, including a group of black students who were arrested after boarding a city bus and deliberately sitting in the "whites-only" seats.[79] Gilbert and the Savannah movement in the 1940s thus offered an alternative model to the Auburn Avenue Strategy. It was an alternative that involved taking greater risks but also one that promised more rapid and substantial rewards. Those who were active in the Savannah movement justified it on these grounds. Wesley Law, head of the NAACP Youth Council under Gilbert and later statewide director of the NAACP, cited the achievements in Savannah as having produced a far more liberal climate than existed in Atlanta, which he derisively labeled "a cracker town." Law also challenged the centrality of A. T. Walden and Atlanta's leadership in generating black political influence in Georgia, arguing instead that "it was Gilbert who led blacks into the future."[80]

The different approaches that were favored by the black leadership in Atlanta and Savannah in the 1940s broadly represented the major strategic tension within Georgia's civil rights movement. While the tension was very real—both politically and personally—the two approaches were variations on a theme rather than polar opposites. Walden's pragmatism did not mean that he lacked determination or courage; Gilbert's militancy did not equate to an inability to compromise with white political leaders. Ultimately, the chief difference between the two men and the approaches they represented was not whether desegregation and black political influence should be achieved, but what the best strategy for achieving these goals was. The overall influence of advocates of direct-action protests versus supporters of the Auburn Avenue Strategy would ebb and flow over the next thirty years according to the political climate in the state, but the essential debate remained the same. In the 1950s, it would be Walden's preferred strategy of restrained activism that held sway; in the 1960s, momentum shifted back toward the use of direct-action protests. Each of these approaches had a critical impact on postwar Georgia.

*   *   *

As was the case for the South as a whole, Georgia in 1946 was in the midst of a comprehensive and irreversible transformation of its social and economic structure. The proportion of agricultural workers in the state was in decline. In 1940, a third of Georgia's workforce still worked in agriculture; by 1960, that would be down to 10 percent. White-collar employment rose sharply over the same period.[81] The black population in the state declined absolutely, from 45 percent in 1910 to 35 percent in 1950, but it also became more urbanized, more educated, and more able to vote.[82] Per capita income levels also rose for all Georgians, from 62 percent of the national average in 1942, to 70 percent in 1953 and 74 percent by 1962.[83]

As was the case for the rest of the South, Georgia had also been affected by the political and cultural changes of the New Deal and World War II. By 1942, thanks to New Deal programs and wartime spending, the federal government was providing 10 percent of the state's revenue; by 1953, the figure had risen to 17 percent. The relative growth of the federal government's role in funding state spending was part of an overall growth in government spending in Georgia. In 1942, state spending per capita was $35.19. Fifteen years later, the figure had risen to $187.18 (a real-terms increase of approximately 200 percent).[84] In addition, the alternating traumas and triumphs of depression and war had changed how Georgians saw themselves and the world: some were driven to demand reform, others to defend tradition, but none could escape the changes in political culture in the postwar world.

In light of all these changes, there was really no way that politics in Georgia would be able to restore the status quo ante. Regular Democrats spoke up for the state's traditional political constituencies, but sensed that they were facing a challenge of unprecedented scale. Loyalist Democrats and the civil rights movement sought to speak for the new and growing constituencies that the social and economic changes of the previous decade had empowered on the political stage. The stage was therefore set in 1946 for an election campaign that pitted the two opposing factions within the state Democratic Party against each other, with both seeking to respond to the emerging presence of the civil rights movement. The 1946 elections in Georgia would revolve around the state's growing demographic and economic divisions, arguments over the New Deal and government activism, and the future of white supremacy as well as the one-party system itself. The eventual victory by Regular Democrats was a serious setback for Loyalist hopes, a setback whose impact on Loyalists was "all the worse because it need not have been."[85] Nonetheless, despite the hopes of Gene Talmadge, it proved to be only a setback, rather than a crushing defeat. In fact, the elections of 1946 turned out to be just the opening round in a three-decade struggle to provide a conclusive answer to the central question posed by Kytle and MacKay: "Who Runs Georgia?"

2

Politics in Georgia before *Brown*

1946–1954

The Democratic Party can no more win today unless it is the liberal party than
it has been able to win in the past when it has not been the liberal party.

U.S. representative Helen Douglas Mankin (D-GA), 1946

The 1946 Democratic primary in Georgia was expected to be a close contest even before a single candidate entered the race. In part, this was due
to an intense personal rivalry between two of the state's leading political
figures. In the previous gubernatorial contest, Ellis Arnall had handed
Gene Talmadge his only defeat in an election for statewide office. It was
widely expected that Talmadge would seek to avenge this defeat at the
first opportunity. Talmadge's wounded ego was clearly a factor, but there
was more to his determination to regain the governor's office than simply personal pique. He and Arnall were also sharply at odds over public
policy. To Talmadge and his Regular supporters, Arnall's modernizing
agenda as governor threatened to undermine the institutions and tradi-
tions that they held most dear; to Arnall and his Loyalist allies, Talmadge
represented everything that was holding the South back from economic
prosperity and social peace. As a result, even though Arnall was constitutionally ineligible to run for a second consecutive term, both sides saw
the 1946 contest as a critical test of which of the two men's agendas would
gain the initiative in defining the postwar world.

Simultaneous contests in other southern states also suggested it would
be a close race in Georgia. Throughout the region, Democrats were split
between Loyalists supporting economic modernization of the South and
Regulars worried about the threat modernization posed to Jim Crow.
Overall, results in 1946 gave hope to both factions. Loyalists could be
satisfied with Sid McMath's "G.I. Revolt" that gave him control of the city
government in Hot Springs, Arkansas, and would serve as a springboard

for his elevation to the statehouse two years later. They could further be pleased at the victory in Alabama's gubernatorial contest of James E. "Big Jim" Folsom, who had stressed modernization and political reform in his campaign. On the other hand, Regulars could take heart from the elections of Fielding Wright and J. Strom Thurmond as governors of Mississippi and South Carolina, respectively. In short, supporters of both Arnall and Talmadge had cause to be optimistic but also reason to anticipate a tight race.

The collective expectation that the 1946 primary in Georgia would be a pivotal test of each faction's strength was ultimately born out both by the closeness and the impact of the result. Even before the gubernatorial campaign officially started, however, a special congressional election in the state's Fifth Congressional District in February 1946 provided a dramatic prologue that raised the stakes further for the summer contest. In 1942, the Fifth District, based around Atlanta and containing the most politically active black population as well as the most urbanized and educated white electorate of any of Georgia's districts, had strongly supported Arnall. Still, Regular Democrats were confident they would win the special election. They were so confident, in fact, that their chosen candidate, Tom Camp, decided to forego the county-unit system in the special election and relied on being able to secure an overall plurality to win.[1]

Much to Camp's surprise, and to the general shock of Regulars across the state, he was defeated by state representative Helen Douglas Mankin of Fulton County. The defeat was particularly jarring for Regulars, as Mankin's views placed her firmly within the liberal wing of the Loyalist faction. In the General Assembly, Mankin had supported spending more money on educational programs and had spoken up for "good government" reform, women's rights, and greater tolerance for labor unions. At various times, she had sponsored legislation extending the school year as a way to provide Georgia's children with higher levels of education; backed making secret ballots available in Georgia elections to prevent electoral fraud; promoted laws to give women greater legal rights within marriage; and campaigned alongside union leaders for the creation of a state department of labor.[2] Given how closely this coincided with Arnall's own priorities, it was no surprise that he warmly endorsed her candidacy.[3]

On race, Mankin subscribed to the general Loyalist view that prosperity would alleviate social and racial tensions. As her biographer put it, Mankin believed that "when [the South] gained its economic health,

then interracial adjustments would naturally follow."[4] Like many Loyalists, Mankin was also keen to maintain discreet contacts with black political leaders. During the 1946 campaign, Mankin talked with the black
leadership in Atlanta and won their private support. In part, this was because she was the only candidate willing to meet with them. It was understood by all sides that these contacts could not be overt. Accordingly,
word of Mankin's meeting was not disseminated to black communities in
Atlanta until the night before the election.[5] Aside from her clandestine efforts to secure black support, Mankin preferred not to address race if she
could avoid it. She shared the hope of one of her supporters that if "we all
kept quiet about it, [racial tensions] might go away—or something."[6] As
Mankin's campaign manager, Helen Bullard, later noted, she had no idea
what Mankin actually thought about race in 1946, only that she did not
want to talk about it.[7]

Atlanta's black leadership in turn overlooked Mankin's reluctance to
publicly support racial change in exchange for the chance to demonstrate
their political muscle. Jacob Henderson, who registered black voters
on behalf of Mankin, had generally warm things to say about her as an
individual. Above all, Henderson argued, the effectiveness of the voter
mobilization efforts he helped organize for the special election ensured
that "from that point on, the boys didn't ignore us."[8] Clarence Bacote,
a civil rights activist and historian at Atlanta University, was similarly
understanding about Mankin's silence on race. Bacote recalled that even
Mankin only ever agreed to nighttime meetings with black leaders so as to
conceal these contacts from her white opponents. Still, Bacote's recount-
ing of the tale is primarily a gleeful description of having blindsided the
city's white establishment.[9]

Both Henderson and Bacote had good reason to be pleased with their
efforts. Once the results were in, it was clear that votes from the black districts of Atlanta had given Mankin her plurality.[10] Overall, Mankin owed
her election to the so-called populist coalition of blacks, poor whites, and
labor unions that southern liberals had been seeking for generations.[11]
Her triumph was both a surprise and an achievement with lasting consequences. Her victory suggested to Loyalists across Georgia that they
might be on the cusp of ousting the Regulars from office. Furthermore,
Mankin's achievement was also noteworthy on account of her being the
first woman elected to Congress from Georgia. The fact that her campaign

had also been run by a woman, Helen Bullard, only added to the sense of change that her election represented.

And yet for all that Loyalists and black political leaders had to celebrate in Mankin's victory, her success also contained warning signs for the future. As soon as it became known that the ballots of black voters had been crucial to Mankin's victory, Regulars seized on the issue to warn white voters of the dangers of voting for Loyalist candidates. Gene Talmadge took to referring to Mankin as "the belle of Ashby Street," in reference to the main street in the majority-black precinct that had put her over the top. The nickname also drew attention to Mankin's gender in a none-too-subtle attempt to impugn both Mankin's closeness to black voters and to raise the specter of the ultimate sexual taboo of a white woman associating with black men.

Mankin also had to deal with a lack of support from some Loyalists who thought that she was too liberal. In particular, her affinity for labor unions made some uncomfortable. Frances Pauley, the head of the Georgia League of Women Voters (GLWV), commented that for many white Georgians, "it was almost as bad to have your picture taken with somebody with the union as it was to be taken with a black."[12] Others were uneasy at Mankin's perceived lack of femininity. It was no secret that Mankin enjoyed a drink, or that she smoked and was not averse to swearing. All of this would have been unremarkable for any male politician of the time (indeed, it would have been more remarkable for a male politician not to have those traits), but in Mankin's case some deemed it inappropriate. Hamilton Lokey, a fellow Loyalist state legislator, admitted to having reservations about Mankin because "she was a rather strident woman" who "didn't have the soft, genteel . . . the storybook class of a southern lady." Instead, "she was rather aggressive."[13]

Overall, Mankin's election and the subsequent reaction to it helped set the tone for the next decade and beyond. Her ability to win black support and finesse questions of race through progressive color blindness so as to advocate for economic modernization and political reform was something other Loyalists would seek to emulate. Similarly, the Regular opposition to her as an advocate for black interests who was disrespectful toward the cultural norms of the traditional white South was representative of many later efforts to mobilize a white backlash against Loyalist candidates. In the short run, the backlash successfully ended Mankin's tenure in Congress and severely hampered civil rights activity, but it did not restore the Regulars to uncontested control of the state party, and it could not shut down black political mobilization entirely. Instead, it ushered in a period of stalemate, where the two Democratic factions established broad and stable coalitions of support that evenly split the Georgia electorate in the period between the end of the war and the U.S. Supreme Court's 1954 ruling in *Brown v. Board of Education*. In hindsight, however, it became clear that even though her congressional career lasted less than twelve months, Mankin had fired the opening shot in what was a lengthy and tumultuous contest for control of the Democratic Party in Georgia.

The 1946 Primaries

A key factor in Talmadge's 1942 defeat by Ellis Arnall was Talmadge's controversial intervention in the affairs of the University of Georgia. As governor, Talmadge had pressured the Board of Regents to dismiss two faculty members on suspicion of racial liberalism. Following their ejection, the state's university system had its accreditation withdrawn. In the subsequent primary, Arnall attacked Talmadge as thus having jeopardized the state's educational system. The way Talmadge saw it, he had been standing up for white supremacy and had been thwarted by the urban intelligentsia, who could not be trusted to defend segregation. Talmadge also believed that although Georgia's voters had rejected him in 1942, fundamentally they still shared his commitment to Jim Crow. As such, when the U.S. Supreme Court upheld a lower court ruling invalidating the all-white primary in Georgia in April 1946 and Arnall refused to contest the decision, Talmadge believed he had found the issue that would return him to the statehouse. Four days after the Supreme Court's decision, Talmadge announced his candidacy. Restoring the white primary was his number one campaign promise.[14]

In anticipation of Talmadge's likely candidacy, Arnall set about finding a candidate who would continue the agenda Arnall had pursued as governor. That Arnall's agenda had left a major impact on the state was something not even his detractors could deny. Indeed, Arnall's success in getting so much of his agenda approved was a major reason why Regulars hoped Talmadge would win the election and reverse the tide. During his four years in office, Arnall had spread rural electrification throughout the state, extended the school year, and liberalized the state's notoriously harsh penal system.[15] In order to bring about political reform, Arnall also persuaded the General Assembly to repeal the poll tax and draft a new state constitution in 1945.[16] Arnall had used his term as governor to try and reorder the state's political priorities, and the 1946 contest would reveal to what extent he had brought Georgia's voters along with him.

Ultimately, Arnall recruited Cobb County businessman James V. Carmichael as his chosen successor. Carmichael, who had served two terms in the General Assembly prior to 1946, was the embodiment of a southern modernizer. The highly acclaimed manager of the Bell Aircraft plant in the rapidly growing town of Marietta, Carmichael had also been a member of the commission appointed by Governor Arnall to update the state constitution and had served as director of Georgia's Department of Revenue.[17] Only thirty-six at the time he announced his candidacy, he presented himself as a youthful alternative to the visibly ailing Talmadge. Overall, Carmichael's persona as described by Talmadge's biographer was everything a Loyalist could hope to be: "progressive, hard-working, intelligent, prosperous, adaptive to change and somewhat liberal."[18]

During the campaign, Carmichael stuck to the central themes of the Loyalist agenda. In his opening campaign rally, Carmichael offered himself as the candidate of "good government" against the "old gang-type government" that Talmadge represented.[19] The Cobb County Good Government Club paid Carmichael's filing fee, and "B-29" clubs, named in honor of the most famous aircraft produced at the Bell plant, were set up to advocate for Carmichael and his promise to bring "as many new industries as we can" to the state. Such economic boosterism was central to Carmichael's campaign message. In speech after speech, Carmichael explicitly linked the state's economic prospects to the condition of its education system and the willingness of the state government to actively and energetically involve itself in ensuring that new businesses would want "to come to Georgia."[20]

If Carmichael could have had his way, he would undoubtedly have wanted economic progress to be the focal point of the election. However, given his opponent's plans and the undoubted political sensitivity of the issue of black voting, there was no chance the white primary would not feature in the campaign. In response, Carmichael tried to neutralize the issue by expressing support for segregation, but also for the rule of law. As such, on the one hand, Carmichael consistently stated his opposition to integration and even took credit for having helped to keep segregation protected in the 1945 state constitution.[21] And yet Carmichael was also adamant that he would not seek to defy the Supreme Court's decision, repeatedly describing it as the "law of the land." In Carmichael's view, it was a decision that no one could overturn, and as this meant that black voting was constitutional, blacks should be allowed to vote.[22] By neither criticizing segregation nor encouraging resistance to the Supreme Court's decision, Carmichael was following the path of progressive color blindness—passively endorsing the notion of equal rights while offering little to actively bring that equality about.

Overall, Carmichael's stance on race indicated that even white Georgians drawn to economic modernization did not like the idea of supporting civil rights. Of course, they did not like to be thought of as racists either, and so it was helpful to all concerned that Carmichael "kept the issue neatly under the rug."[23] But Carmichael was also facing pressure from black Georgians, who after all had provided the impetus to abolish the white primary in the first place.

Like Mankin, Carmichael wanted support from black voters. However, the most he was willing to do in public to attract them was to state his opposition to overturning the white primary ruling. Privately, he was willing to go a little farther. His campaign engaged in clandestine efforts to reach out to the black leadership involving elaborately staged "chance meetings" between Carmichael and black political leaders. Perhaps the best illustration of how this strategy worked was the borderline farcical but politically very productive meeting that took place between Carmichael and A. T. Walden in the service elevator of the Piedmont Hotel in downtown Atlanta. The meeting had been arranged by future state senator Osgood Williams. As unusual a meeting place as this was, it led to an agreement between Carmichael and Walden that the latter would deliver black support to the former in exchange for a pledge that a Carmichael administration would listen to black concerns.[24]

There was one issue where Carmichael departed from Loyalist orthodoxy: his support for the county-unit system. Pragmatically, this made sense. The primary was going to be decided by voters in dozens of small counties who benefited from county-unit voting. They were unlikely to support a candidate who opposed it. Still, Carmichael's position was somewhat ironic, as the county-unit system represented the greatest barrier to Loyalist success in statewide primary contests. Once the election was done, Carmichael recanted his support of county-unit voting and would later describe it as the single biggest obstacle to the Loyalist agenda as a whole.[25]

The barrier presented by the county-unit system was problematic enough for Carmichael in the governor's race; it proved even more damaging for Helen Douglas Mankin in her bid to be renominated in the Fifth District. As in the special election, Mankin ran as a supporter of New Deal politics in the nation and a continuation of the Arnall administration's policies in Georgia. She stressed her support for federal aid to education and federal support for economic development projects in Georgia. Mankin campaigned particularly hard for the votes of teachers and labor union members. She also reached out to the growing number of veterans returning home to Atlanta as part of general postwar demobilization.[26] Once again, Mankin arranged surreptitious meetings with black political leaders, and—like Carmichael—she refused to either repudiate black voters or to openly support civil rights.[27] This time, however, the Regular Democrats in charge of the Fifth District executive committee ruled that the primary winner would be determined by county-unit voting.[28] This meant that Mankin's expected large majority in Fulton County could be offset by losing the other two counties in the Fifth District—DeKalb and Rockdale—even though they contained only 25 percent of her constituents.

To oppose Mankin, Regulars selected Judge James C. Davis, a candidate so firmly traditionalist that documents surfaced during and after the campaign linking him to the Ku Klux Klan (KKK) and other Far Right groups.[29] Nonetheless, despite his unsavory associations and the violent tendencies of some who supported him, even Mankin's biographer acknowledges that Davis "played it cool" on race during the campaign. Instead, he spoke of the need for a balanced budget, a more efficient government, and efforts to speed up the process of converting from a wartime economy to peacetime prosperity.[30] Such "coolness" did not mean that Davis eschewed playing on voters' racial concerns altogether. While Davis's rhetoric was restrained (by his own standards), he was not averse to hinting that Mankin was in league with black voters and their left-wing allies. For instance, one Davis campaign leaflet charged that Mankin was relying on the "negro vote" to win and had been endorsed by the Communist Party and the CIO.[31]

Talmadge proved far less reticent on race in his statewide campaign than Davis was in Atlanta, in part no doubt a reflection of the more pro-Regular balance of the statewide electorate. In fact, the Fifth District race proved useful to Talmadge, who argued that Mankin's brief term in Congress and potential reelection was an indication of the dangers facing the state if white supremacy was compromised and black voters were allowed to shape Georgia's politics.[32] Nonetheless, even Talmadge's campaign advisers were aware that commitment to white supremacy might not by itself be enough to win the election. Accordingly, Talmadge adopted a campaign platform that, on everything except racial issues, was markedly more progressive than anything he had ever run on before. It called for raising teachers' pay by 50 percent, increasing state funding for rural medical facilities, and a major road-building program. The platform had been drawn up by the candidate's son, Herman, who argued that "a more liberal approach and a dampening of the racial issue" was necessary for his father to win. The degree to which the 1946 platform marked a new direction for Gene Talmadge can be inferred from his supposed response on reading it—"good god almighty! Who wrote this stuff?"—before Herman persuaded him it was necessary to embrace at least parts of the Loyalist agenda in order to adjust to the new political climate.[33]

Once the campaign began in earnest, however, Talmadge's old habits proved hard to break. As polling day approached, he focused ever more on race and ever less on the rest of his platform. The white primary, Talmadge declared, had been abolished by "radical communist and alien influences"; he told black voters to stay away from the polls as "neither U.S. Attorneys nor Jimmy Carmichael" would be able to protect them there; and he warned that the state faced the prospect of having its entire system of segregation dismantled if Carmichael won.[34] As his focus on race grew to the exclusion of other concerns that voters had, Talmadge risked alienating substantial numbers of Georgians.[35]

The results of the primary did indeed suggest that Talmadge's constituency was much narrower than he might have hoped and far smaller than in his heyday. That Talmadge trailed Carmichael in the popular vote was a powerful indicator that racial conservatism alone was not sufficient to carry majority support in postwar Georgia. On the other hand, it was not a clear triumph for Carmichael either, as although he secured a plurality over the other candidates, he was still short of 50 percent. This in turn suggested that even with repeated assurances of support for segregation, the Loyalists' program of economic modernization also lacked majority support. As such, the 1946 primary was ambiguous in determining which

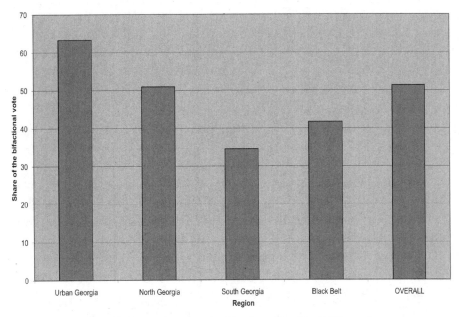

Figure 1. Share of bifactional vote received by Carmichael in 1946 by region.

of the two factions had the political wind at its back. The county-unit system only heightened the ambiguity. Carmichael won 313,384 votes to Talmadge's 297,245, but as Talmadge captured 242 unit votes to Carmichael's 146, Talmadge became the nominee. A similar phenomenon occurred in the Fifth District, where Mankin's clear win in the popular vote (56 to 44 percent) was negated by the county-unit tally. As expected, Mankin carried Fulton County (six unit votes), but her narrow loss in neighboring DeKalb County (six unit votes) and heavy defeat in tiny Rockdale County (two unit votes) left Davis the winner by eight to six overall.

While the 1946 results were unclear about whose agenda had the upper hand *overall* among Georgia's voters, they did reveal the demographic and regional divisions that would form the basis for the political constituencies of the Regular and Loyalist factions for the next thirty years. In geographic terms, figure 1 shows that Carmichael did best in Georgia's urban counties (63.3 percent) and in north Georgia (50.9 percent).[36] As shown in figure 2, Carmichael also carried the most populous counties in the state (with 59 percent of the vote) and those with the fastest-growing populations (60.1 percent).[37] Carmichael also won counties with the highest median incomes (60.2 percent) and the highest average years of schooling completed (59.4 percent). By a smaller margin, Carmichael also carried

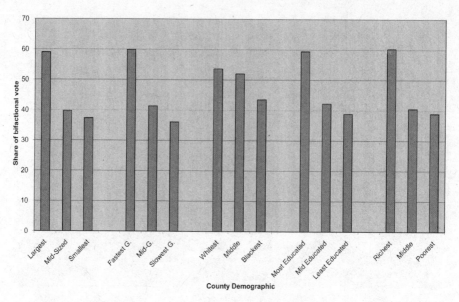

Figure 2. Share of vote for Carmichael by county demographic, 1946 Democratic primary.

those counties with the proportionately smallest black population (53.6 percent). In contrast to Carmichael, Talmadge easily carried the state's smallest counties (63.4 percent), those experiencing the slowest rate of absolute population growth (65.2 percent), those with the lowest median income (60.8 percent), those with the lowest average years of schooling (62.2 percent), and those with the proportionately highest black populations (57 percent). Geographically speaking, Talmadge won in south Georgia (65.5 percent) and the Black Belt (58.3 percent).

In sum, the 1946 primary showcased the political tensions within Georgia at the end of World War II. Taking the state as a whole, political support for modernization and traditionalism were evenly matched, but that support varied widely according to region and demographics. Both Regulars and Loyalists could draw some comfort from these results, but both also could see cause for concern. The civil rights movement was in a similar position. The end of the white primary and the mobilization of black voters had played a decisive role in the campaign, but it had also given Talmadge his main campaign issue, and the backlash against black Georgians that was expected to follow his election threatened to undo much of what civil rights activists had achieved. Ultimately, the fact that Talmadge and Davis prevailed—however narrowly and undemocratically—meant that the immediate impact of 1946 was to put the Regulars back in power, but on a shaky foundation. Over the course of the next few years, they sought to shore up that foundation while Loyalists and civil rights activists tried to undermine it.

Degrees of Loyalty: The National Democratic Party, Race, and the 1948 Elections

The manner in which Regulars and Loyalists had campaigned in 1946 suggested that both recognized there were not enough "true believers" on either side to guarantee a statewide victory and that many Georgians had sympathies with aspects of both modernizing and traditionalist messages—hence Loyalists hedging on the county-unit system and avoiding any mention of civil rights; hence Regulars endorsing some government expansion and more money for education. Two years later, the national Democratic Party was the cause of a similar dilemma. Regulars distrusted the national leadership, found it useful as a foil to attack during election campaigns, and were opposed to many of its policy priorities. As such, when the Dixiecrats broke away from the national party on exactly this basis, one might have expected to see an exodus of Regulars flocking to their standard. Similarly, given their admiration for the New Deal and desire to reshape the South in its image, one might have expected Loyalists to mount a vigorous defense of President Truman and the Democratic ticket.

In fact, neither faction reacted in such a straightforward way. To be sure, some Regulars joined the Dixiecrats and some Loyalists actively campaigned for Harry Truman, but most were reluctant to commit absolutely to one or the other. Many on each side recognized that white Georgian's attitudes toward the national Democratic Party were more ambivalent than either outright rejection or total embrace. Additionally, Regulars had to consider the potential political cost of being tagged as "disloyal" and forfeiting access to patronage and influence in Congress, while Loyalists had to worry about being tagged as "lackeys" to an increasingly unpopular White House.

Tension between Regular Democrats and the national party leadership had been building for several decades prior to the 1948 campaign, but not until the postwar years did it result in an open sectional rupture. Since at least the 1920s, culturally traditionalist southern Democrats had been uncomfortable at the anti-Prohibition, urban, Catholic image of the non-southern wing of the party.[38] So strong was this internal tension that when Al Smith, the Catholic mayor of New York and an avowed "wet," won the party's nomination in 1928, it broke the Solid South wide open.[39] As the New Deal grew in size during the 1930s, southern conservatives began to chafe both at the economic philosophy behind it and its implications for southern race relations.[40] In several southern states, disaffected Regulars, including Gene Talmadge, had launched efforts to deny Roosevelt electoral support after 1936, but FDR proved to be immensely popular with southern voters.

When President Truman therefore announced the formation of a presidential commission to recommend civil rights laws and then endorsed its proposals in early 1948, he was not suddenly creating turmoil in an otherwise tranquil sectional relationship within the Democratic Party. And yet Truman's move was significant because it explicitly injected race into the long-festering sectional tension. Additionally, it did so just as Regulars were facing an increased level of political competition from Loyalists at the state level. When the 1948 Democratic National Convention then adopted a civil rights plank that was even stronger than what the president had asked for, it proved to be the last straw: several Regular delegates walked out of the convention on the spot. A few weeks later, those same Regulars convened in Birmingham, Alabama, and nominated Governors Thurmond of South Carolina and Wright of Mississippi as States' Rights Democratic ("Dixiecrat") candidates in the presidential election. The Dixiecrats' immediate strategy was twofold: first, to reestablish their authority in the national party; second, to shore up their own standing within the South.

What followed across the South was an internal struggle within state Democratic organizations over whether Dixiecrats would be able to put Thurmond's name on the ballot as the "official" Democratic candidate. In those states where Thurmond succeeded in doing so, he won; in those where he was unsuccessful, Truman won.[41] Initially, Dixiecrats had high hopes that Georgia's Regulars would help deliver the state's electoral votes to Thurmond. However, the situation in Georgia was complicated as a result of aftershocks of the 1946 primary. Although Gene Talmadge had been elected governor, he died before taking office. This resulted in a months-long dispute over the succession until the Georgia Supreme

Court ruled that lieutenant governor M. E. Thompson would serve as acting governor until a special election could be held in September 1948. The court's decision in favor of Thompson, a Loyalist, meant that the state party machinery was not as overwhelmingly in Regular hands as it would have been if Talmadge had survived.

Had Gene Talmadge been in office, he would surely have thrown in his lot with the Dixiecrats. After all, he had tried to organize a bolt from the party as far back as 1936. Herman Talmadge, by contrast, was more reluctant. Herman had already demonstrated a more pragmatic streak while running his father's 1946 campaign, and although he was preparing to make opposition to Truman's civil rights program a central plank of his 1948 special election campaign, he was uncertain whether to side with the Dixiecrats. The advice he received from other Regulars was mixed. Charles Bloch urged Herman to support Thurmond, but James Peters warned that any such move could lead to Loyalists such as Ellis Arnall and E. D. Rivers regaining control of the state party. Peters was worried that if Talmadge endorsed Thurmond, Arnall and his supporters would run against Dixiecrats as having deserted the party.[42]

Thompson also faced a difficult decision over how to respond to the Dixiecrats. Although he had denounced the proposals of Truman's Civil Rights Commission, Thompson still publicly endorsed Truman for president and tried to critique Talmadge for disloyalty. In turn, Talmadge used Thompson's support for Truman as a way to heighten white fears that Thompson might support desegregation.[43] The fact that Talmadge was able to win the primary by running on anti-Truman sentiment, but still considered it too politically risky to break with the Democratic Party and join the Dixiecrats, speaks to the dilemma the national party was causing Georgia's politicians in 1948.

As Talmadge refused to take Truman's name off the ballot, Georgia provides a better gage of the extent and demographic base of Dixiecrat support than those states where Thurmond's name was listed in the Democratic column. Overall, Thurmond won 20.9 percent of the vote in Georgia, compared to Truman's 60.8 percent and Republican Thomas E. Dewey's 18.3 percent. Some of the distribution in Dixiecrat support was predictable for an arch-Regular group dedicated to preserving segregation. Thurmond ran best in counties with the highest black populations (29.7 percent) and in the Black Belt (30 percent). Thurmond also did better in counties with low median incomes than high ones, which also matched up with both Talmadges' performances in the 1946 and 1948 gubernatorial contests.

And yet other patterns of Dixiecrat support did not match the typical Regular coalition. Thurmond ran just as well in Georgia's largest, smallest, and mid-size counties—a very different pattern from Regular gubernatorial candidates. He ran better in the state's fastest- and slowest-growing counties than he did in those experiencing middling population growth. He did better in those counties with the highest and lowest median years of education than he did in those closer to the state average. He ran ahead of his statewide total in otherwise anti-Regular urban Georgia (22.6 percent) and nearly as well there as in arch-Regular south Georgia (24.8 percent). North Georgia, by contrast, proved singularly unreceptive to the Dixiecrat appeal, giving Thurmond only 10.7 percent support. This meant that for the only time in statewide contests between 1946 and 1962, the breakdown of voting in north Georgia was farthest from, rather than closest to, the actual breakdown of votes across the state.[44]

The relatively weak relationship between Thurmond's support and the Regular coalition is further illustrated by the low rate of correlation between the two. The Pearson correlation coefficient between the level of support a county gave to Thurmond and the support it gave to Herman Talmadge in the gubernatorial primary was a positive but unimpressive 0.372. To be sure, the fact that Talmadge's support correlated positively with Thurmond and negatively (-0.254) with Truman's suggested that core Regular voters were more inclined to vote Dixiecrat than others. But compared to the very strong correlation between support for Herman Talmadge in 1948 and Eugene Talmadge in 1946 (0.726), the Regular-Dixiecrat connection was far more ambivalent.

The absence of any overriding correlation between support for the Dixiecrats in 1948 and the Regular-Loyalist split in the Georgia Democratic Party was in turn indicative of the mixed impact of Thurmond's campaign across the South as a whole. The Dixiecrats failed to carry any southern state where they had not gained control of the state party organization, and as the case of Georgia demonstrated, they could not count on the united support of Regular leaders even as they rhetorically positioned themselves as the defenders of the Regular cause. On the other hand, that only 20 percent of Georgia's voters supported the Dixiecrats did not mean that this was the limit of opposition to civil rights or dislike for the national Democratic Party. Overall, the Dixiecrats showed that the tension between state and national Democrats was a divisive and complex part of the debate over the direction of postwar Georgia, but they provided only an ambiguous indication of how the tension or the debate would be resolved.

The appropriate relationship with the national Democratic Party was also a tendentious issue for black Georgians, if for different reasons than in the case of Thompson and Talmadge. Deciding whom to support in a statewide primary was a relatively easy decision for black leaders: back the candidate whose election would most likely advance black influence. As there was no possibility that a Republican in the 1940s was going to win any statewide office, even Republican black leaders were happy to dedicate their resources to mobilizing black voters for the Democratic primaries. On the national stage, though, partisan differences within the black community were more significant. Each party had powerful black leaders in Georgia. For the Republicans, these included John Wesley Dobbs and John Calhoun, while A. T. Walden in Atlanta and Mark Gilbert in Savannah headed the most powerful black Democratic organizations. These partisan tensions were serious. In trying to persuade Atlanta's black leadership to form a single, united organization for coordinating black political support, Jacob Henderson described the partisan differences as the most difficult to overcome. Walden and Dobbs would "spend an awful lot of time fighting each other" based on their partisan rivalries, and the only way Henderson was able to convince them to cooperate in forming the Atlanta Negro Voters League (ANVL) in 1949 was by making sure that there were cochairs for every position so that both parties would be equally represented. Walden and Dobbs were named as joint heads of the organization as part of this compromise.[45]

While the ANVL and other organizations made bipartisan cooperation at the state and local levels possible, black leaders in both parties were simultaneously trying to use black voting strength as a way to gain leverage and influence within their national organizations. In trying to win over Georgia's black electorate to their side, both sides held a mixed hand. For Dobbs and Calhoun, it was straightforward enough to point at the Georgia Democratic Party as the source of segregation and violence against blacks and to argue that, as the "party of Lincoln," Republicans deserved black support. On the other hand, even with segregation written into its programs, the New Deal was popular with southern black voters, and once President Truman announced his support for a civil rights program in 1948, this also provided a plausible reason for black voters to overlook the sins of the state party in favor of the promises of the national one. Georgia's black Republicans responded to the inclusion of civil rights in the national Democratic platform by arguing it was just talk to win black support. The *Atlanta Daily World* made this case when it urged its readers to back Eisenhower in 1952 to punish the Democrats for having done nothing on civil rights since 1948.[46]

Black Democrats faced the opposite problem. For Walden, the decision of the national party to endorse civil rights was a very welcome development, not only because it made selling black voters on Democratic presidential candidates that much easier but also because it gave Walden additional leverage when negotiating with Loyalists over accepting some desegregation. At the same time, Walden knew that making the case for Democratic support in terms of Truman's support for civil rights would make life very difficult for the Loyalists with whom he was trying to build alliances at the state level. There was also the presence of Regular Democrats to contend with, who were the biggest roadblock to the civil rights legislation that the national party leadership had endorsed. Walden's preferred approach in 1948 and beyond was to focus on the economic benefits that the Democratic Party had provided for black voters, while noting only that the national leadership was not hostile to civil rights. In this way, Walden also found himself drawn to progressive color blindness, which served as a useful means to advocate for the Democratic Party among black voters and also for Walden himself to gain influence and power within the party.

Despite the upheaval of the "Dixiecrat Revolt," the outcome of the 1948 elections did not appear obviously different from what had gone before in Georgia. In the presidential contest, the Democratic ticket prevailed by a large margin. In the gubernatorial primary, a Regular candidate vowing to keep blacks in their place won a comfortable victory. And yet by the same token, the events of 1948 were an important political watershed in postwar Georgia. The national Democratic Party's decision to explicitly oppose the central tenet of the Regulars' agenda had ripple effects for all the participants in Georgia politics.

Restoring Regular Dominance? Georgia Politics, 1948–1954

Following the Regular victories in the 1946 primaries, Arthur Powell Sr., an Atlanta attorney, wrote to congratulate James Davis on his success over Helen Douglas Mankin. Along with the congratulations, however, Powell sounded a note of caution. Powell was troubled that "many good white citizens" had voted for Mankin, even though he was pleased that "a large majority" of whites had backed Davis. Still, Powell warned, if white supremacy and the one-party system were to be preserved, such divisions in the white community could not be allowed to continue: "[this] is no time for a minority of the [white] people to continue to vote for Mrs. Mankin, so that the Negroes can elect her, thus making the Negro vote the balance of power . . . now is a time for the white people to stand together."[47]

Powell's letter neatly summarized the crux of the problem facing Regular Democrats in the 1940s and early 1950s. On the one hand, victories in the 1946 and 1948 primaries had demonstrated that there was strong support among white voters for the traditionalism the Regulars stood for. On the other hand, the closeness of the results, and the dependence on the workings of the county-unit system in the case of 1946, suggested that nearly as many voters were drawn to the modernist appeals of their Loyalist opponents. It was clear, in other words, that "the white people" were not standing together, and this made the Regulars' position precarious. If Regular dominance of state politics was going to be restored and the Solid South preserved, it would be necessary to reduce the Loyalists' appeal among white voters and restrict the growth in the number of black voters.

Accordingly, once Herman Talmadge became governor in 1948, he and his Regular allies set out to do just that. Talmadge pursued three interrelated strategies: first, extend the county-unit system to include general elections and to try and write the system into the state constitution; second, roll back the gains made by Georgia's black political leadership through voter registration drives, especially in the urban centers of Savannah and Atlanta; and third, convince a clear majority of white voters that the maintenance of segregation was of paramount importance and could be achieved without sacrificing the state's education system or its economic prospects. This final aim would require a mixture of carrot and stick: specifically, it meant providing extra resources for Georgia's schools while simultaneously passing laws that would prevent those schools from ever being desegregated.

To the extent that Regulars were able to implement these policies and get white voters to "stand together," their success can be seen as a sign of the strength of traditionalism within Georgia. And yet the policies the Regulars adopted also revealed the insecurity of their position. The attempt to extend the blatantly undemocratic rules of county-unit voting and the rigorous provisions against dissent put into the laws designed to preserve segregation all suggested that Regular Democrats feared they were presiding over an electorate only superficially united behind them: they acted as if the only way to preserve their version of democracy was to prevent the people getting their hands on it.

During his six years as governor, Herman Talmadge made two efforts to convince Georgians they should allow the county-unit system to be extended. In 1949, he initiated a statewide referendum on a constitutional amendment that would have required general elections in Georgia to be decided by county-unit votes. Georgians voted on the amendment in November 1950 and defeated it by 164,337 (55 percent) to 134,292 (45 percent).[48] In 1952, Talmadge tried again, this time with an amendment that would have required all candidates in a general election to have been nominated in a party primary. As primaries would have to take place under county-unit rules and were very expensive to hold, this measure was clearly intended to choke off Republican growth and to prevent Democrats who lost in the primary running as independent candidates in the general election.[49] Once again, a referendum was held; once again, the measure was voted down, this time by 309,170 (52.5 percent) to 279,882 (47.5 percent).[50]

In both of these campaigns, Regulars equated defending the county-unit system with defending segregation. A prominent example of this was the widely circulated pamphlet *Your Stake in the County-unit Amendment*, which was written for the 1952 referendum campaign. According to *Your Stake*, approval of the amendment would prevent "mixed schools," rule by corrupt political bosses, and the spread of organized crime. By contrast, supporting the amendment meant supporting integration and wanting the "bloc vote" (that is, black voters) to control Georgia's politics. The pamphlet then listed several prominent men and women, mostly from Atlanta, who were part of this "pro-integration" group and contained several pictures of black men dancing with white women with the implication that such debauchery was unthinkable so long as the county-unit system was in place. Even more pointed was the claim that the only reason Georgians had such excellent representatives in Congress was the "protection afforded the white people by the county-unit system." *Your Stake* ended with an endorsement of the amendment by Governor Talmadge, in which he warned of dire consequences should the amendment be voted down, concluding that "the white people of this state must repel by their votes these threats to our homes, our children, our institutions, our daily lives and our fortunes."[51]

The link between the county-unit system and the preservation of white supremacy could hardly have been more explicit. Nonetheless, despite the overwhelming support of the Georgia political establishment, the governor was not able to convince the voters to go along with him. Instead, the opposition to extending the county-unit system, led by Loyalists who saw it as an outdated anachronism, and civil rights leaders who saw it as a bulwark of white supremacy, secured comfortable majorities on both occasions. Loyalists chose to frame the issue as one of "good government," which also turned out to be good politics. Working alongside ostensibly nonpartisan groups, such as the GLWV, Loyalists ignored the question of white supremacy altogether and argued instead that extending the county-unit system represented a threat to democracy.[52]

The GLWV had opposed the county-unit system since the 1930s, so its involvement in both the 1950 and 1952 campaigns was not a surprise. In May 1950, the GLWV justified its opposition to the county-unit amendment by calling it an affront to fairness and part of a series of events that was putting democracy "on trial throughout the world."[53] In 1952, the GLWV adopted a similar position, arguing that extending the county-unit system was one of "four steps" Talmadge was taking to establish not only one-party rule but also one-man rule in the state. Such a political system, the GLWV argued, would be devastating to Georgia's future.[54]

Although the GLWV did not officially side with either faction in the Democratic Party, the support it solicited and received from key Loyalists in the referenda was a clear sign that it sympathized with the modernizers' agenda. Similarly, the involvement of so many Loyalists in the campaigns against the county-unit amendments underscored that these referenda were a continuation of the Regular-Loyalist split. Among those who campaigned against the amendments were Atlanta's mayor Hartsfield, James Carmichael, Helen Douglas Mankin, and Helen Bullard.[55] Additionally,

Morris Abram, an attorney who filed multiple suits in federal court against the county-unit system from 1947 to 1964 and who challenged James C. Davis in a primary election in 1954, was a key organizer in the anti-county-unit campaigns.[56] C. Baxter Jones, who ran against Davis as a Loyalist in 1952, also worked for a "no" vote on the amendments, as did Charles Weltner, who eventually defeated Davis in 1962 and for whom this was a first taste of active politics.[57] In the General Assembly, Loyalist state legislators, including James MacKay, Osgood Williams, and Atlanta's Everett Millican, all took to the floor of the state house to speak against county-unit voting.[58]

The breakdown of the vote in the two referenda further demonstrated the continuity with the factional contest within the Georgia Democratic Party. As figures 3 and 4 illustrate, the demographic and geographic divisions from 1946 were evident in the returns from 1950 and 1952. In each case, where Regular candidates had previously done well, support for extending the county-unit system was high; the reverse was true in pro-Loyalist parts of Georgia. That both votes resulted in defeats for the county-unit system was furthermore a clear sign of the precarious status of the Regular majority. These defeats take on even more significance when one considers the natural advantages of the proamendment forces. First, it was almost taken for granted that voters would approve constitutional amendments. The 1950 and 1952 ballots saw a total of eighty-three amendments for voters to decide on. Of these, eighty were approved. Other than the two county-unit amendments, the only other one defeated concerned raising the salaries of elected officials.[59] Georgia voters were also clearly motivated to vote. Both times, turnout on the county-unit amendment was higher than on any other amendment. In 1952, nearly 590,000 voters cast ballots, compared to 566,000 in the very competitive 1950 Democratic primary.[60] The proamendment campaigns, although lacking the support of the major urban newspapers, also outspent the opponents of the county-unit system both times—by a ratio of five to one according to one analyst of the 1952 campaign.[61]

Black political leaders also opposed the county-unit amendments, but their campaigns against them were often low-key and generally tried to frame the issue in nonracial terms. This reflected an attempt to balance the desire to get black voters out to vote against the amendments with a recognition that allowing the referenda to be seen as a vote on black civil rights might throw support to the pro-county-unit side. Accordingly,

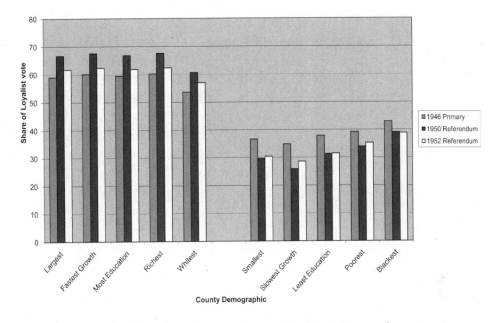

Figure 3. Loyalist share of vote by county demographic, 1946 primary and county-unit referenda.

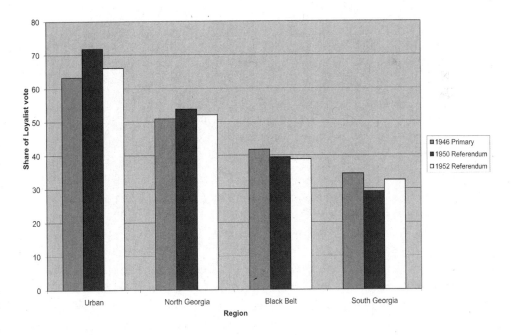

Figure 4. Loyalist share of vote by region, 1946 primary and county-unit referenda.

while Grace Towns Hamilton worked closely with Morris Abram in Fulton and DeKalb counties, and while appeals to vote against the county-unit system signed by prominent black leaders such as Rev. William Holmes Borders, Martin Luther King Sr., A. T. Walden, and Morehouse professor Benjamin Mays appeared in several newspapers, opposition to the county-unit system in public was not generally stated in terms of a critique of racism.[62] Instead, the rhetoric of good government and the antidemocratic nature of county-unit voting were emphasized, as when Walden explained that his opposition to the 1952 amendment was "not because I am a Negro, but because I am a Georgian who believes that Georgians should have a right to self-government and a free general election."[63]

Walden and other black leaders were more active in preserving and extending the gains made in black voter registration and using that to seek negotiating power with white politicians over desegregation. Regulars recognized this as a threat to their political power and took steps to try and scale back black political influence. The methods Talmadge and his supporters adopted were not particularly subtle, but they were nonetheless effective in many parts of the state. On the one hand, violence and intimidation (both physical and economic) were employed to prevent blacks from attempting to register to vote. Laws were also passed that made it easier to strike previously qualified voters from the rolls, and the range of questions that a prospective voter was expected to answer in order to register was expanded.[64] Being known as an advocate of black voting could on occasion be fatal, as in the case of Thomas Brewer, who was shot to death by a white storeowner in Columbus in February 1956.

For all their efforts, however, the best that Regulars could manage was to slow the growth of black voting strength in Georgia; they were not able to reduce it. The estimated number of black voters in the state rose from 125,000 in 1946 to 145,000 in 1952, and 160,000 in 1956. This was not a uniform rise. In his breakdown of the figures for the ANVL, John Calhoun noted that there had been reductions in the number of black voters in two of Georgia's ten congressional districts, which had been offset overall by gains in the other eight.[65] In part, the numbers had kept rising because some of the more restrictive measures Talmadge and his allies wanted to adopt proved too much for even segregationists in the General Assembly to support. For example, a law that would have required compulsory re-registration for all voters every few years was stopped because of the burdens it would have placed on white voters.[66]

Overall, though, the continued increase in black voting strength should be credited primarily to the continued efforts by civil rights organizations in the face of a more hostile state political leadership than had existed when Arnall or Thompson was governor. The ANVL in particular was among the most successful organizations in expanding black electoral influence in Georgia prior to *Brown*. It claimed there were 10,000 black voters in the city when it was founded in 1949, a number that rose to 27,500 by 1958 and 35,000 by 1960.[67] The impact on city politics was immediate. According to John Calhoun, Mayor Hartsfield received 85 percent of the black vote in 1949 in a race that he won with a majority of just 102. Such was the importance of the black vote in Atlanta from then on that the cloak-and-dagger tactics of 1946 were no longer necessary. As Calhoun wrote to the ANVL board analyzing the organization's role during the 1949 mayoral election, "it became the consensus of opinion that we need no longer have to endorse in secret, but an open campaign would win." What was more, Hartsfield agreed with this sentiment.[68]

From then on, the ANVL convened public meetings for candidates in municipal and state elections to speak in front of black audiences and field questions from black voters. Gradually, Loyalist candidates came round to the idea that an endorsement from the ANVL was something worth seeking. The same approach for pressuring white candidates was adopted by William Randall Sr. in Macon under the auspices of the Macon Voters League. According to Randall, because black voters held the "balance of power" in the city, Macon's legislators in the General Assembly were more progressive on racial matters than most.[69]

A key reason why Loyalists were happy to cooperate with the ANVL and like-minded groups was that these groups were consistently gradualist in their policy agenda. The ANVL was also publicly ambivalent on some of the more contentious racial issues. Even white newspapers acknowledged the slow pace of change the ANVL was pushing for, though this willingness to accept half a loaf in exchange for a seat at the table made the ANVL a source of frustration among civil rights activists who wanted a more confrontational approach.[70] Nonetheless, for A. T. Walden, the seat at the table was key. It was worth being patient if it meant getting the ear of those in power in the Democratic Party. To this end, Walden and his like-minded black leaders continued to find the language of progressive color blindness valuable and downplayed the race-based nature of their goals.

One such ally of Walden was Claudius Turner, a black activist from Mc-Intosh County in coastal south Georgia. Turner's view of the role of race in Georgia politics was one with which every Loyalist Democrat would have agreed. In a letter to Walden, Turner noted that white voters were often "hypnotized by the cry of 'nigger, nigger, nigger'" and that it was the job of civil rights activists to take "that hypnotic spell off as many whites as possible." Doing so would require a high level of "skill in indirection" that could be achieved only if "as far as possible our answers and statements" were never "racial or minority statements." Instead, black leaders should stress the idea that they were concerned with the "well-being of the entire citizenry of the state." This would "undermine the fear-psychosis of most whites," who would soon realize that blacks wanted "the same things politically that whites want." "Under such political psychology," Turner concluded, "democratic integration would set in," and black political influence would be firmly established.[71]

Turner's views were entirely in synch with Walden's, who wrote an effusive reply that praised Turner for so accurately "sensing the political situation which confronts us." Walden also asked Turner to take charge of the local branch of the Georgia Association of Democratic Clubs, which was another of Walden's organizations.[72] For his own part, Walden deployed the kind of strategy that Turner described to such effect that he was recruited by Loyalist and national Democrats as a party spokesman. In 1952, Walden was appointed a southern regional director for the presidential campaign of Adlai Stevenson with the specific task of mobilizing black support for the Democratic ticket in the South.[73] In the form of a newspaper, the *Georgia Plain Dealer,* Walden called for black voters to back Stevenson in boilerplate Loyalist language. Walden claimed that while the Republicans had freed the slaves in 1863, they now stood for "rich, privileged corporations," and black voters should trust the Democrats to put food on the table in 1953.[74] Furthermore, if southern blacks voted Republican, they would forfeit "many basic gains for the common man" achieved by Democrats "over the past twenty years."[75]

His determination to establish a black presence in the Democratic Party at this time occasionally put Walden in a difficult position, such as when he grudgingly gave public support to James C. Davis after Davis's renomination in the 1952 primary.[76] Such were the demands of party loyalty, but Walden was willing to pay this price in exchange for influence with the party. Within Atlanta, growing black electoral influence enabled Walden and Miles Amos to win election to the Atlanta Democratic Party Executive Committee in 1953. Five years later, Walden would beat a white candidate in a bid to join the Fulton County Democratic Executive Committee, and in 1962 he was elevated to the Statewide Executive Committee.

On one policy area, however, Walden and Loyalists had more trouble finding common ground. It was perhaps the most delicate racial issue of all: the schools. For all the compromises he was willing to make on other issues, Walden and the NAACP were determined to press for better treatment of blacks in Georgia's schools, though they did not initially press for integration. In August 1949, the NAACP filed suit in Irwin County in rural south Georgia demanding that the "equal" part of "separate but equal" be honored. In 1950, the U.S. Supreme Court, in the *Sweatt v. Painter* and *McLaurin v. Oklahoma* cases, struck down state laws requiring segregation in higher education. Within a month of these decisions, the Atlanta NAACP filed suit in *Aaron v. Cook* demanding that the Atlanta school board either equalize or desegregate its education system. Slowly but surely, pressure was building on the constitutional viability of the southern school systems.

For Loyalists and Regulars alike, segregation in the schools was a highly emotional issue, but for different reasons. To Loyalists, good schools were an absolute necessity. Most of them preferred segregated schools, but would countenance desegregation if it was unavoidable. Better that than not having a public school system. Nonetheless, Loyalists worried that other white Georgians might not agree. The schools were the most sensitive public space for white southerners. The idea of desegregated education brought forth not just fears of race-mixing, but also long-standing concerns over black sexuality as well as that most emotive of political subjects—the fate of the children. The perfect storm of segregationist fears that desegregation of the schools produced was neatly captured in President Eisenhower's reported statement to Chief Justice Warren on the eve of the *Brown* ruling: "all they [white parents] are concerned about is to see that their sweet little girls are not required to sit in schools alongside some big black bucks."[77] As a result, Loyalists were worried that if segregated schools were declared unconstitutional, white Georgians would choose to close the schools down.

Loyalists had good reason to be worried. Even before *Aaron v. Cook* was filed, Regulars had taken steps toward putting the state on a collision course with the federal courts. In August 1950, Roy Harris persuaded the state Democratic convention to declare the *Sweatt* and *McLaurin* decisions to be null and void in Georgia. In 1951, Harris, who had been one of public education's strongest boosters in the state just a few years earlier, began advocating for a private school system to avoid desegregated education. That same year, the General Assembly passed a law granting the governor the authority to cut off state funds for any educational institution that did not maintain segregation.[78]

Two years later, seeking to safeguard the option of abolishing the public school system should the Supreme Court rule against segregation in the pending *Brown* decision, Talmadge called on Harris and Charles Bloch to provide advice on an amendment to the state constitution. In December 1953, such an amendment was drafted to allow the state to provide grants-in-aid to pay for private tuition in the event that the public schools were closed. As Thomas O'Brien has noted in his study of Georgia's massive resistance laws, the measures that Talmadge proposed for education were essentially a blank check: "Georgia's state leadership was asking the state's citizens for a permit to do anything they saw fit with the public school system, including abolish it."[79]

And yet for all their bravado and vows of defiance, Regulars were also worried about the likely consequences of a showdown with the federal courts over desegregation. They were also aware of the support among white voters for improving the public school system. Indeed, between them, Roy Harris and Herman Talmadge had vastly expanded state funding for education in Georgia. Harris had crafted a plan—the Minimum Foundation for Public Education (MFPE)—which Talmadge used as the blueprint for asking the General Assembly to establish a 3 percent sales tax. Intended to substantially increase funding for Georgia's schools, the tax was approved in April 1951.[80] Such was the public support for extra funding that by 1955 Georgia was devoting more of its budget to education than any other state in the Union.[81] The combination of promising a better funded school system, while also putting in place measures that would allow that system to be abolished, threatened to produce an irresolvable dilemma for the Regulars if the federal courts ever ruled that it was a choice between "schools or segregation."

Both factions of the Democratic Party therefore had reason to hope that the federal courts would not compel such a choice to be made. As a result, neither had much cause to be pleased at the *Brown* decision in May 1954. Even Georgia's civil rights movement was hesitant over how to proceed. No major effort was made to file a lawsuit calling for integration until 1958. Nonetheless, *Brown* had a significant impact on Georgia's politics. In the short term, it allowed Regulars to rally the white electorate behind a policy of massive resistance to civil rights. The reasoning behind the resistance was little different from Gene Talmadge's opposition to ending the white primary in 1946, but *Brown* gave the issue a greater salience with white voters than had existed over the previous ten years.

The result was the disintegration of the Loyalist faction at the ballot box. First came the Democratic primary in September 1954. Five candidates were competing for the gubernatorial nomination, of whom three—Marvin Griffin, Fred Hand, and Tom Linder—were Regulars, and two—M. E. Thompson and Charlie Gowen—were Loyalists. Although both Thompson and Gowen expressed opposition to Talmadge's "private schools amendment," both also promised they could keep the schools segregated and criticized *Brown*.[82] Of the Regulars, Griffin and Hand backed the private schools amendment, while only Linder expressed his skepticism as to its value. Linder claimed he doubted that Georgia's voters would actually be "willing to surrender the public schools."[83] However, his own outlook was hardly any more conciliatory: Linder proposed that all parents in Georgia be sent a questionnaire asking if they approved or disapproved of segregated education. Those who disapproved of segregation would then be given a state-funded psychiatric examination.[84]

The outcome of the primary was a heavy defeat for the Loyalist candidates, who secured just 37.1 percent of the vote between them. M. E. Thompson managed to win the support of less than half of the voters who had backed him in 1950.[85] A second indication of the momentum shift toward the Regulars in the wake of *Brown* was the outcome of the referendum on allowing privatization of the public schools. The proposal was passed by 210,478 (53.7 percent) to 181,148 (46.3 percent).[86] Although the breakdown in the voting followed established Regular-Loyalist divisions, it also revealed a sharp rise in support for the Regulars' position in traditionally pro-Loyalist areas. For example, 67.6 percent of voters in the counties with the highest median incomes voted against the county-unit system in 1950, but only 53.2 percent voted against the private school amendment in 1954. In urban counties, 71.8 percent of voters had voted against the Regular position in 1950; only 56.6 percent did so four years later. In both these cases, this represented a drop in support nearly twice the overall decline of 8.7 percentage points in Loyalist support across the state as a whole.

Overall, *Brown* changed the dynamics of Georgia politics, but in terms of momentum, not trajectory. It was a pivot point, not a turning point. By elevating race to the number one concern of the electorate, it moved the political debate onto territory that favored Regulars. Loyalists hoped to keep the debate centered on education and the economy, but in the wake of *Brown* this proved to be impossible for several years. As a result, the stalemate between the two Democratic factions that had characterized the first postwar decade in Georgia politics was broken. From 1946 to 1954, there had been seven statewide votes that pitted the two factions against each other—four primaries and three referenda. Loyalists had won clear victories in two (the county-unit amendments), and Regulars had done so in three (the 1948 and 1954 primaries and the private schools amendment). The remaining two races (1946 and 1950 primaries) resulted in one plurality for each faction, but by the slimmest of margins.

In other words, results from this period suggested an evenly divided electorate. Other than in the 1954 primary, neither faction's share of the vote ever dipped below 45 percent in any contest, and the five-candidate field in 1954 marked it as something of an outlier. The core demographic and geographic characteristics of each faction's voting coalition also remained consistent during this time. The only reason that Regulars had such a hold on the governor's mansion during this time was the county-unit system, which produced lopsided Regular majorities of 242 to 146 in 1946, 312 to 98 in 1950, and 295 to 115 in 1954, even though the winning candidate in each case received 43 percent, 49.3 percent, and 36.9 percent of the popular vote, respectively. This level of political competition disappeared in the years after *Brown*. In 1958, the Regular candidate, Ernest Vandiver Jr., won the gubernatorial primary with over 80 percent support.

Nonetheless, although *Brown* tipped the scales in the Regulars favor in the short term, it did not change the underlying political dynamic. Even during their time in the electoral wilderness, Loyalists would continue to formulate their opposition to the Regulars in terms of the language of progressive color blindness and the overall agenda of a modernized New

South. Regulars would continue to emphasize the need for absolute commitment to white supremacy and defense of traditionalism. Each faction was primarily interested in defending one of two things Georgia's white electorate cared about very deeply—schools and segregation. So long as voters were not compelled to choose between the two, their support for massive resistance was strong. But once the civil rights movement succeeded in forcing a showdown over whether to actually follow through with massive resistance and close the schools, the familiar divisions of the postwar years reappeared. While *Brown* therefore temporarily provided the Regulars with a political trump card, it would ultimately prove to be a short-lived advantage.

3

Contesting Massive Resistance

1954–1962

I will not vote to destroy a living institution in order to preserve a dying one.

State representative Hamilton Lokey (D-Fulton County), 1956

The "Statement on Constitutional Principles" that Georgia's senior U.S. senator Walter George read into the *Congressional Record* on March 11, 1956, was intended to be a defining moment in the white South's confrontation with the federal government over school desegregation. More popularly known as the "Southern Manifesto," the two-page document was written as a rallying cry against the *Brown* decision and purported to represent the settled and undivided opinion of a defiant white South. In his speech, George read into the *Record* the Manifesto's praise for those state legislatures that had vowed to "resist forced integration by any lawful means" and called on all white southerners to work to "bring about a reversal" of *Brown*. George also endorsed the Manifesto's claim that the *Brown* ruling was unconstitutional, had no "legal basis," and was a "clear abuse of judicial power." According to the Manifesto, the Supreme Court had exceeded its authority, and hence the ruling was invalid. In espousing this view, the Manifesto was not just endorsing the gathering momentum behind "massive resistance" to desegregation; it was all but demanding that such resistance receive the support of every white southerner.[1]

The Manifesto encapsulated the Regular position as it was being presented to southern voters in the mid-1950s. By placing race at the center of the political discussion and framing resistance to the Supreme Court as a defense of southern tradition, the Manifesto was intended to define the debate over desegregation in terms that would be favorable to the Regulars' arguments. Ideally, it would place Loyalists on the defensive in southern elections, while the national Democratic leadership would be on notice that supporting school desegregation would jeopardize a majority of the party's southern support. By seeking to create an impression of unassailable white southern unity, the Manifesto's authors were therefore speaking to both a national and a regional audience.

Superficially, the Manifesto's authors were very successful in their aims. Certainly the overwhelming support of the southern congressional delegation for the Manifesto lent plausibility to the claim that it spoke on behalf of white southern opinion: nineteen out of twenty-two southern senators and 81 out of 105 southern representatives signed the document.[2] This in turn reflected a larger shift within southern politics toward electing Regular Democrats committed to massive resistance after 1954. According to Earl Black's analysis, only two out of the fourteen gubernatorial races held in the South from 1950 to 1954 had produced victories for the most racially conservative candidate. By 1956, however, that trend was reversing, and the Manifesto represented this shift in the political climate.[3] Loyalists who disliked the Manifesto had to worry that a failure to sign would invite defeat in their next primary by a pro-Manifesto opponent. In some cases, as with U.S. representative Brooks Hays of Arkansas, such a threat was explicitly made in order to persuade him to sign.[4] For the sake of his reelection prospects, Hays was wise to do so. In the years after the Manifesto was published, winning a southern election almost anywhere required a commitment to massive resistance. Even in the supposedly more progressive Rim South, those who opposed defying the federal courts found themselves ever more isolated in their attempts to avoid state legislatures passing "interposition resolutions" that declared federal court rulings on desegregation to be null and void.[5]

Collectively, the support for the Manifesto, the dominance of southern electoral contests by Regular candidates, and the spread of massive resistance throughout the South all suggested a consensus among white southerners that desegregation would not be permitted to occur. In fact, this appearance of unity was a facade, and no such consensus existed. For a few years in most southern states, massive resistance generated landslide victories for Regular candidates and reduced Loyalists to also-rans at the ballot box. During that time, the civil rights movement came under sustained legal, political, and sometimes physical assault across the South, and many states passed laws intended to thwart *Brown* by privatizing or closing the school system. Nonetheless, for all the sound and fury that massive resistance generated, it proved to be a short-lived movement that represented an aberration in the development of postwar southern politics. By the early 1960s, the familiar political divisions of the postwar years had reappeared, and attempts to implement massive resistance had failed. In truth, massive resistance had only ever been likely to survive unchallenged so long as it was political posturing. Once it required executing as a policy, many of its erstwhile supporters balked at the consequences. In contrast to the hopes of the Southern Manifesto's authors, complying with the law through token desegregation proved to be more palatable to the majority of southerners than preserving white supremacy through closing the schools.

Yet just as the popularity massive resistance enjoyed at its peak should not lead us to overstate the depth of support it had among white southerners, so the rapidity of its fall should not lead us to understate the effort it took to bring it down. While there was always a good chance that white southerners would be hesitant to abandon public education for the sake of Jim Crow if actually forced to choose between the two, it was still necessary for supporters of desegregation to ensure that such a choice had to be made. This became a top priority of the civil rights movement in the aftermath of *Brown* and was a vital step toward the ending of massive resistance. By pushing the federal courts to order desegregation, civil rights activists forced the hand of those who feared the economic and social consequences of abandoning the public school system. This included most Loyalists, but also some leaders of a reemergent southern Republicanism. Few of them welcomed having to make this choice, but once they realized they had to choose there was no doubt in their minds that open schools was the first priority. Once again, Loyalists and their allies deployed progressive color blindness in order to win support for their position, and once again it proved a valuable tool in finessing the issue of race in the postwar South.

Ultimately, the contest over massive resistance illustrated several themes central to postwar southern politics, and its fall resulted in significant consequences for the civil rights movement and both political parties. First, it demonstrated once again that the central dynamic in the postwar South was the relationship between Loyalist Democrats and the civil rights movement. Massive resistance ended when the civil rights movement forced Loyalist Democrats to campaign against it. In turn, the end of massive resistance created an opening for Loyalists to regain the initiative in the contest for control of the Georgia Democratic Party. The end of massive resistance also undermined the central premise of the

Regulars' leadership: their ability to maintain the color line at all costs. For the civil rights movement, the end of massive resistance represented a considerable success, though still only a partial one. While civil rights activists were able to push a critical portion of the white southern population toward accepting an end to complete segregation, this also meant desegregation would take place on terms that these same white southerners found acceptable—that is, in a limited and strictly controlled fashion.

Second, the debate over massive resistance highlighted again how both Regular and Loyalist Democrats recognized that the basic agenda of the other had considerable support among the southern population, and how both factions formulated their political strategies accordingly. This was true even though Loyalists were a negligible presence in electoral contests during the massive resistance years. In fact, the Regular co-option of sizable portions of the Loyalist agenda even as massive resistance was in full swing was a critical part of shoring up their electoral dominance at the time. Similarly, even though Loyalists and their allies were ultimately successful in undermining massive resistance, they recognized that racial and social traditionalism was still popular, and sought not to challenge it any more than necessary. In short, despite the lopsided election results in the late 1950s, both modernizers and traditionalists acted as if they knew that neither could ultimately prevail by appealing only to their own base of supporters.

In Georgia, massive resistance lasted from around 1954 until 1961, although final ratification of its demise by the electorate did not occur until the 1962 Democratic primary. It reached its political peak in the 1958 gubernatorial election, when Ernest Vandiver was elected on a pledge that "no, not one" black child would ever be allowed to go to a white school on his watch. Vandiver also vowed to preserve the county-unit system, another familiar Regular priority. With no Loyalist opponent to challenge him, he captured more than 80 percent of the popular vote and carried all but six counties. And yet within two years of taking the oath of office, Vandiver found himself asking the General Assembly to repeal the massive resistance laws and allow token desegregation to take place. A year later, the county-unit system, on the verge of being struck down by the U.S. Supreme Court, was abandoned by the state party. In the 1962 primary to succeed Vandiver, Loyalist Carl Sanders prevailed over former governor Griffin by a landslide. The political structure that Vandiver had vowed to defend with a huge popular mandate had not even survived his term in office—proof positive of the shallow nature of the apparent consensus behind massive resistance.

In April 1959, a pessimistic Richard Russell had predicted dire consequences for the Regulars should massive resistance be ended. In a letter to Ross Sharpe of Lyons, Georgia, the senator argued that so long as massive resistance and the county-unit system were maintained, the Regulars would "get along all right." If, however, these pillars of Regular dominance were to fall, "the country boys are finished."[6] In truth, even after the events of 1961 and 1962, Regulars continued to represent a sizable portion of the Georgia electorate, so Russell's assessment was unduly fatalistic. However, seen in terms of the control of the Georgia Democratic Party that Regulars had enjoyed in the previous sixteen years, the "country boys" who had been running it were indeed "finished." Their one-time dominance would never be restored. Ending massive resistance broke their hold on the state Democratic Party.

All-In: The Regulars Gamble on Massive Resistance

The election of Marvin Griffin and the passage of the private schools amendment in 1954 provided Regulars with the political authority and the political momentum necessary to make massive resistance the official policy of the state. They proceeded to do so by passing laws that sought to snuff out any possibility that school desegregation might occur in Georgia. Most of these laws sailed through the General Assembly with only token opposition. The near-unanimous support that massive resistance enjoyed among Georgia's elected representatives reflected the collapse of the Loyalist faction as an electoral force after 1954. Regulars were enjoying the kind of dominance in Georgia politics they had not had since before World War II, and they used the opportunity to flex their political muscle. They were able to establish a legal framework in Georgia under which desegregation was to all intents and purposes illegal, and anyone who attempted to implement it could expect the state to take action against them.

As uncontested as the rise of massive resistance was, however, it rested on an enormous bluff, which if it were ever called would bring the whole edifice crumbling down. The bluff in question was that for all their talk of defiance, there were only a handful of Regulars who had any enthusiasm for actually implementing what massive resistance potentially called for: the closure of the public school system. While Regular leaders were confident that the overwhelming majority of white Georgians would prefer segregated education to be maintained, they were far less confident that a similar majority would be willing to see public education abolished. Massive resistance was therefore only capable of creating the illusion of consensus in Georgia so long as it was a combination of symbolic defiance and rhetoric.

In order to sustain massive resistance, Regulars did everything possible to prevent their bluff being called. First and foremost, this meant trying to shut down the civil rights movement so that civil rights activists would not be able to secure a federal court ruling requiring desegregation in Georgia. In the absence of such a ruling, Georgia would never have to face the choice between backing down from massive resistance or abandoning its public school system. Indirectly, Regulars also hoped that putting pressure on the civil rights movement would roll back or halt the rise in black voter registration across the state. As far as Regulars were concerned, the more black voters there were, the greater would be the share of the state's electorate willing to comply with *Brown*. To Regulars, keeping Georgia's electorate as white as possible was therefore both philosophically desirable and politically beneficial.

As the most important civil rights organization in Georgia in the 1950s, the NAACP was the organization most likely to be able to secure a federal desegregation order and was therefore the one that Regular leaders were most eager to target. State attorney general Eugene Cook accordingly proposed laws to the General Assembly that would restrict the ability of the NAACP to operate. In August 1956, Cook demanded that the NAACP hand over its membership files and financial records to the state. When John Calhoun refused to comply, he was jailed for contempt of court, becoming the first black southern leader of the NAACP to be jailed during massive resistance.[7] In January 1957, Cook backed measures that would declare the NAACP "subversive" to the Georgia Constitution and requested U.S. attorney general (and known civil rights supporter) Herbert Brownell to declare the NAACP a subversive organization nationwide.[8] Later that summer, in a clear attempt to cripple the organization financially, state revenue commissioner T. V. "Red" Williams presented the NAACP with a demand for eleven years' worth of back taxes.[9] Collectively, these and other measures showed how keen Regular leaders were to put an end to the legal challenges to Georgia's segregation laws. For a while, their efforts appeared successful. In May 1956, the NAACP announced it was dropping *Aaron v. Cook*, the lawsuit challenging racial discrimination in education it had pursued for six years.[10] The following year, black educator Horace Ward gave up on his attempt to integrate the University of Georgia law school. By the end of 1957, there were no extant lawsuits calling for the enforcement of *Brown* in Georgia.[11]

The simultaneous attempts to crack down on black voter registration were a continuation of the efforts sponsored by Herman Talmadge in the 1940s. Regulars were able to do the most damage to voter registration efforts in rural Georgia, particularly in the Black Belt. A combination of legal measures that made it tougher for anyone whom the registrar did not want to vote to register, economic intimidation from white landowners and businessmen, and outright physical violence persuaded many civil rights activists to abandon voter registration drives. The impact of this was reflected by the fact that after 1952 rural Georgia lagged behind even Mississippi and Alabama in the share of its black population that was registered to vote.[12] Perhaps the most brutal incident that illustrated the risks facing black activists in Georgia during massive resistance was the murder of Thomas Brewer in Columbus four weeks before the Southern Manifesto was presented to Congress. The shooting of Brewer, the head of the local NAACP and a critical figure in initiating the lawsuit that overturned Georgia's white primary, caused civil rights activists in Columbus to back off their voter registration drive.[13]

Ultimately, however, Regulars were only able to slow down or restrict black activism; they could not stop it entirely. The potential for a desegregation order therefore remained a threat. As a result, Regulars also had to worry about the reaction of the white population if such an order were ever issued. In particular, Governor Griffin and Attorney General Cook were worried that the school boards in and around Atlanta might, if given the option, agree to comply with *Brown* rather than close their schools. If this happened, it would undermine, perhaps fatally, the statewide unity on which massive resistance depended in order to succeed. Accordingly, Griffin and Cook set about making desegregation a practical impossibility. Their aim was to create a set of laws such that even if a local school board wanted to comply with *Brown*, it would not legally be able to do so. In taking these steps, supporters of massive resistance were tacitly admitting that they did not believe their white constituents were quite as united in their commitment to white supremacy as the Southern Manifesto had implied.

The Regulars' preferred plan in response to a desegregation order remained the replacement of the public school system with state-subsidized private schools. The 1954 amendment had made such a plan constitutionally possible, and in February 1956 the General Assembly approved the funds for it. In January 1957, Governor Griffin requested and received the power to suspend compulsory attendance laws when desegregation was ordered, as well as the authority to deploy troops to prevent desegregation taking place.[14] With federal court rulings in the fall of 1958 striking down attempts by Arkansas governor Orval Faubus to prevent desegregation, further laws were adopted in 1959 in Georgia to shore up massive resistance. These new laws mandated Governor Vandiver to close any school ordered to desegregate, provided state funding for school boards to hire legal counsel to defend segregation, and denied school districts the right to use taxpayers' money to operate desegregated facilities.[15]

The rationale behind these measures was similar to that of the "Doomsday Device" director Stanley Kubrick imagined in *Dr. Strangelove*.[16] In order to make massive resistance credible, it required laws that contained universal, automatic sanctions if desegregation were ever attempted. The chance that someone might waver in their commitment to massive resistance was thereby eliminated. This concentration of powers in the hands of the governor and the *requirement* that he use them illustrated the lack of faith massive resistance leaders had in local officials in some parts of Georgia, most especially the state capital. Sometimes this lack of faith led to even more alarming suggestions, such as the law proposed by Cook that would have made complying with any desegregation order in Georgia a capital offense.[17]

Ensuring that the state had the authority to implement massive resistance removed the threat that Loyalist leaders at the local level might agree to desegregation. In order to shore up popular support for their agenda among voters generally, Regulars resorted to political carrots rather than sticks. Aware that a sizable portion of Georgia's voters were now expecting far more from their state government in terms of public services, Regular governors co-opted parts of the Loyalist agenda to appeal to them. The hope was that such a strategy would win the backing of voters who were supportive of racial traditionalism but who also expected economic modernization.

Accordingly, while Marvin Griffin's and Herman Talmadge's public stances on race were very similar to Gene Talmadge's, both Griffin and the younger Talmadge had a very different attitude toward the role of government. Both had raised taxes in order to fund extra spending on public education. Griffin had promised not to raise taxes during his 1954 campaign, but the public pressure for raising teachers' pay and increasing school funding proved too strong to resist.[18] The cause of this change in outlook from the Regular administrations of the 1930s can be traced to three overlapping motivations. First, some Regulars agreed with the Loyalist belief that a good public education system would provide economic benefits. Roy Harris was a good example of this mind-set, though he believed such benefits could also be achieved in a segregated system.[19] A second motivation was a concern that the "separate but equal" school system would be struck down unless some effort was made to genuinely equalize white and black facilities. As white parents would not likely support a reduction in resources for their schools, this meant spending more money on education generally. Herman Talmadge subscribed to this view. Finally, there was the politically pragmatic belief that the state's electorate would only be reliably supportive of the Regulars' racial agenda if they were guaranteed a sound educational system. This was the view of former state party chairman James S. Peters, who warned Harris in a public letter that if the schools were not kept open and well-funded, voters would turn to Loyalist candidates instead.[20] This final concern represented a further dilemma for supporters of massive resistance and exposed a division within the Regular leadership. The more pragmatic Regulars, such as Peters, Ernest Vandiver, and, eventually, Herman Talmadge, were inclined to hold out against desegregation as long as they possibly could, but were wary of the political consequences of closing the public school system. By contrast, Regular hardliners such as Harris and Charles Bloch were determined that the "no, not one" promise of Vandiver's 1958 campaign must be upheld even at the cost of ending public education.

That even the leadership of the massive resistance movement was divided over whether to carry out its threats if push came to shove was a further sign of just how superficial the unity of white opinion in Georgia was after the *Brown* decision. But even if the Regulars had been entirely united, there was no realistic chance that they could forever suppress the political divisions that had been evident in the 1940s. This is not to say that their efforts to do so were without impact. Although neither the civil rights movement nor Loyalist Democrats could be eliminated as a political presence, they were firmly on the back foot during the late 1950s. Nor was it the case that massive resistance was inevitably bound to fail. To bring it down, the civil rights movement had to be proactive in forcing Georgia to choose between public schools and segregation, and whites supportive of economic modernization had to find a politically viable way to advocate open schools. At its core, massive resistance may therefore have been a high-stakes bluff, but it was still one that required its opponents to have a hand strong enough to enable them to call it.

Marching along Auburn Avenue: Black Activism during Massive Resistance

Historian Stephen Tuck describes the 1950s as "years of retrenchment" for the civil rights movement in Georgia.[21] In terms of the scope and style of the black activism that took place during the years of massive resistance, this characterization cannot be disputed. Whereas the 1940s had seen voter registration drives and desegregation campaigns all across Georgia, once the Regulars gained control of the levers of power civil rights activity stalled or fell away in much of the state outside of Atlanta and Savannah.[22] Even Atlanta's black leadership seemed to have been cowed by the presence of massive resistance in the mid-1950s. Such was certainly the impression created by dropping the pending lawsuits against segregated schools and not filing any new ones.[23] Nonetheless, even though black activism was more muted and less widespread than in the 1940s, that which did occur was still central to bringing down massive resistance and for setting the stage for the renewed momentum of black protests in the 1960s.

For most of the 1950s, the Auburn Avenue Strategy was the preferred strategy of Georgia's black leadership. That it emerged as such was largely because massive resistance had closed off most other approaches. The Auburn Avenue leadership operated on the premise that there were enough white Georgians who would accept gradual desegregation if the alternative was closed schools—an assessment that turned out to be accurate. As such, limited though black activism was in the 1950s, it proved sufficient to call the Regulars' bluff by securing court rulings that guaranteed a showdown over massive resistance. In addition, the rising number of black voters in urban areas also created a powerful incentive for white politicians in Georgia's cities to moderate their opposition to racial change. These were both immensely significant achievements. At the same time, the relatively slow pace of change that the Auburn Avenue approach accepted fueled a sense of frustration among younger black activists that in turn widened the generational divide in Georgia's civil rights movement. Having played a pivotal role in undermining massive resistance, Auburn Avenue's leaders also found that support for their gradualist style of politics was also under threat as a result.

A. T. Walden, who was nearly seventy years old by the time of the *Brown* decision, remained the embodiment of the Auburn Avenue leadership. Walden was still primarily interested in focusing his activism on voter registration and on increasing black influence in the Democratic Party. Walden hoped to demonstrate to Loyalists that black voters were a powerful voting bloc, but that they were willing to pursue gradual change when it came to race relations and were therefore an electoral asset rather than a threat. Accordingly, it was important not to push too hard on school desegregation. Although Walden ultimately hoped that the *Brown* decision would be implemented, he was willing to hold back on demands that it be enforced so as not to destabilize his relations with Loyalist leaders. As head of the ANVL and a key member of several other statewide civil rights groups, Walden therefore pursued an agenda that focused on registering more black voters and getting elected officials to listen to black concerns while not rocking the boat by pushing for radical racial change. This made him an ideal political conduit to the black community for the Loyalist leadership, and Walden was in turn rewarded by increasing influence within Loyalist circles.

Within Atlanta, Walden hoped to parlay the rising number of black voters into political influence. The ANVL's endorsement, which had been growing in value since 1949, became ever more coveted, just as Walden had hoped it would. By the mid-1950s, Loyalist candidates were actively seeking an audience with the ANVL. Luther Alverson, a former state legislator and candidate for reelection to the Fulton Superior Court, wrote to Walden in August 1956 expressing his "pleasure" at being invited to an ANVL meeting and stressed his keenness to attend. Randy Dodd, a candidate for Fulton County sheriff, replied to Walden's invitation with a somewhat clumsily worded attempt to thank Walden for informing "your people" about civic affairs, but also with the request for ANVL support on account of Dodd's promise to "render a service to all people as all people elect me. I will be impartial and fair to all regardless of race, creed or color."[24]

This level of interaction with white candidates was a far cry from arranging furtive encounters in hotel service elevators, and public contacts between black voters and white political candidates soon become more routine than remarkable—a development reflected in the matter-of-fact tone of the report sent to Walden on the ANVL's "screening" of three mayoral candidates and twenty-eight hopefuls for city council in August 1961.[25] The growing presence of black voters virtually required white candidates to pay attention and thus raised the incentive for them to court black support. This was a politically simple calculation, but it had significant consequences for how white politicians would react to black concerns. As Robert Thompson, housing director of the Atlanta Urban League, sardonically noted, "when we got more vote[s], we made a whole lot of Christians out of the white people."[26]

Walden enthusiastically supported the quiet revolution in interracial political dialogue that black voter registration produced, but he was more circumspect on the more sensitive question of school desegregation. While Walden supported *Brown* in principle, he was willing to acquiesce to white leaders' requests for time to consider their response. His attitude on this was evident even before the *Brown* ruling was handed down. A February 1954 report of the ANVL's Committee on Objectives set out Walden's priorities. The report called for the creation of an interracial Council on Human Relations, black membership of several citywide bodies, and the right for blacks to apply for such city jobs as fireman and sanitary inspector. On the question of the likely ruling on *Brown*, however, the report suggested nothing further than an "initiation of studies on procedures for implementing the pending decision of the U.S. Supreme Court on public schools."[27] The following year, when Walden requested a meeting with Mayor Hartsfield to discuss ANVL concerns, the list of topics that Walden proposed included parks policy, the proposed Council on Human Relations, and the appointment of black firemen, but said nothing about schools.[28]

Hartsfield and other Loyalists were quite happy to discuss Walden's agenda items. They were also quite happy to "study" indefinitely the issue of desegregating Atlanta's schools, as it meant neither formally rejecting nor actually implementing the *Brown* decision—the perfect color-blind position. Walden even went so far as to promise to hold off on any legal action for the duration of the "study" the Atlanta school board promised it would hold—a move that caused considerable frustration among younger black leaders who wanted things to move faster. The eventual report on *Brown* from the Atlanta school board was not released until September 1957, more than three years after the ruling. Even then, while not vowing resistance, the board concluded that more time would be needed to draw up an implementation plan.[29] Walden's approach on school desegregation further legitimized him as a black leader to do business with in the eyes of Loyalists, but was doing little to challenge the status quo on education.

Even by the standards of the Auburn Avenue Strategy, Walden's approach was conservative. Yet, as he was reluctant to change course, it fell to others within the Auburn Avenue establishment to adopt a more assertive approach. John Calhoun was among those who called for a more confrontational strategy to achieve school desegregation, albeit one that still focused on the courts. Calhoun personally took the lead in initiating a new lawsuit against segregation in Atlanta's schools that ultimately secured the crucial federal court order demanding compliance with *Brown*. Rumors of Calhoun's intentions were circulating in the media by the end of 1957, and in January 1958 *Calhoun v. Latimer* was filed, calling for Atlanta to desegregate its high schools.[30] Calhoun's role in bringing this suit was almost certainly a contributory factor to his being specifically targeted by state officials in their campaign against the NAACP. Such interference was to no avail. Despite Eugene Cook's efforts on behalf of the state to keep the suit out of the federal courts, the attorney general was formally rebuffed in May 1958. The eventual outcome was just what Calhoun had hoped for. In June 1959, federal judge Frank Hooper ruled that Atlanta must draw up a desegregation plan by December 1 of that year.[31]

Hooper's ruling was only one of several legal developments in 1959 that made it clear Georgia would soon have to decide whether to implement its massive resistance laws. Also in 1959, a separate case brought by a black applicant to Georgia State College resulted in a ruling that segregation in Georgia's higher education system must be ended.[32] Separately during that summer, Charlayne Hunter and Hamilton Holmes began the process of attempting to desegregate the University of Georgia, which would eventually become the case (*Holmes v. Danmer*) over which the fate of massive resistance in the state would be decided. Although it took a further two years of lawsuits, political maneuvers, and federal court rulings before the final confrontation took place, it was clear from 1959 onward that a showdown over massive resistance was unavoidable—a showdown that would not have occurred had it not been for black political activism.

However limited and cautious the Auburn Avenue Strategy had therefore been, it nonetheless succeeded in two critical respects. It made black voters in Georgia a sufficiently large group that white politicians in the urban parts of the state could not afford to ignore them, and it generated a court ruling on *Brown* that forced both Regulars and Loyalists to take positions—against public education and for desegregation, respectively—that they would have preferred to avoid. This may have been as much as could reasonably have been hoped for amid the hostile context of massive resistance, but there was no hiding the fact that in an effort to gain access to mainstream political channels, the Auburn Avenue leaders had been reluctant to confront segregation via direct-action protests. This was arguably good politics, but it was not producing change fast enough for a younger generation of black Georgians.

Even as the showdown with massive resistance loomed, this generational tension became evident. Some of the old guard acknowledged that this was inevitable. Jacob Henderson, who had been so critical to launching the ANVL in the 1940s, reflected that "at that particular time [1960], I was a little too old" to be leading the charge against Jim Crow. Instead, Henderson said, much of the older generation looked at the student movement and concluded, "Well, that's their ballgame."[33] A less sentimental message was conveyed by one black man, who wrote to Walden in 1961 that he was no longer willing to defer to the ANVL's leadership: "You guided us when we were mere political babes. This we appreciate, but we are big boys now and wish to think for ourselves, if you don't mind."[34] Even after massive resistance collapsed, the Auburn Avenue Strategy that Walden and Calhoun had pursued would continue to be influential among black Georgians, especially those who aspired to close links with white political leaders. But it would never again be as dominant as it had been during the 1950s. Massive resistance had made it the only sustainable option as far as many black leaders were concerned. As cracks in the Regulars' dominance began to appear after 1960, more confrontational approaches began to dominate the civil rights movement in Georgia.

Voices in the (Sub)Urban Wilderness: Loyalists and Republicans

Until the civil rights movement's legal successes in 1959, political opposition to massive resistance from white Georgians was minimal. This is
not to say that massive resistance had uncritical support—the 45 percent
who voted against the private schools amendment in 1954 can at least be
marked down as representing voters with reservations—but so long as the
possibility persisted that massive resistance might succeed in thwarting
the *Brown* ruling without having to close the public schools, few political
figures were willing to speak out against it. Like the civil rights movement,
open political opposition to the Regular agenda was confined largely to
urban and suburban areas of the state, particularly Atlanta. Even there,
outright opposition to massive resistance was a minority view until school
closings became a real proposition. Nonetheless, although their voices
were small in number and would need the civil rights movement to push
the situation to a crisis before they could be heard, the few Loyalists willing to speak out and the leaders of the reemerging Republican Party were
laying down important markers for future political contests—particularly in the way both drew on the rhetoric of color blindness to try and
carve out a political position from which they could challenge the Regular
agenda.

The political impotence of Georgia's Loyalists in the years after 1954
was vividly illustrated by the "men's room walkout" in the General Assembly that left state representative Hamilton Lokey of Fulton County as
the accidental hero of the anti-Regular forces. Lokey was part of a group
that became known to their opponents as the "sinister seven." These seven
legislators were the only reliable votes in the General Assembly against
massive resistance laws. In the early months of 1956, these seven men—
Lokey, James MacKay, Muggsy Smith, and Fred Bentley from Atlanta and
its suburbs; Bill Gunter and Bill Williams from Gainesville in north Georgia; and Bernard Nightingale from Brunswick on the Atlantic coast—
were growing frustrated at their lack of political influence.[35] They found
themselves repeatedly casting token votes in opposition to interposition
resolutions and laws enabling school closures, none of which made any
difference to the final outcome. On one occasion, they decided as a group
to stay in the men's room during a vote rather than engage in a futile
gesture of opposition. The idea was to portray the General Assembly as a
toothless rubber stamp for Governor Griffin. Unfortunately, nobody told

Lokey of the plan, and so, with his colleagues hiding in the bathroom, he appeared in the chamber to cast the lone "no" vote for the day.[36]

Over the following days, Lokey attracted a brief flurry of attention from the anti–massive resistance sections of the media, which praised his nerve and heroism without mentioning the unintentional nature of it. As flattering as Lokey found the adulation, the farcical context of how it came to pass demonstrated how eager opponents of massive resistance were to find and lionize Democratic politicians willing to criticize it but also just how weak this opposition was within the Democratic Party: when your collective might can be comfortably accommodated in a handful of toilet stalls, it is hard to mount much of a challenge. Nonetheless, while Lokey may have become an accidental leader for Loyalists, he was actually well suited for the role, not only because he was genuinely passionate about the risk that he believed massive resistance posed to public education but also because he was not a radical figure operating on the ideological fringes of Georgia politics. Lokey was a fairly conventional Loyalist, albeit with a willingness to engage in unconventional behavior, and an ideal man to carry the flag for Loyalists during what amounted to their wilderness years.

Lokey had been elected to the Georgia House in 1952 following the retirement of his friend, Luther Alverson. A war veteran and attorney, Lokey was ideologically disposed toward the "good government" outlook that represented the dominant strain of Loyalist thought. Like many others in that school of thought, he was somewhere between lukewarm and skeptical toward labor unions. In fact, his first campaign for the General Assembly was in opposition to a man Lokey later referred to as the "labor representative" backed by the local unions.[37] Like many good government advocates, his political priorities were education, economic progress, and political reform, not racial justice or redistribution of wealth.

Lokey's objections to massive resistance stemmed from his belief that it represented an outdated mind-set, not an immoral one. Prior to 1954, this had been a familiar Loyalist argument, but in the years thereafter, few political figures were willing to make this case. Lokey was therefore exceptional not for what he thought, but for his willingness to say it in public. The strongest public expression of Lokey's views appeared in February 1956 in the "Public Schools Declaration" he coauthored with his fellow member of the "sinister seven," James MacKay. The "Declaration" was published in opposition to the imminent adoption of the private schools plan. It opposed the private schools plan by stressing the importance of education, not the need for racial justice.

The "Declaration" began by warning that "anything that harms the public schools does irreparable harm to the future of our children and our state." In line with color-blind thinking, the "Declaration" also took a swipe at the effort to suppress the discussion of other issues by appealing to race, saying that attempts were under way to "deny the rights of peaceful assembly, petition, or open discussion." In acknowledgment of the popularity of segregation, the "Declaration" concluded with a general endorsement of "our traditional way of life," but warned against using this as a justification for ending public education.[38] This was partly intended as political cover. Just as Regulars worried about being seen as antieducation or antigrowth, so Lokey and others worried about being seen as antisegregation. Defending the "traditional way of life" reflected a continuing Loyalist willingness, eagerness even, to pledge support for segregation so long as it did not threaten public education. As Everett Millican, the Loyalist state senator from Fulton County, put it, "I was as much for segregation as anyone; but if it had to be a choice between segregation and not having the kids go to school, then, I was in favor of letting the kids go to school."[39]

That the "Declaration" omitted any mention of race, support for *Brown*, or support for desegregation generally was a typical tactic for advocates of progressive color blindness. Looking back on it later in life, Lokey conceded this was a deliberate ploy, confirming it had been his intention for the "Declaration" not to "say one word about integration or desegregation."[40] While this made good political sense at the time, in his autobiography Lokey nonetheless admitted to being horrified at just how hesitant he and his Loyalist colleagues had been in the 1950s: "As I reread today the speech[es] I made . . . I am appalled at how gingerly I tried to make my points, at how careful I was to use language that would not offend."[41] Looking back from the perspective of today, the Loyalist opposition to closing the schools does indeed seem rather timid and meek. In this regard, it was, like the caution of the Auburn Avenue leaders, a sign of the minimal political space that opponents of massive resistance believed they had to work in.

And yet even though Lokey's stance—carefully inoffensive as it was—did not resonate with many Georgians initially, the "open schools" argument that lay at the heart of the "Declaration" would be the one that brought down massive resistance a few years later. It paved the way for, and helped rationalize, token desegregation as an alternative to massive resistance. In 1956, with no looming crisis over school closures, Lokey's arguments attracted little support. However, by the end of 1958, with *Calhoun v. Latimer* working its way through the courts, Lokey and other Loyalists found that their open schools position was gaining more sympathetic responses from their audiences.[42] After the federal court rulings in 1959, such sympathy and support grew exponentially. Lokey, MacKay, and the rest of the "sinister seven" became key figures in mobilizing public opinion against massive resistance. By 1962, the open schools position had become popular enough among Georgia Democrats that Carl Sanders, a state senator from Augusta, drew on it to win a landslide victory in the Democratic primary. This result must have been particularly satisfying to Lokey, given that it came at the expense of former governor Griffin, who in 1956 had appeared to be in complete control of the political landscape.

Writing of these events some forty years later, Lokey claimed always to have suspected that support for open schools was far more widespread in the state than the handful of Loyalists who joined him in speaking out in 1956.[43] Subsequent events certainly suggested this was the case, but Loyalists alone cannot take the credit for this. Although the one-party system had long rendered it a politically irrelevant group, during the 1950s the Georgia Republican Party began to experience a steady gain in support. Most of this new support was coming from high-income, highly educated, urban and suburban parts of the state, and it was being drawn toward a form of Republicanism that also rejected massive resistance: a form of Republicanism based on winning power through a "suburban strategy." Although Georgia's Republicans managed no electoral breakthrough during the 1950s, by developing the broad outlines of the "suburban strategy," they were laying down an important marker not only for future partisan competition in the South but also for the ongoing debate within the southern GOP over how to achieve majority status in the region.

Electoral disappointment was not the only thing that Republicans and Loyalists had in common during the 1950s: in fact, there was considerable overlap between the core worldview of the two groups. Both were motivated primarily by the modernizing impulse in southern politics, although for different reasons. Both thought that race was a politically disruptive issue and so were drawn to the politics of color blindness, although as a result of different political calculations. Such similarities were in part a reflection of the fact that at the time both were pursuing demographically similar voters. Where they nonetheless differed from each other was their outlook on economics and government activism. While Republicans who believed in a suburban strategy accepted that a large part of the New Deal would be a permanent fixture in American life, they were skeptical over any plans to expand government further. Instead, they pitched their appeal to the economic aspirations of individual southern suburbanites—low taxes, limited government regulation of business, independence from urban control, and preservation of what they deemed to be their "property rights" (and property values). They were, in short, Eisenhower Republicans, both literally and ideologically. Their appearance in the 1950s was therefore no coincidence, and it was entirely fitting that they first attracted serious attention for the role they played in securing Eisenhower the 1952 presidential nomination over conservative favorite Robert A. Taft.

In contrast to the adherents of the "southern strategy" who would make up the other major faction in postwar southern Republicanism, race did not feature explicitly in the suburban strategy. This did not mean, however, that race was irrelevant to their political calculations. In many ways, the absence of race in the suburban strategy was as telling as the general absence of nonwhites in southern suburbia. It had not been overlooked; it had simply been excluded as an unwelcome intrusion. The impulse to ignore race was perfectly explicable: after all, many whites who moved to the suburbs during the postwar years were hoping to "leave behind" the racial problems of the cities. Some of them did so for explicitly racial reasons, but many others had more ambiguous racial views. They may have associated integrated neighborhoods with social problems and lower property values, and been unwilling to bus their children to integrate schools, but they would not have wanted to think of themselves as doing so for racist reasons. For some this was a perfectly sincere belief, for others it was rationalization or self-delusion; but either way, politically the effect was the same: candidates who were tagged as going after the "white backlash" too explicitly risked alienating significant numbers of suburban supporters who did not want to feel they were supporting a racist candidate.[44]

Suburban strategists therefore had an incentive to pursue color-blind politics. Generally speaking—and there were individual exceptions—suburban strategy Republicans wanted to avoid talking about race so that they would not be tagged as "too white" (that is, racist) by the electorate; by contrast, Loyalists wanted to avoid it in order to avoid being tagged as "too black." From the 1960s onward, the Republican Party in Georgia would be divided between supporters of suburban versus southern strategies. In the 1950s, political realities meant that only a suburban strategy was feasible. With Regulars in control of the Democratic Party and the state government, and with no organized Republican presence in most of rural Georgia, there was little to be gained by pursuing rural and small-town voters with an appeal to the white backlash even if Republican leaders had wanted to. As it was, few of those in charge of the party in the 1950s wanted to follow such an approach. For some, this was due to a genuine abhorrence of racial segregation. Nan Pendergrast, one of fifteen charter members of a "Draft Eisenhower" movement in Georgia and editor of the Republican Party newsletter, ascribed her Republicanism to the GOP being one of only two "integrated public organization[s] in the state of Georgia." According to Pendergrast, "the Democratic Party was the white primary, the very essence of bigotry."[45] Elbert Tuttle, the chair of the Georgia GOP in the late 1940s and later a federal judge who issued several prodesegregation decisions, was of a similar mind-set. Others were less engaged in efforts to change southern race relations, but were still hostile to the massive resistance movement. Among these were Tuttle's successor as state chairman, Bill Shartzer, and the state treasurer and future Internal Revenue Service (IRS) commissioner, Randolph Thrower.

A further important factor mitigating against a Republican endorsement of massive resistance was the influence of black leaders in the party. John Calhoun in particular had the political skills, contacts, and ability to get out the vote that made him not just the most influential black Republican, but arguably the most effective operative within the state party as a whole. Certainly as far as Nan Pendergrast was concerned, Calhoun was far more clued in on how to wage successful politics than many of the other leaders: "he thought we were, all of us, from Elbert Tuttle down, impossibly naive, and didn't know what it was all about."[46] Other black leaders who remained or became significant influences within the Georgia GOP included Martin Luther King Sr., John Wesley Dobbs, and C. A. Scott, editor of the influential *Atlanta Daily World*. It was thus sound political strategy for Republicans to avoid alienating black supporters.

As a result of these various considerations, Georgia's Republicans focused their attention in the 1950s on the state's Fifth Congressional

District. It contained more urban and suburban voters than any other district; it had the largest number of registered black voters of any Georgia district; and it was home to a disproportionately high number of high-income and college-educated voters—all groups assumed to be "gettable" for Republican candidates. Based on previous elections, the Fifth also seemed promising. In 1952, its three counties had given Eisenhower 40.5 percent support, which was more than 10 percent ahead of his statewide average. Finally, as it was represented in Congress by James Davis, Republicans could hope to peel off support from Loyalist Democrats who had resented his presence there since 1946.

In 1954, the Republicans made their first serious effort to unseat Davis. They nominated Charlie Moye, an Atlanta-based attorney, as their candidate. Moye was a member of the state party's executive committee and was chairman of the party in DeKalb County. In 1952, he had run unsuccessfully for the state legislature in DeKalb.[47] During his 1954 congressional campaign, Moye stressed his support for the economic policies of the Eisenhower administration and positioned himself as a business-friendly candidate who would bring prosperity to the district.[48] Seeking to take advantage of the sectional tension within the Democratic Party, Moye presented himself as more progressive than Davis but more conservative than the Democratic Party in Washington. In this vein, Moye's campaign praised Eisenhower for having halted the slide toward "socialism" in Washington, while also criticizing Davis as being too reactionary by pointing to his opposition to Social Security and hostility to the United Nations.[49] Moye also opposed county-unit voting and called for a two-party system, framing his stance on both issues as representing a modern, forward-looking position.[50]

As far as race was concerned, Moye espoused a color-blind approach, simultaneously distancing himself from massive resistance while not openly supporting the civil rights movement. Moye spoke out against the private schools amendment, basing his objections not on the need to respect *Brown*, but on the damage that private schools would do to meritocratic values. Moye said he could not support the amendment, as the end of public education would result in the son of "a janitor" being unable to attend school with the "son of a corporation president."[51] That the Fifth District voted against the amendment by 58.2 to 41.4 percent even as the measure carried the state by 53.7 to 46.3 percent suggests Moye had accurately reflected the view of his electorate.[52]

Despite this, however, Moye still lost to Davis, polling 29,911 votes to the Democrat's 54,069—a margin of 64 to 36 percent. In the absence of any earlier congressional campaign of note to compare this to, it is hard to say if such a showing was creditable or disappointing. It was certainly several points below Eisenhower's support in the district two years previously, but Moye had nothing like Eisenhower's name recognition and stature, so that is not necessarily a reasonable benchmark. At the very least, Moye's showing was not negligible.

Certainly his fellow Republicans were encouraged by it. In 1956, Randolph Thrower challenged Davis using the same themes as Moye. Thrower's stump speeches regularly focused on his opposition to the county-unit system, the need for two-party politics, and the economic growth of the Eisenhower years. Additionally, Thrower rejected the politics of massive resistance and implicitly criticized Davis by promising that "not for one vote, or one thousand votes, or a hundred thousand votes will I become a peddler of hatred and rancor and bitterness."[53] Refusing to engage in the rhetoric of massive resistance did not mean Thrower spoke up for civil rights: rather, he was also hoping to ignore race altogether. Despite the growing strength of massive resistance over the previous two years that should have made the climate tougher for such an approach, Thrower improved on Moye's absolute and relative vote, losing to Davis by 85,292 to 58,777 (59.2 to 40.8 percent). Strikingly, though, Thrower ran marginally ahead of Eisenhower's showing in the Fifth District that year, not just relatively (40.8 to 40.5 percent) but also in total votes received (58,777 to 57,429). This reversed the normal pattern of southern Republicanism in the 1950s, where Eisenhower ran ahead of his party's congressional candidates, and was testament to Thrower's qualities as a candidate. In 1958, Thrower planned to challenge Davis again, a rematch that would have been intriguing given the Republican's promise that he would make Davis's racial views and support for massive resistance his number one campaign issue.[54] Unfortunately for the GOP, Thrower was kept off the ballot after the filing deadline was unexpectedly (and discreetly) moved forward by the Democratic secretary of state.[55]

Even though there had been no breakthrough victory for them to celebrate during the 1950s, Georgia's Republicans could still look back on a decade that had witnessed sustained growth in Republican support. The nature and pace of this growth were evident from the party's performance in presidential contests. From 18.9 percent support in 1948, the Republican ticket improved its showing to 30.3 percent in 1952, 33.7 percent in 1956, and 37.9 percent in 1960. In total, there were nearly 200,000 more Georgians willing to vote for Richard M. Nixon in 1960 than Thomas E. Dewey in 1948. Of those 200,000 new Republicans, more than 60 percent were from the fifteen counties that contained the state's most populous urban and suburban areas (counties that accounted for approximately 45 percent of the state's voters). By contrast, south Georgia and the Black Belt, the heart of Regular strength, had 30 percent of the state electorate, but contributed just over 20 percent of the new Republican voters and gave Nixon only 26.8 percent support in 1960.

In the medium term, the growing Republican strength would become a cause of grave concern for Loyalist Democrats. With Regulars in control, however, the attitude for most of the 1950s was to make common cause against the shared enemy. Hamilton Lokey spoke warmly of the time "Randolph" ran for Congress, while Nan Pendergrast freely admitted having crossed party lines to support Baxter Jones in 1952 and Morris Abram in 1954 during their primary campaigns against Davis. She justified disregarding party allegiance by explaining that she simply "loathed" Davis.[56] And yet for all the enmity toward Regular incumbents, neither Loyalists nor Republicans had been able to dislodge them from power, even in Atlanta. Only after the NAACP secured the desegregation order from Judge Hooper were the color-blind arguments each had advanced against massive resistance able to gain traction and undermine the white unity on segregation the Regulars had cultivated.

HOPE at the Grassroots

As Georgia's moment of decision on massive resistance approached, neither Loyalists nor Republicans were well placed to lead the opposition to closing the public schools. Regulars dominated the General Assembly and controlled the governor's office, which were the two institutions where the decision on whether to comply with Judge Hooper's court ruling would be made. Hooper's ruling had initially included a deadline for compliance of the beginning of the 1960 school year. However, the next gubernatorial contest was not until 1962. This meant that massive resistance could not be blocked through defeating it at election time; instead, it would be necessary to persuade Governor Vandiver and a majority of the General

Assembly not to go ahead with the very measures they had promised to implement in order to win office.[57]

Unable to rely on electoral politics to prevail, opponents of massive resistance mobilized through a pressure group: Help Our Public Education (HOPE). Initially formed in Atlanta in December 1958, HOPE saw its membership expand every time the moment of crisis got nearer. By the summer of 1960, it was recognized by supporters and opponents alike as the most significant white organization calling for massive resistance to be abandoned. By the end of 1961, HOPE's arguments had become official state policy, and massive resistance was no more. Although HOPE had not made the end of massive resistance in Georgia inevitable, it had played a crucial role in two respects: it had established beyond any doubt that white opinion was divided on the question of massive resistance; and it had helped create a viable political alternative to closing the schools for Georgia's political leadership.

These were both impressive achievements in their own right and vindicated those civil rights leaders who had predicted that many whites were not willing to pay the price that massive resistance demanded.[58] At the same time, HOPE's achievements also came with a significant cost for the goals of civil rights leaders: by advancing a color-blind argument against closing the schools, the decision to allow desegregation to proceed was justified on grounds that were based on white, suburban concerns about education. Racial justice was barely considered. The civil rights movement had forced white Georgians to make an uncomfortable choice about segregation, but white Georgians were able to limit the racial consequences of making that choice.

HOPE's decision to base its campaign on progressive color blindness was quite deliberate. From the outset, its leaders made it clear that they did not want a public debate over Jim Crow versus desegregation, or racism versus civil rights. Instead, they wanted to frame the choice as being between the "reasonable discussion" over public education that HOPE was promoting and the "shouting and hysteria" of massive resistors.[59] A HOPE press release from December 1959 made the point even more explicitly: "HOPE . . . has deliberately steered clear of controversy, re: the pros and cons of the moral issue."[60] Muriel Lokey, Hamilton's wife and one of HOPE's founding members, later justified this silence on the "moral issue" by describing it as so "touchy" that "in the climate of those years

. . . we just knew it was a total loss to make any impression on changing anybody's minds publicly by coming out with statements that segregation was wrong."[61] Both Lokeys were evidently uncomfortable about the consequences of this, but they stuck to it as two, of HOPE's leading spokespersons. Hamilton Lokey gave a speech in Savannah to the League of Women Voters where he stressed his personal support for segregation and expressly declared that there was no moral issue about race to be considered.[62] Although he knew this was a disingenuous claim, he believed it was politically necessary, justifying it to Nan Pendergrast, also a senior figure within HOPE, on the grounds that "halitosis is better than no breath at all."[63]

HOPE's desire to avoid discussing race was also reflected in the decision by its leadership that HOPE should be a whites-only organization. This was a painful decision for several of its leading activists, including in particular Frances Pauley, who had vowed never to be part of a segregated organization.[64] Muriel Lokey justified the whites-only position as purely pragmatic, explaining that "we just kind of thought that since our job was to persuade white people . . . it wasn't necessarily our job to take black people around with us." Lokey subsequently said she believed this attitude had been "naive and immature," recalling in particular the nervous panic she felt over what to do when HOPE received a check from Don Hollowell, a black lawyer, political ally, and friend of many HOPE activists.[65] As personally discomforting as it was to some of its members, HOPE stuck to the whites-only policy. It was a further example of just how race-conscious white southerners thought they had to be in order to avoid having to address race as a political or moral issue.

HOPE's intentional color blindness was also shaped by the broader recognition by southern modernizers that much of their potential support on issues of economics and education came from people who were still socially and culturally traditionalist. By not criticizing segregation, they wanted to avoid alienating racial traditionalists. HOPE made use of a similar ploy in the way it used traditional conceptions of southern womanhood in order to advance its case. The leadership and spokespersons of the organization were overwhelmingly women, and its public image was deliberately feminine and maternal. This was intended to lend credibility to their cause and to make HOPE harder to oppose. By stressing their status as mothers and framing their objection to massive resistance in terms of the harm it would do to their children, HOPE was able to present its campaign as apolitical. Furthermore, by portraying themselves this way, HOPE activists were able to present themselves as very "traditional" women worrying about the kind of things that traditional white southern women were supposed to be worrying about.

Accordingly, HOPE was more than happy to have its members presented in the press as nonthreatening, attractive, motherly figures. Muriel Lokey was described as a "petite mother of five"; Nan Pendergrast was "Atlanta's best-looking mother of six"; fellow HOPE activist Maxine Friedman and the organization's director Fran Breeden were, respectively, a "tall, attractive, dark-haired" mother of three and a "chic society matron." Such descriptions fit perfectly the image HOPE wanted to present of itself as being, in Matthew Lassiter's words, "explicitly apolitical and implicitly maternal."[66]

Such an image was also helpful in making sure that their concerns would be heard, because it put Regular leaders in an awkward position. Segregated schools had long been defended as necessary in order to protect the purity of what Mississippi judge Tom Brady had referred to in 1954 as the most "angelic thing" on earth: a "well-bred Southern woman, or her blue-eyed, golden-haired little girl."[67] And yet now, through HOPE, these same "well-bred southern women" were implicitly asking for segregated schools to be abandoned. Their culturally exalted status thus made them much harder for Regulars to attack, and HOPE's activists frequently used this to their advantage. Frances Pauley recounted the shock Richard Russell experienced when she led a group of HOPE supporters to see him. The senator could not believe that members of the Rotary Club and the United Church Women would not support keeping the schools segregated.[68] When Governor Vandiver initially refused to meet with a HOPE delegation on grounds of their political agenda, the women accused him of a lack of chivalry, and a closed-door meeting was hastily arranged.[69]

As politically astute as such tactics were, and while they may have succeeded in persuading many that HOPE's leadership were politically disinterested mothers, the image was patently misleading. To acknowledge the deception is not to criticize it; rather, it is to recognize that HOPE's members were far more politically engaged than their deliberately constructed image suggested. In many ways, this should not be surprising: such a savvy apolitical image was best cultivated by politically experienced people. Almost to a woman, HOPE's leading figures were veterans of the hard-fought political battles of the previous fifteen years. Muriel Lokey had served in the leadership of the GLWV for many years, as had Nan Pendergrast even as she was simultaneously helping to reestablish the Republican Party in Georgia. Frances Pauley and Eliza Paschall were veterans of the anti-county-unit campaigns and were well connected within the Loyalist leadership, and behind the scenes was the constant presence of Helen Bullard, who Pendergrast remembered as "a wonderful, wise old tortoise in the background telling us what to do next—as wise a lady as I ever knew."[70]

Utilizing the traditional conception of their gender in this way and avoiding a direct critique of segregation by no means meant that HOPE was destined to win the argument, but it made it far more likely that their voices would be heard. There was clearly a sizable constituency that was receptive to the open schools position, but it needed to be organized. Drawing on their previous experience in statewide political activity, the founders of HOPE made themselves the preeminent anti–massive resistance organization in Georgia. The initial meeting of HOPE in December 1958 was attended by just seventeen people, all from Atlanta. By January 1960, the group had presented a petition against massive resistance containing 10,000 signatures and had a mailing list of some 20,000 names across Georgia.[71] Alongside Atlanta, HOPE chapters were mobilized in Athens, Savannah, Brunswick, and Columbus, as well as in several other small towns. All of these chapters made lobbying their local state legislators a key priority.[72]

HOPE's ability to attract support grew with every federal court decision that moved a showdown over massive resistance closer. When Judge Hooper approved a desegregation plan for Atlanta in early 1960, Vandiver responded by appointing a commission under prominent banker and attorney John A. Sibley to recommend a course of action to the General Assembly. This was an obvious attempt by Vandiver to buy more time. The Sibley Commission held hearings across the state, and it was largely HOPE chapters that coordinated witnesses to appear and speak out against closing the schools. Even though the 1,600 witnesses split approximately two to one in favor of maintaining massive resistance, the commission report backed HOPE's position that keeping the schools open was more important than preserving segregation.[73]

HOPE's campaign had made the Sibley Commission necessary, and the commission's report had in turn endorsed HOPE's arguments. This meant that the governor had some political cover should he choose to abandon massive resistance, but it did not mean that HOPE was in a position to force Vandiver's hand. For a start, HOPE was not the only grassroots organization to take a stand on massive resistance; in fact, it was not even the only group that claimed to speak for "respectable" middle-class citizens within Atlanta. A countergroup, the Metropolitan Association for Segregated Education (MASE), also held rallies throughout 1960 arguing *for* massive resistance to desegregated schools and also claiming the mantle of "respectability" in its arguments. Given that, as Kevin Kruse estimates, white middle-class voters had cast a majority of their ballots for the 1954 private schools amendment, it is very likely that MASE represented a larger proportion of the white middle-class than HOPE did.[74] Nonetheless, the very fact that massive resistors had felt the need to organize MASE in response to HOPE, and that by 1960 the divide over massive resistance in the state was seen as HOPE versus Vandiver and the General Assembly, is a good indicator of how successful HOPE had been in shaping the political debate in Georgia. That Vandiver ultimately chose to adopt HOPE's recommendation when the showdown came only further underscored the group's influence.

While it was ostensibly a nonpartisan organization, HOPE should really be seen as an organization of Loyalist Democrats by another name, though it also contained a number of suburban Republicans. The only meaningful difference between HOPE and the Loyalists was that HOPE did not field candidates at election time and had nothing to say on the relationship between state and national Democrats. Otherwise, the two groups were virtually indistinguishable. The arguments HOPE deployed against closing the schools used the same color-blind rhetoric as Loyalists had used to oppose Regulars from 1946 to 1954, and that Loyalists and Republicans had used less successfully from 1954 to 1959. Not only that, but the arguments were often being made by the same people. The leading figures in HOPE all had past experience as campaigning for or deep personal connections to key Loyalist Democrats, and many Loyalist politicians were in turn active supporters of HOPE. In this sense, the personnel, arguments, and scale of influence that HOPE achieved from 1958 to 1960 were a sure sign that the Loyalist weakness after *Brown* was temporary rather than terminal. As the events of the next two years would demonstrate, the Regulars would soon be on the defensive—something that had not seemed likely at the time of HOPE's founding.

Showdown and Aftermath

The location of the crisis that brought massive resistance in Georgia to an end came as a surprise to many, as did the swiftness with which the events played out. Ever since the NAACP had filed *Aaron v. Cook* in 1950 the assumption had been that Atlanta would be where any showdown happened. Judge Hooper's court orders had all focused on Atlanta, and the premise behind HOPE, the Sibley Commission, and the renewed massive resistance laws of 1958 to 1959 was that the confrontation would take place in the state capital. It was therefore something of a shock when the showdown actually took place in Athens. On January 6, 1961, a federal court ruled that the two black students who had filed *Holmes v. Danner* in August 1960 must be admitted to the University of Georgia. On January 9, the state's request for a stay of the order was dismissed, which meant that the law as it stood required Vandiver to close the state's flagship university. The governor had at most a few days to decide whether to implement the laws he had only recently championed or to request their repeal. Several days of frantic discussion followed between the governor and his staff, members of the General Assembly, and senior political and business figures from around the state. Then, on January 18, Vandiver appeared before the General Assembly to ask for the massive resistance laws to be repealed. By the first week of February, his request had been implemented.[75]

Precisely what persuaded Vandiver to abandon massive resistance will never be known for sure, and the benefit of hindsight should not lead us to conclude that it was obvious he would decide this way. That said, there had been clear signs that, his 1958 campaign rhetoric notwithstanding, Vandiver was part of the pragmatic wing of the Regular leadership and harbored serious reservations about actually following through on massive resistance. Just weeks after he was elected, Vandiver had instructed future U.S. attorney general Griffin Bell to evaluate the plans other southern states were considering to see if any would allow segregation to be maintained without closing the schools. Sadly for Vandiver, Bell reached a dispiriting conclusion, reporting back that "none of [the other states] had a plan that would work." In fact, as far as Bell was concerned, "there was no [such] plan" that could withstand judicial review.[76]

Vandiver's motivation behind appointing the Sibley Commission in the spring of 1960 was similarly indicative of a reluctance to pursue massive resistance to the extent of closing the schools. A further sign of this reluctance were the regular clandestine meetings arranged by Herman Talmadge that Vandiver attended to discuss issues involving desegregation with selected black leaders, such as Martin Luther King Sr. All of these actions suggested that Vandiver agreed with Herman Talmadge and James Peters that closing the schools was, at best, an extremely high-risk strategy. This was in marked contrast to the attitude of more militant Regulars such as Charles Bloch or Roy Harris, both of whom stuck to the position that integration of any kind was infinitely worse than a private school system.[77]

Clearly, Georgia's Regular leadership was divided over how to react to the crisis in Athens. It was therefore no surprise that Vandiver's decision resulted in heated denunciations from Regulars who accused him of failing to hold the line on desegregation. Public opinion in general was also divided, as the respective campaigns of HOPE and MASE and the debates in front of the Sibley Commission had demonstrated. There is unfortunately no way to know for certain how Georgians would have voted on ending massive resistance in January 1961 had they been given the chance, although opinion polls suggested there was still a majority that favored massive resistance.[78] On the other hand, such polls may have been reflecting a "heat of the moment" sentiment. At least this is a reasonable conclusion to draw from the closest thing we have to a verdict on the popularity of Vandiver's decision—the 1962 Democratic primary.

The 1962 primary was the first since 1950 that featured a clear-cut factional contest between just two candidates. Marvin Griffin, making a bid to return to office, campaigned as an unreconstructed Regular. He was opposed by Carl Sanders, who in January 1961 had been one of the first members of the General Assembly to call for the massive resistance laws to be repealed rather than forcing the closure of the University of Georgia.[79] During the 1962 campaign, Sanders made his rejection of massive resistance clear, pledging that "while I am Governor we are going to obey the laws, we are not going to resist federal court orders with violence and we are not going to close any schools."[80] Sanders's position was little different from that advocated by James Carmichael in 1946: Georgia needed to focus on economic progress and education, and not obsess over racial issues.

Sanders was also helped by having Vandiver's support over Griffin and that Griffin was tainted by several corruption scandals. Even with these advantages, the final result—a lopsided victory for Sanders by 59.6 percent to 40.4 percent—suggested Georgians were prepared to accept token desegregation in exchange for open schools. It was also unquestionably a huge drop in the apparently unassailable Regular strength the results of 1958 had implied. In a further sign of how the tide had turned against the Regulars over the previous four years, the county-unit system had been abandoned for the primary just as it was on the verge of being struck down by the U.S. Supreme Court. This made 1962 the first statewide primary in Georgia not to be determined by county-unit rules since 1908. This was heartening enough for Loyalists, but it speaks further to the scale of Sanders's victory that even though his vote was heaviest in the most populated counties, he would have won even if the county-unit system had remained in place.

Aside from the scale of Sanders's victory and the fact that it was the first Loyalist success in a gubernatorial contest since 1942, the most striking feature of the 1962 primary was the similarity between the breakdown of the vote for Sanders versus Griffin and the breakdown for Carmichael versus Talmadge. As figures 5 and 6 show, the demographic and regional patterns in the results had barely changed. Like Carmichael, Sanders won the state's largest (67.5 percent), fastest-growing (63.3 percent), most-educated (66.4 percent), and richest (67.5 percent) counties. He also won in urban areas (70.4 percent) and in north Georgia (57.7 percent), as well as in counties with the smallest black populations (62.8 percent). Like Talmadge in 1946, Griffin won the smaller (58.1 percent), less-educated (57.1 percent), poorer (58.9 percent), and slowest-growing (56.7 percent) counties. Griffin also carried the Black Belt (55.6 percent) and south Georgia (53 percent), along with those parts of the state with the highest black population (55.2 percent).

Overall, Sanders outperformed Carmichael by around 8.2 percent of the bifactional vote statewide, which was close to his improvement over the Loyalists' 1946 showing in most of the demographic and regional categories (a notable exception was south Georgia, where Sanders improved on Carmichael's showing by over 12 percentage points and polled 47 percent—an exceptionally high score for a Loyalist).

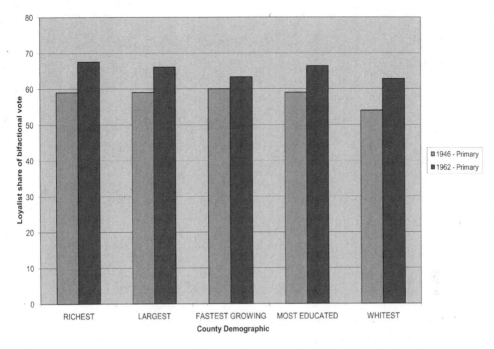

Figure 5. Loyalist vote by county demographic, 1946 and 1962 Democratic primaries.

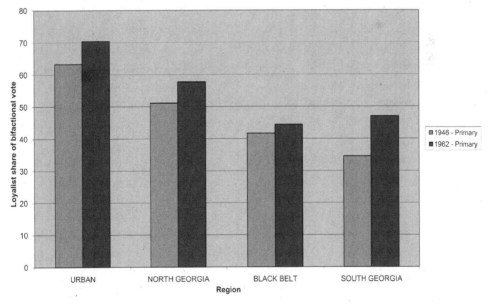

Figure 6. Loyalist vote by region, 1946 and 1962 Democratic primaries.

What Sanders's victory represented was neither the end of race as a political issue nor the death of Regular influence in either state politics or the Democratic Party. However, it did represent a public acceptance of token desegregation as an alternative to massive resistance. It also showed that the absence of Loyalist success in the mid-to-late 1950s was a temporary hiatus caused by the exceptional circumstances of massive resistance, not the killing off of the opposition to the Regulars of the 1940s. There was simply too much continuity between the demographic and regional basis of Sanders's support and the political positions he took, and the basis of support and positions of the Arnall-era Democrats during the pre-*Brown* period.

Nonetheless, this did not mean that the status quo ante had been restored. The end of massive resistance and the county-unit system had generated political momentum for the Loyalists, but it had also provided new opportunities for the civil rights movement and the Republican Party to increase their influence in state politics. This meant that as well as trying to consolidate their authority within the state party, Loyalists faced two additional challenges. They needed to refine their stance on racial change in order to respond to the more assertive and comprehensive assaults on segregation from a new generation of black activists; and they needed to build a party organization capable of fighting off the growing presence of the GOP. What was more, all of this would have to happen while the national party moved ever closer to an all-out embrace of federally mandated desegregation. In the contest over massive resistance in Georgia, Loyalists, prompted by the civil rights movement, had ultimately prevailed, but their immediate reward was to face a politically turbulent decade where race—the issue they wanted to eliminate from southern political discussion—remained center stage.

4

"A Truly Democratic Party"

1962–1966

I want to see the Democratic Party become honest in Georgia, so that those who are masquerading as Democrats within the party now will be forced to either form a party of their own or join the Republican Party where they actually belong.

State senator Erwin Mitchell (D-DeKalb County), 1961

There were ample reasons for Georgia's Loyalists to be very satisfied with the way things were going in the early 1960s. In November 1960, John F. Kennedy won Georgia by a larger margin than any other state except Rhode Island. In the winter of 1961, massive resistance was repealed, and token school desegregation followed in Atlanta that fall without serious incident. In 1962, the county-unit system was abandoned, and Carl Sanders was elected governor by a landslide after campaigning on the twin promises of economic modernization and open schools. It is hard to imagine what more Loyalists could realistically have hoped for. And yet senior Loyalists remained anxious about the future. Their anxiety was captured in a December 1962 letter sent by J. B. Fuqua, the newly appointed Georgia Democratic Party chairman, to Claudia Duffell, a Loyalist member of the Fifth Congressional District Democratic Executive Committee. Despite all the positive developments of the previous few years, and even though Sanders had been elected governor only weeks earlier, Fuqua wrote Duffell that it was urgently necessary that the state party be "rejuvenated." In particular, Fuqua warned, it would soon be necessary for "a decision [to] be made as to whether the Georgia Democratic Party brings into its ranks the Negro voter, who now represents a sizeable factor in our state."[1]

Fuqua's concerns were an indication of how the Loyalists' position in 1962 mirrored that of the Regulars in 1946. In that earlier moment,

Regulars had been returned to statewide office, but were immediately compelled to take measures to address the vulnerabilities in their position. Sixteen years later, Loyalists were similarly aware that while they had gained the political initiative, this did not mean future success was guaranteed. As Fuqua suspected, and as subsequent events would confirm, the string of victories that Loyalists enjoyed between 1960 and 1962 did not represent a final resolution of the struggle to shape postwar Georgia. Instead, they were a prelude to the most politically fluid and uncertain period in the state's postwar history: a period during which Loyalists experienced successes and setbacks in seemingly equal measure.

Fuqua's call for the party to be "rejuvenated" was a recognition of the challenges Loyalists faced. The most critical remained the civil rights movement. Although the end of massive resistance represented a grudging acceptance by most white Georgians that limited desegregation was a price worth paying for open schools, this did not mean that there was much support for doing anything more than the bare minimum that compliance with the law required. Such minimal compliance would have suited most Loyalists just fine, but if they hoped that civil rights activists would accept the kind of stage-managed token desegregation that Atlanta had undertaken in September 1961 as a sufficient rate of change in the racial order, they were quickly disabused of that notion.

Even before massive resistance ended, the civil rights movement had begun to take a more confrontational approach. The Auburn Avenue Strategy of back-channel negotiations and the so-called Atlanta Way of addressing racial issues by getting white and black community leaders to hammer out compromises that were then handed down as fait accompli to their constituents began to lose ground after the rise of student protest movements in the winter of 1960.[2] At this time, a new generation of black leaders both expanded the targets of civil rights protests and changed the style of those protests. Within Georgia, the student movement in Atlanta and the campaign of the Southern Christian Leadership Conference (SCLC) in Albany attracted the most attention, even though they were not necessarily as successful as lesser known protests elsewhere.[3] Nonetheless, the very presence of direct-action protests, successful or otherwise, presented Loyalists with a thorny political challenge.

In the first place, direct-action protests inevitably sparked white resistance, which in turn ensured that race remained at the center of political debate.[4] As white resistance escalated, pressure grew for the passage of federal civil rights legislation. This again left Loyalists with a choice they did not want: either support the desegregation of public accommodations or tacitly condone the violent opposition to it. The former remained unpopular with white voters, while siding with the resistance would certainly alienate the growing number of black voters and, more problematically, risked tarnishing the state's image in the eyes of investors. On the other hand, while direct-action protests certainly caused a serious political headache for Loyalists, they also created an opening to adjust to limited desegregation. This was the result of a secondary impact the protests had: they exacerbated the generational tensions within Georgia's politically active black population. While such senior figures as A. T. Walden, William Holmes Borders, and Martin Luther King Sr. provided support and legal assistance for some of the protests, they were also frequently at loggerheads with the student leadership over whether to continue the sit-ins and store boycotts.[5] Leaders of the Atlanta student movement, such as Lonnie King, Herschelle Sullivan, Ben Brown, and Julian Bond, regularly encountered resistance to their activities from established black leaders and institutions, particularly in the editorials of C. A. Scott's *Atlanta Daily World*.[6] Loyalists took advantage of these divisions to criticize the students and direct-action protests while simultaneously aligning themselves with the "respectable" black leadership in order to demonstrate that they were not hostile to black voters as a whole.

In doing so, Loyalists again used progressive color blindness, though they deployed it in a manner that was subtly yet significantly different from earlier. Whereas in the 1940s the courtship of black voters had been clandestine, and in the 1950s acceptance of desegregation had been justified in terms of preventing disaster befalling the state, by the 1960s Loyalists were pivoting toward positively flaunting their associations with "respectable" black leaders. In particular, once Loyalists decided that Jim Crow was in its death throes, they came to believe that acquiescing in its demise and publicizing their willingness to seek good race relations through cooperating with selected parts of the black community made good political sense. This attitude represented a transitional moment between the postwar Loyalists' fear of being seen as prodesegregation in the 1940s and the New South Democrats openly celebrating the value of desegregation to southern progress in the 1970s. This approach reflected the evolution of an existing strategy rather than a new departure; at the same time, it answered in the affirmative Fuqua's question about whether to make the "Negro voter" an integral part of the Georgia Democratic Party.

Loyalists faced two further challenges in the early 1960s. The first was how to maintain a functional relationship with the national Democratic Party; the second was how to respond to the rising strength of the Republican Party. While John Kennedy had easily carried Georgia, there was no hiding the ominous signs that support for the national Democratic Party in Georgia was on very tenuous ground. Many parts of the state that voted for Kennedy were the same parts that routinely backed Regular candidates who vowed to fight the national party's agenda. This was not encouraging for the long term. As Numan Bartley put it in his survey of postwar Georgia politics, this represented "a political absurdity that could not forever endure."[7]

Additional cause for concern for Loyalists was the nonbinding referendum sponsored by Regulars in September 1960 over whether the Democratic electors chosen at the presidential election should be required to vote for Kennedy or should remain "free"—that is, unpledged to any candidate. The result was a 55 to 45 percent majority in favor of unpledged electors.[8] Had the result of the referendum been honored, Georgia's electors would likely have followed the lead of Mississippi's unpledged electors and cast their presidential ballots for U.S. senator Harry Byrd of Virginia. Loyalists could therefore be grateful that Governor Vandiver changed his mind on the issue after a private meeting with Kennedy and decided to withdraw his support from the "free electors" campaign. Instead, Vandiver endorsed Kennedy's candidacy.[9]

Loyalists were nonetheless alarmed at what they saw as a repeat of the Dixiecrat campaign of 1948 and suspected Regulars were intending to use the state party organization to actively sabotage the Democrats' presidential ticket. In order to prevent this from happening, a group of Loyalists established the Democratic Forum in March 1960. Their intention was to raise funds for and support the candidates of the national Democratic Party.[10] The Democratic Forum attracted several prominent figures from within the Loyalist ranks, including Helen Bullard; A. T. Walden; Ivan Allen Jr., who in 1961 would be elected mayor of Atlanta; and Charles Weltner, a young attorney who was gearing up for a primary challenge against Congressman James Davis in 1962. Once Kennedy was nominated, the Democratic Forum arranged crowds for his visits to Georgia and held a series of fund-raisers. True to Loyalist tradition, it engaged in color-blind politics. Blacks were members of the group, and a Kennedy campaign event the Democratic Forum hosted at Atlanta's Hungry Club became the state's first officially integrated fund-raiser, but the question of racial equality was never explicitly raised as a goal of the organization.[11] Instead, as Weltner wrote to Senator Russell in a vain attempt to gain his support for the organization, the core principle of the Democratic Forum was that it stood "four-square for party loyalty."[12]

The Democratic Forum was one of the first of a series of organizations that Loyalists established over the coming decade to "rejuvenate" the state party. As well as the problem of the Regulars' attacks on the national party, Loyalists also worried that the state party organization had become moribund. They saw this as a huge liability for Democrats once two-party competition began in earnest, as Loyalists were certain it soon would. In the most populous parts of the state, Republicans were already making serious inroads. Although Nixon trailed Kennedy by 25 percentage points statewide, he was less than 5 points behind in urban and suburban counties. Within Atlanta, Nixon was only 3.6 points adrift, thanks in part to the estimated 57 percent support he received from the city's black voters.[13] In General Assembly contests, Republicans were registering increased support in urban and suburban districts, and in 1962 they picked up state senate seats in Atlanta, Savannah, and Macon. Given that these were the same parts of the state that Loyalists relied on for their support, there was an understandable anxiety at the inexorable rise of an organized Republican opposition and the absence of an effective Democratic organization through which to push back.

To address this trio of challenges, Loyalists built on the themes they had developed to advance their agenda in the 1940s and 1950s, but tried to augment them in a way that recognized the increased militancy of the civil rights movement and the changing nature of partisan competition in the 1960s. The experiences of three individuals who were active at different levels of Georgia politics illustrate the various ways in which Loyalists responded to the political climate of the early 1960s.

The first was Charles Weltner, who was elected to Congress in 1962. As a congressman, Weltner came to support civil rights legislation as necessary, but adamantly insisted that he was not a civil rights advocate. The second was Melba Williams, a Democratic activist from Atlanta's suburbs who saw firsthand the growing GOP strength around her and the lack of a Democratic organization to challenge it. The third was Governor Sanders.

In his dual capacities as titular head of the state party and the state's liaison to the Kennedy and Johnson administrations, Sanders faced perhaps the hardest task of all: he had to maintain a working relationship with a national party about to endorse civil rights laws, adjust to the growing black political presence in both state politics and the Georgia Democratic Party, and yet not exacerbate tensions within the state party to such a degree that it would rupture and hand the state over to the GOP.

As might be expected in such trying and uncertain political circumstances, each of these three individuals experienced a mixed record in achieving their goals. By the end of the decade, Weltner, Williams, and Sanders could all point to considerable achievements, but each had also experienced significant political defeats. In this sense, what the three of them collectively experienced not only spoke to the particular situation facing Georgia Loyalists in the early 1960s but also to the uncertainty and fluidity that existed in southern politics as a whole at this time. Nonetheless, for all this uncertainty, and for all the personal disappointments these three Loyalists suffered, they were laying the groundwork for the emergence of what Democratic National Committee (DNC) chairman John Bailey termed a "truly Democratic Party" during a visit to Atlanta in 1965. In the 1970s, it was this "truly Democratic Party" that Weltner, Williams, and Sanders helped create that would dominate the political landscape in Georgia.[14]

Charles Weltner: Pragmatic Idealist

Charles Weltner was not a typical politician. His career was full of contradictions and tensions that make it hard to do him justice by using conventional political labels to describe him. Even as the only member of Congress from the Deep South to vote in favor of the 1964 Civil Rights Act on final passage, and one of the few to unequivocally condemn the white violence in Birmingham during 1963, Weltner nonetheless, even in retirement, refused to identify himself as a supporter of civil rights. As a white southern member of HUAC, Weltner called for an investigation into the activities of the KKK—a new departure for the otherwise largely anti-Communist HUAC—only to subsequently befriend Calvin Craig, the Klan's leader at the time. A firm believer in the need for a modern, forward-looking approach to politics, Weltner could also exhibit an old-fashioned distaste for the kind of political compromises modern politics required, as shown most dramatically when he withdrew from his reelection campaign in October 1966 following the nomination of Lester Maddox as the Democratic candidate for governor.[15]

Nonetheless, despite such politically unorthodox behavior, and even though he was in office only four years, Weltner was at the heart of Loyalist activities in Georgia in the 1960s and also embodied the continuity of those activities with the Loyalist agenda of the 1940s and 1950s. Throughout his career, Weltner spoke up for the economic and political modernization of the South, repeatedly contrasting his own stances against what he interpreted as the reactionary and outdated policies supported by Regular Democrats. When taking on the Republican Party, Weltner portrayed its candidates as opposing the kind of activist government he thought was needed to bring progress to the South. Weltner also often charged that his opponents were stirring up racial resentments in order to distract voters from more pressing concerns. In short, for all his political eccentricities, Weltner was the very model of a modern Georgia Loyalist.

Weltner's background provided him with good credentials for a future as a Loyalist politician. His father, Philip Weltner, had been a vocal opponent of Eugene Talmadge in the 1930s, having resigned from the University of Georgia Board of Regents in 1935 over the key Loyalist issue of whether to expand funding for education (Talmadge was refusing to allow federal funds to be appropriated for that purpose). Following an unsuccessful effort to run a candidate to unseat Talmadge in 1936, Philip Weltner continued to critique the one-party system's prioritization of race over all other concerns.[16] Charles Weltner shared his father's dim view of the shallowness of the one-party South, telling one interviewer in 1986 that Georgia politics in the 1940s was "like soap opera . . . it was all personalities. There weren't any issues, it was just talk." In a further oral history in 1991, Weltner described the same period as having "nothing to do with public policy, it just had to do with who was gonna rule."[17]

After graduating from Columbia Law School in 1950, and having become a critic of the county-unit system (but not of segregation) during his time there, Weltner returned to Atlanta to practice law and spent five years working in the same law firm as Ellis Arnall.[18] Weltner first became politically active during the second referendum on the county-unit system in 1952, where he volunteered for the anti-county-unit campaign. From 1954 onward, he also campaigned against the closing of the public school system and worked on several Loyalist campaigns against James

Davis in various Fifth District primaries. The political contacts he made during the 1950s led Weltner to get involved with the Democratic Forum in 1960.[19] Weltner later argued that setting up an organization such as the Democratic Forum was necessary; indeed, it was overdue, as the national party was in danger of becoming a "foreign element" in Georgia due to the increasing hostility it faced from the Regular leadership of the state party.[20]

In December 1961, Weltner announced that he planned to challenge Davis in the 1962 primary. Given the continued existence of the county-unit system, this was something of a long shot.[21] Fortunately for Weltner, the county-unit system was abandoned prior to the first round of primaries in 1962—had it not been, he would have lost—and he was able to defeat Davis. During the campaign, Weltner positioned himself as the forward-thinking candidate and portrayed Davis as being out of touch. By doing so, Weltner echoed the larger Loyalist narrative of their cause being about modernization versus the Regulars' traditionalism. Weltner attacked Davis for being "tied to the past," for having views that belonged "in the nineteenth century," and for having failed to adapt to the modern age, with the congressman's opposition to activist government being singled out as the best evidence for this.[22] Davis recognized the potential damage such charges could do to him and reined in his attacks on big government. Instead, Davis emphasized the federal money he claimed to have brought to Atlanta in the form of government services and funding for the Buford Dam.[23]

On the question of race, Weltner said nothing in favor of desegregation, though he attacked Davis as a Klan sympathizer. Weltner also picked up the support of established black leaders such as Grace Towns Hamilton and A. T. Walden, as well as newer black politicians such as Leroy Johnson, who in November 1962 became the first black man elected to the Georgia General Assembly since 1908.[24] Overall, Weltner's own description of the change he and his fellow Loyalists tried to bring to Georgia politics neatly sums up the way he portrayed himself as juxtaposed with the Regular Democrats as a whole: "We didn't have galluses [suspenders], and we didn't wear boondockers [military-style boots], and we didn't chew tobacco. We didn't have a bunch of hound-dogs following us around, we didn't drive pickup trucks with gun racks in them. We were new."[25]

After defeating Davis in a runoff primary, Weltner faced Republican James O'Callaghan in the general election. Hoping to take advantage of the unpopularity of the national Democratic Party's policies in Georgia, O'Callaghan portrayed Weltner as being too close to liberal Democrats in Washington. In the weeks leading up to polling day, O'Callaghan claimed that Georgia's traditionally Democratic voters did not support the New Frontier's "big government" political ideology, and by implication dared Weltner to declare his support for Medicare, which Weltner pointedly refused to do.[26] Later, the Republican argued that Fifth District voters were more in tune with the national Democrats of thirty-five to forty years earlier, but that their principles were now represented by the GOP. Again, Weltner refused to be drawn on specific aspects of the national party's agenda that he supported—a sure sign he believed this was a political trap.[27]

While Weltner could afford to be coy about supporting specific Democratic policies, he still wanted to present himself as a loyal Democrat—but it was a loyalty he preferred to assert in more general terms. On at least two occasions when asked his opinion of the national party, Weltner replied simply that he was "proud" to be a Democrat and to be nominated on the party's ticket.[28] On other occasions, Weltner hinted at his general support for the policies of the national party, though he usually did so by speaking up for a general belief in government activism, rather than an endorsement of any specific policies. However, when asked whether he was more of a Kennedy Democrat or a Harry Byrd Democrat, Weltner unequivocally stated his political beliefs were far closer to Kennedy's.[29]

From time to time Weltner was more specific, such as his endorsement of federal urban renewal programs, which he argued had "removed hovels of misery" from Georgia. Overall, however, he preferred to focus on attacking O'Callaghan for the programs the Republican might want to cut, especially in the defense industry.[30] A week before the election, Weltner accused O'Callaghan of wanting to cut all federal programs by 10 percent. O'Callaghan responded by saying that only "non-essential" programs would be cut, without offering any clear sense of which programs those were.[31] Just as Weltner was wary of being tagged as too closely identified with the specific programs of the national party, so O'Callaghan was evidently more comfortable talking about "small government" in the abstract rather than identifying actual spending he wanted to eliminate.

On polling day, Weltner prevailed by the comfortable margin of 65 to 35 percent. His arrival in Congress coincided with the high point of congressional activity on civil rights. Whereas up to that point Weltner had been able to avoid much discussion of race, by the summer of 1963, with national media focusing on weeks of violence in Birmingham and Governor Wallace's efforts to thwart the desegregation of the University Alabama, the issue was becoming harder to finesse. Weltner's private feelings on the issue of race at this time are unclear, but while he was clearly discomforted by the violence in Alabama, it was not the immorality of segregation that ultimately persuaded him to speak out against it. Rather, Weltner was motivated by the damage he believed that racial resistance was doing to southern progress.

Accordingly, in the aftermath of the Sixteenth Street Church bombing in Birmingham in September 1963, Weltner condemned it as the result of a failure of leadership, not as a sign of the need for desegregation. In a widely reported speech, Weltner declared, "I know why it happened. It happened because those chosen to lead have failed to lead. Those whose task it is to speak have stood mute. And in so doing we have permitted the voice of the South to preach defiance and disorder. We have stood by, leaving the field to reckless and violent men."[32] These were strong words from an elected southern official, but Weltner was still framing the incident as an indictment of racist violence, rather than a call for civil rights. As Weltner later explained, "There was a connection [with the civil rights movement] but I was talking about murder," going on to add, "I want you to understand that I did the best I could to slip and slide and avoid that whole race issue . . . last thing I wanted to do was to be a civil rights advocate or leader. I just wanted to get, you know, to dodge around it."[33]

During the congressional debates over the 1964 Civil Rights Act, Weltner found himself in an even more delicate position. Even as he had condemned the violence in Birmingham, Weltner was on record as opposing the desegregation of public accommodations that the Civil Rights Act called for. When the House of Representatives approved the act in February 1964 with the public accommodations section still intact, Weltner voted against it.[34] Yet when the bill returned from the Senate in June 1964, Weltner broke ranks and voted for the act on final passage, even though the public accommodations section remained. Weltner felt pushed to take a stand because he believed that opposition to the Civil Rights Act would threaten southern progress. In explaining his change of heart, Weltner invoked the need to adapt rather than endlessly resist inevitable change: "I will add my voice to those who seek reasoned and conciliatory adjustment to a new reality. . . . We must not remain forever bound to another lost cause."[35]

The reasons Weltner gave for supporting the 1964 Civil Rights Act were consistent with his general Loyalist beliefs, but there were also political calculations he had to consider, calculations that many southern Democrats would face after the mid-1960s. In particular, Weltner had to consider his own prospects for reelection in 1964. In February 1964, the Fifth District had been redrawn in such a way as to increase the share of black voters to 29 percent, and it was anticipated that Weltner would face a primary challenge from state senator James Wesberry, who was much more forthright in his support for desegregation than Weltner.[36] Weltner therefore had a clear incentive to appeal to black voters by voting for the Civil Rights Act, though there was also the risk of alienating white voters as a result. Weltner subsequently admitted that he was not sure whether supporting the 1964 act would help or hurt him. He did concede, however, that even though "I was afraid [voting for] it would defeat me," it turned out "not to be as bad as I thought."[37] In both the primary and the general election, Weltner attracted well over 90 percent of the black vote, which proved sufficient to renominate and reelect him by fairly comfortable margins despite losing the white vote to his opponents. This combination of overwhelming black support and a sizable minority of white support that Weltner and many of his fellow Loyalists relied on in the mid-1960s remains the typical electoral coalition for southern Democrats to this day.[38]

During his second term, Weltner continued on his trajectory toward ever more open support for civil rights measures and the Johnson administration. In February 1965, Weltner persuaded HUAC to investigate the Klan, a move that gained a burst of publicity following the KKK's involvement in the murder of white civil rights activist Viola Liuzzo in Selma the following month. Also in 1965, Weltner voted in support of the Voting Rights Act. He was also one of only two members of the Georgia delegation to vote with President Johnson more than half of the time during the 1965–1966 congressional session (the other was James MacKay, who was elected from the Fourth District in 1964). This included supporting the controversial open-housing section of the 1966 civil rights bill. In his 1966 reelection campaign, Weltner was far more assertive about his racially progressive credentials and openly accused his Republican opponent, Fletcher Thompson, of being the ideological descendant of Marvin Griffin and Roy Harris. Thompson, Weltner claimed, was willing to sacrifice the South's economic growth on the altar of racial reaction.[39]

Just over a month prior to polling day, however, Weltner pulled the plug on his own political career. After the extraordinary twists and turns of the 1966 primary season had left the arch-Regular Lester Maddox as the Democrats' nominee for governor, Weltner withdrew from the race. His reasoning was that he did not want to be on the same party ticket as a man whom he saw as his antithesis. The two men were indeed opposites on everything from ideology to personality, a fact illustrated by the symbolic differences in the two events that had brought them the most attention during their political careers. Weltner had received headline coverage when he voted with northern Democrats for final passage of the 1964 Civil Rights Act—here was a white southerner willing to move on from his region's past; just days later, Maddox made front-page news by brandishing an ax handle and a pistol at a group of black ministers seeking to test the new law at his Atlanta restaurant—here was a white southerner determined not to let go. When Maddox won the runoff against Weltner's former law partner Ellis Arnall on September 28, 1966, Weltner asked for a pledge that Maddox would support the national party's presidential nominee in 1968. When no such pledge was forthcoming, Weltner determined he could not endorse his party's nominee for governor, and so would have to withdraw from the Democratic ticket. Explaining his decision to reporters, Weltner told them, "I cannot compromise with hate. I cannot vote for Lester Maddox."[40]

In taking this step, Weltner evidenced a purist streak that had been apparent throughout his career. Like many Loyalists, he believed that the continued presence of Regulars such as Maddox in the party was a political liability. Like many Loyalists, he had come to accept desegregation as a way of moving the South forward rather than out of a concern for racial justice. Like many Loyalists would do during Maddox's term as governor, it appeared he was willing to excuse Maddox's excesses provided he would work for the national ticket in 1968. And yet adopting a far more rigorous reading than anyone else of the pro forma loyalty pledge that all Democratic candidates were expected to sign, and ignoring the long history in Georgia politics of candidates who did not formally endorse each other being on the same ticket (including himself and Governor Sanders in 1962, despite both having virtually identical policy beliefs), he took the exceptional step of withdrawing from the contest.

His hastily chosen replacement, Archie Lindsey, subsequently lost the seat to Fletcher Thompson in November. In the Fourth District, James MacKay also lost to his Republican challenger, Ben Blackburn, a man Weltner considered little more than a reasonably personable, reactionary wing nut.[41] Weltner's withdrawal did play an important part in sparking a Loyalist backlash against Maddox's nomination, but it proved to be the end of Weltner's career in elected office. In 1968, he attempted to regain his old seat, but was defeated by Thompson. In 1973, he ran for mayor of Atlanta, but finished third in the primary and did not make the runoff. He continued to be active in Loyalist circles, helping to raise funds for the Young Democrats and speaking at events organized by Georgia Democrats who opposed Governor Maddox. Later in life, he returned to public office as a judge on the Georgia Supreme Court, where he served until his death from cancer at the age of fifty-five in 1992.

Measuring the precise impact of Charles Weltner, or any one individual, on Georgia's postwar political development is not really possible. Overall, Weltner's importance was not any lasting personal accomplishment as such; rather it was the manner in which his beliefs and actions reflected the dilemmas Loyalists found themselves having to confront during the transition from one- to two-party politics and the kind of solutions they would come up with. On race, Weltner embodied the desire to avoid the issue that was characteristic of progressive color blindness: "I didn't want to fool with any civil rights issue. Last thing I saw myself as was a civil rights advocate; and I still don't see myself as a civil rights advocate."[42] On the question of relations with the national party, Weltner formulated as well as anyone the delicate balance between party loyalty and independence that Loyalists had to strike. In 1966, he predicted that "ultimately, the only way the Southern Democrat can move is toward the party's national program," though for the time being, they would have to retain "far more independence than Democrats from other sections, where two-party politics is fully developed."[43] Above all, Weltner represented the overarching hope of all Loyalists that they could get beyond the traditional politics of the Solid South and, once the questions of civil rights and party loyalty had been resolved, that they would be able to "move on to the unfinished task of building a New South."[44]

The DeKalb County Democrats: Party Building at the Grassroots

Although he embodied many of the political trends of the time, Charles Weltner was clearly a somewhat idiosyncratic individual; by contrast, Melba Williams was a far more typical figure for the postwar South—albeit one who committed an exceptional amount of time and effort to party politics. Williams was a white, suburban, middle-class woman, and therefore part of several demographic groups with increasing political relevance after World War II. Born in Alabama, Williams moved to Georgia in 1949 to become a schoolteacher in DeKalb County, just east of metropolitan Atlanta. As the debates over massive resistance became more heated, Williams began to take a more active role in Democratic Party politics. From 1958 onward, she held a series of positions on county and statewide Democratic committees, so that by the time of President Kennedy's inauguration she was a well-known figure among party activists in DeKalb County and was an obvious candidate to help with party-building efforts in the county.

As a Loyalist residing in DeKalb County, Williams was on the sharp edge of the disappearing Solid South. During the 1950s, DeKalb County became a battleground county that gave above-average support to Republican candidates at all levels. In the 1960 presidential election, Richard Nixon won 49.9 percent of the vote in DeKalb County, cutting the Democratic margin of victory in the county from over 14,000 votes in 1956 to just 70. In fact, initial returns suggested that Nixon had carried DeKalb County, and it was only after local Democrats insisted that the votes be retallied that Kennedy was declared the winner.[45] When vigorous efforts by Republicans in the Atlanta suburbs to win local contests were added to these election results, it was understandable that Democrats in DeKalb County should be concerned over growing partisan competition. Particularly alarming to Williams and her fellow activists was the complete absence of a viable party organization to work through in order to mobilize against the Republican challenge.

This absence of grassroots party organizations was a feature of Democratic politics across Georgia. Generally speaking, rank-and-file Democrats had very little say in the way the party was run. The members of the State Executive Committee were appointed by the state party chairman, who in turn was appointed by the governor. Delegates to national party conventions were likewise selected by these same two men. At the county level, power rested with the county commissioners and the local Democratic Executive Committee, which was nominally elected, but generally operated as a closed shop. There was, in practice, no such thing as being a "member" of the Democratic Party in Georgia; one could register as a Democrat and take part in primaries, but there were few local organizations to join or take part in. The upshot of this was that when election time rolled around, whether the Democratic apparatus in any given county would undertake to work for the Democratic candidates depended very much on the attitude of the county Democratic Executive Committee. As far as Melba Williams was concerned, the DeKalb County Executive Committee's commitment to the party left a lot to be desired.

A further issue that frustrated all residents of DeKalb County in the early 1960s, regardless of partisan loyalties, was the continued disfranchisement the county suffered from as a result of malapportionment and the county-unit system. From 1950 to 1960, the situation had gotten worse. DeKalb County's population increased by 120,387 (88.3 percent) over the decade. This made it the number one county in Georgia for absolute population growth, the number two county for relative population growth, and the number two county (behind Fulton County) in terms of total population in 1960. Despite this, DeKalb County still had only six unit votes in Democratic primaries, meaning that its more than 225,000 residents were less valuable to any candidate than the barely 10,000 residents of the state's four smallest counties. Additionally, DeKalb County had only three representatives in the state house and one state senator, whom it shared with two other counties.

There were, in other words, both partisan and structural concerns that led to the decision by Williams and her fellow Loyalists to launch a new grassroots organization in October 1961. Williams became secretary of the group, which termed itself the DeKalb County Democrats. An initial statement of purpose described the group's primary goals as being to espouse the "values" of the national Democratic Party and to provide support to the national and state party's candidates at election time. In addition to this, the DeKalb County Democrats also set out to campaign in favor of reapportionment within Georgia and an end to county-unit voting. They did so, even though this would mean greater representation for parts of the state where Republicans were relatively strong, which made likely a higher Republican presence in the General Assembly.[46]

In fact, the DeKalb County Democrats were not opposed to some

Republican presence in Georgia, as they hoped that a two-party system would siphon off disloyal Regulars from the Democratic Party. In their submission to the 1961 Georgia Election Laws Commission, the DeKalb County Democrats openly declared that they would "welcome a two-party system in Georgia."[47] It was this same desire that prompted DeKalb County's state senator Erwin Mitchell to declare his support for reapportionment in a speech in February 1961 by saying that he hoped it would lead to "those who are masquerading as Democrats within the party" being forced to "either form a party of their own or join the Republican Party where they actually belong."[48]

By late 1962, the DeKalb County Democrats had got their wish. The county-unit system was gone, and, after being compelled to do so by the federal courts, the General Assembly voted to reapportion the state senate, increasing DeKalb County's representation to three.[49] A further reapportionment of the state house was mandated by the courts in 1965, which increased urban and suburban representation in the General Assembly. To compete for the newly created state senate districts, the GOP announced in 1962 that it would hold its first-ever primaries. Sixteen Republicans put their names forward as candidates. Of those, nine were running in either Fulton County or DeKalb County, and the other seven were all either from other urban and suburban counties or from rural areas in north Georgia, thus showing that the centers of Republicanism had not changed much since the early 1950s.[50] None of the Republican candidates were successful in DeKalb County in 1962, though the GOP did defeat Hamilton Lokey in neighboring Fulton County.[51] However, even the elections in DeKalb County were more competitive than in previous cycles, which suggested that the DeKalb County Democrats were right to believe a more vigorous and reliable party organization would be needed in the future.

Following the 1962 elections, Melba Williams was appointed to the State Democratic Executive Committee. In that role, she began encouraging J. B. Fuqua to pursue reorganization of the state party along the lines of the DeKalb County Democrats. Just weeks after Fuqua took office, Williams wrote to inform him of their organization's purpose of wanting to "support the principles of the Democratic Party" and to elect the best Democrats to office.[52] Williams was thus a kindred spirit for Fuqua in his desire to see the Georgia Democratic Party "rejuvenated."[53]

The approach that Williams had in mind involved a greater effort to reach out to women, the young, and black voters. In May 1963, Williams wrote to Fuqua setting out the steps that she and the DeKalb County Democrats believed needed to be taken. She welcomed Fuqua's decision to appoint two black Democrats—Leroy Johnson and the evergreen A. T. Walden—to the State Executive Committee. Williams specifically drew attention to the claims made by several Republicans in Atlanta that the Democratic Party was taking black voters for granted. She told Fuqua that she was confident that Johnson and Walden, by counteracting this appeal, would "make an effective contribution to our party in the state." Nonetheless, she cautioned, "there is much [else] that must be done to initiate a real Democratic Party organization." To achieve this, Williams returned to the theme of building the party at the grass roots, suggesting a monthly newsletter and discussion within the state party executive on "the formation of sub-committees to work on such problems as the formation of women's groups and clubs, student and young people's clubs [and] Negro voter organizations."[54] A few weeks later, Williams repeated this message to Fuqua, urging again the creation of an organizational effort to mobilize women on behalf of the Democratic Party, to which Fuqua responded by saying that such an effort was under way under the leadership of Georgia's Democratic national committeewoman, Marjorie Thurman.[55]

Williams's concern over Republican efforts to reach out to traditionally neglected voters made good sense. While Barry Goldwater's presidential candidacy significantly increased the traditionalist influence within the Georgia Republican Party after 1964, and sharply diminished its ability to attract black support, in the early 1960s the Republican leadership in Atlanta made sustained efforts to mobilize support among African Americans and women. The base of Republican strength was still in those parts of the state that had voted against massive resistance measures, and Republicans from Atlanta continued to state their willingness to accept racial change in exchange for economic progress and social stability.[56] Added to this, there remained several powerful black Republican leaders in the state capital, most especially John Calhoun and C. A. Scott, who aligned themselves with the moderate GOP faction, and expected their interests to be represented there.

A snapshot of the image and agenda these moderate Republicans wanted to project can be found in the minutes of the Fulton County Republican Planning Committee, which was chaired by Atlanta alderman Rodney Mims Cook and of which John Calhoun was also a member. The

Planning Committee's remit was to map out political strategy for the Fulton County GOP. It recommended that Georgia's Republicans embrace what Cook termed "progressive conservatism."[57] On the question of the public schools, the committee suggested the model for Georgia to follow was the compliance with *Brown* of North Carolina, not the massive resistance of Arkansas and Louisiana.[58] In 1963, the Fulton County Republicans published the pamphlet *Operation Breakthrough*, which dealt specifically with the need to appeal to women voters. It noted that Republican women had organized the drive to recruit permanent activists in Atlanta after the 1960 election and argued that the GOP needed to understand the political strength, and seek the vote of, "the hand that rocks the cradle."[59]

On civil rights, Fulton County Republicans adopted the stance of favoring equal rights, deploring those who sought to deny them, but remaining ambivalent on whether any new civil rights laws were necessary to bring equality about. In February 1963, state chairman Jack Dorsey made clear his intention to seek the black vote for the Republicans. Dorsey admitted he was disappointed that James O'Callaghan had not picked up the same level of black support against Weltner in 1962 as Richard Nixon had against Kennedy in 1960, but he nonetheless said he thought the black vote might yet return to the GOP. Dorsey argued that "the Republican Party for years has recognized the rights of Negroes and has done more to promote those rights than the Georgia Democratic Party."[60] In July 1963, Cook's Fulton County organization proposed a resolution to the state party convention emphasizing the Republican Party's belief in equal rights and condemning the state Democrats for "the injection of the struggle for these rights into the area of political expediency."[61] Just how enthusiastic these Republicans were about social integration is open to question, but they were clearly seeking to avoid being seen as hostile to black advancement so as to be able to attract black support. It was therefore understandable that Williams should seek to counter these efforts.

The statewide newsletter that Williams advocated was eventually established as the *Georgia Democrat*, but even before this she took matters into her own hands in DeKalb County. In August 1963, she persuaded the DeKalb County Democrats to pay for a subscription to the DNC's monthly publication, *The Democrat*, for all Democratic officials in DeKalb County. In the letters to the county officials notifying them of this subscription, Kelsey Howington, the president of the DeKalb County Democrats, stressed again the twin themes of the need for grassroots strength and party loyalty. Howington wrote, "We hope that this and other contacts between [the DeKalb County Democrats] and party leaders will help us co-ordinate our efforts to strengthen our party organization in DeKalb County, as well as to allow us to conform such efforts to basic principles and objectives set by our state and national [Democratic] committees."[62]

As the concern she expressed over GOP efforts to reach out to black voters indicated, Williams intended to keep track of what the partisan opposition was doing. In the summer of 1963, she, along with many, was speculating over a likely contest between President Kennedy and Barry Goldwater in 1964 and wanted to lay the ground for a successful Democratic effort in DeKalb County. Accordingly, she wrote to Charles Weltner, asking for some background information on Goldwater that could be used in the election and thanked the congressman when he sent it, admitting that although she was "not sure yet . . . what use I will make of it," she was determined "to be ready to answer the opposition."[63] Williams also reported to Fuqua on the president's reelection prospects in DeKalb County, telling him optimistically in August 1963 that "the anti-Kennedy sentiment is decreasing" but also repeating her call for a more vigorous effort on the president's behalf in Georgia: "We Democrats must not hide our heads in the sand. . . . [We must] remind people of all the Democratic Party has done for the rank and file voter."[64] Fuqua appreciated Williams's commitment to the cause, telling her that he wished other Democratic organizations were as active in their efforts as the one in DeKalb County.[65]

By the following year, other senior Democrats were joining Fuqua in their praise of Williams and the DeKalb County Democrats. In January 1964, Williams received letters from Fuqua and Governor Sanders congratulating her on her efforts to create what Sanders termed a "functioning" Democratic Party in DeKalb County.[66] Soon thereafter, the organization renamed itself the "Democratic Party of DeKalb County" and was presented with an official charter from Governor Sanders on behalf of the state party.[67] In June 1964, the rebranded organization wrote to the White House asking—somewhat optimistically—if President Johnson might want to attend its opening meeting. While such a presidential visit was highly unlikely, replies were nonetheless sent to the DeKalb County organizers from White House Special Assistant Kenneth O'Donnell and on behalf of Lyndon Johnson. Both O'Donnell and Johnson expressed their enthusiasm for the type of party structure that was being built in DeKalb County, with Johnson congratulating the DeKalb County Democrats on "launching a strong and vigorous new party organization."[68]

Despite the efforts of the DeKalb County Democrats, the 1964 elections produced at best mixed results. In the presidential contest, even though Lyndon Johnson gained an impressive 13,000 more votes than Kennedy's total in 1960, Barry Goldwater added an even more impressive 25,000 votes to Nixon's showing and carried DeKalb County handily. The picture was brighter farther down the ticket. The recently redrawn Fourth Congressional District—whose presence was a testament to the changing population structure of the state—elected James MacKay to the U.S. House by a comfortable margin. At the state legislative level, although Democrats lost two of the county's three state senate seats to the GOP, they held on to all three seats in the Georgia House.

Overall, the 1964 results were a clear sign of growing Republican strength in DeKalb County, but the Democratic Party of DeKalb County remained bullish over its long-term chances of reshaping the county's politics and the Georgia Democratic Party along Loyalist lines. When the DeKalb County Democrats held their first official county convention in July 1966, their sense of how valuable it had been to develop a grassroots party organization in the county was palpable. The keynote address was given by Governor Sanders—which was a sign of the level of recognition that Williams and her organization had received from the state party—however, it was James MacKay's speech that best summed up the sense of achievement of those present. MacKay told the delegates that they had "fought successfully for a new Democracy in Georgia." Furthermore, Mackay argued, it was "the first chance we've had to be effective Democrats," as it represented a breakaway from the Regular control of the county Democratic structure. MacKay termed the Regulars "nominal Democrats," and warned that just because such Democrats had "held sway in the past" was no reason that such nominal Democrats would be tolerated in the future.[69]

MacKay's point was further illustrated by the comments of two local political activists with diverging views on what it meant to be a Democrat. On the eve of the 1966 convention, Mrs. Charles J. Alford wrote to Kelsey Howington, handing in her resignation as a vice president of the county Democratic Party. Alford's dislike of the emphasis on loyalty to the national party and support for progressive polices was readily apparent in the way she signed off her letter, "with best wishes for, and loyalty to, a *conservative* Democratic Party."[70] By contrast, George H. Carley, a newly elected state house member from DeKalb County, gave a more upbeat assessment of this move away from Regular conservatism. Carley wrote Howington that the convention had been extremely valuable and positive, and that, above all, the spirit of the delegates was "an indication that we are becoming the party we need to be in order to meet the Republican threat."[71]

Despite the high spirits of mid-1966, the fortunes of Loyalist Democrats in DeKalb County over the next few years did not live up to the hopes of MacKay and Carley. Just as it had done to Charles Weltner, the nomination of Lester Maddox represented the exact opposite of what Melba Williams and the DeKalb County activists were hoping for. Additionally, the success of electing James MacKay to Congress proved to be all too fleeting, as he lost his reelection bid in November 1966. In the state legislative contests, Republicans also continued to gain ground, winning four of the newly expanded twelve House districts in the special elections of 1965.[72] Melba Williams was also to suffer personal political disappointment. After moving to Athens in 1968, she became an active supporter of Carl Sanders in the 1970 Democratic gubernatorial primary, only to see the former governor defeated by Jimmy Carter.

Discouraging as these setbacks were, they did not mean that the activities of the DeKalb County Democrats were ineffective, or worse, irrelevant. True, there was significant Republican growth in DeKalb County during the 1960s, but given the county's demographics—high-income, highly educated, suburban, and still very white—this was unavoidable, given the general growth in Republican strength in such areas across the South and the nation.[73] Furthermore, even if the DeKalb County Democrats had only a marginal effect on slowing this growth, it is hard to believe that they actually did any harm by their actions. Quite the contrary—after all, at the very least, they had created a lasting party organization, which still operates in the county to this day with the same goals as when it was founded.[74] What is more, despite the defeats of the mid-1960s, Loyalists began to fare better in DeKalb County by the early 1970s, which became most clearly evident in the 1974 victory of Elliot Levitas over Ben Blackburn, the Republican who had unseated James MacKay. Levitas had first been elected to the Georgia House of Representatives with the support of the Democratic Party of DeKalb County during the special elections held in 1965 and, unlike MacKay, would go on to hold his seat in Congress for more than a decade.

Above all, though, the lasting significance of the Democratic Party of DeKalb County, along with other similar groups of Loyalists across the state, was the way its message of grassroots activism, party organization, and advocacy for incorporating black voters into the party eventually filtered up to the highest echelons of the state leadership and won some notable converts on the way—none more notable, perhaps, than former governor Herman Talmadge, who had since been elected to the U.S. Senate in 1956. Even at the height of massive resistance, Talmadge had maintained contacts with black political leaders. Ben Brown, a black student leader elected to the General Assembly in 1965, recalled that when he had spent time touring rural Georgia trying to encourage blacks to vote, he had frequently run into Robert Parks, a black man who acted as Herman Talmadge's recruiter among black voters in rural areas. Brown added that while Parks had spent most of his time working for Talmadge in the 1950s by staying behind the scenes, his successor in the 1960s, Curtis Atkinson, had been placed much more visibly "up front" by the senator.[75] For all his previous bluster about the evils of black voting, even Herman Talmadge was not unappreciative of its electoral power, and within four months of the passage of the 1965 Voting Rights Act, he was appearing at the Atlanta Hungry Club soliciting black support.[76]

In the wake of the 1966 congressional losses to the Republicans, the chairman of the Fulton County Democratic Party, Jack Turner, had written to the DNC asking for assistance in winning the black vote. Turner attributed the defeats of Lindsey and MacKay to a low turnout among black voters in general and around a third of those who did vote supporting the Republicans. Turner asked the DNC to hire George Booker, a former assistant to Charles Weltner, in order to help keep black residents of Fulton County in the Democratic column.[77] Turner, like Melba Williams, was a committed Loyalist. The Fulton County Democratic Party had the same goals as the Democratic Party of DeKalb County, and Turner used the same arguments for hiring Booker that Williams had made to Fuqua about the need to attract black voters. What was especially notable, however, was that two days after Turner's letter, Senator Talmadge wrote to DNC chairman Bailey, also asking for Booker to be appointed and making essentially the same argument. Talmadge's letter illustrated how the arguments being made by grassroots Loyalists to try and move the state party away from its traditional hostility to black voters had now been fully accepted, if for pragmatic rather than moral reasons, by one of the erstwhile leading exponents of that hostility. In his letter, Talmadge wrote:

> I understand that Mr. Booker has performed well in Fulton County and has generally been able to get the vote out for the Democratic ticket in Negro areas. We certainly do not want Negroes to change their voting habits, which in the recent past have been Democratic. The Fulton County people have convinced me that this may very well happen unless there is a neutral Negro organizer in Atlanta on almost a full-time basis. I, of course, would be delighted for Mr. Booker to organize, insofar as is possible, other Negro communities in Georgia for the purpose of encouraging them to vote Democratic. A tremendous amount of money was placed in the hands of the Republicans this last time, and they spent it freely in the Negro community.[78]

The tone and argument that Talmadge deployed demonstrated the significance of grassroots organization in making the state Democratic Party face up to the new political competition of the 1960s. It was the grassroots Fulton County Democratic Party that persuaded Talmadge that employing a full-time black organizer was necessary to ward off the Republican threat. It was the necessity of organizing at the grass roots rather than relying on the old party structure that was behind Talmadge's request. In this sense, even if Melba Williams and her colleagues did not manage to reverse the tide of Republican growth in DeKalb County that had first motivated them to organize in 1961, they had nonetheless shown the ability of grassroots action to shape the thinking of even pragmatic Regulars within the state party leadership.

Carl Sanders: In the Eye of the Storm

Throughout his 1962 primary campaign against Marvin Griffin and subsequent tenure as governor, Carl Sanders stuck to the Loyalists' modernizing message with such consistency that one biographer termed him the "spokesman of the New South."[79] A college graduate, World War II veteran, and lawyer, Sanders's background was, like Charles Weltner's, tailor-made for a career as a modernizing southern politician. Prior to his run for governor, Sanders had represented Augusta as both a state representative and a state senator. During his time in the General Assembly, Sanders became increasingly critical of massive resistance, which he argued was interfering with the state's economic and political development. It was this belief that led him to be one of the first senior political figures in the state to come out against the closure of the University of Georgia during the desegregation showdown in Athens in January 1961.[80] Given his political views, it was no surprise that once he became governor, local activists such as Melba Williams, fellow Loyalist politicians such as Charles Weltner, and national Democratic leaders such as President Johnson all saw Sanders as an important ally in their efforts to end the Regulars' preeminence in the Georgia Democratic Party.

Sanders is an important example of how the Loyalist positions of Weltner and Williams could be parlayed into statewide electoral success in Georgia. In comparison to the other two, however, Sanders had both greater powers and greater responsibilities. As governor, he had considerable patronage at his disposal, in terms of both party and state offices, and equally considerable informal powers of persuasion, which he could use to advance his policy agenda. On the other hand, as head of the state party, he had to be mindful not to push too hard or too fast on any given divisive issue, so as not to jeopardize party unity. As governor, Sanders was also a key intermediary between the national and state Democratic parties, which further limited his room for maneuver.

Nowhere were the possibilities and constraints that Sanders faced as a Loyalist southern Governor better illustrated than on the question of incorporating black voters into the Georgia Democratic Party. Like Weltner and Williams, Sanders believed that the future of both the Democratic Party and the Loyalist agenda would be best served by abandoning the Regulars' hostility to incorporating black voters into the Democrats' political coalition. Yet Sanders did not want to be identified as a promoter of either civil rights or massive resistance, an attitude encapsulated in his 1962 campaign pledge to resist both "race-baiting" and "race-mixing."[81]

Instead of engaging with civil rights, Sanders hoped to strengthen Loyalist ties to the black community by encouraging political relationships with black leaders without focusing on issues that would be seen as specifically black concerns. The hope was this would strengthen the appeal of

Loyalist candidates within the black community without driving away too many white supporters. This approach depended on forging relationships with black leaders who were willing to press for racial change primarily through negotiation and gradual accommodation rather than through direct action. Ideally, such leaders would also support the Loyalist contention that racial inequalities would best be solved be improving the economic prospects of all Georgia citizens. The viability of this approach was put to the test as soon as Sanders took office. The reapportionment of the state senate in 1962 had increased Fulton County's representation in that body from one to seven. In the heavily black Thirty-eighth District, the Democrats nominated Leroy Johnson, a lawyer and former public school teacher, and the Republicans selected T. M. Alexander, who ran an insurance business in Atlanta. Both candidates were black, ensuring that when the General Assembly reconvened in 1963, it would have its first black member in over fifty years. Johnson's victory in the general election meant that it would be a Democrat who broke this particular color line.[82]

As Johnson's political style and beliefs were close to the Loyalist ideal, state Democratic leaders were keen to promote and praise Johnson as an example of black leadership and to minimize the possibilities for racial tension arising from his election. When he arrived in the General Assembly, the viewing galleries were desegregated at his request, he was given several prominent committee assignments, and he was even invited to visit Senator Talmadge's family farm.[83] This did not mean that Johnson's arrival in the General Assembly provoked no ill-feelings from the existing membership. On the contrary, he was socially ostracized by many Regular legislators and also faced criticism from more militant black leaders for being insufficiently assertive.[84] And yet the fact that he was criticized both by the student protestors and supporters of massive resistance only served to heighten Loyalist interest in promoting Johnson as a valuable asset to the party. To this end, Fuqua sent a copy of one of Johnson's speeches to White House aide Jack Valenti, commenting, somewhat patronizingly, that it was evidence that "we have trained our Negro State Senator right" as "even when he gets on the other side of the country he talks like a good Democrat, and he really is."[85]

The reapportionment of the Georgia House in 1965 also resulted in an increase in black legislators—seven were elected from Fulton County alone—and the varying receptions given to them confirmed just what kind of black leaders Loyalists hoped to cultivate. The Loyalist ideal in this case was represented by Grace Towns Hamilton, who was already well known to many of them as the strong-willed but (from their perspective) eminently reasonable leader of the Atlanta Urban League. As they had done with Leroy Johnson, Loyalist leaders were keen to show that they were willing to do business with Hamilton. At the first session she attended, House Speaker George T. Smith assigned her "seat no. 1" in the chamber and gave her prominent seats on important committees.[86] In a letter to President Johnson, Ralph McGill, by 1965 a firm supporter of the Loyalist cause, singled Hamilton out as a "very exceptional woman" with whom the White House should consider working.[87] Thanks in part to the advocacy of Georgia Loyalists on their behalf, both Leroy Johnson and Grace Towns Hamilton attended the White House on several occasions, and in 1966 President Johnson appointed Hamilton to the Presidential Commission on Recreation and Natural Beauty.[88]

In contrast to the cooperative approach Loyalists took with Johnson and Hamilton, the case of Julian Bond demonstrated the very different reaction a more "radical" black politician would get. Although Bond was hardly more radical in his overall political beliefs than several of the other black legislators elected in 1965—Bond's fellow student activist and state legislator Ben Brown later recalled that Bond had no real reputation as a radical prior to that year's elections—he made several statements strongly critical of the Vietnam War that were interpreted by some as indicating questionable patriotism.[89] In response, the General Assembly voted in January 1966 to deny Bond his seat. In sharp contrast to the cooperative approach he pursued with Johnson and Hamilton, Carl Sanders publicly endorsed keeping Bond out of the state legislature. By a vote of 184 to 12, the Georgia House went along with this position.[90] Bond spent the rest of the year trying to have this decision reversed, and in December 1966 the U.S. Supreme Court demanded that he be seated. Nonetheless, as well as illustrating the desire of Sanders and others to disassociate themselves from those perceived as "radical" black activists, the dispute over Julian Bond also had significant long-run consequences. Not only would Bond play a critical role in the tumultuous politics of the grassroots challenge to Governor Maddox after 1966 but also the fact that it was the Vietnam War, rather than race, that sparked the dispute also signaled the appearance of a new issue that would soon rival race as a divisive force among Georgia Democrats.

The arrival on the political scene of elected black politicians like John-son, Hamilton, and Bond required some careful political maneuvering, but the moment that truly tested Sanders's ability to strike the balance on race that he was looking for was the 1964 Democratic National Conven-tion in Atlantic City.[91] In a telling irony given that it would ultimately cause Sanders no end of trouble, the most divisive racial issue at the con-vention came about because Democrats in Mississippi had been unable to reach the kinds of accommodations with black leaders that Sanders had helped to engineer in Georgia. Regulars in Mississippi still had a strangle-hold on the state Democratic Party in 1964 and had systematically ex-cluded blacks and nearly all Loyalists from selecting the delegates to the Democratic National Convention. The result was the nomination of an all-white delegation made up overwhelmingly of people who supported massive resistance and were planning to endorse Republican candidate Barry Goldwater in the general election. This meant that from the na-tional party's perspective, the official Democratic Party of Mississippi was, in the words of one historian, little more than "a gangrenous appendage that would soon have to be severed for the welfare of the whole."[92]

The response of civil rights workers and Loyalist activists in Missis-sippi was to form their own organization and nominate their own del-egates—interracial and committed to supporting President Johnson's reelection—to go to the national convention as representatives of the Mississippi Freedom Democratic Party (MFDP). The MFDP delegates then petitioned the Credentials Committee to throw out the Regular slate and seat them instead. Superficially, Sanders might have been expected to sympathize with the MFDP's objectives, and perhaps, deep down, he did. After all, the MFDP was taking on just the kind of ultraconservative, race-obsessed, traditionalist politicians Sanders disliked. In the immedi-ate context of 1964, however, the appearance of the MFDP was a most unwelcome development as far as Sanders was concerned, as it threatened to force him to make the choice all Loyalists hoped to avoid: whether to side with Regular Democrats or civil rights activists on the issue of racial equality. It was Sanders's nightmare scenario—his own version of Hob-son's choice—and as he helped Lyndon Johnson try to find a compromise solution to the MFDP's challenge, Sanders found himself faced only with uncomfortable options.

Sanders and Johnson were discussing the MFDP by phone at least a month prior to the convention. Johnson told Sanders that he was under pressure from northern union leaders and Democratic governors not to accept the credentials of Mississippi's Regulars. On the other hand, Johnson noted, other southern delegations would not be able to stay if a "bunch of Negroes" were seated instead. Sanders replied that he thought a "coalition of reasonable states in the South" could be put together to stand apart from the Mississippi Regulars and George Wallace, who was talking of orchestrating a walkout from the convention. Sanders then asked Johnson to make some sort of statement that the federal government would not "deliberately cram civil rights" down the white South's throat, though he realized such a statement may not be possible for the president. Johnson, as was to be expected, avoided committing himself to do so.[93]

As the convention approached, the two men talked repeatedly about the problem. Along with Texas governor John Connally, Sanders became one of Johnson's southern point men on the MFDP issue. In early August, Sanders addressed the question of the black vote in Georgia. In a typically Loyalist move, and in marked contrast to the Regular leadership in Mississippi, Sanders selected four black delegates to attend the convention as part of Georgia's delegation. All of them were impeccably "moderate" in their view on civil rights. In an indication that there was as at least as much political expediency as moral commitment in his decision, Sanders commented to Johnson that he had gotten a good reaction in the state to his choosing "four nigger delegates." The governor was also pleased to report that voter registration among Georgia's black community was rising and that this should help the president. He also detailed an exchange with conservative Georgia Democrats who wanted to sit out the convention and the election campaign, in which Sanders had warned them that they were in effect "going to sit idly by and cut [their] own throat" by handing elections at all levels to the Republicans.[94]

Sanders was clearly frustrated by supporters of Goldwater, including the Mississippi Regulars, trying to pass themselves off as Democrats. In particular, Sanders singled out Governor Wallace of Alabama. Complaining that Wallace was going to be given a slot to speak at the Platform Committee in favor of repealing the Civil Rights Act, Sanders argued that this was simply giving him a forum to express pro-Goldwater sentiments. The convention should be run, said Sanders, on the basis of "if you're a Democrat, you can come, but if you're not, we don't want to hear from you."[95]

Yet for all their agreement on the value of black voter registration, close cooperation with moderate black leaders, getting conservatives to campaign for the Johnson ticket, and the undesirability of keeping closet Republicans in the party, the governor and president nonetheless took sharply different stances in their overall assessment of the MFDP. With the convention already under way, and still urgently seeking a compromise that would keep civil rights activists and the Loyalist South happy, Johnson said of the MFDP that, to be honest, "they ought to be members of the Mississippi delegation." Sanders, having accepted that the Mississippi Regulars were out to disrupt the convention, nonetheless demurred on this point, saying that MFDP members should have been included only "if they are Democrats."[96]

At this point, Johnson became audibly agitated, snapping back at Sanders, "They *are* Democrats, and by God they tried to attend the [Mississippi Democratic] Convention and pistols kept them out. These people *begged* to be let in." Sanders, still skeptical, warned that people would say the "nigras" had taken over the Democratic Party if the MFDP were given any seats at all. Johnson dismissively replied that "two niggers" could not take over the party, and in any case, Sanders's delegation had four. Sanders protested that his four were "good, loyal Democrats," while the MFDP was just a "rump group." Johnson retorted that the MFDP delegates were also loyal Democrats and that some symbolic MFDP presence was not going to hurt anyone in any southern state. Finally, in an exasperated tone, Johnson informed Sanders that "you and I just can't survive our modern political life with these goddamn fellas [the Regulars] down there that are eating them [civil rights workers] for breakfast every morning. They gotta quit that." As far as the president was concerned, the Mississippi Democrats "gotta let [blacks] vote . . . however much we love [U.S. senators] Eastland and Stennis." If Mississippi's Democrats "won't let one [black] man go to a precinct convention, we got to put a stop to that." Sanders quickly moved the conversation on from this point, and it ended shortly afterward. As a final comment, Johnson wondered aloud why any reasonable southern leaders would want to associate themselves with the actions of Mississippi's Regulars. After all, the president commented, "there's laws they are violating."[97]

This conversation, particularly Johnson's closing rhetorical question, crystallized not just the immediate dilemma facing the Democrats at the

1964 convention but also the entire question of how to respond to the changing patterns of southern politics and the civil rights movement. The logic Johnson used to explain why the Regulars were of little value to the Democratic Party was hard to refute, as was his belief that Democrats had to lean toward siding with the demand for black voting rights. Likewise, Sanders's aggravation at pro-Goldwater Democrats was an extension of that, and both men were echoing ideas southern Loyalists had been developing for twenty years. And yet neither Johnson nor especially Sanders could quite bring himself to make a clean break and banish the Regulars from the party.

Eventually, the agreed-on compromise for the MFDP was that two of their members would be seated as delegates at-large. The Mississippi Regulars would retain their seats provided they swore an oath to support the national Democratic ticket and promised that all future delegations would be chosen in a nonracially exclusive manner. This was too much for all but three of the forty-four Regular Mississippi delegates to accept, and they walked out of the convention. However, the vast majority of southern delegates, including all the Georgians, stayed put. To this extent, Sanders could be relieved that, as it were, the line had held, but the end of the convention did not signal the end of his problems. Instead, he now had to pivot from avoiding a damaging walkout over civil rights to trying to persuade senior members of the Georgia state party to campaign for the Democratic ticket.

Above all, Sanders wanted to secure the cooperation of the state's two U.S. senators, Richard Russell and Herman Talmadge, in Johnson's re-election campaign. Neither Russell nor Talmadge was inclined to work for Johnson, and Sanders and Fuqua feared the impact this would have on the Democratic vote. At one point, it was even thought possible that Russell would go so far as to endorse Goldwater. In July 1964, Fuqua sent the White House a newspaper article containing several positive quotes Russell had given about the Republican candidate, which, Fuqua worried, "in the minds of [Russell's] followers . . . amounts to an outright endorsement of Senator Goldwater." Fuqua went on to warn that the silence of so many of the state's congressmen who had been helped by Johnson was a serious problem and that the Democratic "banner" in Georgia was being carried only by Governor Sanders and those who had been "publicly loyal" throughout the Kennedy-Johnson administrations.[98]

Russell did not endorse Goldwater, but his refusal to work for the Democratic ticket remained a concern. Shortly after the Democratic convention, Sanders spoke with Johnson and vice presidential candidate Hubert Humphrey about trying to set up an event in Georgia at which Russell could be persuaded to appear with Humphrey in order to find out if "he's going to play on the team."[99] Many in Georgia hoped Johnson would be able to use his long-standing friendship with Russell to persuade the senator to campaign on the president's behalf. State senator Julian Webb, a Loyalist from southwest Georgia, wrote to let Johnson know that "even one speech in this state by Senator Russell in support of [Johnson-Humphrey] . . . would eliminate any question about Georgia's support of the Democratic Party" in the election.[100] But Russell remained unpersuaded. As on every occasion after 1952, other than a brief foray into the campaign of 1960, Russell went no further than to say he personally would vote the straight Democratic ticket. In October 1964, Russell went on a tour of military installations. Russell ostensibly undertook the tour in his capacity as chairman of the Senate Armed Services Committee, but it was hard to escape the conclusion that his real motive was to avoid being pressured to campaign for Lyndon Johnson.

Sanders, Johnson, and Fuqua probably suspected that persuading Russell was a hopeless task, but they had reason to be more hopeful with Herman Talmadge. Talmadge had proven himself willing to cooperate with the Johnson administration in the Senate on a series of "War on Poverty" measures. White House aides also hoped Talmadge's closer connection with members of the state government might be turned to Johnson's advantage by persuading senior Georgia officials to join the campaign trail. White House Special Assistant Lawrence O'Brien met with Ninth District U.S. representative Phil Landrum to discuss campaign strategy in Georgia and reported back to the president that several key Democrats in the state government owed their positions to Talmadge and would likely campaign for Johnson if Talmadge requested them to: "they would perhaps move if he [Talmadge] moved."[101] Two weeks before the election, Special Assistant to the President Douglass Cater had a conversation with George Goodwin, the president of the First National Bank in Atlanta, who warned that Johnson, Weltner, and MacKay all faced an uphill struggle in Georgia. It was Goodwin's opinion that "the only man who can save the situation is Herman Talmadge," but only Johnson had enough leverage to get Talmadge to break his silence.[102] Talmadge, however, proved to be no less intractable than Russell, and the Johnson-Humphrey campaign in Georgia had to make do without the open backing of two of the three most senior Democrats in the state. In the end, Sanders was left to plow an often lonely furrow on behalf of the president.

The absence of a united state party effort to campaign for Lyndon Johnson in Georgia was seized on by other Loyalists after the election as the critical factor allowing the state to be carried by Goldwater. Ellis Arnall wrote to Johnson shortly after the outcome, congratulating him on his national landslide, but speaking also of the sadness that "100% Georgia Democrats" felt at the behavior of "misguided Democrats" in the state.[103] Also espousing the idea that more could have been achieved if more Georgia Democrats had been willing to campaign for the president, Ernest Vandiver sent a clipping to the White House from his one-time ally Roy Harris, in which Harris said that but for the efforts of the "Sanders-Vandiver" machine, Goldwater would have carried the state by an even wider margin.[104] State senator H. "Mac" Conway of DeKalb County, who was unseated in 1964 by a "Goldwater Republican," also wrote Johnson saying he could not imagine "better circumstances" in which to lose than "being identified with the President of my country and the Governor of my state." Conway echoed Vandiver's claim that but for the efforts of Sanders and other Loyalists, the Republican margin would have been even larger.[105] Georgia public safety commissioner Walter McDonald was even more critical of the state party figures who had left Sanders out on his own, laying the blame for Johnson's defeat "upon the office-holders and beneficiaries of the Democratic Party from the very top to the very bottom."[106]

Whether a more unified state party would have been enough to blunt Goldwater's appeal to Georgia voters in 1964 is debatable, but it is hard to believe that Johnson was not hurt to a significant degree by so many party leaders sitting on their hands. Whatever impact this had, however, there was no hiding the unprecedented nature of the voting patterns in Georgia that year. Goldwater did improve on Nixon's 1960 showing in urban and north Georgia—the two most Republican regions of the state—by 6.6 percent and 13.2 percent, respectively. However, he outdid Nixon even more in the Black Belt (by 34 percent) and south Georgia (by 35.1 percent), where local Republican candidates were generally nonexistent. Likewise, while there was a significant overlap between Goldwater's victory and earlier Regular victories in Democratic primaries—the Republican won handily in the blackest, poorest, and slowest-growing counties—there were also notable differences. Unlike, for example, the 1948 Democratic primary, where Herman Talmadge prevailed by a similar statewide margin as Goldwater did in 1964, in the latter contest there were Republican majorities in the largest, fastest-growing, most-educated, and richest counties—something Talmadge was never able to achieve. While Goldwater therefore made inroads in parts of the state and in certain demographics where Republicans had not previously been competitive, and while his well-known opposition to the 1964 Civil Rights Act unquestionably helped him in doing so, his defeat of Lyndon Johnson in Georgia was more complex than simply an updated version of the Regular-Loyalist divide of the 1940s and 1950s. Instead, the result reflected the fluidity in partisan allegiance that would characterize the emergence of two-party politics in Georgia over the course of the next few years.

Despite his inability to secure a victory for Lyndon Johnson in Georgia, and despite still having to expend a good deal of political energy simply trying, in his own words, to "keep the [Georgia] Democratic Party intact," Carl Sanders still had reason to be at least partially satisfied with the state of things by the end of his term.[107] His efforts to manage the continued desegregation of the state party and to prevent civil rights disputes in general from turning violent had been largely successful, despite occasional flashpoints such as over the seating of Julian Bond.[108] Nevertheless, Sanders, like Charles Weltner and Melba Williams, would also suffer political disappointment even as so many things he had advocated were coming about. While he was constitutionally barred from seeking reelection as governor in 1966, there is little doubt that he would have preferred almost anyone rather than Lester Maddox to be his successor.

But if 1966 was a disappointing year for Sanders, 1970 would turn out to be even worse. Running as the heavy favorite against Jimmy Carter, Sanders presented himself as the architect and advocate of the economic and political modernization that Georgia had experienced during the 1960s. Despite this message, and despite high favorability ratings for his time as governor and advantages in name recognition and funding, Sanders was defeated by the ambiguously traditionalist but distinctly "common man" campaign of Jimmy Carter. Given the highly personalized and occasionally racially charged strategy that Carter used to defeat him, it was presumably only small comfort for Sanders that Carter would go on to become the capstone of the Loyalist Democrats' efforts to reshape the South's politics in the manner Sanders had campaigned for during his own career.[109]

*   *   *

The experiences of Charles Weltner, Melba Williams, and Carl Sanders provide a snapshot of the challenges facing Loyalists in the early 1960s. Over the course of the decade, congressman, party activist, and governor all experienced political success and political frustration, with the greatest period of sustained success coming at the very beginning of the decade and the greatest frustrations occurring toward its end. And yet even though by the end of 1970 the most politically active parts of their careers had passed, and in the cases of Weltner and Sanders had been abruptly curtailed by electoral defeat, the kind of politics that they had been working toward—a "rejuvenated" state Democratic Party that had incorporated the "Negro voter," that promoted a firmly modernist agenda on economics and education, that was no longer in a state of constant political warfare with the national party, and that still remained the majority party in state politics—was also soon to be firmly entrenched in Georgia.

This paradox of their long-term substantive success alongside their short-term individual failures is a further way in which the personal travails of these three figures speak to two critical aspects of the Loyalist experience during this time. First, for all the setbacks they suffered, Georgia's Loyalists in the 1960s continued to lay the groundwork for the emergence of a modernized New South politics in the 1970s; and second, the Regular-Loyalist divisions in the Georgia Democratic Party, the tensions over the relationship with the national Democratic Party, the continued rise of black political influence, and the reemergence of the GOP as a viable political entity had created a highly volatile political environment that made the short-term prospects of any one political figure or message very hard to predict.

This latter point was most clearly demonstrated by the exceptionally unpredictable election campaigns of 1966. In July of that year, the Democratic Party of DeKalb County was holding its county convention at which James MacKay celebrated a newfound capacity to take on the Republican Party, Charles Weltner was touring his district taking shots at his Republican opponent while facing only token opposition in the Democratic primary, and Carl Sanders was delivering an upbeat assessment to Lyndon

Johnson of the strength and unity of the Georgia Democratic Party, light-heartedly telling the president that he had concluded that maybe "it ain't such a bad thing to be a Democrat."[110] Six months later, MacKay, Weltner, and Sanders were all out of office, the Republicans had witnessed their best-ever performance in state and congressional elections in Georgia, and the state's Democrats were more divided than they had been at any point over the previous twenty years. For all that had therefore been accomplished in building the "truly Democratic Party" in Georgia by 1966, there remained a great deal of work left to do.

5

"The Damndest Mess"

1966

As I'm sure you know, this fellow [Lester Maddox] is bad news.

Lee White, special assistant to Lyndon Johnson, 1966

At first glance, it would be hard to find a better case study for the devastating impact of the white backlash on the Democratic Party's fortunes in the South than the election of Lester Maddox as governor of Georgia in 1966. In contrast to Carl Sanders, who had sought to limit the political impact of racial tensions and to minimize the hostility of white Georgians toward the national Democratic Party and the federal government, Maddox based his campaign on a direct appeal to these tensions and hostilities. While Sanders had advocated obeying the law and accommodation to racial change rather than massive resistance, and had worked closely with Lyndon Johnson to paper over the regional schism in the Democratic Party, Lester Maddox had picketed the White House during the passage of the Civil Rights Acts of 1964 and Voting Rights Act of 1965, and he had openly supported Barry Goldwater in the 1964 presidential election. Maddox's vehement opposition to desegregation was summed up in a telegram he sent to the White House in 1964 in which he urged Johnson not to sign the Civil Rights Act, and instead to "rebuke the socialists, racial agitators and communists" who had "invaded" the South and, being little better than "communists and savages," had inflicted "death, injury, rape and social and economic harm" on white southerners.[1]

Not only did Maddox therefore embody the rhetoric and agenda of the white backlash and ride it successfully to the highest office in the state, he did so by defeating Ellis Arnall, the very personification of the 1940s southern liberalism that the backlash is credited with undermining. In the process, Maddox's candidacy also threatened to split the Georgia Democratic Party, and thereby helped Georgia's Republicans to elect two congressmen to the U.S. House and to come within an electoral regulation of capturing the statehouse for the first time since 1872. In short, in just a few brief months, and with no experience in office and no political machine or financial backing of any substance, Lester Maddox appeared to undo all the gains Loyalists had made over the previous generation, and he did so simply by tapping into the continued racial and cultural resentments harbored by white Georgians. The optimism that Loyalists had felt as late as the mid-summer of 1966 that such resentments were dying out as a political force lay in tatters by the end of the year, even though the combination of reapportionment, the end of county-unit voting, and demographic shifts in the state's population should have moved the underlying political structure firmly in their favor.

It is therefore no wonder that the white backlash aspect of Maddox's election has received so much attention.[2] And yet to speak of the 1966 election only in terms of how it illustrated the strength of this backlash is to leave the story incomplete on two counts. First, presenting Maddox's election as an inevitable, or at the very least a natural, response to the political events of the 1960s overlooks the fact that his success in the 1966 campaign was essentially a political fluke. To describe it as such is not to claim that it was inexplicable or insignificant; nor is to dismiss the white backlash Maddox appealed to as politically irrelevant. Rather, the justification for terming Maddox's election a fluke is that it depended on a series of unanticipated and unpredictable events occurring: the withdrawal of former governor Vandiver, the presumptive favorite, from the race; the decision by Herman Talmadge not to enter the contest; a narrow second-place finish for Maddox in the first Democratic primary; highly unusual voting patterns in Maddox's runoff victory; and a grassroots write-in effort during the general election that denied his Republican opponent a critical number of votes. Had any of these highly contingent events turned out differently, the election result would in turn have been very different. There was, in short, nothing inevitable about Maddox's victory.

Second, the fact that Maddox won has led to a tendency to ignore or neglect the arguments his opponents were making on the basis that these arguments must have been ineffective. Yet in terms of shaping post–Jim Crow politics in Georgia, the arguments of those who campaigned against Maddox would be far more critical than the white backlash or the southern strategy. As the years following Maddox's election demonstrated, advocating accommodation with the civil rights movement proved to be the most effective means for the Georgia Democratic Party to beat back the Republican challenge that had seemed poised to take over the state in 1966. In short, the fluke nature of the 1966 elections in Georgia highlights the central ambiguity of the white backlash; namely, that while it is true that Maddox could not have won had there not been a white backlash for him to appeal to, it was a highly unpredictable political force that could just as easily backfire on those who sought to exploit it. Ultimately, it would be the resulting backlash *against* Maddox, rather than the white backlash itself, that would be the most consequential legacy of the 1966 election.

Overall, rather than seeing the 1966 election as demonstrating the omnipotence of the politics of backlash, it should be viewed both as an illustration of the fluidity and volatility of the political climate in the mid-1960s South as two-party politics established itself as the successor to the one-party system, and yet also, despite this volatility, as an indication of the lasting significance and continuity of the political coalitions that had developed in postwar Georgia. It was a highly ambiguous election, but a significant one nonetheless. From one perspective, it was simply political chaos. Dominated by colorful personalities, with major candidates dropping in and out of the race, new grassroots organizations apparently springing out of nowhere, and seemingly freakish voting returns refusing to conform to conventional political wisdom, the contest illustrated once again the critical importance for any election campaign of "events, dear boy, events."[3]

From another perspective, however, the 1966 electoral cycle provided an important guide to long-term trends in Georgia politics. The basic factional split within the Democratic Party endured, but it was being shaken up by the presence of a sustained Republican presence in state contests. Jimmy Carter first appeared on the political radar as a result of his performance in the 1966 primaries. The subsequent dilemmas of both parties in Georgia also became evident during the course of the contest. For the Democrats, 1966 reinforced both the perils of ignoring the "common man" populism and continued strength of social traditionalism that Maddox had based his campaign on (a realization that was critical to Carter's later political career), as well as the futility of trying to outflank the GOP on the right. For the Republicans, the results, especially when compared to the returns from the 1964 presidential contest, left open the question of whether the southern strategy championed by converted Regulars and hard-line traditionalists or the suburban strategy of conservative color blindness and free-market economics that had been the dominant approach in the 1950s would be more effective in the two-party South. Of course, many of these lessons would not become evident until after the dust of the campaign had settled. As such, and given the seemingly endless twists and turns that took place over the course of the year, it is understandable that even as seasoned a veteran of Georgia politics as Richard Russell should describe the process to Lyndon Johnson as "the damndest mess I have ever seen."[4] It did indeed appear very messy, but at the same time it was highly revealing about the state of Georgia politics in the mid-1960s.

The Truly Democratic Party Continued

As late as May 1966, there was little reason to believe that Georgia's gubernatorial election that year would produce anything out of the ordinary. True, it seemed certain that the Republican Party would run a properly financed statewide campaign for the first time in living memory. The GOP had also recruited a credible candidate: former Democrat, now Republican congressman Howard "Bo" Callaway. However, with the Democrats set to nominate Vandiver as their candidate, it did not seem that Callaway, or any other Republican, could win. In May, Vandiver's return to the statehouse was viewed favorably by more than 70 percent of Georgia voters, and he was not considered vulnerable in either the Democratic primary or in the general election.[5]

As well as being popular with the electorate, Vandiver was also a candidate acceptable to both factions of the state party. Although he had first been elected governor in 1958 as a Regular, he had revealed himself to have more pragmatic inclinations than many of his more zealous supporters had hoped for. Indeed, his willingness to abandon massive resistance in 1961 coupled with his public support for both the Kennedy campaign in 1960 and the Johnson campaign in 1964 meant that he was acceptable to Loyalists. Nonetheless, as a critic of federal desegregation guidelines, the "bungling bureaucrats" enforcing them, and many, though not all, Great Society social programs, he was also acceptable to many Regulars.[6] As a result, even though former governor Ellis Arnall, still a Loyalist icon twenty years after he left office, and Lester Maddox, at that point chiefly famous for his use of an ax handle to keep his Atlanta restaurant segregated after the 1964 Civil Rights Act, were also declared candidates for the Democratic nomination, a second term for Vandiver seemed to be a foregone conclusion.

The sanguine attitude among Democratic leaders toward the likely outcome of the 1966 election was also evident in the pace and scope of party reform that had taken place since Lyndon Johnson's defeat in Georgia during the 1964 election. It was not that Loyalists did not understand the need to take action against continued pro-Republican Regulars in the party, but their timetable for implementing any changes in the wake of Johnson's defeat was geared around the president's presumed 1968 reelection campaign, not the 1966 contest. Accordingly, when second-term state senator Jimmy Carter was appointed by Loyalist party leaders to chair a committee on reform of the state party in December 1964, the idea was that new rules would be adopted by 1968. These rules were intended to ensure that strong action would be possible against people in the party calling themselves Democrats who refused to support national Democratic candidates and instead allied themselves with Republicans. People such as Lester Maddox, for example.

Among the reforms that Carter's committee considered were stricter rules allowing for the expulsion of Democratic office-holders who worked for Republican candidates, binding loyalty oaths for Democratic primary candidates not to support Republicans in the general election, and holding party primaries on the same day. This last step was necessary, according to Public Safety Commissioner Walter McDonald, so as to prevent Republicans voting in Democratic primaries in order to nominate a weak Democratic candidate "in the hope of being able to beat him in the General Election."[7] That there was considerable support among Loyalists for these sorts of changes is clear, as most of them were adopted in some form by the state party during Carter's own term as governor. However, when the state Democratic Executive Committee met in late 1965 to consider the recommendations of the Carter Committee, they adopted only modest reforms, with a view to making more substantial changes at a later date.[8] A further sign that there was little contemplation given to the need for reform ahead of the 1966 elections was that those changes that were made, with the full support of Governor Sanders and Chairman Fuqua, were geared at strengthening the powers of the governor to enforce party discipline—a move they, as Loyalists, would hardly have proposed had they at all anticipated that the incoming governor would be a man whose idea of party discipline was so diametrically opposed to their own.[9]

That only relatively modest changes were made and that they were often based on concentrating greater power in the hands of the governor were decisions that Loyalists would soon regret in light of the electoral chaos that unfolded during 1966. The catalyst for this chaos was Vandiver's withdrawal from the campaign in May 1966 after he suffered a mild heart attack. As a consequence, Arnall and Maddox went from mildly interesting diversions to being the front-runners for the Democratic nomination, with each occupying the most extreme positions of their respective factions. Arnall, still the bête noire of Regular Democrats, assumed the status of favorite, and his rhetoric left little doubt as to where he stood on the tendentious question of party loyalty. In July 1966, he proclaimed to an audience in Atlanta, "I'm a local Democrat, a state Democrat and a national Democrat, and anyone who doesn't like it can go to hell!"[10] Despite the fact that he expressed the beliefs of the Loyalist Democrats as strongly as anyone, Arnall's candidacy and potential nomination presented even those sympathetic to him with a dilemma. In particular, there was a concern that Arnall, for all his political talents, was too divisive a figure within the state party and would trigger large-scale defections to Callaway from Democratic voters. As Carl Sanders put it to Lyndon Johnson, Arnall was a man with a "great deal of forensic ability," but given his unflinching endorsement of liberal policies and the political climate in Georgia in the wake of the 1964 election, it was likely that Callaway would "massacre" him.[11]

On the other hand, Loyalists viewed Lester Maddox as a hysterical demagogue who would seriously embarrass the party and encourage racial violence in the state. Even some Regulars who disliked Arnall intensely were not enamored with Maddox, whose rabble-rousing they considered a threat to order. As one Georgian wrote to Senator Russell's office, even as a conservative Democrat, "I personally can't stomach the ax handle [Maddox] in the #1 spot."[12] Vandiver's withdrawal took out of the running the ideal compromise candidate for Georgia's Democrats in 1966. Now, with Arnall and Maddox as the only choices, each expressing the absolute position of his faction, neither side was convinced its candidate could or should win. As a result, Democrats from across the party had an interest in persuading others to enter the race.

Desperately Seeking Someone: The Talmadge Fiasco

The first to put his name forward as a replacement for Vandiver was Herman Talmadge. It is quite possible that Talmadge had received advance knowledge of Vandiver's withdrawal, given their close political and personal relationship; in any case, he announced on the day of Vandiver's withdrawal that he would be willing to be a candidate if the people of Georgia wanted him to return. He invited Georgians to express their opinions to him.[13] It is clear that many were caught off guard by Talmadge's actions. Governor Sanders implied to President Johnson that Talmadge spoke only to Vandiver and his Senate staff before making his announcement.[14] What is less clear is what exactly happened next. Evidently, Talmadge received a barrage of telegrams, postcards, and letters over the next few days from constituents expressing their opinions. Claiming to be responding to what Georgians were telling him, Talmadge announced on May 23 that he was withdrawing his name from consideration.[15] What lay behind Talmadge's decision to withdraw is harder to discern. Both contemporary observers and subsequent analysts have offered up a series of possible motives. The explanations include Talmadge being told by Atlanta's political "kingmakers" that they wanted him in the Senate and would give him no money for a gubernatorial campaign, or that he simply did not fancy his chances of success.[16] Whatever the true reason, the responses Talmadge received from his fellow Georgians certainly indicated that the political climate in the state was unsettled, and it is hard to believe that Talmadge was reassured about his chances for success from reading what his constituents told him.

Perhaps most striking was the unexpected nature and origins of both hostile and favorable reactions to his suggested reentry into state politics. There is no doubt that many of the telegrams and letters—probably the majority—were generally supportive of Talmadge's candidacy. Many of them informed the senator he would be welcomed by the state's voters, or, at the very least, that they would support him in whatever decision he chose to make.[17] Such was the prevailing opinion among many officials within the Democratic Party, who apparently hoped that Talmadge's candidacy would "[hurl] back the rising tide of Republicanism" in Georgia.[18] The Catoosa County Democratic Executive Committee held a vote of its members and requested that Talmadge run for governor.[19] Future governor and then state legislator Joe Frank Harris also urged Talmadge to return "at a time when our Democratic Party needs a boost." Former General Assembly majority leader Frank Twitty likewise expressed his support.[20]

Less expected, perhaps, were the endorsements from former political opponents, including leading Loyalists. Prominent among these was Hamilton Lokey, who wrote to express his hope that Talmadge would enter the race. Recognizing that their former differences might make them odd political bedfellows, Lokey extended an offer that he was prepared to "actively campaign for you, keep my mouth shut, or campaign for your opponent, which ever course you feel will be of the greatest assistance to you." The Loyalist vice-chairman of the Fulton County Democratic Party, which represented those who had formed the basis of anti-Talmadge activism in the 1950s, also offered his help to Talmadge in the forthcoming primary.[21]

This is not an exhaustive sample of the various Democratic officials and representatives who wrote to Talmadge, and nor was their support universal. However, the overwhelming opinion among public figures and party activists who wrote to Talmadge, whether allies or former opponents, was that he should run. That they should all be urging him to return regardless of previous (or ongoing) political disagreements highlighted the dilemma Vandiver's withdrawal had created and just how badly many Georgia Democrats wanted to find a candidate they could unite behind. In the end, however, despite this apparent unity of purpose, there was considerable truth in the analysis of Walter Davis of Lithonia, who wrote Talmadge, "True, all the Democratic politicians welcomed your announcement but they are the only ones who did."[22]

In contrast to the united opinion of Democratic officials, the response Talmadge received from the grassroots was far more mixed, and often much more hostile. One form of complaint was that Talmadge was a patsy for President Johnson. The fear many expressed was that Johnson was trying to put "his man" in the statehouse, and then have Carl Sanders elevated to the U.S. Senate. As one telegram succinctly put it, "Can Not Support your Sell out to Johnson." Other Georgians echoed this point: "say it ain't so Herman, you haven't really sold out," lamented Rose Johnson of Macon. "Six Registered Voters" suggested that as "you and Betty [Talmadge] helped put LBJ in," Talmadge should "stay in Washington with him—you deserve each other."[23] Federal Judge Frank Scarlett was more delicate, warning Talmadge that many saw him as having made a deal with Johnson, and that the perception of this association "is not going to help you a bit in these sections [south Georgia]."[24] On the one hand, the idea that a man who had spoken out against the national Democratic leadership for the best part of twenty years, who had once been among the best-known segregationists in the nation, and who had done almost nothing to help the national Democratic campaign in 1964 could yet be seen as having "sold out" to the White House seems absurd. On the other hand, it revealed just how unpredictable a political force the white backlash was— logically speaking, those who were most vicious in their condemnation of Talmadge's proposed return to Georgia were those one might have expected to have been his core base of support. In public relations terms, the Talmadge episode was evidently something of a fiasco; certainly the Atlanta press reported it as such.[25] The outcome, however, was to leave Arnall as the putative front-runner, with Maddox snapping at his heels—a situation that remained unsatisfactory to many.

Spoiled for Choice: The First Primary

Between Vandiver's withdrawal and Talmadge's decision not to enter the race in May and the Democratic primary in September, three other candidates entered the race. James Gray, a newspaper editor from Albany in southwest Georgia, represented himself as the choice of conservative business interests. Despite having served as state Democratic Party chairman from 1959 to 1962, Gray had supported Eisenhower for president in 1952 and 1956 and Barry Goldwater in 1964. His credentials, as far as Loyalists were concerned, were therefore highly suspect. Gray was also racially conservative, though, unlike Maddox, he was not calling for renewed massive resistance to the federal civil rights laws. Gray fit perfectly the Loyalist archetype of a Regular who really ought to be in the Republican Party. The Regulars also had another candidate in Vandiver's former lieutenant governor Garland Byrd, who was more difficult to pin down ideologically. Byrd had held elective office for a long period of time, unlike either Gray or Maddox, but was as much a political "fixer" as an ideologue. He had, along with other Regulars, supported the massive resistance measures and shown no sympathy toward civil rights. On the other hand, he was neither as histrionic in his attacks on the national party as Maddox nor as brazenly pro-Republican as Gray. In fact, Byrd had run unsuccessfully as the Democratic candidate against Bo Callaway in the

Third Congressional District in 1964, and once he was eliminated in the September primary, would endorse Ellis Arnall over Maddox.[26]

The final candidate to enter the race was state senator Jimmy Carter. First elected to the General Assembly in 1962, Carter was something of a political enigma. Given that he went on to become president of the United States, historians and biographers have understandably been interested in examining his early career for clues about the motivations for his later actions on the national stage. However, the consensus, if one exists on this subject, is that it is very hard to tell precisely what Carter's views were prior to his term as governor of Georgia.[27] In part, this is because of the apparent inconsistencies in his image that he presented between his first campaign for governor in 1966 and his subsequent successful run in 1970. Yet even allowing for the vagueness of his policy positions, and his ambivalence on racial issues, even in 1966 Carter fit the classic profile of a Georgia Loyalist.

In 1961, Carter had been approached by Sumter County Attorney Warren Fortson (brother of Georgia secretary of state Ben Fortson) to run against the highly conservative congressman E. L. "Tic" Forrester in the 1962 Democratic primary in the Third District. Fortson's motivation was the well-established Loyalist position that Forrester was a reactionary liability who was hindering the emergence of modern, progressive politics.[28] Carter declined and ran for the General Assembly instead. Once elected, he became closely involved with Loyalist efforts to establish a more reliable party apparatus in Georgia, in particular in his position as head of the special committee on organizing the state party.[29] In his private correspondence with senior party figures, Carter frequently echoed key Loyalist themes. He developed friendly relations with Congressmen Weltner and MacKay, as well as Leroy Johnson, to whom Carter wrote in 1965, "I suspect that you will never fully realize how much your service [in the General Assembly] has meant to our whole state."[30]

After Bo Callaway won the Third District as a Republican in 1964, Carter decided he would challenge him for the seat in 1966. Like many Loyalists, Carter was keen to prevent Georgia from becoming a Republican-controlled state. With Callaway on the verge of abandoning the Third District to run for governor, Carter wrote to Herman Talmadge, asking the senator to lend his assistance to "prevent our entire state government from being won by the Republicans."[31] Carter's concern over the Republican Party was the same as the general concern of Georgia's

Loyalists—namely, that the GOP was too conservative. Carter's views on this are apparent in a letter he wrote to the head of the Young Democrats in Georgia after he was informed they had invited Senator Edward Kennedy to speak at their convention. Carter supported the invitation, telling the Young Democrats' Will Wallace, "We entirely need someone like [Kennedy] to help us here in Georgia now and help to save us from the Goldwater-ites and the Birchers. We are over-run with them down here."[32] The same message was repeated in a letter Carter wrote directly to Senator Kennedy.[33]

With Callaway now running for governor, and with Vandiver having dropped out, Carter entered the gubernatorial race. Even though he would criticize Arnall as being too liberal, Carter ran a Loyalist campaign. Without endorsing civil rights laws or further school desegregation, he nonetheless openly campaigned for the black vote, seeking to portray himself, according to Peter Bourne, as "a candidate who [had] the respect of a majority of the responsible Negro and white voters."[34] Beyond that, Harold Henderson noted, Carter was also making his appeal in 1966 as "the only Democratic candidate capable of uniting a badly divided party and achieving victory over the Republican challenger," a theme he would subsequently echo not only in his second campaign for governor in 1970 but also in his primary campaign for the Democratic presidential nomination in 1976.[35]

It was therefore a five-way choice that voters in the Democratic primary faced on September 14, 1966, when just four months earlier they would most likely have anticipated ratifying Ernest Vandiver's return to office. The choice ranged from the unswervingly loyal Ellis Arnall, through the loyal but more circumspect Jimmy Carter, to the establishment conservatives Gray and Byrd, and finally to the insurgent conservative Maddox. Assuming, therefore, that Arnall and Carter represented the Loyalist wing of the party, while Byrd, Gray, and Maddox represented the Regulars, the first primary revealed familiar divisions in the Democratic electorate, as shown in figures 7 and 8. Between them, Carter and Arnall polled 51.1 percent of the votes cast while the remaining three candidates picked up 48.9 percent. As the Loyalist candidates, the Arnall-Carter vote was, as expected, strongest in the largest (57.8 percent), fastest-growing (58.3 percent), most-educated (57.3 percent), richest (58.5 percent), and whitest (54.6 percent) counties. Equally predictably, they did best in Georgia's urban areas (60.4 percent) and the northern part of the state

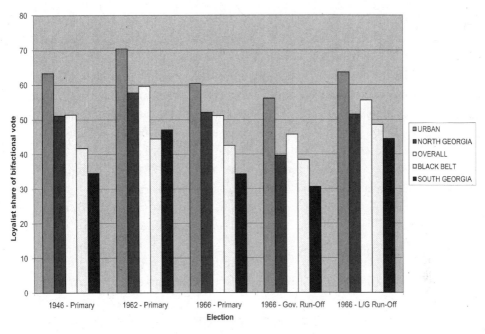

Figure 7. Loyalist vote by region, 1946–1966.

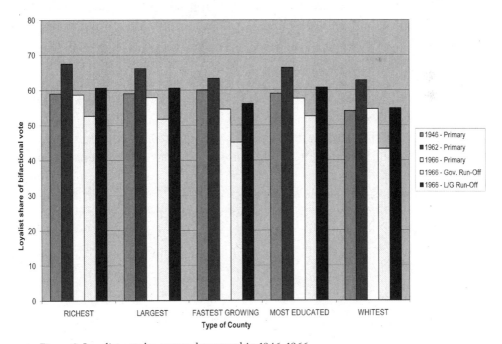

Figure 8. Loyalist vote by county demographic, 1946–1966.

(52 percent). The Maddox-Gray-Byrd vote was highest in the smallest (63 percent), slowest-growing (57.7 percent), least-educated (57.1 percent), poorest (63.7 percent), and blackest (56.8 percent) counties. And just as Regular candidates had been doing for decades, they prevailed in south Georgia (65.7 percent) and the Black Belt (57.6 percent).[36] Overall, Arnall came out on top with a little under 30 percent of the votes—a disappointing outcome given his status as perceived front-runner—and would face second-placed Lester Maddox in a runoff.

Another noteworthy feature of the results was that only a small shift in votes would have been required to put Carter into second place and into a runoff with Arnall.[37] Such a result would have produced an entirely different narrative for the subsequent runoff and general elections. Carter would have had a very good chance against Arnall, and a race between Carter and Callaway would have been the perfect testing ground for the appeal of a Loyalist Democrat against a conservative Republican in the immediate aftermath of the major federal civil rights laws. Based on similar contests in the rest of the South, who would have prevailed is tough to know for sure. In Virginia in 1965, Mills Godwin had been elected governor as a recently converted Loyalist Democrat (and soon to be Republican), but Godwin's opponent that year had been the racially moderate Republican Linwood Holton. In 1966, South Carolina Loyalist Robert McNair was elected governor, as was the repentant segregationist Buford Ellington in Tennessee (although Ellington faced no serious opponent). On the other hand, in Florida, conservative Republican Claude Kirk won the statehouse over Loyalist Robert King High, while in Arkansas another racially moderate Republican, Winthrop Rockefeller, defeated Regular Democrat James Johnson.[38] While the varied outcomes of southern gubernatorial elections in the mid-1960s therefore offer no firm prediction for who would have been favored in a Carter-Callaway matchup, they do illustrate just how unsettled party politics in the South was at this time. The one thing that can be said for sure about a contest between either Arnall or Carter and Callaway in Georgia, however, is that, whatever the result, it would have produced a very different political atmosphere in the state over the following four years than occurred as a result of Maddox's victory.

The Runoff

Even after Maddox finished second in the primary, the idea that he might ultimately become governor remained preposterous to many. As the Democratic National Committee's analyst of the primary wrote to the White House, "The feeling is Arnall would clobber Maddox in the run-off."[39] Nonetheless, all recognized that the runoff contest offered a clear-cut contrast in candidates. Maddox and Arnall were opposites in person-ality, agenda, and campaign style. Both men ran a campaign based on the key themes of their respective factions within the Democratic Party. In typically Loyalist fashion, Arnall warned that Maddox would damage the ability of Georgia to make economic progress and maintain racial calm. According to Arnall, a vote for Maddox was a vote for "strife" and "hate," and against "responsible government." If Maddox became gover-nor, Georgia would become a "laughing stock," and there would be no chance to "bring new industry to our state and move Georgia forward." Rather than risk a Maddox administration, Arnall urged voters to support his own desire to create a "positive, forward-looking state government."[40] Maddox responded to Arnall's charges by drawing on the central themes of previous Regular campaigns. To Maddox, Arnall represented "sellout liberalism" and was the "granddaddy of forced racial integration." Unsur-prisingly, Maddox claimed, Arnall's status as an integrationist and "wild socialist" had guaranteed him the support of the "bloc vote" (that is, black Georgians). Furthermore, Arnall was also linked in Maddox's newspaper advertisements to "LBJ, Humphrey, Socialism, MLK & SNCC [the Stu-dent Non-Violent Coordinating Committee]."[41]

In the runoff, Maddox defeated Arnall by 54.3 percent to 45.7 percent. Once again the vote broke down largely along established patterns of Reg-ular and Loyalist support (see figures 1 and 2). There were, however, some unusual aspects of the result that underscore the difficulty of assessing the role of the white backlash in Maddox's success. For instance, there was the curious pattern of voting in north Georgia, which had been the bellwether region for statewide contests since World War II. In every statewide refer-endum and contested gubernatorial primary held between 1946 and the first primary in 1966, north Georgia had always gone with the winning candidate or the winning side in the referendum. In each case, the amount of support the winning side received from north Georgia was, on aver-age, only 1.1 percent different from the statewide total and on only one occasion (the 1954 primary) more than 2 percent different.[42] As a result, north Georgia had several times supported Loyalist candidates and causes even during the massive resistance years. Additionally, in 1964, the northern part of the state had voted for Lyndon Johnson by 55.6 percent to 44.4 percent, even as Johnson polled only 45.9 percent of the vote statewide. Simply put, north Georgia was not considered natural "backlash country." And yet while Arnall's support across the other three regions of the state was approximately 3.5 percent lower than the combined Arnall-Carter vote in the first primary, in north Georgia it was down by more than 12 percent.[43]

Why north Georgia's voters reacted in this way is difficult to know for sure. Intuitively, one might assume that Maddox's "common man" appeal may have led him to run better than expected in north Georgia against Arnall's upscale, establishment-backed campaign. However, the comparison between north Georgia's voting in the runoff as opposed to the first primary is inconclusive on this point. Maddox improved on the Regulars' showing in all demographic categories in north Georgia, but he actually gained more support in high-income counties (15.5 percent) than in low-income ones (7.1 percent). The differential between the Regular showing in the high- and low-income counties also disappeared. While in the first primary there was a sharp drop-off in support for Maddox, Gray, and Byrd as one went up from low- to high-income counties (56.9 to 44.4 percent), in the runoff there was only a slight difference (63 to 59.9 percent). Ranking the north Georgia counties by education level produces similarly ambiguous results, although in this case the differential between low- and high-education counties was negligible to begin with (a less than 3 percent spread in either primary).

It is similarly hard to find any clear explanation from the racial makeup of the counties. Regulars did better by approximately 2.5 percent in the primary in north Georgia counties with the highest black populations than with the lowest; Maddox improved that edge to a 4.1 percent difference in the runoff, but even then he ran best in the counties with a black population of middling proportion (62.4 percent) than in either the blackest (60.7 percent) or whitest (56.6 percent) counties. Such aggregate analysis by county cannot rule out that, at the individual level, it was poorer, less-educated white voters living close to black populations who shifted to Maddox in the runoff, but it provides no evidence to suggest this was the case. Whatever factor was turning north Georgia voters against Ellis Arnall, it seemed to be equally strong across all demographic categories, and demonstrated once more the fluidity of the political climate in 1966.

There was also the question of the mysterious 42,000 additional votes that were cast in the runoff—mysterious, because runoffs usually had lower turnouts than primaries. Many Loyalists suspected the difference was explained by Republicans "crossing over" and voting in the Democratic primary in order to nominate the weaker candidate. Ralph McGill estimated in the *Atlanta Constitution* that around 75,000 Republicans had taken advantage of Georgia's open primary law to back Maddox in the hope that Callaway would defeat him.[44] There is some evidence for this. Fellow journalist Bruce Galphin noted that in fifty-five counties, Maddox received more votes in the runoff against Arnall than he did in the general election against Callaway, even though turnout was higher in the latter contest. As Harold Henderson has pointed out, however, the Georgia Republican Party was preparing Callaway to run as the conservative against the liberal Arnall. They believed this was their best chance of victory, and Maddox's success meant a complete change of strategy from what they had prepared.[45]

Legitimate as Henderson's objections are in terms of dismissing an *organized* Republican effort to get Maddox nominated, the missing votes that Galphin observed are nonetheless intriguing. Evidently, tens of thousands of people who had voted for Maddox in the runoff cast their ballots for Callaway in the general election.[46] To concede that these voters were not acting at the behest of the state Republican Party does not rule out that they were motivated by the same basic intention that Loyalists accused them of—that is, casting votes for Maddox to eliminate even the possibility of Arnall beating Callaway, and then casting their general election ballot for Callaway as the better of two essentially agreeable choices. Even some Democrats voted on this basis. Ernest Vandiver claimed that he voted for Maddox in the runoff with the intent of subsequently supporting Callaway, based on his view that Maddox would be an easier opponent for the Republican than Arnall was.[47]

The final complication for assessing the meaning of the 1966 runoff was the result of the simultaneous runoff for lieutenant governor, which involved a contest between the Regular incumbent, Peter Zack Geer, and the Loyalist Speaker of the Georgia House of Representatives, George T. Smith. As Maddox did with Arnall, Geer tried to paint Smith as a "lackey" to Loyalist Democrats and a "captive" of the national party.[48] By contrast, Smith, like Arnall, emphasized boosting Georgia's industrial development and focusing on economic progress rather than race.[49] The total number of votes cast in each election was very similar (around 816,000 in the race for governor; around 806,000 in the race for lieutenant governor). The overwhelming majority of Georgia Democrats going to the polls evidently voted in both contests. Yet while Maddox defeated Arnall by 8 points, Smith prevailed over Geer by 56 to 44 percent, and, unlike Arnall, Smith won a majority of the votes in the north of the state. Clearly, then, being a Loyalist in 1966 did not mean inevitable defeat, and appealing to the white backlash was no guarantor of electoral victory either in north Georgia or the state as a whole.

The General Election

As if the primary campaign had not been turbulent enough, the general election campaign did little to restore any sense of normality to the proceedings. The next twist in the story took place at the grassroots, where dissatisfaction with the possibility of Maddox being the next governor, or even simply being the Democratic nominee, was strongest. Given that Maddox was the very antithesis of what Loyalists had worked for over the previous twenty years, it was not surprising that they were extremely unhappy at his nomination, but there were also several Regulars who could not support the idea of a man Vandiver labeled a "pipsqueak" being in charge of the state.[50] Actually doing something to counter Maddox, however, was highly problematic. Disenchanted Democrats had three options. The first, and seemingly most likely, was to hold their nose and vote for Callaway. In terms of overall ideology, there did not appear to be any great difference between the Republican and the Democrat, but it was plausible to argue, even for those who did not consider themselves as conservative as either candidate, that Callaway was the lesser of two evils, as he would not engage in violent resistance to enacted laws in the way Maddox had done with his ax handle in July 1964.

On the other hand, to elect Callaway would be to put the powers of state patronage into the hands of the Republican Party for four years. While the Democratic Party could hope not to nominate Maddox or someone of his ilk in 1970, Callaway might by then have built up a formidable Republican campaign machine that would be difficult to overcome. To avoid this, it might be better to vote for Maddox, keep the state in Democratic hands, and make sure that a more suitable candidate was nominated the next time around. This, of course, meant hoping that Maddox would not do irreparable damage to the Democratic Party or the state in the meantime.

The final option was to organize a write-in campaign for a third candidate.[51] This, too, was very risky. Not only did it stand no realistic chance of successfully electing someone other than Callaway or Maddox but also to associate with a campaign against the Democratic nominee was to invite charges of disloyalty, making such a move particularly problematic for those who styled themselves as Loyalists. Working outside the party also precluded any chance of an alliance with elected Democratic officials, however distasteful they considered Maddox's beliefs to be. The only potential value of a write-in campaign, other than the ability to cast a vote that was ideologically unproblematic to the conscience of the voter, was that it might deprive the actual winner of a sense of legitimacy and that a strong showing for a write-in candidate would provide a base for preventing a future Maddox candidacy occurring.

Given this unenviable set of choices, it is not surprising that anti-Maddox Democrats offered a rather disjointed series of responses to his nomination. Two ad hoc groups developed for those Democrats unwilling to support Maddox. The first adopted the name "Democrats For Callaway" (DFC). The DFC argued that Maddox as governor would be a threat to order and economic progress and therefore it would be better to vote for Callaway as a lesser evil. The second titled itself "Write-In Georgia" (WIG) and rejected the idea that Callaway was a lesser evil in any meaningful sense. Rather, WIG espoused the ideological positions of the Loyalist Democrats and argued that a stand had to be made for government activism, racial moderation, and opposition to the general conservatism of the Republican Party.

As unusual and varied as the responses of Georgia's Democrats to Maddox's nomination were, a poll taken in October 1966 suggested their uncertainty mirrored that of Georgia's voters. Conducted by Penetration Research, the survey claimed Callaway led Maddox by 42 percent to 34 percent, with a substantial 24 percent of voters undecided. Of the undecided voters, more than a third said they planned to vote for neither candidate, which the poll concluded indicated "strong alienation" on the part of moderates. The poll went on to note that the healthy lead Callaway had enjoyed over Maddox among all white voters in August had been reversed, and he now trailed the Democrat substantially in rural areas. What was odd about these results, though, was that "the Republican maintains a healthy lead over Maddox among voters who supported [President Johnson] two years ago, but the Democrat presently runs almost even with him among former Goldwater backers." In other words, seemingly half of those who preferred Goldwater to Johnson in 1964 now preferred to vote Democratic rather than back a Goldwater Republican, while many of those who had been prepared to support the president in 1964 now favored one of the chief acolytes of Johnson's opponent—a further indication that partisan allegiance in Georgia in 1966 was unusually fluid.[52]

Against this backdrop, and in competition with the regular Democratic organization and the state Republican Party, the DFC and WIG set out to make their pitch to the voters. The DFC's key personnel were white political leaders who feared the impact a revival of massive resistance would have on Georgia. Chaired by Judge Robert Heard, prominent DFC members included Vandiver and John Sibley, the author of the 1960 report that advocated ending massive resistance to school desegregation. The DFC also attracted support from members of the Auburn Avenue leadership, Rufus Clement of the Atlanta Board of Education, and some 250 black ministers from the state capital who endorsed Callaway on the same basis as the DFC.[53] Just as significant, there was also support from some who had opposed abandoning massive resistance in 1961 but who now considered Maddox undesirable. Most prominent among these was Charles Bloch.[54]

Within days of Maddox's nomination, the DFC took its case to the public. One memo to supporters called for an emphasis on Callaway's ability to maintain law and order and stressed how important it was to reach out to black voters by noting Callaway's opposition to violence by racist whites. This was a particularly interesting argument, insofar as emphasizing law and order is often seen as a coded appeal to white voters' fear of black violence, yet here it was being deployed as an appeal to white *and* black voters' fears of *white* violence. The argument that Maddox was a threat to order was also the central pitch of John Sibley during a speech he gave on October 24. Sibley praised Vandiver for having desegregated Georgia's schools "within the bounds of the law and not in defiance of the law, to the lasting welfare of all the people in the state." Sibley's focus on law and order was also evident in his criticism of Maddox for his ax-handle protest. Sibley argued that prior to the 1964 Civil Rights Act's passage, Maddox would have been justified, but once it became law, "they [blacks] were within their rights and entitled to be served." Robert Heard also stressed themes of order and economic progress on the eve of the election, arguing it was "in the state's interests to give Bo Callaway a mandate for law and order, responsible government and peaceful conditions for progress."[55]

Ostensibly, the DFC existed only for the purpose of contesting the 1966 election. For all its intentional transience, however, the DFC's brief appearance on the political scene was significant, though this was due more to what its existence revealed than what the group actually achieved. Above all, it cast doubt on the ability of a Georgia Democrat to attract much support by seeking to outflank his or her Republican opponent on the right. That many business leaders were involved in the DFC, as well as conservative political heavyweights such as Charles Bloch, suggested that in a choice between two right-wingers, many people who were racially conservative were no longer attracted by the candidate vowing the greatest resistance to racial change. Given the Republican Party's greater ability to claim the conservative mantle on nonracial issues, the clear preference of many prominent conservatives for Callaway over Maddox did not bode well for attempts to maintain the Georgia Democratic Party as the more conservative political option.

If the DFC presented Maddox as a threat to order and growth, then the WIG campaign portrayed him as a threat to progressive politics. Reluctant to support a conservative Republican, grassroots Loyalists were understandably drawn to the idea of working for a candidate they could represent as one of their own. The impetus for such an effort gained considerable momentum following the decision by Helen Bullard and two of her friends, Charlotte Smith and Betty Platt, to call an exploratory meeting to discuss the possibility of a write-in campaign to oppose Maddox.[56] Five hundred people attended the meeting, far more than the venue could hold. Encouraged by this high turnout, a steering committee was appointed to find a candidate to support. Several names were considered, including Talmadge, George T. Smith, Arnall, and Carter. It soon became clear that persuading anyone to accept the status of a write-in candidate was going to be extremely difficult. Smith and Carter said that they would repudiate any effort to campaign on their behalf; Talmadge was considered unlikely to agree; and eventually Arnall was chosen as the candidate, almost by default.[57]

Around this time, two men who would play a major role in the development of the Georgia Democratic Party over the coming years joined WIG: E. T. "Al" Kehrer, the Southern Region civil rights director of the American Federation of Labor–Congress of Industrial Organizations (AFL-CIO); and Rev. John B. Morris, an Episcopal priest from Atlanta who had been actively involved in attempts to desegregate Episcopal schools in the city. Kehrer and Morris became the campaign managers for the organization and immediately made it clear that they had long-term ambitions for WIG beyond the 1966 election. In particular, they hoped to pursue two key priorities. First, WIG was unapologetic, though not uncritical, in its support of the national Democratic Party and accordingly worked for the development of a state party that was firmly Loyalist. Second, WIG hoped that the Georgia Democratic Party would thereby become an instrument for implementing progressive politics in contrast to a conservative Republican Party.

Kehrer stressed the first of these two themes in a memo to WIG activists shortly after the group was founded. In it, he warned that 1966 would not be the end of the story, and that the "radical right" Democrats that Maddox represented would still be in charge of the state party machinery whatever happened. Therefore opposition to Maddox must continue beyond the election, otherwise "the resulting vacuum could very well have disastrous results for the Democratic Party and the future of our State." Morris made clear his fears over a "polished" Goldwater conservatism becoming dominant in the state in the absence of a progressive Democratic Party. Without a more liberal political vision as opposition, Morris argued, such conservatism "will be more difficult" to erase from Georgia. Civil rights activist Hosea Williams also joined WIG and tried to rally black support for the write-in away from the claims of Rufus Clement and other black leaders involved in the DFC. Eventually, Williams was able to get the Georgia Voters League and the Georgia Association of Democratic Clubs, the two largest black voter organizations in the state, to endorse WIG during the last week of the campaign.[58]

Although there was considerable enthusiasm among WIG activists, the group did face a genuine problem in being unable to persuade key Loyalist leaders to join their efforts. Even those who were rumored to be unenthusiastic about Maddox's candidacy, such as Jimmy Carter, would not bolt the party. Charles Weltner, much to WIG activists' frustration, described their campaign as a "lost cause."[59] Governor Sanders, whose distaste for Maddox was widely reported, also refused to align himself with WIG, responding to Morris's call for him to support the effort to combat Maddox with the explanation that "I am a loyal Democrat and will give my support to the Democratic nominee in the coming election."[60] Even Arnall distanced himself from the effort on his behalf, though there is evidence that he was not displeased at its existence. In correspondence with Morris, he noted that "many good Georgians" would be unhappy over the choice of Maddox or Callaway, but said he could not be an official candidate of any sort.[61] In fact, there was a lot of pressure on Arnall to publicly repudiate WIG, something Arnall refused to do.[62] As such, while WIG activists may have hoped that Arnall would lend his open support to their efforts, he performed a considerable service simply by keeping quiet. An open repudiation would almost certainly have crippled the movement.

As was the case with the DFC, WIG found itself in a highly unusual position. From the outset, WIG justified its existence on the basis that Maddox did not represent all Democrats in Georgia, and yet its primary objective was to prevent a Callaway victory. What was more, the group's core base of support consisted of Loyalists, yet its chosen method of advancing the Loyalist cause was to seek the defeat of the legitimately selected nominee of the state party. Unlike the DFC, WIG could hold out no hope of direct electoral success. Like their DFC counterparts, however, WIG members saw themselves as belonging to an organization pursuing a cause that would be continued beyond election day. It was only in the context of being part of a longer-term struggle over the direction of the state Democratic Party and Georgia politics that the motivation of WIG's activists makes sense. Seen in this light, the contribution of WIG to Georgia politics, seemingly only marginal in terms of the votes it attracted at the ballot box, was that it built on and extended the ideas of an earlier generation of Loyalists and set in motion the backlash against Maddox that would limit the degree of control he would be able to exercise over the state party.

As fate would have it, the activities of WIG, allied with a quirk in Georgia's electoral system, did deny victory to Bo Callaway, which the Arnall supporters had hoped it would. Overall, however, 1966 was not a good year for Loyalists. Between them, Callaway and Maddox each attracted around 47 percent of the popular vote, with Callaway holding a small lead. Maddox, as was to be expected, ran well in those parts of the state where Regular Democrats had always run well, though again, the behavior of north Georgia was notable. In what was an unusual enough development in itself, Maddox actually lost support in the other three regions of the state between the runoff and the general election—in total, he received around 17,000 fewer votes from urban, south Georgia, and Black Belt counties against Callaway than he had against Arnall. In north Georgia, however, he *gained* around 26,000 votes.

From the Republican perspective, the comparison with Goldwater in 1964, as illustrated in figures 9 and 10, also provided ambiguous lessons for the future. Even though Callaway had been a Regular Democrat who switched to the Republicans because of Goldwater's candidacy, he did best in traditionally Loyalist areas. In fact, Callaway *improved* on Goldwater's showing among the largest, fastest-growing, most-educated, and richest counties, while Republican support collapsed in the smaller, poorer, less-educated, and proportionately blackest counties.[63] Regionally, only urban Georgia gave a majority of its votes to both Callaway and Goldwater, but this was the part of the state that, since 1946, had been least receptive to white backlash politics. For the Georgia Republican Party, determining the political strategy that these results suggested would be most successful would prove to be no easy task. The alternating southern strategy and suburban strategy appeals that the party tried in the 1970s are a telling illustration of how difficult a question this was to resolve.[64]

As for WIG, it had succeeded in persuading around 50,000 people, or approximately 5.5 percent of the final tally, to mark their ballots for Arnall.[65] In the absence of any similar campaigns featuring such a write-in effort, it is hard to gage whether this was an impressive or a disappointing outcome. Given that the write-in votes generally came from areas where Callaway was stronger than Maddox, the overall effect of these votes for Arnall was most likely to prevent the Republican securing a majority. Under state law, this meant the election would be decided in the General Assembly, which, dominated as it was by Democrats, was universally expected to pick Maddox as the winner, and it duly did. As well as having Maddox as governor for four years, Loyalists also had to come to terms with losing Weltner and James MacKay's congressional seats to Republicans. Given the political views of the people who were elected in their stead along with Maddox, it is hard to disagree with Numan Bartley's

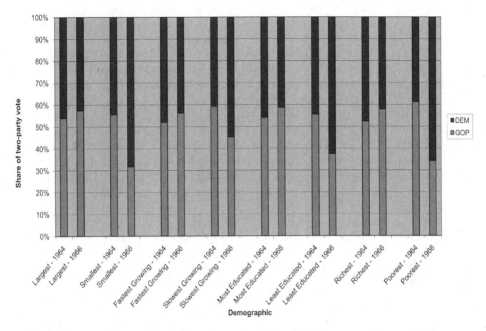

Figure 9. Republican and Democratic votes in 1964 and 1966 by county demographic.

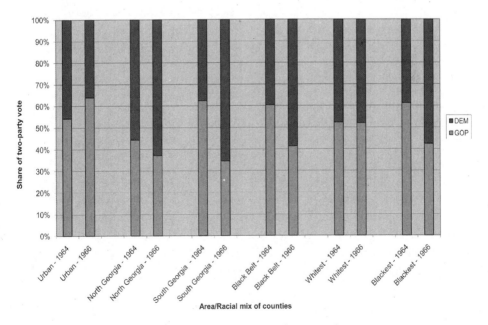

Figure 10. Republican and Democratic votes in 1964 by area and race.

assessment of Georgians in 1966 as having "challenged the rule of the moderates."[66]

Nonetheless, reading too concrete a set of sentiments into the actions of the Georgia electorate at this time is highly problematic. There was no inevitability about a Maddox victory in 1966, though given the political climate it was not as outlandish a prospect as many observers had initially thought. Still, but for a series of events that could have gone differently—Vandiver's heart attack and withdrawal from the race in May, Jimmy Carter's narrow failure to qualify for the runoff, and various twists and turns in the campaigns of Arnall, Callaway, and Maddox—Georgia might have ended up with any one of these men as governor in January 1967. Each would have left a very different judgment to be drawn about the state's mind-set if he had won. In this regard, the 1966 election truly was "the damndest mess" that Russell had described—a series of unpredictable events, colorful personalities, and freakish voting returns.

Amid the chaos, however, there was also clarity. There was no longer any possibility of denying the Republican Party's presence as a conservative political force in Georgia. As Maddox's attempt to outflank Callaway by appealing to segregationist sentiment showed, for the Democrats to adopt such a position was extremely hazardous to party unity. Moreover, despite all the twists and turns of the electoral cycle, the basic continuity of arguments about appropriate relations with the national Democratic Party and the level of accommodation to civil rights remained constant, and would continue to determine the evolution of the two-party system in Georgia. Finally, in placing at the head of the state Democratic Party a man who represented an attempt to reverse the direction the party had embarked on after 1961, the outcome of 1966 virtually guaranteed a showdown between Maddox and Loyalists over control of the state party. In fact, in light of the depressing electoral results they had just endured, the prospect of that showdown was one of the key things that kept Loyalists energized. As a result, for all the notoriety he has achieved, Lester Maddox represented an aberration in Georgia's political development rather than an indication of what was to come. The crucial backlash for Georgia was not the one that put Maddox in office, but the one that developed in response to his candidacy and would eventually end his political career.

6

The Loyalist Backlash

1966–1971

Are we the Democratic Party which has provided great leadership in bringing progress to the southern region; or are we to favor in Georgia the Dixiecrat faction which fought for white supremacy, the white primary, segregation and all that has blighted our region?

Rev. John B. Morris, 1968

There was at least one thing opponents and supporters of Lester Maddox could agree on: the sight of the "ax handle" taking the oath of office as governor of Georgia in January 1967 was confirmation of what an exceptional and unpredictable eight months of politics Georgia had been through. Additionally, most of those present at the inauguration would likely further have agreed that, love him or loathe him, at least Maddox's political views were a known quantity. As one voter told the *New York Times*'s Gene Roberts, "one thing about ol' Lester . . . you know where he stands."[1] In light of this, pro- and anti-Maddox Georgians were surely equally surprised to hear the new governor deliver an inaugural speech devoid of any of the white backlash rhetoric that had first catapulted him to notoriety and on which he had based his campaign. Instead, Maddox used his speech to call for moderation and reconciliation—neither of which were characteristics he was known for. Little wonder, then, that the *New York Times* chose to headline Roberts's report on the inauguration, "Will the Real Maddox Please Stand Up?"[2]

That Maddox's first day as governor should have produced this kind of surprise and confusion as to what his intentions in office were was nonetheless entirely appropriate. For one thing, it served as a reminder that Maddox remained a highly unpredictable individual, capable of making snap decisions and changing tack on an issue with little or no warning even to his aides and supporters. This made him a difficult person to work with. The unexpected nature of Maddox's inaugural also served as a powerful reminder that Georgia politics remained in a deeply unsettled state, even with the 1966 campaign over. Indeed, in many ways, the period after Maddox became governor was more disruptive to the Georgia Democratic Party than the election itself.

The source of the continued political instability was caused by more than just the quirks in Maddox's own personality. Equally important was the backlash against Maddox led by veterans of the 1966 write-in campaign. By early 1967, WIG activists had set up a new organization, the Georgia Democratic Forum (GDF), to continue their efforts to drive Maddox and his fellow Regulars out of the state Democratic Party. The GDF's leaders set about trying to undermine Maddox's position as head of the state party by offering themselves to the DNC as an alternative, loyal party organization for national Democrats to work with.

For the long run, the GDF set as its goals the final marginalization of Regulars in the state party, an acceptance and endorsement of the end of segregation, and the advancement of a broadly progressive agenda in the state—all goals that were logical extensions or echoes of familiar ambitions of Loyalist Democrats. More immediately, those in the GDF set themselves the challenge of unseating the delegation that Maddox would appoint to attend the 1968 Democratic National Convention in Chicago. That they were actually able to achieve this, albeit thanks in considerable part to Maddox's own actions at the convention, was a considerable accomplishment. On the other hand, that the unseating of the Maddox delegation came about in a manner that none of the GDF's founders could have predicted (or indeed, in many cases, would have wanted) meant it remained an ambiguous victory. Ultimately, the GDF's aims, successes, and setbacks were critical not just for the way they reflected and contributed to the political turbulence of the late 1960s but also because they set the stage for the emergence of the New South Democrats as the dominant force in Georgia politics.

Additionally, the GDF demonstrated how the core issues that Georgia's Democrats had been contesting since the end of World War II remained central to understanding the state's politics in the 1960s. Ideologically, the GDF represented the more liberal wing of the Loyalist faction, but its leaders were still well within the mainstream of Loyalist thought. Just as he had been during the WIG campaign of 1966, Ellis Arnall was the political leader closest to the GDF's collective heart, but the group was pragmatic enough to support and work with such establishment Loyalist figures as Carl Sanders and, eventually, Jimmy Carter. A further way in which the GDF represented continuity with what had come before was that the group used similar approaches and strategies as earlier pro-Loyalist activist groups, such as HOPE, the DeKalb County Democrats, or the GDF's own namesake from 1960, the Democratic Forum. Above all, the GDF shared with these earlier groups a desire to frame themselves as the forces of progress willing to adjust to the new reality, as opposed to the forces of backwardness and demagoguery represented by the Regular Democrats.

In what would prove to be a further indicator of the future, the GDF campaign against Maddox also found itself blindsided by a new and divisive political issue that would plague the Democratic Party for the next generation: the war in Vietnam. For the GDF, and for Loyalists generally, Vietnam presented a dilemma almost as great as civil rights. Foreign policy had not been a particularly divisive issue for the older generation of Loyalists in the 1940s. Most of them were veterans of World War II and firm believers in the values of American intervention abroad. They had embraced the core tenets of the "Cold War liberalism" that rejected the criticism of American foreign policy voiced by former vice president Henry Wallace in his 1948 presidential campaign. By the end of the 1960s, the progressive consensus on America's role in the world was crumbling, and a growing number of Loyalists, often from the postwar generation, were determined to prevent any Democrat who did not repudiate the Vietnam War from getting the presidential nomination. In 1968, this intra-Loyalist tension nearly derailed the effort to unseat Maddox. Ever since 1968, the shadow of Vietnam has both energized and haunted the Democratic Party at all levels of politics.

If Vietnam was an issue that plagued Democrats across the spectrum, the eventual fallout from the Chicago convention showdown within Georgia contained a particularly unfortunate irony for the GDF. The GDF played the leading role in challenging the Maddox delegation, and did so without any significant assistance from either the national party leadership or senior Loyalist leaders within the state. And yet after Maddox was unseated at Chicago and the Regular Democratic leadership was left in disarray, it was not the Loyalists of the GDF who reaped the benefits. Instead, the subsequent electoral cycle demonstrated once again the truth in politics of the adage that "he who wields the dagger rarely wins the crown," for while the GDF could take heart that the two leading candidates in the 1970 Democratic primary, Carl Sanders and Jimmy Carter, were Loyalists, both were from the more centrist wing of the Loyalist faction, and neither was willing to adopt as progressive an agenda as the GDF was advocating. From the GDF's perspective, New South Democrats such as Carter were infinitely preferable to Regulars such as Maddox, but while those in the GDF had helped create the conditions that made Carter's election possible, they had also hoped for more of their own agenda to be realized.

Nonetheless, despite these significant qualifications to the GDF's success at the 1968 convention and beyond, most Georgia Loyalists could still look back on 1966 from the vantage point of 1970 and be happy to have recovered the political initiative they had lost so abruptly four years previously. The 1970 Democratic primary was not just contested by two Loyalists, it was also contested by two candidates who both deployed the rhetoric of modernization and progressive color blindness. Not only that, but the ill-fated efforts by the Republican Party in 1970 to implement a southern strategy in order to win power across the South failed either to revive race as the central issue of southern election campaigns or to win many southern elections for GOP candidates.[3] Indeed, the Republican who attempted to succeed Maddox by following the dictums of the southern strategy did not even make it through his own party's primary, despite having been the heavy favorite when the campaign began. By 1970, the politics of the New South had arrived in Georgia.

"The Riddle of Lester Maddox"

When Bruce Galphin titled his 1968 profile of Georgia's governor "the riddle of Lester Maddox," the riddle he had in mind was Maddox's obvious and virulent racism coupled with his ability to work with African Americans once he was in office.[4] Such apparent contradictions in his racial attitudes certainly confirmed what a complex personality Maddox was, but this particular "riddle" was not unique to him. It was very common in Georgia politics, and indeed southern politics as a whole, for even diehard segregationists to evince either personal kindness toward individual African Americans or to employ them as part of their political machines. A more particular and more consequential "riddle" that Maddox presented was how his fellow Democrats, at the state or national level, should deal with him now that he was in the statehouse. This riddle was particularly vexing for the national party leadership and Loyalists in Georgia, who had to construct their response to Maddox by recognizing him as head of the state party, while knowing he had reached that position by casting them as "the enemy."

Those working for the national Democratic administration in Washington faced the more delicate judgment call. They needed to determine whether or how they were going to work with a man who had built his political image on opposition to national Democratic policies. This was no easy decision to make. In part, this was because those in the White House were unclear about what they hoped to achieve, but it was also because they had little direct knowledge of Maddox on which to base their goals. Prior to his election as governor, most White House aides knew Maddox only as a rabble-rouser who need not be taken seriously. When President Johnson's civil rights aide Lee White had dismissed Maddox as "bad news" in January 1966, he had suggested that any further correspondence from him be filed without reply.[5] In January 1967, however, the "bad news" held elected office as a Democratic governor and appeared to be putting out feelers of reconciliation to the Johnson White House.[6]

In order to establish what Maddox's intentions were, the White House relied on Joseph Bowman, a Georgian who was assistant to the secretary of the treasury. Soon after Maddox's inaugural, Bowman informed the White House that the governor was keen to set up a meeting with Lyndon Johnson. In Bowman's view, Maddox was seeking "to establish himself as a moderate liberal—rather than carrying the [George] Wallace-type label." In passing along Bowman's advice to White House Appointments Secretary Marvin Watson, Henry Wilson, Bowman's contact at the White House, nonetheless expressed skepticism over the governor's intention, noting there was a need to consider "how cautiously the President feels compelled to play with Maddox."[7] Despite Wilson's reservations, in the early months of 1967 the White House entertained a cautious optimism that differences with Maddox could be smoothed over. Two visits to the White House by Maddox in January and February 1967 seemed to provide some basis for continuing this hope. In the aftermath of his second visit, Maddox let it be known that the positive impressions he received had led him to cancel the idea of holding a "George Wallace Day" during Wallace's visit to address the Georgia General Assembly. At this point, Wallace was widely expected to run for the White House in 1968 on an anti-Johnson, white backlash ticket, and the White House was understandably keen to minimize Regular Democrats giving him any support.[8]

The high water mark of the efforts by the national party leadership to bring Maddox on board came in April 1967 with a visit to Georgia by Vice President Humphrey. Humphrey's report on the visit detailed the extent of the efforts undertaken to court Maddox. In his report, the vice president explained how he had made "a strong effort to convince [Maddox] that under all circumstances he should remain in the Democratic Party next year, and not bolt with [George] Wallace." In order to persuade Maddox of this, the vice president explained, "I told him that a Republican President would be just as tough on the [enforcement of school desegregation] 'guidelines.'" That Humphrey, a known civil rights supporter and advocate of vigorous enforcement of *Brown*, should be making this kind of appeal to a civil rights opponent such as Maddox speaks volumes for the seriousness with which the vice president was going about winning over the governor. Humphrey continued his pitch with an appeal to Maddox to be a "hero" by helping the Democrats carry the South in 1968. Humphrey described the visit's atmosphere as "courteous" and "hospitable," although he also noted that Maddox was an "unpredictable man." Finally, Humphrey recounted conversations he had with other Democrats in Georgia. Based on these, he claimed, "the general attitude on the part of liberal and moderate Georgians is one of watchful waiting, with some notes of very cautious optimism."[9]

With the benefit of hindsight, any sort of optimism regarding Maddox's desire to compromise with the national party leadership seems naive, but in the early months of 1967 it was easy to understand why Humphrey and others in the White House might have been deceived. This was the period of the so-called new Maddox when the governor appeared to have decided that he needed to reach out to Loyalists and the national leadership. As well as an inaugural address that was moderate in tone, Maddox met with groups of black legislators in Georgia and appointed several men as political aides who were known not to share his skepticism of civil rights and hostility toward the federal government. By the late summer, however, the veneer had slipped. Bruce Galphin pinpoints a speech Maddox gave on August 4, 1967, as the end of the "new Maddox." In it, Maddox returned to the rhetoric of the white backlash, denouncing Lyndon Johnson's "socialistic welfare schemes" and arguing that government collusion with Communism had helped spark riots in American cities. The moderates in his administration, appointed to such acclaim just six months earlier, began to leave in droves, feeling that they could restrain the governor no longer.[10] Also in August 1967, Maddox began to openly boost a Wallace presidential campaign, even suggesting that he would sign a third-party petition to get him on the ballot in Georgia.[11] Whether in direct response to these developments or for other reasons, the Johnson administration ceased its overt courtship of Maddox after this point, and his personal visits to the White House were discontinued.

The veterans of WIG were never as optimistic as the White House over Maddox's intentions. They had more experience of Maddox's rhetoric and also had less of a vested interest in seeking to "make" the governor loyal. Nonetheless, during the initial stages of the establishment of the GDF, their moves were also cautious, at times even conciliatory, toward Maddox and his supporters. Some of this was because the GDF hoped to get support from the national party and so did not want to be seen as troublemakers, but there was also a hope that stressing their willingness to cooperate with Maddox *in principle* might allow the GDF to broaden its base beyond the dedicated activists of WIG and to attract more establishment Loyalist figures who were sympathetic to GDF's goals but were loathe to openly split from the official state party.

Accordingly, in the weeks after it was formed the GDF began with at least a rhetorical commitment to supplementing, rather than supplanting, the state organization. John Morris, who, along with Al Kehrer, had taken the lead in establishing the GDF as a successor to the WIG campaign they had helped manage, emphasized the nonconfrontational outlook of the group in a letter he wrote to DNC chairman John Bailey in April 1967 informing Bailey of the GDF's founding. Morris described the GDF as an attempt to mobilize grassroots support for the national party and said he would be interested in discussing the status of such a group with the DNC. Pointing to sympathetic contacts with Georgia's national committeewoman Marjorie Thurman and Charles Weltner, Morris promised that the GDF would remain loyal to the Democratic ticket no matter what Maddox's position turned out to be.[12]

At the same time, Morris also wrote to Senators Russell and Talmadge as well as Governor Maddox, inviting them to address the meeting of the new grassroots organization, ostensibly as a sign that the GDF was open to everyone.[13] Predictably, none of the three agreed to attend. Just as predictably, for all of Morris's conciliatory language, news of the GDF's establishment brought immediate charges of disloyalty. Georgia's national committeeman William Trotter wrote to Morris accusing him of undermining the Democratic Party. In reply, Morris stated he was not attempting to create a third party and claimed instead that the GDF had two main goals, both of which were in the long-term interests of the party: to remove "Dixiecrat" (that is, Regular) influence from the state party and to mobilize at the grass roots to prevent Republicans taking over state politics.[14]

The GDF held its inaugural meeting in May 1967 in Macon, with some 300 delegates from twenty-three counties in attendance. Al Kehrer was elected chairman of the organization. Morris, who was selected to be on the executive committee, immediately wrote John Bailey an optimistic report of the event and passed on information about the meeting to George T. Smith, Carl Sanders, and Ellis Arnall.[15] Although they had not formally ruled out working with Maddox, there are several indications that by this time the GDF no longer considered it even a nominal possibility. In an invitation to Senator Robert Kennedy to address the founding meeting of the GDF, Morris mentioned the correspondence with Maddox, Talmadge, and Russell, but argued that they would hardly welcome a group seeking to "build a loyalist Democratic Party in contrast to the Dixiecrat-type tradition."[16] Morris's skepticism toward the prospects of cooperation with the governor was further hinted at in a letter to Joe Sports, Maddox's executive director of the state party. Morris asked Sports for promotional material for the GDF, including "Vote Democratic '68" stickers, which, he sardonically added, "I assume exist."[17]

For his part, Maddox made his attitude toward the GDF clear during the summer of 1967. Responding to comments by Lieutenant Governor Smith that it was time to start emphasizing the positives about the national party and pledge loyalty to it, Maddox declared that any Georgia Democrat expressing such praise for the national leadership was "either stupid or a fool or a coward or a traitor."[18] By the end of 1967, Maddox had made it clear that he saw the national party and its supporters in Georgia as his opponents. The national party and the GDF accordingly began to prepare themselves for what was now an inevitable flashpoint: the status of the delegation that Maddox would appoint to the 1968 Democratic National Convention. If the political maneuverings of 1967 between Maddox, the

Loyalists, and the White House had made one thing clear, it was that resolving this matter was unlikely to be straightforward.

Showdown in Chicago

Anyone assessing the chances of success for the GDF's challenge to the Georgia delegation at the Democratic National Convention, without the support of the national party, would surely have offered only long odds at best. In contrast to the substantial political resources available to the other principals most interested in the outcome, the White House and Maddox, the GDF could rely on little more than the enthusiasm of its members and the small, voluntary financial contributions it could attract from its core supporters. And yet the GDF prevailed. However, as is the case with many political victories, the GDF's success came at a price. Although the war in Vietnam was not an issue GDF leaders had either expected or wanted to address, its emergence during the summer of 1968 as a politically divisive force within the Loyalist coalition represented a powerful new fault line in the Democratic Party. As a result, although Loyalists entered the 1968 convention united in their opposition to Lester Maddox, there was no hiding that sharp divisions over Vietnam meant they also emerged from Chicago badly damaged by internal schisms.

At the start of 1968, such schisms were not yet apparent; indeed, it had not seemed that Vietnam would be a particularly problematic issue for the GDF to deal with. Rather, it was the continuing indifference and at times obstructionism of the national party leadership that was the biggest headache for Morris and Kehrer. Although the White House had by now given up on the hope of making Maddox a "team player" in time for the 1968 election, it had not given up hope of forestalling an endorsement by Maddox and Georgia Democratic leaders of George Wallace. Both the DNC and the White House also had two further reasons for seeking a working relationship with the Georgia leadership, even if not with Maddox directly. First, they did not want a repeat of the MFDP crisis of 1964 and hoped to ensure compliance with the nondiscrimination and party loyalty requirements for state delegations by negotiating with state party leaders rather than by coercing them. Second, once Lyndon Johnson dropped out of the race for the Democratic nomination in March 1968, the Democratic establishment, which now supported Humphrey to lead the ticket, hoped to get support from southern delegations to counter the backers of Senators Eugene McCarthy and Robert Kennedy, both of whom were running as opponents of the Vietnam War.

Accordingly, Humphrey supporters set out to find people they could work with in the Georgia state party. Two of the most promising were state party chairman James Gray, appointed by Maddox to the same post he had held under Ernest Vandiver, and Phil Campbell, the state's commissioner of agriculture. Both were senior political figures in Georgia, but both were also Regulars. The vice president met with Campbell and Gray during the spring of 1968, and it was widely believed that both were slated to run Humphrey's campaign in Georgia after the convention. An obvious corollary to working with Campbell and Gray was that Humphrey could have no part in aiding the efforts of the GDF to unseat the delegation that Gray and Campbell would be part of.[19] That Humphrey's decision not to work with the GDF was tactically adjusted to Georgia rather than a blanket policy across the South can be seen by the way that he gave his full backing to the attempt by grassroots Loyalists in Mississippi to unseat the Regular delegation in that state. Humphrey evidently considered Mississippi's Regular Democrats a lost cause, but he held out hope of cooperation from Georgia's leaders.

Humphrey's attempt to ally himself with senior Regulars in Georgia had significant consequences. Even though it was surely motivated by the desire to avoid internal dissent within the Democratic Party, it actually exacerbated tensions on two fronts: first, between Regulars in Georgia; and second, between the GDF and the DNC. Within the state party leadership, the prospective deal between Humphrey, Gray, and Campbell, essentially a nonaggression pact, caused a public rift between those willing to accept the vice president as the presidential nominee and those who wanted to throw their support to George Wallace. Chief among the latter group was the governor. At least one moment of tension between Maddox and Gray had already occurred in public before any official discussions between Gray and Humphrey had taken place. Gray told the press in late 1967 that the Georgia delegation would likely support whichever candidate was nominated. Maddox responded that this was "a lot of bull" and warned Gray and others to stop making pledges of loyalty to Lyndon Johnson.[20] The tension between party leaders was again highlighted by Lieutenant Governor Smith's intervention on Gray's behalf a few days later. Smith blamed irresponsible state party leaders for ruining the standing of the national Democratic Party in Georgia: "How in the world could this happen? Let's face it, we are responsible for it. We've been running against the national Democratic Party all along."[21] To Maddox's evident discomfort, Gray continued to make efforts to shore up support for the national ticket within the state party. In May 1968, the chairman went so far as to compel a member of the Cobb County Democratic Executive Committee to step down, as he was a pledged Wallace elector.[22]

As well as causing ructions between Gray and Maddox, Humphrey's actions also further frustrated the efforts of the GDF to gain national party support. While the formal decision to challenge the Georgia delegation was not made until the summer of 1968, it was quite clear that such a challenge was more than probable from farther back than that. It was equally clear that the national party did not welcome such a challenge. In December 1967, John Morris wrote to John Bailey asking for information about the rules a legitimate state delegation had to comply with in order to be seated at Chicago. This was clearly an attempt to establish on what grounds a Maddox-appointed delegation might be challenged. Morris's request was not acknowledged, and it took several more letters in January and February 1968 followed by a registered post mailing of all the correspondence over the three-month period before Bailey issued a perfunctory response in March.[23]

The foot-dragging, reluctant attitude of the national party leadership was also evident in the actions of New Jersey governor Richard Hughes. As chair of the Credentials Committee, Hughes was in charge of setting the rules for the 1968 convention. By January 1968 at the latest, Hughes had been told that there was a very good chance that a formal challenge to Georgia's delegation would be made.[24] Yet when in July the challenge was publicly declared, Hughes's initial response was to say that Maddox would not likely be unseated and that the Credentials Committee would only seriously consider challenges to state delegations from Alabama and Mississippi. Hughes's statement prompted an angry telegram to Hughes from John Morris and an open letter from University of Georgia professor Phinizy Spalding, who was helping to organize Eugene McCarthy's campaign in Georgia.[25] Within a few days, under pressure from civil rights groups and their supporters in the press, Hughes reversed himself. He subsequently claimed, somewhat unconvincingly, that his comments had been made before he had seen the paperwork on Georgia. Hughes said he had never wanted to suggest that a proper challenge would not be taken seriously.[26]

The presence of an intransigent governor and a lack of support from Humphrey and the national party generally made life substantially more difficult and frustrating for the GDF. This frustration was heightened by a sense among the GDF's organizers that they were being snubbed by the very people they were trying to help. As far as many Loyalists were concerned, attempting to work with Maddox and Gray—while understandably tempting as a temporary fix for the 1968 election—was not going to help create the party unity the national leadership hoped for. Instead, it would leave the Democratic Party in Georgia in tatters for the long term. Of particular concern to the GDF was the repeated habit among certain state party officials of working only for those Democrats in the state of whom they approved—a long-standing Loyalist complaint. In making their pitch to the national party for support, this was a theme that Morris, Kehrer, and those working for Senator McCarthy in Georgia stressed repeatedly. Morris told Governor Hughes that Maddox was almost certain to support George Wallace, and that the multiple Loyalist groups within the southern states were the ones who offered the best chance of turning back "Dixiecrat resurgence" in the South. Al Kehrer, in trying to get information out of Chairman Bailey, wrote in frustration at the willingness of the DNC to work with the Regular Georgia leadership, adding that the GDF would work for the 1968 ticket "even when titular heads of the Georgia Democratic Party have long since flown the coup [sic]." In the complaint against Hughes's initial dismissal of the Georgia Loyalists' challenge, Phinizy Spalding protested that "by pulling the rug out" from under the Loyalists, Hughes was presenting Wallace supporters with "the opportunity to take over completely the Democratic Party" in the state.[27]

Such Loyalist arguments had long-term political logic on their side. When given the choice between state organizations willing to work for the national party and state organizations whose support would always be in doubt, the choice was obvious. From the national party leadership's point of view, this logic should only have been strengthened by the clear positioning of the Republican Party as the more conservative of the two on social and economic issues. As the national Democratic Party became firmly more progressive than the GOP, it should have been natural for it to seek out local parties that were also more progressive in the political contexts of their respective states. These long-term forces, however, while clearly evident by 1968, counted for less than they might have in the face of the perceived short-term needs of Humphrey and the national party of avoiding an intraparty squabble at the Chicago convention. As such, the GDF had to formulate its challenge to Maddox without the help it had hoped for.

If the ambivalence of the national party was discouraging, Morris noted that similar efforts in other southern states encouraged the idea of a challenge. GDF leaders were in regular contact with Claude Ramsey, the AFL-CIO official in Mississippi who had tried to organize the Mississippi Democratic Conference for Loyalist Democrats in 1965, and with John Cashin of the National Democratic Party of Alabama, who sought to challenge the Wallace-backing members of the Regular delegation there.[28] While the efforts in all three states took different paths, they all shared similar motivations, and the GDF was keen to coordinate efforts across state lines.[29] Their correspondence shows that the GDF members were not the only ones who were disappointed at the lack of assistance from the national party. Even Ramsey, whose challenge Humphrey publicly supported, complained of a lack of interest from the DNC, remarking of Chairman Bailey's attitude, "apparently us little Democrats don't rate."[30]

As Morris and Kehrer continued to gather information about how to challenge a delegation's credentials, they identified two areas where the delegation likely to be chosen by Maddox might be vulnerable to a GDF complaint. The DNC's rules for selecting delegates included a demand that all delegates be "bona fide" Democrats who were willing to work for the party's best interests. Additionally, the process for choosing delegates was to be "representative" and should give rank-and-file Democrats in each state an opportunity to participate in the selection. The Convention Call concluded with the warning that if either of these conditions was violated by a state delegation, it would be recommended to the Credentials Committee that it "declare the seats [allocated to that state] to be vacant and fill those with a delegation broadly representative of the Democrats of that state."[31]

The slate Maddox was likely to choose was on shaky ground on both criteria. In terms of being "bona fide" Democrats, the GDF could point to the persistent disloyalty of those likely to be in the delegation, especially Maddox himself. As for being "representative," the process of selection in Georgia was in clear violation of the intention of the DNC. Under Rule 55 of the state party constitution, Georgia's delegation was selected by the state chairman with advice from the governor. The governor's input, while technically only "advice," was rarely ignored, so Georgia's representation at Chicago would essentially be chosen by just two men: Maddox and Gray.

The Georgia delegation was due to be announced at the beginning of July 1968. In June, the GDF established a steering committee to consider the logistics of a challenge. The steering committee's position paper on the challenge, prepared by John Morris, expressed confidence that on the question of being "representative," the GDF would have a strong case against Maddox's nominees. As for being "bona fide" Democrats, however, Morris anticipated (correctly) that the GDF could face a problem if Maddox and Gray named some people to the delegation whose track records of supporting national Democratic tickets were unquestionable. In this case, Morris warned, it might be necessary for the GDF to challenge specific members of the delegation, rather than the delegation as a whole—a far weaker position to take to the Credentials Committee.[32]

A few days later, Gray published his list of Georgia delegates. It did contain some well-known Loyalists, including Lieutenant Governor Smith and John Greer, the chairman of the independent Fulton County Democrats who had publicly supported WIG. It also included African Americans—containing more, in fact, than any previous Georgia delegation—some of whom, like William Randall of Macon, were known to be opposed to Maddox. Nonetheless, despite these concessions, the delegation was top-heavy with people who backed Goldwater in 1964 and contained many who had made supportive comments about Wallace in 1968. Carl Sanders was conspicuously absent, a decision that attracted scorn from some newspapers sympathetic to the Loyalists' aims.[33] Morris's warning that a slate containing some Loyalists might be offered had been prescient. Nonetheless, a further meeting of the GDF Executive Committee was held on July 6 at which the formal decision to proceed was made. On July 9, a memo was circulated to all GDF members announcing that the entire Georgia delegation would be challenged. DNC chairman Bailey was informed of the decision that same day.[34]

In his memo announcing the decision to proceed with the challenge, Morris also touched on a further difficulty facing the GDF: the need to broaden its base. Despite all its activism, in the early summer of 1968 the GDF could still only claim to speak directly for a small segment of Georgia's politically active population. Accordingly, it was announced that a statewide convention of "Loyal Democrats" would be held in Macon in order to select a strong and credible set of delegates to challenge the Regulars. The convention was declared open to all registered voters in Georgia who would pledge to support the national Democratic ticket in November.

During the meeting at Macon, the threat posed to the Loyalists' efforts by divisions over Vietnam became evident. While Humphrey had shunned any official contact with the GDF or other grassroots Loyalist groups in Georgia, one of his antiwar opponents for the Democratic nomination, Eugene McCarthy, took the opposite approach. Most of the GDF leadership were sympathetic to Humphrey, but were frustrated at the lack of support they were getting from him. By contrast, McCarthy supporters had active help from the senator's campaign staff in sending representatives to Macon and selecting a pro-McCarthy slate to challenge Maddox. To that end, two professors at the University of Georgia, Robert Griffiths and Phinizy Spalding, who were leaders of a pro-McCarthy, anti–Vietnam War organization in Clarke County, set out to mobilize their supporters to take control of the Macon meeting. While the GDF was mainly concerned with challenging the state party leadership, the McCarthy campaign was also interested in taking on the national party on the issue of the war.

Although it is too simplistic a categorization for describing the full nature of the underlying basis of Loyalist divisions over Vietnam, there was no doubt that on some level it represented a tension between the more politically pragmatic outlook of the original GDF members, who were willing to work within existing political structures wherever possible, and the more politically idealistic "New Politics" outlook of the McCarthy supporters, who considered many of these existing political structures to be responsible for all that was wrong with American politics. Such was the attitude, for instance, of Robert Griffiths, who was asked in June 1968 to serve on the GDF Executive Committee by Kehrer, but rejected taking part in the organization, calling it "pretty much of a jerry-built group, made up of Atlanta 'liberals' and a number of black politicians."[35] Griffiths was also critical of the willingness of the GDF to engage in old-fashioned political compromises rather than take clear, principled stands on the issues. Unlike the GDF, Griffiths said, McCarthy's supporters were "willing to endure minority party status—both in Georgia and in the nation—as a means of purging the Democratic Party of its more conservative elements."[36]

Their suspicion of "old" politics notwithstanding, both the national and local McCarthy campaigns were nonetheless aware of the potential political benefits of controlling the insurgent delegation being sent to Chicago. Joseph Rauh, a veteran of the MFDP struggle and now working as campaign manager for McCarthy, coordinated with Griffiths and Spalding and other pro-McCarthy figures to encourage a strong turnout at the Macon convention. In a mass mailing to McCarthy supporters in Georgia, the disarray in the pro-Humphrey ranks was seen as a great opportunity, which would allow McCarthy to come away with "at least 40%" of the delegates and give him an "excellent chance of taking half the seats."[37]

When the Loyalist gathering at Macon began on August 10, it soon became acrimonious. The McCarthy campaign had indeed turned out more people at the convention and had the votes on the floor to control it. After his suggestion of a sixty-to-forty delegation split in favor of Humphrey was rejected, Kehrer resigned as chairman of the convention, and several other GDF leaders walked out with him (John Morris did not). It was left to Savannah minister James Hooten to try and restore order. The convention chose a delegation with a majority of McCarthy supporters headed by Hooten and Julian Bond. It was made up of twenty-one African American delegates and twenty-one whites. The choice of Bond as head of the delegation was a sign of how far out of the political mainstream the Macon convention was willing to go. In the 1970s and 1980s, Bond would become a widely respected member of Georgia's Democratic leadership, but in 1968 it would have been hard to come up with a more controversial figure to head the delegation. At that stage, Bond was still primarily known for his public stance against the Vietnam War. Bitter memories (both from his supporters and opponents) of his resulting expulsion from the General Assembly during 1966 still lingered. The effect of his election as head of the Loyalist delegation in 1968 was that the choice being presented to the Credentials Committee in Chicago of a delegation headed by Maddox or one headed by Bond could not have been more stark, or less appealing, to either the national party leadership or the political establishment in Georgia.

What happened at Macon was therefore a further illustration of the political fluidity of the late 1960s. The Loyalist delegation chosen at Macon was by no means inevitably going to be a pro-McCarthy group dominated by the most liberal element of the Georgia Democratic Party. That it became such was due to indifference from Humphrey's campaign, intransigence on the part of Lester Maddox, and superior organization on behalf of the McCarthy supporters. A further twist to the events was then provided by the ultimate unpredictable factor—the personal whims of Lester Maddox. On August 17, four days before the Credentials Committee was due to hear the Georgia challenge, Maddox announced he was putting himself forward as an official candidate for the Democratic presidential nomination. This decision—made without consulting any of the delegates he had appointed—immediately shifted everyone's calculations. At a stroke, the existing Georgia delegation became useless to Humphrey as it was now certain to back Maddox at the convention. There was now little incentive for the vice president to pressure the Credentials Committee to defend the Regulars, especially as that would now mean explicitly defending Maddox. The entry of Maddox into the race also undercut Gray's negotiating position with Humphrey, as he was clearly no longer able to deliver the delegation to the vice president.

On August 21, the Credentials Committee heard testimony from the insurgents justifying their challenge. John Morris appealed once more to the DNC to help in the battle against "resurgent Dixiecrat racialism," which he argued was hurting the Democratic Party in Georgia. Morris concluded his argument by promising, "we [the Loyalist delegation] are unified in our intentions to support the nominees of this Convention: that is 100% more than Lester Maddox's group can say."[38] Julian Bond testified that Maddox discriminated against blacks within the party, 94 percent of whom, Bond pointed out, had voted for Lyndon Johnson in 1964.[39]

The Credentials Committee decided to split Georgia's seats between the Regulars and the Loyalists, giving each group twenty-one seats apiece. After a brief discussion within the Loyalist group, a list of twenty-one delegates was put forward. The compromise was not, however, acceptable to the Regular leadership, including Gray and Phil Campbell, who walked out of the convention claiming they had been betrayed. Back home in Georgia, Al Kehrer continued to protest the manner in which the GDF campaign had been (in his eyes) hijacked, while in Chicago, Julian Bond, the enfant terrible of Georgia politics, was formally nominated by a Wisconsin delegate for vice president, even though Bond was several years too young to be eligible for the nomination. It was therefore with considerable justification that John Morris could reflect on the events at Chicago and conclude that "once more Georgia politics had been turned upside down."[40]

From Chicago to Jimmy Carter

The events at Chicago had been fractious enough, but the fallout and its impact on the 1968 elections resulted in even more unhappy times for Loyalists in Georgia. Immediately after the convention, five long-serving Democratic officials, including former Humphrey ally Phil Campbell, announced they were switching to the Republican Party. Lester Maddox did indeed support George Wallace's campaign under the aegis of the American Independent Party, and Herman Talmadge, while able to defend his Senate seat against a token Republican challenge, did little to help Hubert Humphrey carry Georgia. The actual election returns were equally distressing from a Loyalist perspective. In the race for the presidency, George Wallace carried Georgia with a plurality of 42.8 percent, against 30.4 percent for Republican Richard Nixon and 26.8 percent for Humphrey (an all-time low for a Democratic presidential candidate in Georgia). The comeback attempts of James MacKay and Charles Weltner in the Fourth and Fifth Congressional districts, respectively, both failed. The joy at unseating Maddox at Chicago was soon replaced by concern at the electoral consequences, which seemingly verified Robert Griffith's worry after the convention that "we may have won the battle, I'm not so sure about the war."[41]

The breakdown of the Georgia returns from the 1968 presidential election showed why Griffiths was worried. There was no hiding the dismal level of support the national Democratic ticket received. In a decade where the state's population rose by close to 650,000 residents, and where in 1968 more than 500,000 additional Georgians went to the polls compared to 1960, Hubert Humphrey received nearly 125,000 fewer votes than John Kennedy had eight years previously. Aside from African American voters, Humphrey did not do well with any demographic or regional category in the state. His best showing was the 30.8 percent support he received from the state's urban counties and the 31.8 percent he attracted in counties with the highest proportion of black residents. In no other category or region did Humphrey register 30 percent of the vote, and in none of them did he finish ahead of both Nixon and Wallace. Perhaps the only hint—and it was the merest hint at that—of comforting news was that in some areas of the state where he and Nixon both trailed Wallace, Humphrey ran better than the Republican. Still, it was likely beyond even

Humphrey's legendary capacity for optimism to consider this as anything other than the thinnest sliver of a silver lining.[42]

While there was no hiding the bad news for Hubert Humphrey, the appropriate levels of joy and disappointment the other two candidates should feel was not so obvious. Nixon in particular could draw contrasting conclusions from the results in Georgia. On the plus side, he, like Barry Goldwater four years earlier, had outpolled his Democratic opponent, albeit by only around four percentage points compared to Goldwater's ten. Similarly, Nixon could be pleased that he led both Humphrey and Wallace among urban voters in Georgia, though his plurality was only 37.9 percent (more than ten points down from what he had achieved among urban voters in Georgia in 1960). Additionally, in psychological terms, Nixon and the Republicans could interpret the Wallace victory in Georgia as being rooted more in anti-Democrat sentiment than in hostility to the Republicans: such, at least, was the analysis put forward by Kevin Phillips in his widely read *The Emerging Republican Majority* just a year after the election.

Still, it was surely troubling for Georgia Republicans that they had been unable to hang on to the gains in presidential support for the GOP over the previous sixteen years. Nixon's 30.4 percent support was not only lower than Goldwater's, it was also lower than Nixon had managed in 1960; in fact, it was virtually identical to the showing by Eisenhower in 1952 (30.3 percent). Even beyond the headline numbers, the breakdown of the vote for Nixon and Eisenhower was also very similar; certainly it was far more similar than the comparison between the vote for Nixon in 1968 and Goldwater in 1964. The correlation between Republican voting by county in 1952 and 1968 was a significantly positive 0.54, while that between 1964 and 1968 was a mildly negative 0.243. The Nixon vote, in other words, represented the established base of Republicanism in postwar Georgia—large, urban and suburban, high-income, highly educated counties with proportionately high white populations. The presidential contest of 1968 suggested that this base had not changed or expanded all that much over the previous twenty years.

The 1968 General Assembly elections confirmed this impression. After the 1968 contests, Republicans still accounted for only seven state senators out of fifty-six, and only 28 members of the Georgia House out of 204. In the Senate, this actually represented a decline from the previous General

Assembly. Going into the 1968 elections, Republicans trailed Democrats forty-five to eight in the upper chamber, with one Independent. In 1968, the Republicans actually lost three seats to the Democrats—all in major cities (Savannah, Columbus, and Atlanta)—and while they picked up one seat from an Independent, and one more thanks to an expansion of the Senate from fifty-four to fifty-six members, they now trailed the Democrats by forty-nine to seven going into the 1969 legislative session. The picture was different in the House, where, despite the surprising loss of a House seat in Fannin County, Republicans picked up a total of five seats, leaving them trailing the Democrats by 173 to 28, with a handful of Independents also present.[43]

Common to both sets of results, however, were the areas of the state where Republicans did well. In total, 9 of Georgia's 159 counties were represented by at least one Republican in either the Senate or the House or both. Three of these counties (Dawson, Forsyth, and Hall) were jointly represented in a single district in the state house by a Republican, meaning that thirty-four of the thirty-five Republicans in the General Assembly were from six urban and suburban counties. These six counties were among the most populous in the state. They accounted for around 35 percent of all the votes cast in the 1968 presidential contest and had provided more than 45 percent of Nixon's total vote. The upshot of all this was that at the end of the 1960s, Republicanism in Georgia was still at its core an urban and suburban phenomenon. This would be born out time and again in statewide contests in the 1970s and 1980s, but it represented the basis of the strategic dilemma Georgia's Republicans would face in post–Jim Crow politics: namely, with a party based in the parts of the state that had generally favored economic modernization over racial traditionalism, just how far could the GOP afford to go in using the white backlash to add Wallace supporters to its base without alienating its suburban supporters?

These Wallace supporters had every reason to be pleased that their candidate had carried Georgia, yet they might also have reflected with some concern on the fact that their victory was less than total. Finishing twelve points ahead of Richard Nixon and nearly sixteen ahead of Hubert Humphrey was no mean feat, and Wallace had done so by tapping into the same white backlash vote as Lester Maddox had done two years previously. Yet Wallace, like Maddox, had not managed a majority of the popular vote. In a three-way race, 42.8 percent is an impressive result. Nonetheless, Wallace had attracted 2.5 percent less of the vote than

Lyndon Johnson managed when losing the state in 1964 and a full 12.5 percent less than Barry Goldwater had managed when winning it. Wallace's total also suggested that a comfortable majority of Georgia's voters were unconvinced of the appeal of undiluted white backlash politics and that there was also a sizable anti-Wallace vote. This was further indicated by the strongly negative correlation between Wallace's vote and that of both Nixon (-0.699) and Humphrey (-0.656), while the correlation between the two major party candidates was nonexistent (-0.04). A final troubling aspect of the results for Wallace's supporters was that while he had run up lopsided majorities in several demographic and regional categories, these were the least populated parts of Georgia, and their share of the total statewide vote was declining with every election cycle. Overall, while Wallace had the most to cheer about, his victory had come by way of a points decision rather than a knock-out.

In light of the 1968 results in Georgia, Robert Griffiths's concern that the Loyalist success at Chicago might prove fleeting was understandable. In truth, however, the convention represented a decisive momentum shift in favor of Loyalists within the Georgia Democratic Party, even if it took a few years for the scale of this shift to become clear. For one thing, the showdown in Chicago had helped move the national party toward a more proactive approach to marginalizing Regular influence in the southern state parties. In particular, the McGovern Commission, which was commissioned by the Chicago convention to review the selection procedures for state delegations, pushed for new party rules that would require state parties to create more open and inclusive structures and to engage in more loyal behavior. When the commission came to Georgia to hold hearings in 1969, Loyalists of all stripes, including Carl Sanders, Atlanta's mayor Ivan Allen, Julian Bond, and Al Kehrer, appeared before it to support the call for party reform. While these various witnesses disagreed over the scale of the reforms required, all agreed with the spirit of a rhetorical question put to the commission by John Gregg, a Democratic activist from Cobb County, "How can a strong Democratic Party be built while excluding those who hold the viewpoint of the national party?"[44]

The pressure to reform the party structure was also felt by the leadership within Georgia. At a meeting in February 1970 in Atlanta to discuss suitable procedures for selecting future delegations to national conventions, William Trotter and Marjorie Thurman agreed that a repeat of Chicago must be avoided. John Morris warned that if there was no "mandatory procedure" to allow the grass roots to take part in selecting the Georgia delegation, there would be no way to avoid another showdown.[45] Even James Gray was prepared to appoint a committee to recommend reforms to the delegate-selection process, although he evidently had little appetite for the project. When the committee reported a few months later, Gray rejected out of hand even the fairly modest proposals it made. Gray's actions led to accusations from the GDF that he was behaving in just the "dictatorial" fashion the national party had condemned. Kehrer warned that if Gray's actions were not reversed by 1972, there would be a further challenge to Georgia's delegation.[46]

It was against this background that the 1970 election season took place in Georgia. In a sign of the political momentum turning in favor of Georgia's Loyalists, there was no prominent Regular running in the Democratic gubernatorial primary. Instead, Jimmy Bentley, the comptroller general who had become a Republican in 1968, was the closest to a Regular candidate, and he was running in the GOP primary. Bentley was supposed to reap the benefits of the southern strategy that the national Republican leadership was urging GOP candidates to adopt in the South that year, but as it turned out, the most significant trend in 1970 was not a resurgent southern Republicanism, but rather the rise of the New South Democrat.

The man who would become the national embodiment of this New South Democrat, Jimmy Carter, was considered the underdog in his primary race against Carl Sanders. Carter's strategy in 1970 was controversial in terms of just how far he was willing to go to win white votes by appealing to race. At various times during the year, he went out of his way to express his admiration for Lester Maddox and at one point said that he would be proud to invite George Wallace, who was running his last race-baiting primary campaign in Alabama that same year, to speak at the state capitol.[47] By contrast, Sanders openly worked with the NAACP and the SCLC and made a pledge not to allow "Wallace-type" politics back into Georgia.[48] When photos appeared of Sanders having champagne poured over his head by an African American basketball player, this was interpreted by many as a "nudge-nudge, wink-wink" attempt to win racially conservative white support for Carter.[49]

Despite these racial undertones, it would be false to suggest that Carter was simply rehashing appeals to white solidarity from the days of massive resistance. While Carter did criticize some black leaders, whom he claimed traded money for votes, he was also careful to cultivate black support, and his appeal was based far more on populism than it was on race. This in turn reflected Carter's assessment that the best hope for Democrats in the two-party South was to compete for the votes of those who might otherwise be susceptible to a white backlash appeal without, as historian Randy Sanders put it, "calling direct attention to race."[50] As a result, whenever Carter praised Maddox or Wallace, it was never for their stand on resisting desegregation. Rather, he admired Maddox for his "compassion for the common man."[51] Carter also refused to endorse the resistance to the school desegregation rulings of 1969 and 1970 that Maddox and Wallace called for, and he repeatedly criticized Maddox's calls for schools to be closed rather than desegregated.[52]

Appeals by Carter to populism, rather than racial resentment, were much more obvious, not least in his dismissal of the well-dressed Sanders as "cuff-links Carl." Accusing Sanders of having been in the pocket of corporations and big business, and having personally profited from his time as governor, Carter promised to be "a Governor who will speak up for all of Georgia—not a powerful few; a Governor who will speak up for all of Georgia—not just those with selfish financial and political interests."[53] Such populist rhetoric became a staple of the Carter campaign. In August, he promised to be an equalizing force between the "haves and the have nots, the rich and poor, black and white." A few weeks later, Carter said black voters would not be a "bloc" this time, because unlike in previous races, there was no Griffin, Goldwater, or Maddox whom they would see as hostile to their interests.[54] In terms of his policy proposals, even though he disassociated himself from some of the "ultra-liberals" in his party, Carter was squarely in the New Deal, activist tradition of expanding government services to meet social needs. At various times during the campaign he advocated providing more money for public schools, providing extra funding for the education of mentally ill children, and using state funds to further environmental protection measures.[55]

Sanders ran far stronger than Carter among black voters, not just in the first primary when black candidate C. B. King also drew a large proportion of the black vote, but also in their subsequent runoff. Sanders also positioned himself as more overtly willing to advance black interests, including promises to appoint black members to the state boards of paroles and welfare.[56] While Sanders may therefore be considered to have had a more racially progressive image than Carter, on issues of substance there was little difference between him and Carter. Neither supported busing, neither supported defying federal court orders implementing school desegregation, and both supported the controversial measure introduced by IRS commissioner (and former Georgia Republican congressional candidate) Randolph Thrower to strip segregated private schools of their tax-exempt status.[57] Overall, neither said much about race at all, except to state a belief in the need for the equal treatment of all individuals. Overall, they both exemplified progressive color blindness, with Sanders a shade more liberal than Carter. The biggest difference between himself and Sanders, Carter argued, was that Sanders was a privileged, rich, perma-tanned attorney who was out of touch with ordinary people. In fact, references to Sanders's tan were perhaps the closest Carter came to making any direct pitch to Georgia's voters based on skin color.

The tone and result of the Democratic runoff were signs both of the never-to-be-reversed ascendancy of Loyalists within the state party and also what the contours of a successful New South coalition would look like for Georgia Democrats. By merging a largely de-racialized appeal to social traditionalism with a populist-tinged appeal for activist government, Carter demonstrated that a properly tailored Loyalist message could attract heavy support in traditionally Regular areas; by winning every demographic and regional category of counties against Sanders, Carter also showed this could be achieved without causing a party schism.[58] This New South Democratic coalition would be the basis both for maintaining Democratic majorities at the regional level for the next generation and for the successful campaign by Carter in 1976 that brought the New South to the White House.

In contrast to the contest between Carter and Sanders, the Republican primary between Jimmy Bentley and TV journalist Hal Suit contained far more obvious differences in attitudes on race. Bentley was considered by the GOP county chairmen to be a heavy favorite against the neophyte Suit at the start of the year.[59] Bentley ran as the southern strategy candidate, endorsed from Washington by Bo Callaway, who was now working on southern campaigns for the Nixon White House. Bentley's television ads focused on his opposition to busing, using images that were so menacing and racially charged that the *Atlanta Constitution*'s Bill Shipp sarcastically reassured the candidate after watching such an ad, "Don't worry, Jimmy, all good white folks know exactly what you mean in that television piece."[60] Bentley also gave public support to anti-integration "freedom of [school] choice" plans and launched a much-publicized "tell Nixon and Spiro to Stop [busing for racial balance]" campaign just days before the primary.[61]

In contrast, Suit, while never saying anything that openly welcomed school desegregation, refused to go along with Bentley's rhetoric and responded to questions on the issue by saying that the schools must be kept open and desegregation could not be reversed.[62] Like Carter and Sanders, Suit seemed to be going out of his way not to mention race at all, and when he did, like the Democrats, it was to stress his belief in equal rights for all without discussing what he meant by "equal," or, for that matter, "rights." From the outset of his campaign, Suit defined himself as "conservative—but liberal on the race issue."[63] The Suit-Bentley race was a good illustration of the tension within the Georgia Republican Party over whether to subscribe to the southern strategy or the suburban strategy. Additional tension was evident in the anger of several prominent Georgia Republicans at what they saw as a presumptuous endorsement of Bentley by national party leaders; Georgia Republican chairman Wiley Wadsen, Fletcher Thompson, and former party chairman G. Paul Jones all worked for Suit because of their resentment at the national leadership's attempts to impose a candidate on them.[64]

Suit's use of the suburban strategy was also apparent in his stance on cultural issues. As conservative as his economic views were, when it came to so-called red-button social issues, Suit's stances were fairly progressive. Suit favored legalized gambling and gun control, and opposed the death penalty. His socially progressive attitude even resulted in him having to give an interview denying that his lack of church membership made him an atheist.[65] None of this, however, prevented Suit from resoundingly defeating Bentley in the primary. Around 107,000 Republicans took part— barely one-eighth of the number of voters who voted in the Democratic runoff—and of those, nearly 63,000 chose Suit. Leaving aside the less than 5 percent of the ballots that went to a fringe candidate, Suit received 61 percent of the vote to Bentley's 39 percent. The breakdown of the primary vote was further affirmation of the continued urban and suburban nature of the GOP's base, and, within that base, of the importance to Georgia Republicanism of Atlanta and its environs. This was illustrated by the fact that Suit received more votes in Fulton, DeKalb, and Cobb counties— urban Atlanta and its largest suburbs—than Bentley received across the entire state. Had the contest been held without these three counties, Suit would have trailed Bentley. As it was, Fulton, DeKalb, and Cobb counties contributed 54.6 percent of the Republican primary electorate (compared to only 23.8 percent of voters in the Democratic runoff), and urban and suburban counties overall accounted for 74.6 percent, meaning his majorities in the state capital enabled Suit to win by a landslide.[66] That Suit not only won the Republican primary but did so handily, despite being not just the presumed underdog at the outset but also the very antithesis of what the southern strategy was supposed to produce, suggested that many Georgia Republicans were also keen to move beyond a political rhetoric fixated on racial appeals: they, too, were receptive to color-blind politics in 1970.

The general election contest between Carter and Suit was similarly noteworthy for the absence of any major appeals to the white backlash. Suit did go so far as to call mandatory desegregation "a social experiment that has failed," but went on in the same interview to say he did not want to turn back the clock and recognized that the appropriate "middle of the road" approach would require continuing efforts at desegregation.[67] Suit's main line of attack against Carter was that the Democrat was a tax-raising, free-spending "liberal in conservative clothing."[68] Carter, by contrast, set out his stall as a reform-minded Loyalist. At the state Democratic convention he endorsed allowing local parties to pick 75 percent of the state executive committee and called for a presidential preference primary for the 1972 election.[69] While Carter made no public effort to reach out to the GDF, he did win warm praise from Andrew Young, who had just become the first black candidate nominated for Congress by the Georgia Democratic Party since Reconstruction, and who defended Carter at the GDF annual convention as a man who "attracts people of all persuasions."[70]

On polling day, Carter cruised to an easy victory over Suit. Carter's coalition in the general election was similar to the one he had assembled against Sanders.[71] He led Suit in every region of the state, except urban and suburban Georgia, where he trailed the Republican 48.8 percent to 51.2 percent. As well as overwhelming majorities among low-income (79.3 percent), low-education (72.7 percent), and heavily black (77 percent) counties, Carter also won the largest (53.1 percent), richest (52 percent), most-educated (52.4 percent), and whitest (51.3 percent) counties. The only other category where Suit was ahead was in counties that had seen the largest rise in median income during the 1960s, where he led Carter by 51.1 percent to 48.9 percent. Carter's success also emphasized the danger of seeing the Wallace voters of 1968 as simply "Republicans in waiting." Instead, the Carter-Suit contest suggested they remained undecided in their overall loyalties. Those areas of Georgia that had gone for Wallace in 1968 went for Carter in 1970—the correlation coefficient of their votes by county was a strong 0.643. By contrast, the Republican vote did not change much relative to 1968; the correlation between Suit's and Nixon's support was an even higher 0.826.

Carter outpolled Suit by 59.3 percent to 40.7 percent—a margin of nearly 200,000 votes and a victory of sufficient magnitude to restore Democratic spirits after the turmoil of 1966 and 1968. For all the pleasure Loyalists could take from these various results, however, the 1970 election cycle did not leave the horizon entirely trouble-free. In a sign that the Regular faction still had some life left in it, Lester Maddox was elected as lieutenant governor over George T. Smith in the Democratic primary and then Republican state senator Frank Miller (of DeKalb) in November. Miller's description of Maddox as a "left-wing, free-spending liberal" who "consistently supported socialistic legislation" did not have sufficient credibility to deny the outgoing governor the state's second-highest office.[72]

Still, although many Loyalists, from Julian Bond to Melba Williams, would have preferred Carl Sanders to be governor, the Carter strategy and success were in many ways a vindication of the strategies these same Loyalists had been advocating throughout the previous decade. By contrast, 1970 was a bad year for Republicans in Georgia. Not only did their candidate lose the statehouse in a landslide, but the GOP also suffered a net loss of one seat in the state senate and six in the state house. As if to further cheer Loyalists, the five Democrats who had switched to the Republican Party after the 1968 convention were all out of office by the end of 1970, either through retirement or defeat at the polls. Their years of experience in office were not enough to survive the switch in party label, something that speaks against the idea that southern Republican growth was so slow at this time because they had insufficiently qualified candidates. In 1970, these five former Democrats could hardly have been more qualified, but they were of no assistance to the Republican Party in Georgia.

The election of Jimmy Carter did not by any means resolve all the instability in Georgia's politics that accompanied the rise of two-party politics. The one thing it did settle, however, was that the Democratic Party in Georgia would no longer oppose the core aims of the civil rights movement—equality before the law and the absence of overt racial discrimination—and in fact would embrace these values as its own. Carter's inaugural address in January 1971 could not have made this clearer. In comments that were reported as highly significant throughout the nation, the new governor told Georgians "quite frankly that the time for racial discrimination is over."[73] The importance of this statement was not lost on the listening journalists. An appropriate summary of the significance of what Carter said was offered by Bill Shipp, who noted that "in the era of the Talmadges and the Vandivers, Carter's speech would have been denounced as the talk of wild-eyed liberals or Communists or race-mixers or worse." In January 1971, however, Shipp concluded, "Carter's inaugural address sounded simply like the proper words at the proper time."[74]

7

The New South in State and Nation

1971–1976

I think the greatest thing that ever happened to the South was the passage of the Civil Rights Act.

Jimmy Carter, Democratic presidential nominee, 1976

Jimmy Carter's election as president in November 1976 is often dismissed as a post-Watergate blip in a period of conservative ascendancy—a victory that revealed more about the unique political atmosphere following the downfall of Richard Nixon than it did about the underlying political dynamics of the time. Indeed, several observers believed Carter owed his election largely to fortuitous circumstances and not to any particular qualifications or substance he possessed. As one anonymous critic put it, "any Democrat" could have won in 1976; Carter reaching the White House was simply proof that "any Democrat did."[1] Watergate was clearly a major boost to Democratic candidates during the 1974 and 1976 election cycles, and continuing resentment against Nixon's dishonesty was a major political tailwind for Carter's campaign. Nonetheless, while Carter definitely benefited from a sizable amount of good fortune, his election was also a demonstration of the strength and significance within Georgia, the South, and the nation as a whole of the New South political coalition that Loyalist Democrats had spent a generation seeking to establish.

During the 1970s, New South Democrats established themselves as the dominant political force within Georgia and in most of the South. They did so while advocating political priorities that were identical in spirit to those of the Loyalist Democrats in the 1940s. Like the Loyalists, New South Democrats promoted economic modernization, government activism, and racial moderation; like the Loyalists, New South Democrats used progressive color blindness to build a biracial coalition and to paint their Regular or Republican opponents as racial extremists; and like the

Loyalists, New South Democrats believed in limiting sectional tension within the national Democratic Party.

In electoral terms, the link between the two was more complicated. On the one hand, there were definite continuities: for instance, both Loyalists and New South Democrats in Georgia needed to attract supermajorities among black voters, and both relied on substantial support from heavily white rural counties in north Georgia in order to win. On the other hand, there were also important differences as a consequence of competition between Democrats and Republicans replacing contests within the Democratic Party as the primary dynamic in Georgia's elections. Whereas Loyalists in the 1940s and 1950s had won the support of high-income, highly educated, white urban and suburban voters, in the 1970s this was the most Republican group in the electorate. Whereas Loyalists had generally depended on majorities in Georgia's metropolitan areas and the northern part of the state to offset Regular majorities in south Georgia and the Black Belt, New South Democrats relied on majorities in urban and rural areas, particularly the Black Belt, to offset Republican strength in the suburbs. The replacement of the Loyalist-Regular division by the Democrat-Republican one had therefore reconfigured the primary electoral division in the state, but in a way that was consistent with established partisan voting patterns. Republicans had certainly grown in strength as Regular Democrats had declined, but the base of support for Republicanism in Georgia was demographically little changed in 1980 from what it had been in 1960. New South Democrats were fighting their electoral battles on a different front from their Loyalist forebears, but the rules of engagement were similar.

Several of the difficulties New South Democrats faced in holding their coalition together were also the same as those Loyalists faced for three decades. Marginalizing race as a political issue and not alienating voters torn between economic modernization and social traditionalism remained paramount concerns. Other difficulties were of a more recent genesis, such as the need to avoid being tagged as "soft" on national defense or too "permissive" on cultural issues. This was a direct result of the political fallout from the Vietnam War and the countercultural beliefs with which antiwar protestors were associated. New South Democrats also found themselves battling demographic trends that were increasing the state's suburban population and producing a wealthier, higher-educated electorate. This last development was more than a little ironic: Loyalists had long argued that more education and economic growth would produce a more progressive politics; now those parts of the state that were the wealthiest and most educated were the base of a conservative Republican Party.

Nonetheless, substantial as these challenges were, New South Democrats were largely successful in meeting them during the 1970s. Central to their success was their ability to dilute the effectiveness of white backlash politics at the state level. In particular, the southern strategy continued to be vulnerable to the political appeal of progressive color blindness. This did not mean that New South Democrats had been able to completely remove race as a factor in southern elections—far from it. Nor did it mean that white southern voters had necessarily developed a more sympathetic attitude toward the issue of black social and economic advancement. It did signify, however, that the majority of the electorate in post–Jim Crow Georgia did not want their political leaders focusing on fighting racially divisive battles and were often more interested in jobs, education, and economic growth. Racial prejudices had not been eliminated, but they had become far less central to southern voting behavior than had once been the case.

As a result of the New South Democrats' success in limiting the potency of racial appeals, Regular Democrats were successfully marginalized—either through retirement, through electoral defeat, or by changing their political alignment—and they became little more than occasional curiosities in the party. The Georgia Republican Party fared little better than the Regulars in combating the New South Democrats. It fell into disarray during the 1970s and remained a minority for long afterward. Politically, even though they were only occasionally able to deliver the state to Democratic candidates in presidential contests, New South Democrats dominated congressional, statewide, and state legislative elections in Georgia from 1970 to 2000.

Rather than seeing Jimmy Carter's election to the presidency in 1976 as an aberration, it is therefore better to see it as the national manifestation of a firmly established regional political coalition that would continue to influence both southern and national politics for many years after Carter left the White House. The rise and fall of Jimmy Carter represents in microcosm the possibilities and pitfalls facing southern Democrats in the wake of the civil rights movement. In 1976, Carter won both the Democratic nomination for president and the White House by appealing to black voters, endorsing the legacy of the civil rights movement, and expressing support for using government to advance economic and social progress. Four years later, Carter was defeated, having been successfully portrayed by Ronald Reagan as insufficiently tough, whether in terms of his handling of economic troubles at home or the series of crises he faced overseas. Thus began a long sequence of Democratic weakness at the presidential level in the South. By contrast, at the regional level, southern Democrats proved far more resilient and better able to resist the attacks that had defeated Carter in 1980. Whether in national or regional contests, however, it was not support for civil rights that was likely to result in Democrats being defeated at the ballot box. In fact, had New South Democrats failed to reach an accommodation with the civil rights movement and desegregation, their political prospects would surely have been far worse.

Resisting the White Backlash

Even before he put together his campaign for the White House, Jimmy Carter's activities as governor of Georgia placed him right at the heart of the New South Democrats' attempts to consolidate their position both within the South and within the national Democratic Party. From the beginning of his tenure in the statehouse, Carter sought to advance his brand of politics within the South and to reestablish the South as a constructive influence within the Democratic Party. Meeting both of these objectives meant navigating the tricky political waters of the white backlash. In order to gain national influence, Carter had to demonstrate he was not the kind of race-baiting southern governor who, personified by George Wallace, had dominated the popular perception of politicians from Dixie in the 1950s and 1960s. On the other hand, in order to maintain his position in the South, Carter could not afford to alienate those voters who were drawn to Wallace. They represented too large a slice of the southern electorate to be ignored. Given these two potentially contradictory imperatives and the need to attract both white and black voters to his side, it made sense for Carter to approach racially divisive issues in such a way as to generate as little tension as possible between his supporters.

There were several racially divisive issues Carter had to address that had significant potential either to create an internal split for his base in Georgia or to revive the sectional split within the national party. The most troublesome was busing. Nothing was a more emotive issue in Georgia politics in the early 1970s than the federal court orders requiring children to be bused across school districts in order to promote integration in public education.

Busing had risen to the top of the political agenda after the federal courts and the federal government stepped up the enforcement of school desegregation rulings in 1969. Georgia was warned that federal funding would be cut off for its schools if serious plans to achieve desegregation were not implemented. With "white flight" exacerbating residential segregation, federal court rulings began to make use of busing to circumvent attempts by municipal bodies to draw school districts along racial lines. It was clear that busing was unpopular with the majority of Georgians (and the overwhelming majority of white Georgians), and it had the clear potential to keep race at the center of the political debate. Carter needed to find a position that was sufficiently skeptical of busing without sounding like Lester Maddox and thereby jeopardizing his credibility on the national stage. This task was not made any easier by the determination of some in the state's Republican leadership to make opposition to busing their central campaign issue.

Carter's efforts to hedge on busing were evident in the way he criticized calls for open-ended boycotts of the public schools in response to busing orders, but also tacitly encouraged white parents to contest (by legal means) those same orders.[2] An illustrative instance of Carter's approach was at the start of the 1972 school year in Augusta, where white residents were unhappy at the busing plan the city was to adopt. Carter indicated he would support a proposed one-day boycott of the schools *as a last resort* if the General Assembly was unable to find a compromise first. At the same time, while critical of the Augusta busing plan, Carter praised the voluntary busing program adopted by Atlanta.[3] Overall, Carter took a "split the difference" position on busing: he criticized its social effects as damaging to low-income parents, but also stated his strong support for the principle of desegregation and openness to "voluntary" busing.[4] This ambivalent stance was evident as early as April 1971, when Carter instructed state attorney general Arthur Bolton to file suit asking for the "racial quotas" called for by the federal courts to be overturned in favor of unitary school systems. Such systems, the governor argued, would be sufficient to ensure the absence of racial discrimination.[5]

Carter's position on busing was further influenced by the need to take account of the actions of Georgia's Republican leadership and George

Wallace. During the summer of 1971, the GOP was preparing the ground for a campaign to capture one of the state's U.S. Senate seats the following year. Prospective candidate Fletcher Thompson and state party chairman Bob Shaw set out to appeal to the white backlash by attacking the Nixon administration's insistence on antidiscrimination measures in public housing projects.[6] Attacks by both Thompson and Shaw on busing soon followed, though unlike Carter, the Republicans made little effort to distinguish their appeals against busing from the legacy of opposition to civil rights. As part of his preparations for a Senate campaign, Thompson launched a statewide speaking tour in September 1971 in which he promised to make opposition to busing and racial quotas in jobs and housing his number one theme. In case the association with the past was missed by his audience, his campaign car blared out a rendition of "Dixie" before and after his speech.[7]

Meanwhile, George Wallace used the 1971 Southern Governors Conference in Miami to call for the South to unite behind an antibusing policy that was barely distinguishable from Thompson's. In response, Carter and Winfield Dunn, the Republican governor of Tennessee, drew up a proposed statement that spoke up for the need to end segregation in education, but criticized busing as a poor way to do this (in the usual color-blind fashion, they did not suggest an alternative method).[8] So long as opposition to busing was coming primarily from conservative Republicans and Democrats such as Wallace, Carter was careful not to align too closely with it. By the 1972 Democratic primary season, however, when national party figures with otherwise strong civil rights credentials—such as Hubert Humphrey or U.S. senator Henry Jackson—began to express skepticism about busing, it was clear that it was no longer just, or even predominantly, a southern issue. As a result, Carter could express reservations about busing without sacrificing his credibility as a national figure.

George Wallace proved to be a more delicate problem. Clearly, Wallace still appealed to a significant portion of the white electorate in the South that considered itself Democratic. Conversely, he was viewed by the national party leadership to be at best a troublemaker and at worst an apostate. If Carter wanted to present himself as the bridge between the South and the national party, he had to take care not to become too closely associated with Wallace; if he wanted to establish himself as a regional spokesman within the South, he could not get too distant from Wallace's base. Unsurprisingly, then, Carter's relationship with Wallace had some difficult moments, and Carter frequently sent out mixed signals to the public as to how similar he and Wallace were in their outlook.

Early in his term, there was already speculation that Carter might be considered a potential vice presidential candidate for 1972. Flushed with their successes in 1970, New South Democrats were keen to stress their progressive credentials as a way to establish their standing with the national party. As Bill Shipp noted with a hint of disbelief in March 1971, "the piney woods of the South are suddenly filled with liberally orientated political leaders."[9] Shipp clearly had Carter in mind within this category. It was an image Carter embraced with his warm welcome of DNC chairman Lawrence O'Brien a few weeks later and his joint statement with fellow New South Democratic governors Reuben Askew (of Florida), Dale Bumpers (of Arkansas), and John West (of South Carolina), that "we can no longer berate the federal government, the Supreme Court and other outsiders for our problems."[10]

Lest this be construed as a direct challenge to Wallace, the Alabama governor was quick to point out that none of those now being hailed as New South leaders had dared to criticize him during their election campaigns. Wallace also reminded reporters that he was still waiting for Carter to live up to his election promise to invite Wallace to speak to Georgia's General Assembly.[11] Wallace further let it be known that he was gearing up for another run at the presidency in 1972, that he still considered himself the voice of the white South, and that he intended to tap into the national hostility to busing to transcend the regional limits on his political appeal.[12]

Carter was publicly ambivalent as to whether he favored a Wallace candidacy. On some occasions, he praised Wallace as being a man capable of ensuring there would be a Democratic nominee who could compete in the South.[13] At other times, Carter claimed he would welcome Wallace running either as an independent or a Democrat, though he stopped short of saying he wanted Wallace to win as either.[14] Just as often, however, Carter and his allies in the state party would reject the notion that Wallace should be seen as a suitable leader for the South. Zell Miller, executive director of the state party, dismissed voting for Wallace as a futile dalliance with a political "pied piper" and argued that the way forward was for the South to follow Jimmy Carter's leadership.[15] When asked whether Wallace represented the "New South," Carter replied, eschewing any further elaboration, with a flat "no."[16] The symbolic height of Carter's ambivalence toward Wallace's candidacy was a moment during the 1972 Democratic presidential primaries when Carter, who was at that point seeking to block the nomination of George McGovern, allowed a Wallace supporter to pin a "Wallace '72" button on the governor's shirt in front of reporters, only to remove it before any photographers arrived.[17]

Carter clearly thought it was important to keep open his links to those who had voted for Wallace, but he also knew that he had to maintain close ties with efforts at party reform and with the black leadership in Georgia. Neither of these two groups would take well to Carter if they saw him simply as Wallace's political successor. At the state Democratic convention in 1970, Carter had voiced support for a democratization of party rules, but had been fairly vague as to specifics. In response, the GDF, which had been vocal on the issue at the convention, agreed to hold off on demanding details until after the general election, provided the group would be included in discussions afterward.[18] GDF chairman James Moore clearly remained suspicious of Carter's intentions, writing repeatedly to state party leaders to warn against any attempt "under the pretense of opening the party to the people, [to] actually perpetuate the old and outmoded system."[19]

Contrary to Moore's fears, however, Carter set about implementing most of the reforms the GDF had been advocating, including a major change to the delegate-selection process for the 1972 Democratic convention. In the spring of 1971, state party chairman Charles Kirbo held a series of meetings across Georgia with party activists to discuss reforming the state party structure. Carter subsequently announced that he wanted the power to choose the delegations for national conventions taken away from him, as the one chosen by Maddox in 1968 had left him feeling "remote" from the Democratic Party.[20] In November 1971, the state party executive committee announced its new method for choosing delegates, which involved forty being chosen at conventions open to all Democrats broken down by congressional district and a further thirteen delegates being chosen at-large at a statewide meeting.[21] That these changes, which Carter endorsed, were what the grassroots reformers had in mind was clear from Julian Bond's reaction. A few days after the new rules were announced, Bond described them as "like landing on the moon on the very first try" and "a 100% improvement over the old method."[22]

Carter's relationship with Georgia's black leadership was also a crucial part of shaping his New South image. Carter had lost the black vote to

Sanders in the 1970 primaries, but it did not take long after his victory in the general election before several black leaders made highly complimentary comments about him. Leroy Johnson spoke of the faith he had in the new governor, which was vindicated when Carter appointed several blacks to government agencies after consulting with Johnson.[23] While Carter seemed more comfortable working with the "establishment" black leadership of Johnson and Grace Towns Hamilton, he was also capable of dealing with the more politically controversial Julian Bond, as was shown by the compromise brokered between Carter and Bond at the 1972 Democratic convention over the delicate issue of who would be part of the final Georgia delegation.[24]

As well as boosting his standing with black voters by associating himself with respected figures in the black community, Carter also moved more and more toward openly aligning himself with the color-blind legacy of the civil rights movement. Early in Carter's term, Leroy Johnson had introduced a bill in the General Assembly to have Martin Luther King Jr.'s birthday declared an official holiday in Georgia. In order to aid the bill's passage, Johnson proposed making it a joint holiday also celebrating the life of Richard Russell, who died in February 1971.[25] The attempt to link Russell's and King's legacies together required the broadest possible definition of color blindness, but it did help Johnson advance the measure to the floor of the General Assembly, even if final passage was not achieved. By January 1973, Carter himself had taken up the cause, and declared that Georgia would henceforth commemorate King's birthday. Carter then publicly signed the official proclamation of the King Holiday in the presence of King's father and Congressman Andrew Young. The language of the proclamation was a perfect example of progressive color blindness, especially with its universalization of King's legacy as transcending any specific racial identity. The governor described King as:

> a man who placed the welfare of his fellow man above his own, and who assumed the burden of demanding of a country that it remedy the iniquities and discrepancies experienced by the black man *and the poor man of whatever color*. I urge the citizens of our state to join together in a tribute to this leader of men who was guided by his dream for a true democracy in which *not race or religion, but character and ability* are the measure and worth of a man [emphasis added].[26]

To further emphasize his association with King a year later, Carter personally oversaw the hanging of a portrait of the civil rights leader in the Georgia state capitol. As well as once more paying tribute to King's ideals, Carter joined with Secretary of State Ben Fortson and a large interracial crowd in singing "We Shall Overcome" on the capitol grounds.[27] By 1974, Carter had evidently come to the conclusion that whatever other associations with liberalism might be dangerous for a Democrat in the South, it was no longer a political liability to openly celebrate the civil rights movement. This was a development of no small significance.

It was furthermore a development that was also evident in the campaigns conducted by Democrats in Georgia in 1972 for the U.S. Senate and in the 1974 contest to succeed Carter as governor. In the senatorial contest of 1972, state representative Sam Nunn came through a bruising Democratic primary to face Fletcher Thompson in the general election. Both Thompson and Nunn claimed the label "conservative," but there were nonetheless clear differences in how the two candidates approached the issue of race. Thompson made no secret of his lack of interest in black votes. When his congressional district was redrawn after the 1970 census so that the black share of the vote rose from 38 percent to 40 percent, Thompson announced he was giving up his district to run for the U.S. Senate, as his district had now become too black for him to win.[28] On the question of busing, Thompson sounded mightily close to the leaders of massive resistance with his call for a statewide boycott of the public schools until the federal courts backed down and rescinded their busing orders.[29]

The Thompson campaign should have been the perfect opportunity for the Republicans to crack the Democratic dominance of Georgia's congressional delegation. In many respects, the race could not have been more promising for the GOP. In total, there were ten Senate seats up for election among the eleven former Confederate states in 1972. Of these, three contained "Old South" Democratic incumbents first elected in the 1940s and able to swamp their Republican challengers with name recognition, seniority, and ideological track records that made portraying them as shills for the liberal wing of the national Democratic Party all but impossible. A further three seats contained Republican incumbents, all of whom were favored to win comfortable victories. Of the other four, one was occupied by a vulnerable Democrat, William Spong of Virginia, who had established a liberal voting record in the Senate and was still serving his first term. The remaining three—in Louisiana, North Carolina, and Georgia—were open seats and thus offered the best prospects, outside of Virginia, for Republican gains.

The lack of a strong incumbent was not Thompson's only advantage. Unlike in Louisiana, Republicans in Georgia were able to run a more experienced and recognized candidate than the Democrats.[30] Thompson had been a prominent figure in Georgia for half a decade, and as a three-term congressman easily outranked in political stature Nunn, a two-term state representative. Additionally, the Thompson campaign was able to raise more money than Nunn, overcoming the problem facing Republicans in the 1950s of running campaigns with insufficient funds. A survey of campaign expenditures conducted shortly before polling day showed the Republican outspending Nunn by $140,000.[31] Finally, Thompson benefited from having a popular incumbent president at the top of the GOP ticket. By contrast, Nunn was running alongside Democratic nominee George McGovern, who would pick up less than a quarter of Georgia's ballots.

The likely ramifications of all this for Georgia's Democrats were as clear as they were troubling. Above all, if Nunn was going to win, it was not going to be by any of the traditional structural advantages that Solid South–era Democrats had enjoyed.[32] Nunn could not simply smother his opponents in the manner that James Eastland, John McClellan, and John Sparkman would do that year in Mississippi, Arkansas, and Alabama, respectively. It was also clear that on race, as well as on almost every issue, Thompson was not going to be outflanked on the right. Nunn was going to have to run as a more progressive candidate than Thompson. Eventually, this became the modus operandi of southern Democrats as a whole (this did not mean that Nunn, or other New South Democrats, now needed to run *as liberals*; but it did mean that they needed to run as *relatively* more liberal than their GOP opponents).

While maintaining his distance from McGovern, Nunn portrayed himself as more favorable to labor interests and more willing to work with black leaders than Thompson. Nunn accused Thompson of running a racist campaign, pointing to the jokes the Republican made about the black support the Democrat was receiving.[33] Nunn, by contrast, said he was going to run a "dignified" campaign that was not going to rely on the racial identity of his supporters or his opponent to win.[34] Returning to this theme a few days later, as Thompson continued to point to the black leaders who were supporting his opponent, Nunn invoked the ethos of New South Democrats, declaring, "I'm not going to run a campaign that's going to divide black and white people in Georgia. That day is past."[35] In a further sign that Nunn was perceived as the more progressive of the two candidates, he was endorsed by the Georgia AFL-CIO two weeks before the election, a decision with which Nunn said he was "delighted."[36] It would be grossly inaccurate to characterize Nunn as running a liberal campaign. On most policy areas, his positions can fairly be described as conservative. There was no doubt, however, that on the issue of race, Nunn was following the progressively color-blind approach of a New South Democrat. On polling day he defeated Thompson by the comfortable margin of 635,970 votes (54 percent) to 542,331 (46 percent).

The breakdown of the vote (see figure 11) showed that while Thompson had improved on Suit's 1970 showing outside of the Republican metropolitan base, the basic pattern of the partisan split had not changed. Thompson, like Suit, carried the state's urban areas (with 50.5 percent of the vote compared to Suit's 51.2 percent). The majorities of both Republicans in the rapidly growing Atlanta suburbs (seven of the top ten fastest-growing counties in the state bordered Atlanta) were also very similar: a 33,000-vote edge for Suit, a 30,000-vote edge for Thompson.[37] In the rest of the state the similarities between 1970 and 1972 were likewise apparent. Nunn, like Carter, ran strongest in counties with lower levels of education, lower median income, and lower rates of income growth; the Black Belt and south Georgia provided both Nunn and Carter with their largest proportionate margins of victory; and both Democrats received more support in counties with high nonwhite populations than those with heavily white populations. Despite these broad similarities between the two elections, there were also indicators that Thompson's decision to pursue the southern strategy that Suit had eschewed made a difference. Statewide, Nunn polled around 5 percent below Carter's showing. In the Black Belt, however, Nunn ran 12 percent behind Carter; in south Georgia, he was 18 percent behind; and in the counties with the highest nonwhite population, he was a full 22 percent behind.

As it is highly unlikely, given Thompson's campaign message, that these changes can be accounted for by black voters switching to the GOP, they suggest that if the white backlash appeal resonated anywhere, it resonated with white voters in these counties. The continued ambiguity of the white backlash, however, is also evident from results elsewhere. Thompson

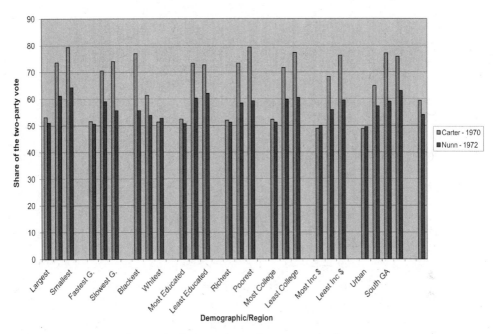

Figure 11. Democratic vote by demographic and region, 1970 and 1972.

improved on Suit's statewide total, but he actually *lost* ground in Georgia's whitest counties. Similarly, while securing a comparable margin of victory in the Atlanta suburbs, Thompson did not do as well in relative terms there as Suit had, even though, with the exception of DeKalb County, these counties were becoming whiter as the decade went on.

In short, while Thompson had expanded the Republican vote overall and done better than Suit in many traditionally Democratic areas, he had not won a majority in any of them, and he had either failed to improve on or actually done worse than Suit in areas where Republican strength was traditionally greatest. As such, Thompson's campaign was suggestive of the costs and benefits for Georgia's Republicans of pursuing the white backlash vote.[38]

Nunn's victory in 1972 showed how a southern strategy Republican candidacy could be successfully opposed in Georgia. Also important in demonstrating how the white backlash could be neutralized in the New South was the 1974 Democratic gubernatorial primary. In that contest, Lester Maddox took on a field of less well known opponents. Maddox's ultimate defeat turned out to have important consequences for national politics. In November 1972, Hamilton Jordan, chief of staff to Jimmy

Carter, wrote Carter a memo outlining plans to win the presidency in 1976. A key aspect of this plan was the marginalization of Maddox as a political figure in Georgia. Jordan argued that if Maddox were reelected in 1974, it would not only suggest that Carter's political clout within his home state was limited, but also, and more fundamentally, it would suggest that the New South image was ephemeral and that Carter had failed to mold a more progressive politics in the state. To emphasize the importance of Maddox's status, Jordan concluded, "I have serious doubts that your [presidential] candidacy would ever get off the ground if Lester Maddox is re-elected Governor."[39]

On the statewide level, the contest against Maddox would provide a good test of whether Georgia's Democratic electorate was now ready to accept the rapprochement with the ideals of the civil rights movement as Carter had defined them at his inaugural in 1971 and his pronouncement of the King Holiday in 1973. As Howell Raines, the political editor of the *Atlanta Constitution*, noted in July 1974, white Georgians still held negative views of blacks and continued to buy into several racial stereotypes. At the same time, they had recently shown themselves to be willing to vote for candidates endorsing equal rights and publicly celebrating support from black leaders. Raines concluded that the 1974 primaries would therefore "provide an interesting readout on the degree to which submerged white racism transfers into votes. A big Lester Maddox victory would indicate that the antiblack vote is not only alive, but lively as well."[40]

Maddox was the clear front-runner. It was widely expected that he would finish ahead of the field in the first primary, but, given the number of candidates on the ballot, it seemed likely a runoff would be necessary. The issue became whether the Maddox vote would be able to expand, or whether the other candidates' votes would transfer to whichever of his opponents made it through to the runoff. Three candidates were considered to have a good chance of challenging Maddox: Bert Lance, the head of the state Highway Department; former U.S. senator David Gambrell; and the majority leader in the state House of Representatives, George Busbee. When the votes were counted, Busbee had secured second place, with around 27 percent of the vote to Maddox's 37 percent. The contrast between the two men was so perfectly characteristic of the differences between the Solid South and the New South that it could have been a caricature. Maddox was flamboyant, unpredictable, and outspoken; Busbee was reserved, cautious, and not given to rhetorical flourishes. This difference was also what Busbee chose to highlight with his campaign's most famous slogan, which described him as "a workhorse, not a show horse."[41]

The difference in their attitudes toward the civil rights movement was also impossible to miss. Maddox said he personally favored segregation, though he did not call for its restoration by law. However, he did speak out forcefully against busing and affirmative action, declaring in his campaign opener that "we're fighting for freedom."[42] When it became clear that he would be facing Busbee in the runoff, Maddox immediately focused on Busbee's black support, alleging that it made the majority leader a suspect candidate. In particular, Maddox focused on Busbee's support from Julian Bond, declaring that from now on he would consider himself to be running against "the two B's—Busbee and Bond."[43]

By contrast, Busbee openly celebrated his black support, though he rarely addressed race as an issue and continually insisted that he was seeking the votes of no racial group in particular.[44] Busbee's own campaign began at a rally in Atlanta, where he was introduced by state representatives Grace Towns Hamilton and Ben Brown.[45] The association between Busbee and Julian Bond that Maddox was so keen to dwell on was a genuine one. Back in 1966, Busbee had been one of the few legislators to vote in favor of Bond being seated in the General Assembly, and Ben Brown later recalled that it was because of their joint awareness of Busbee's past record on race that he and Bond were so active in the 1974 campaign.[46] Days before the first primary, Busbee received and welcomed an endorsement by the NAACP's Political Action Committee.[47] Finally, during the runoff campaign, the Busbee campaign circulated a pamphlet with pictures of Maddox's famous 1964 ax-handle confrontation with civil rights activists, providing in a single photo a powerful image of the combination of recklessness and racism that New South Democrats promised to avoid.[48]

The Busbee campaign also received barely concealed help from Carter, which showed just how eager the governor was to ensure a Maddox defeat. Carter made a series of public pronouncements on Maddox's failings as lieutenant governor, variously accusing him of absenteeism, dereliction of duty, irrelevance, and misuse of state resources.[49] Clearly willing to twist the knife at every opportunity, Carter also weighed in with his thoughts after the first primary that Maddox's 37 percent was a "poor showing."[50] The utter ruthlessness of the Carter-Busbee forces in their attempts to discredit Maddox reached its apex in a dispute over a bill passed by the General Assembly in 1973 to raise politicians' salaries. At the time,

Maddox had opposed the bill vociferously while Busbee had been one of its chief sponsors. The pay raise had only passed the state senate because Maddox's supporters were outnumbered there. Yet during the 1974 campaign, Busbee, Carter, and the *Atlanta Constitution* all accused Maddox of having allowed the bill to pass on his watch as presiding officer in the state senate in order to get himself a pay raise.[51]

It is difficult not to feel a little for Maddox in terms of some of the things he was being accused of, but when Georgia's Democrats went to the polls for the runoff their verdict could hardly have been clearer. Maddox's forecast that he would win 55 to 60 percent of the vote was hugely optimistic; he managed only 40.2 percent to Busbee's 59.8 percent.[52] The results mirrored the long-standing demographic and regional divisions of earlier contests between Regulars and Loyalists, with Maddox either competitive or ahead in rural areas, small counties, low-income counties, and counties with less-educated populations, but trailing by large margins in urban areas and in high-income and highly educated counties. One difference with comparable contests from the previous decade—such as Marvin Griffin's similarly large loss to Carl Sanders in the 1962 primary—was noteworthy, for while Griffin had managed a similar share of the overall vote (40.4 percent) to Maddox's 1974 showing, he had done better in counties with large nonwhite populations, while Maddox was stronger in counties with larger white populations. This reversal can most plausibly be ascribed to the increased black voting in rural areas that followed the 1965 Voting Rights Act and voter registration drives in rural Georgia. Combined, these had helped push black voter registration in the state to just 3 percent below white voter registration by 1972.[53] Aside from that, little had changed in the basic composition of the factional split in Georgia's Democratic Party. However, unlike after 1962, there would be no subsequent revival of the Regular wing of the state party. Maddox's defeat in 1974 also marked the end of a cycle of four consecutive Democratic primaries in which former governors (two Regulars and two Loyalists) had suffered heavy defeats in their bids to return to office. By contrast, since 1974 four of Georgia's five governors—three New South Democrats and one Republican—have been successfully reelected to a second term.[54]

These long-term developments were of course not known to those commenting on the outcome of the 1974 race. Still, many observers were in agreement that the result represented a potentially crucial political moment. Numan Bartley wrote after the election that urban and small-town votes had outnumbered rural votes in a Democratic primary for the first time, and that this might lead to a reduction in the size of the "Wallace-Talmadge" constituency. Bartley remained skeptical, however, that it was a decisive victory, concluding that "the 1974 election may have been more fatal to the political career of Lester Maddox than to 'Maddox Country.'"[55]

Howell Raines was more optimistic, referring to Busbee's triumph as being a "black-white voter coalition so well put together that it produced a genuine landslide."[56] Busbee saw his victory as a vindication of color-blind politics, saying of racial politics as practiced by Maddox, "those days are gone, and I hope they never come back."[57] In the long run, Busbee's victory signaled the last gasp of Regular politics within the Georgia Democratic Party. After Maddox's defeat, it became all but unheard of for a major Democratic politician in the state not to openly seek the endorsements and votes of African Americans.[58] The manner in which Busbee won in 1974 became the blueprint for Georgia Democrats thereafter. To return again to the analysis of Howell Raines, "[Busbee] won with a true coalition, which may be Busbee's gift to Georgia's politics of the future."[59]

Maddox's defeat in 1974 was clearly a major victory for the New South agenda of Busbee, Carter, and their supporters. An added bonus was the simultaneous implosion of the Georgia Republican Party. How much of the GOP's woes could be attributed to Watergate is hard to estimate, but several local factors made it a very quiet year indeed for what Republican gubernatorial candidate Ronnie Thompson, the mayor of Macon, had termed the "silent conservative voice" that was waiting to sweep state Democrats out of power.[60] As it happened, Thompson was part of the problem. That he won the party's gubernatorial nomination despite a history of attacking the state party leadership, a hospitalization for mental illness, and a quixotic desire to keep running in both Republican and Democratic primaries was a strong indication of the disarray in Republican ranks. The day after winning his runoff by just 300 votes, Thompson called on state party chairman Bob Shaw to quit, saying he suspected Shaw of conspiring to prevent the state party from supporting his candidacy.[61] The national Republican leadership considered Thompson so poor a candidate that he was the only one of the party's gubernatorial nominees excluded from a campaign event with President Ford.[62] Once he actually began to campaign against Busbee, Thompson ran as an out-and-out southern strategist, seeking to tag Busbee as the "black candidate" and paint him as a hapless liberal. Like Maddox, Thompson played up

Busbee's connections to Julian Bond, and at one stage accused the Democrat of having "bought" the statewide black vote for $200,000.[63]

Nothing Thompson said made any dent in Busbee's lead, which may have been in part a reflection of the quality of candidate that Thompson was, but equally suggested once again that Republicans had still not found the right strategy to counter the New South Democrats' appeal. This was just as true for the lieutenant governor's race, which was between Democrat Zell Miller and Republican John Savage. Savage was an eminently more credible candidate than Thompson and also deployed a southern strategy. For instance, Savage repeatedly attacked Miller for having supported affirmative action. Miller responded by robustly defending his support of affirmative action. Having said of Savage that "his red neck is showing," Miller set out his position: "I'll talk about my philosophy. I believe in quality education for all persons regardless of color, and if it takes racial quotas to achieve that . . . then I favor them."[64]

On election day, both Miller and Busbee sailed to easy victories. Only in the whitest counties (36.6 percent), the counties with the fastest income growth (35.6 percent), the Atlanta suburbs (37.2 percent), and north Georgia (34.4 percent) did Thompson even manage to get above one-third of the vote (his overall statewide showing was a dismal 31 percent).[65] Democrats were also able to cheer the success of Elliot Levitas—a state legislator with close ties to the DeKalb County Democrats—in defeating four-term congressman Ben Blackburn in the Fourth Congressional District. The Georgia Republican Party had undergone a precipitous decline since the heady days of Bo Callaway's near triumph of 1966. In that year, Callaway attracted over 47 percent of the vote while outpolling Lester Maddox, and two Republican congressmen were elected from the state. In 1970, Hal Suit managed a passable 41 percent against Jimmy Carter, and Fletcher Thompson posted 46 percent against Sam Nunn two years later. In 1974, Ronnie Thompson managed just 31 percent, and the number of Georgia Republicans in Congress dropped back to zero. In the first-ever statewide Republican primary in 1970, more than 100,000 ballots were cast. By the time of the 1974 runoff, the number was down to 22,000.[66] This decline was in spite of the fact that their Democratic opponents were far less conservative in 1970, 1972, and 1974 than they had been in 1966. For a party that was expected to profit politically from the white backlash against the civil rights movement, things were not going according to plan. By contrast, Georgia's New South Democrats had every reason to be pleased with the greatly reduced ability of the politics of the white backlash to garner support for their opponents.

The Vietnam War and the Politics of "Values"

In his study of American liberalism after 1945, John Martin argued that as well as the changing demographics of the nation and the white backlash, two other crucial forces accounted for the decline of the national Democratic majority: "Vietnam and Nixon—so obvious that if one is not careful he will miss the guile of history."[67] Nixon's status as a partisan hate-figure, coupled with his post-Watergate image as a popular symbol for all that is corrupt in American political life, has ensured that whatever damage he may have done to liberalism as an ideology, he had an ambiguous legacy in terms of the political harm he did to the Democratic Party. At least for 1974 and 1976, Nixon was a valuable political asset for Democratic candidates to run against in their campaigns.

By contrast, the Vietnam War revealed a deep divide within the Democratic Party and had a lasting impact on the party's electoral prospects. The schism caused by Vietnam was especially potent, because it left Democrats open to criticism not just for being soft on Communism—this was, after all, not a new charge for conservatives to make—but also for favoring the socially unconventional attitudes of the counterculture that dominated the public image of antiwar protests. Such unorthodox values raised the hackles of social traditionalists, whether or not they approved of the war itself. As a result, Vietnam was about more than just the already divisive question of whether the United States should be fighting a war in Southeast Asia and on what terms it should try to withdraw; Vietnam was also a proxy for the tension between the counterculture and the "silent majority" over what might loosely be termed "American values." Actual support for the war was often a secondary issue. Someone as socially traditionalist as Lester Maddox could make statements saying the war was a mistake and yet still align himself against the values of the antiwar demonstrations.

As far as Maddox and other conservatives were concerned, antiwar protestors were attacking American patriotism. In 1971, the trial of Lieutenant William Calley, who was in charge of the unit responsible for the My Lai massacre, proved to be a flashpoint on this very issue. Shortly after Calley was given a life sentence by a military court for his role at My Lai, southern conservatives such as Wallace, Maddox, and Mississippi governor John Bell Williams held "Rallies for Calley."[68] At these rallies, Calley's conviction was framed as a victory for anti-Americanism, and campaigns were launched to overturn it. Ronnie Thompson went so far as to suggest that as well as being pardoned, Calley should receive the Congressional Medal of Honor for doing "what he was told to do" at My Lai.[69]

The uproar over Calley was symbolic of a wider phenomenon that had begun in the late 1960s. It became a staple of political rhetoric to equate criticizing the war or proposing to cut defense programs as evidence of disloyalty to the nation and a threat to American morality. Even Democrats used this charge against each other. When Ernest Vandiver prepared to challenge U.S. senator David Gambrell in the 1972 Democratic primary, he used Gambrell's alleged "softness" on national defense as his primary line of attack.[70] In June 1971, Vandiver criticized Gambrell for voting against the Supersonic Transport plane, calling this a vote against national security. Rather than cutting defense spending, Vandiver argued, "I believe our people want a return to old-fashioned common sense and old-fashioned patriotism."[71] Vandiver returned to this rhetoric time and again prior to the August 1972 primary.

Carter was evidently troubled by the issue of Vietnam becoming the defining aspect of the 1972 elections given its potential for splitting the Democratic Party. In what was widely interpreted as an attempt to oppose the candidacies of Democratic senators Edmund Muskie and George McGovern, Carter took a resolution to a meeting of his fellow Democratic governors asking that the war not be used as a campaign issue against Richard Nixon.[72] Nixon, by contrast, had already decided that attacking Democrats as unpatriotic would convince white, male southern voters of the Democrats' general weakness (and unmanliness?), which in turn would help them forget the pressure being applied by the Republican administration on school desegregation.[73] Even George Wallace, whose national profile in the 1960s had been due to his stance on civil rights, declared that for his 1972 campaign, national defense was going to be his number one issue with which to attack "liberals."[74]

Carter's attempts to keep Vietnam out of the 1972 election campaign were likely doomed to failure in any case, but likelihood became certainty with McGovern's success in securing the Democratic nomination. McGovern represented the nightmare scenario for New South Democrats precisely because of his commitments to cut defense spending, his criticisms of the military that were accompanied by offers of leniency to those who dodged the draft, and his alleged endorsement of the counter-culture that some of his supporters embodied. This image of McGovern was summarized by the quip that his platform was "acid, amnesty, and abortion." McGovern's strong support for desegregation was also a liability for white southerners, but it would be far too simplistic to attribute his catastrophic showing in the region to this alone. Either Henry Jackson or Hubert Humphrey, who both had considerably more support from southern state party leaders than McGovern, would surely have done better. And yet despite their criticisms of busing, both of these two were strongly identified with the civil rights movement. Carter's own presidential campaigns, the 1980 defeat as much as the 1976 victory, served only to underscore the openness with which southern Democrats could now speak of their support for desegregation. By contrast, McGovern's defeat illustrated the damage that supporting defense cuts and "alternative" cultural lifestyles could do to a politician's popularity among white southerners.

The attempts by Georgia Democrats to distance themselves from McGovern began even before he won the nomination. During the 1972 senatorial primary between Gambrell, Vandiver, and Nunn, none of the three candidates could repudiate McGovern strongly enough. The primary campaign consisted almost entirely of a Dutch auction over who was least like McGovern. Nunn and Vandiver barely devoted any rhetoric to attacking each other, so the contest effectively became the two challengers versus Gambrell. Nunn accused Gambrell of hiring McGovern campaign staffers to work for him in Georgia.[75] Vandiver used the fact that Gambrell and McGovern had both opposed the Supersonic Transport plane to describe the two as "political bedfellows," who wanted not "merely to change the America we know. They want and mean to destroy it."[76] That Gambrell himself described McGovern as a man who had "chosen to maintain his political identity with the intolerant minority who advocated forced school busing for other people's children and who established their political image by kicking the South in the teeth" was not seen by Gambrell's opponents as any reason not to link the two together.[77]

The debate over busing during the primary marked the high point of farce in the campaign. In February 1972, the U.S. Senate had passed a strongly worded antibusing resolution by forty-three to forty, with both Gambrell and Herman Talmadge voting in favor of the motion. On another occasion, Gambrell had voted against a measure designed to curb busing, arguing that it did not go far enough. On these grounds, Nunn accused Gambrell of sharing the probusing views of Edward Kennedy of Massachusetts and Jacob Javits of New York.[78] Once again, it did not seem to matter to Nunn that Gambrell had made opposition to busing the central theme of his rhetoric for over a year. At one point, Gambrell had even tied his votes against busing to a boilerplate, conservative, populist critique of social permissiveness, denouncing busing as a policy that led to the "common man" having "his children . . . bused while the snobs send their children to private schools . . . and on top of all that, the smut peddlers, dope peddlers and rapists are set free on his children by courts that he has paid for."[79]

After Gambrell failed to win a clear majority of votes in the first primary, he was defeated in the runoff by Sam Nunn, who continued to put distance between himself and McGovern. The correct level of distance to hold from McGovern was also a delicate issue for Jimmy Carter, who by this time had national ambitions. Prior to the Democratic National Convention, Carter was part of a "stop McGovern" movement, but once this proved unsuccessful, Carter could not repudiate the national ticket without sacrificing his own reputation for party loyalty. Accordingly, shortly after returning from the Democratic convention, Carter took the only option open to him—he pledged to vote the straight Democratic ticket in November, but would "focus" on congressional and local races; that is, he would not campaign for McGovern.[80] In explaining his stance, Carter made no secret of the fact that he disagreed with most of McGovern's platform (he singled out national defense as a particular concern). Zell Miller also said he would vote for McGovern, but not because he agreed with him. Rather, he did not think four more years of Nixon was something to be "stomached."[81]

Animosity toward McGovern among Democratic leaders in the South was certainly high, but there was also animosity toward McGovern among sections of the Democratic Party across the country that was rooted in similar concerns: the fear that McGovern embodied a radical agenda that focused on cultural issues and ignored "bread and butter" economic concerns while evoking a defeatist image in foreign policy. In this dynamic, southern Democrats found themselves in the unfamiliar position of siding with the party's establishment faction instead of being that establishment's primary cause for concern. The combination of economic boosterism, progressive color blindness, and hawkish foreign policy views that

New South Democrats espoused dovetailed very well with the beliefs of many of the national party's leadership—including Hubert Humphrey, who was McGovern's most dogged challenger in the 1972 primaries. As Bruce Miroff recounts in his analysis of the 1972 election, Humphrey tore into McGovern during a televised debate for proposing to "cut into the very muscle of our national defense" and referred to McGovern's welfare policy as requiring an "unbelievable burden" for American taxpayers.[82] This line of attack was hard to distinguish from the one Nixon would use against McGovern in the fall.

The 1972 campaign produced a countermovement within the Democratic Party ready to blame McGovern's "radicalism" for the electoral landslide he suffered. Four prominent Democrats—Humphrey, Muskie, Jackson, and Shirley Chisholm—appeared together on *Meet the Press* just before the Democratic convention to declare that McGovern would produce an electoral disaster.[83] When such disaster duly materialized, they saw it as confirmation of their warnings (and did not, apparently, see their own public evisceration of McGovern as having played much of a role). The upshot of this was a post-1972 effort to ensure a candidate more to the liking of these anti-McGovern Democrats, many of whom found themselves drawn to the idea—all but unthinkable prior to the late 1960s—of backing a "southern favorite son". as the nominee for 1976.[84]

This is not to say that there was a determination that the next candidate had to be from the South; however, many New South Democrats had precisely the political characteristics that anti-McGovern Democrats believed were necessary for success. Perhaps the most critical of these was that New South Democrats had shown themselves capable of successfully resisting the lines of attack from Republicans on "values" to which McGovern had been subjected. In Georgia, for instance, Republicans had tried to use the issue of "values" against Sam Nunn in 1972 and George Busbee in 1974, but with little success.

Given the image that Nunn had built up during the primary with his denouncements of McGovern for his platform, it was not easy for Fletcher Thompson to attack Nunn directly on values. Instead, the Republican turned his focus on antiwar demonstrators, whom he accused of lacking patriotism and embracing radical social ideas. These demonstrators, Thompson suggested, were likely to support Nunn. On more than one occasion, Thompson advocated putting the actress Jane Fonda on trial for treason following her well-publicized visit to North Vietnam. He evidently hoped this would peel away supporters from Nunn.[85] Similarly, in 1974, as his gubernatorial campaign failed to gain any traction on the issue of race, Ronnie Thompson tried to paint George Busbee as too socially permissive. Just days before the general election, Thompson let rip with the accusation that Busbee would be a "liberalized Governor with way-out plans to enact liberalized abortion laws. I don't think the working people want to be bound into a union in order to work and support their families as Busbee-ism dictates."[86] In neither campaign did these charges prove effective.

Overall, New South Democrats were generally better at deflecting such Republican criticisms because they genuinely were more traditionalist than their nonsouthern colleagues on social issues and more hawkish on national defense. This "tougher" stance on matters related to social issues and defense was evident in the voting behavior of southern Democrats in Congress. As Stanley Berard has noted in his survey of congressional Democrats from 1970 to 1998, while the differences between the voting behavior of southern and nonsouthern Democrats were diminishing on racial issues in the 1970s, and on welfare, education, and the budget in the 1980s, regional differences within the party remained stark on foreign affairs, defense, and social issues well into the 1990s.[87] In short, the fact that so many New South Democrats were *not* seen as dovish and permissive made them a central part of the coalition within the national party that wanted to insulate itself against the kind of attacks that had been so effective in 1972.

At the state level, the political contests in Georgia during the early 1970s contained lessons and warnings for both parties about the politics of values in the New South. For the Republicans, it was clear that while it was often easy to portray national Democrats as antimilitary and socially permissive, it was much harder to do this against New South Democrats. For the GOP in Georgia, neither racial nor cultural conservatism was by itself enough to win the supermajority of southern white voters on which Republican success depended. Yet while New South Democrats could take heart from these developments, they had to be on notice of the threat posed to their position should they ever become perceived as "weak" on national defense or "soft" on "social issues" in the way that several national Democrats were.[88] The potential for cultural and national security issues to divide southern and nonsouthern Democrats has remained powerful to this day—generally more powerful than differences on economic policy; certainly more powerful than the once ever-present sectional divide over race.

Projecting the New South onto the National Stage: The 1976 Carter Campaign

In his foreword to a biography of Helen Douglas Mankin written during the Reagan administration, Ellis Arnall assessed her significance in the context of national politics and concluded that "the conditions that led to Jimmy Carter's acceptance and election as an American president were conditions Helen Douglas Mankin played an important part in bringing about."[89] Arnall was understandably talking up his former protégé's impact. As critical as Mankin had been to the politics of 1940s Georgia, in a ranking of the factors that contributed to Carter's presidential success in 1976, her career would have been pretty far down the list. Still, there was some truth in what Arnall had to say. While the role of any one Loyalist Democrat from a generation earlier may not have amounted to much in terms of shaping the 1976 presidential election, the collective agenda that Mankin and others had advanced since the end of World War II was strikingly evident in Jimmy Carter's run for the White House. The continuing fallout from the Watergate scandal may have been the single biggest contributor to the national political mood in 1976, but Carter's campaign was also a powerful demonstration of the strength of the New South political coalition on the national stage.

From the moment he publicly declared his candidacy in December 1974, Carter centered his campaign rhetoric around themes that both Arnall and Mankin would have found very familiar. In working his way through the primaries to beat out several more high-profile Democrats for his party's nomination and then overcoming President Ford in the general election, Carter deployed the same strategies he and his fellow New South Democrats had successfully used to establish electoral majorities in Georgia and across the South over the previous six years. Finally, the manner in which Carter sought to finesse the internal tensions within the party—particularly over foreign policy and cultural issues—spoke to the central role New South Democrats would play in shaping the future of the Democratic Party over the next several decades.

Securing the nomination was Carter's first challenge. Though well-enough known within the party hierarchy due to some national media attention and his role as chairman of the Democrats' 1974 national campaign committee, Carter was not a well-known political figure for most voters. Famously, he was low-profile enough that none of the panelists recognized him during his December 1973 appearance on *What's My Line* (perhaps even more famously, he was low-profile enough that when he told his mother he was running for president, she responded "President of what?"). The lack of a national image was undoubtedly a challenge he had to overcome, but it also gave Carter a chance to shape his image in a way that would be advantageous to his campaign. A critical goal for Carter was to persuade voters outside the South that he was not another southerner in the mold of George Wallace; yet at the same time, as he was relying on southern support to win the nomination, Carter could not allow any distancing from Wallace to be perceived as a repudiation of the South.

Carter had already been walking a fine line in his personal relationship with Wallace during his term as governor, but Wallace was more popular in Georgia than he was in the nation, so Carter's room for maneuver was more restricted in the arena of national politics. The picture was further complicated by Carter having to compete with Wallace for votes in the Democratic primaries. Carter was warned by Hamilton Jordan as early as November 1972 that while "we should make every effort to court Wallace and gain his friendship and trust," it was likewise important that Carter be seen as "a better qualified and more responsible alternative."[90] Following Jordan's advice, Carter outpolled Wallace in early nonsouthern primaries and then edged him out by 34 to 31 percent in Florida. The Florida triumph was quickly followed by a decisive 54 to 35 percent victory over Wallace in North Carolina, which established Carter as the dominant candidate from the South. Even then, Jordan advised that Wallace be treated with "quiet respect," though it was just as important not to go overboard in regretting his withdrawal and thereby alienating black voters.[91] Carter was able to walk this line and secured Wallace's endorsement at the Democratic convention without (it seemed) giving offense to either black or labor leaders.

Still, dealing with Wallace the individual was only one part of the equation. Distancing himself from Wallace's racial legacy was far more important, and Carter's success in doing so was surely the most significant reason civil rights leaders were willing to support him despite Wallace's endorsement. In 1970, there had been legitimate questions over whether Carter was deploying implicit racial appeals in his campaign against

Sanders, but there was no doubt at all over Carter's strategy for 1976: talk up the achievements of the civil rights movement, praise desegregation, and associate himself as much as possible with improved race relations. The strategy was not executed flawlessly. There were some major stumbles, the most serious of which was Carter's comment endorsing the value of "ethnic purity" in American neighborhoods that were resisting government-backed "black intrusion." Following the understandable protests from civil rights leaders and other Democrats, a chastened Carter had to publicly apologize for a self-described "careless" and "very serious mistake."[92] For critics of Carter, moments such as these were a sign that his true feelings on race were a lot less enlightened than his public persona. They may be right, though only Carter himself can know for sure. Nonetheless, whatever his true feelings on the subject were, his campaign evidently saw it as a misstep, and it was clearly out of line with Carter's overall message on race, which remained rooted in the language of progressive color blindness.

Central to Carter's approach was linking economic and social progress in the South to a decline in racial tension. He also sought to place himself at the center of these developments, as he did in a speech to the Georgia Human Relations Council, where he spoke of how race relations had improved since the Maddox years now that state troopers were not routinely sent out to minor disturbances for the purpose of exacerbating racial tensions.[93] In September 1974, Carter spoke of his support for open housing legislation in Georgia and his opposition to creating racially exclusive housing tracts.[94] When the Voting Rights Act was up for renewal in Congress in 1975, Carter repeatedly made it clear that he supported extending this landmark legislation. Carter couched his endorsement in terms of the benefits it had provided to blacks *and* whites in the South by removing from office racial demagogues who had been a roadblock to southern progress.[95] This was a note he struck when he announced his candidacy for the presidency by declaring it his intention to resist those appealing to people's "fears and prejudices." It was also in line with his frequent declarations that Martin Luther King Jr. had "liberated whites" as well as blacks, because whites had also "been constrained for generations by the pre-occupations of the race issue."[96]

On the still delicate issue of busing, Carter's public position was that mandatory busing was bad, but the complaint was rooted in populism, not racism: "I've never seen a rich kid bused." Additionally, Carter, claimed, it was just as often black parents who told him "we don't want our kids bused anymore to a distant school." And yet while mandatory busing was bad, desegregated education was necessary for social and economic progress. Desegregation, Carter stated, was the "best thing that ever happened to the South in my lifetime." Carter's daughter, Amy, attended a school that was majority black, "and that's the way we like it." The best desegregation policy was voluntary busing where "any child who wants to be bused can be bused at public expense," but "no child is bused against the wishes of the child." As Carter noted, Atlanta had adopted such a plan in 1973 with the support of the federal courts, the local NAACP and SCLC, the white mayor (Sam Massell), and the black vice-mayor (Maynard Jackson). Carter supported it, too. Indeed, Carter suggested, it was time for northern cities to look to Atlanta's model as it was the only one likely to be accepted by "black and white citizens."[97]

From a political standpoint, taking this line was a way of appealing to white voters who were opposed to "forced busing" while also reassuring them that they need not think of their views as racist. At the same time, by talking up the value and significance of desegregation, and calling for black parents to be more involved in school board decisions so that they feel "this is my school system too, it's not just a white folks' school system that my kids have to go to," he was also consciously seeking black support for his busing position as well.[98] Maximizing black support remained central to the Carter strategy. Campaign memos from 1976 make it clear that the Carter team was relying on black support in critical primary contests. Senior aide Stu Eizenstat wrote Carter in March 1976 that with major northern states holding primaries, "the key to [our] victory may well hinge on the size of the black vote which we can turn out for our campaign." Eizenstat argued that Carter's performances in Massachusetts and Florida had shown he had the "inside track" to getting black support, and that if this could be held on to, it would "be a priceless asset which can and will turn close elections our way."[99] Through his endorsement of desegregation, his embrace of the civil rights movement, and his relationships with black leaders, Carter was able to secure this "priceless asset." His ability to win over black voters was critical not just in 1976 but also in his retention of the Democratic nomination in 1980 against the challenge of Edward Kennedy.[100]

His desire to minimize racial tension as a political issue was not the only continuity between Carter and the 1940s Loyalists. His views on the role of government and education were also little different from Ellis Arnall's. Like Arnall, Carter projected an image of fiscal conservatism and support for streamlining government. He boasted of his reorganization of state government that had cut the number of agencies from 300 to 22 (Carter even cited this during his *What's My Line?* appearance when asked about things he had done in his life). At the same time, also like Arnall, Carter stressed his support of activist government, particularly in the realms of education and economic growth. He did not want government to sit idly by; instead, he favored a "dynamic and creative government" that would identify and solve problems facing its citizens. In particular, while he was skeptical of budget deficits, he wanted more to be spent on schools. At various times throughout his campaign, Carter argued that federal spending on education "must be increased," that low-income school districts must be given "supplemental funds," and that Nixon's proposal to ax $174 million in funds for Georgia educational programs must be opposed. There was no bigger priority for government, Carter argued, than "ensuring a quality education for every child."[101] Overall, Carter characterized his agenda as being "about more efficient government, not necessarily smaller government."[102]

Carter's 1976 campaign also tried to bridge gaps within the Democratic Party as a whole. Carter's desire to be seen as a unifying figure within the party was symbolized by his appearance on the national convention stage with George McGovern and George Wallace—a sight that was incongruous enough even before the subsequent group rendition of "We Shall Overcome."[103] The biggest tensions Carter had to worry about were over foreign policy and cultural issues. In seeking to navigate each, Carter reflected the established Loyalist and New South Democrat concern not to alienate culturally traditionalist voters. In trying to hold his coalition together, Carter's approach was to present himself as cautious, but not soft in foreign policy, and traditional, but not reactionary on cultural questions.

Carter tapped into the feelings of the antiwar movement by suggesting that the overall defense budget be cut and by promising not to intervene militarily in other countries unless there was a direct threat to U.S. national security. In particular, Carter acknowledged an important feature of the antiwar movement's indictment of U.S. foreign policy when he accepted that the "attitude of concentrating our own emphasis in foreign policy on the [interests of] white-skinned people" was hurting America's standing in the world.[104] On the other hand, Carter also appealed to the feelings among many Americans that the antiwar movement had denigrated the military. In a speech to the American Legion, Carter spoke of his son Jack's military service in Vietnam as part of a proud family legacy. Yet when Jack returned from duty, "he and the uniform he wore were all too often greeted with scorn and derision" by people for whom "patriotism is out of fashion, or is an object of scorn or jokes." Carter's desire to move beyond the debate over Vietnam without alienating either side was best captured in his proposal to pardon those who dodged the draft. A pardon was preferable to an amnesty, he explained, because "amnesty means what you did is right. A pardon means that what you did—right or wrong—is forgiven." Additionally, a pardon would mean that "we can now agree to respect those differences [over Vietnam] and forget them."[105]

On cultural issues Carter followed a similar path of trying to soothe the fears of all sides. Most of the personal opinions he expressed were traditionalist, but they were almost always qualified by saying that he would not impose those views on others and would execute laws even if they conflicted with his personal values. So, for instance, he informed the National Abortion Rights League that he was "personally opposed" to abortion but he would respect *Roe v. Wade* and would not seek to overturn it via constitutional amendment.[106] On gun control, Carter referenced his own background as a hunter and stated his opposition to "proponents of extreme gun control," while also noting that he accepted the need for some regulations to prevent guns from falling into the hands of dangerous people.[107] Nonetheless, despite his middling stances on most cultural issues, the cultural image Carter presented was of a person with traditional cultural values. His faith was something he discussed openly and frequently; moral lessons passed on to him by his parents were often cited in his speeches; and it was not unusual to hear Carter speak of his concern for the stability of the American family, which he argued was under threat from a "loss of values" in American society.[108]

On November 2, Carter won a two-point victory over President Gerald Ford. While that victory may not have occurred without Watergate, Carter's reliance on support from southern states and the distribution of that support demonstrated both how pivotal the New South coalition was to his election as well as the depth of that coalition's roots.[109] In terms of his home state support, Carter's vote in 1976 (at the county level) had a 0.79 correlation with his gubernatorial election in 1970.[110] As figure 12

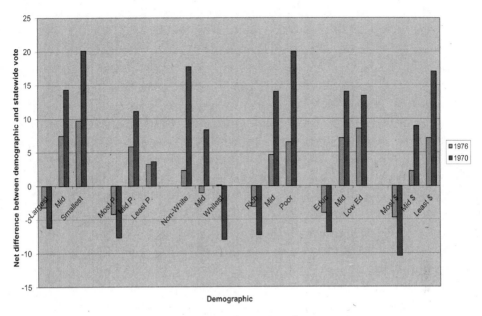

Figure 12. Carter vote by county demographic, 1970 and 1976.

illustrates, the relative edge that Carter held in various demographic categories followed essentially the same pattern in 1976 as in 1970 with one notable discrepancy: in 1970, Carter carried the state's whitest counties, but only barely, and by a smaller margin than he carried those counties with a more "mixed" racial composition. In 1976, his support in the whitest counties in Georgia was far in advance of his support among the more mixed counties, though not as high as it was in the least-white counties. In this regard, the 1976 presidential contest was something of an outlier: by 1980, the partisan pattern within the state of Republicans doing relatively well in the whitest parts of Georgia would be matched in the presidential contest. Still, Democrats at the state level would continue to win majorities among the whitest *rural* counties for several decades, even if those majorities were not as big as in less-white rural counties.

The pattern in Georgia was replicated across the South in 1976. Considering the eleven former Confederate states as a single unit, figure 13 illustrates how Carter's support rose across southern counties as the median income level dropped. Figure 14 illustrates how this was also true for the relationship with years of education completed, and figure 15 charts the level of Carter's support in relation to the proportion of white residents

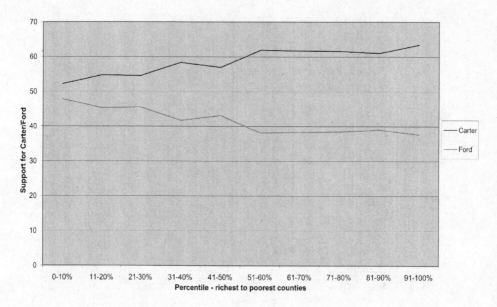

Figure 13. Southern support for Carter and Ford in 1976 by county median income.

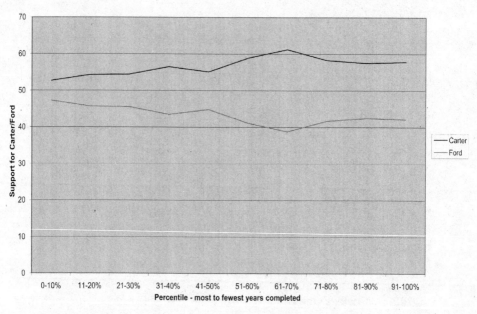

Figure 14. Southern support for Carter and Ford in 1976 by median years of education completed.

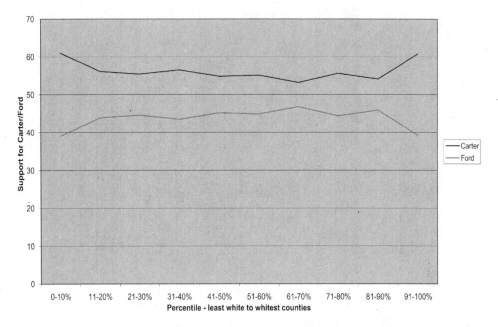

Figure 15. Southern support for Carter and Ford in 1976 by racial composition of county.

in a county. Across the South, Carter did better in the whitest and least-white counties. The overall picture is clear: the coalition that New South Democrats had developed in Georgia to defeat Republican challengers was the same one that delivered Carter a majority of the South's electoral college votes in 1976.

Carter's presidential campaign also spoke to two other significant features of party politics in the New South. First, Carter's victory confirmed that whatever racial prejudices southern voters still held, there was sufficient white support for a candidate openly associating with the leadership of the civil rights movement to sweep ten of the eleven southern states. This was the best performance in the region for any Democrat since Franklin Roosevelt. Furthermore, this occurred *after* Regular influence had been marginalized, so it is hard to believe that many of the southern whites who voted for Carter did so under the misapprehension that he was running as an opponent of civil rights.

Second, as illustrated by figure 16, despite all the political dramas of the previous decade, the election suggested that there was still a good

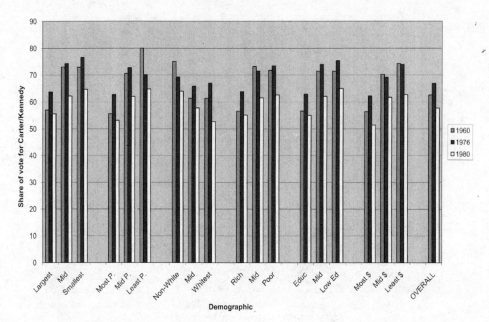

Figure 16. Democratic presidential vote by county demographic in Georgia, 1960, 1976, and 1980.

deal of continuity with the partisan divisions at the presidential level as they existed in 1960. In other words, in both 1976 and 1980, even though Carter won ten of the eleven southern states in the first case and only one in the second, the breakdown of the partisan voting still followed the basic pattern of 1960, which in turn had followed the basic patterns of Eisenhower's two campaigns in the 1950s. In each case, Republican support in Georgia was greatest in the high-income, fast-growing, well-educated counties, and Democratic support rose as median incomes, years of education, and population growth fell. Shafer and Johnston's calculations for the South as a whole also support this conclusion about the sources of Republican strength in the region as of 1980. Reagan was able to outpoll Carter in the South in 1980 by growing the coalition of voters that had voted for Richard Nixon twenty years earlier, rather than by tapping into the parts of the South that had backed Wallace in 1968, most of whom still preferred Carter.[111]

This is not to say that what happened in 1976 and 1980 was a return to the status quo ante. There had been significant changes since 1960, and there were ongoing changes in the relative bases of support for each party beyond 1980. For a start, while the aggregate and relative percentages of Democratic or Republican support may appear very similar in Georgia for 1980 and 1960, there had obviously been a big increase in black voters during that time, a large majority of whom were reliably Democratic in their voting behavior. In other words, the apparent stability in Democratic support over this period in the least-white counties in the state clearly masked a growing Republicanism among white voters being offset by the appearance of a compensating large growth in the number of new black Democratic voters. Nineteen eighty also showed the growing divergence between urban and suburban voting behavior in the state, a split that in 1960 had been relatively small. While Carter carried his home state by 57 to 43 percent in 1980, and won those counties that Numan Bartley had classified as "urban" for postwar Georgia by 55 to 45 percent, Carter's support was actually substantially split between the major metropolitan centers of the state, where he won 61 percent of the vote, and the ring of suburban counties around Atlanta, where he won only 48 percent.

Republican gains in the Atlanta suburbs were also the central factor in the defeat of Herman Talmadge that year. Outside of the Atlanta suburbs, Talmadge was ahead of his Republican challenger, Mack Mattingly, by approximately 110,000 votes with a relative advantage of approximately 10 percent. In the Atlanta suburbs, however, Talmadge was trounced 68 to 32 percent and nearly 140,000 votes. This resulted in a statewide edge for Mattingly of 51 to 49 percent and the election of Georgia's first Republican senator since the 1870s. Had Talmadge been able to improve his showing in the suburbs by just 3 percent, he would have been reelected.

In sum, while there had clearly been changes in the bases of both major parties in Georgia since 1960, the continuity was more striking. Developments since the Nixon-Kennedy contest suggested evolution rather than revolution. The Republican Party in Georgia remained, at its heart, a suburban party, as it had been since it began to grow in the 1950s. The Republican recipe for success in Georgia after the emergence of New South politics was to run up big margins in the suburbs to overcome Democratic majorities in the cities and in rural Georgia. The New South Democrats' success depended on staying competitive with the Republicans in suburban areas and maintaining sufficient margins of victory in the rest of the state to assemble a coalition of over 50 percent of the vote. In short, Democrats needed to replicate what Carter managed to do in 1980; Republicans would seek to emulate Mattingly. To this extent, the 1980 results were a good indicator of how each party would go about winning elections in the state over the next generation. Their only major flaw as a predictive indicator was that they got backward which party would do better at which level of election, for although Carter won Georgia in 1980, the following six Democratic presidential candidates were able to replicate this only once in the following seven elections. Similarly, however, while Mattingly picked up a statewide office for the GOP in 1980, not for another twenty years would Republican candidates be able to achieve consistent success at the state level. For both state and national elections, however, the partisan coalitions that shaped New South politics during the 1970s remained central to understanding the balance of power in Georgia into the twenty-first century.

Conclusion

He wished to Hell "Mother Hubbard" weren't so accurate. He wished to Hell
Darmon spit tobacco juice.

Flannery O'Connor, "The Barber"

The frustrations felt by the central character in Flannery O'Connor's short
story "The Barber" are surely familiar to any number of southern liberals
who have despaired over the years at their region's seemingly pathological
refusal to see their point of view. O'Connor's story takes place during an
election campaign in Georgia that bears a striking resemblance to the pivotal 1946 Democratic primary and revolves around the exchanges between
a small-town professor and his local barber. The barber is an enthusiastic
supporter of Hawkson, a candidate whose positions and passion-filled
rhetoric are reminiscent of Eugene Talmadge, while the professor, Rayber,
supports the more moderate, "rational" candidate, named Darmon. As
the discussions continue, the professor finds himself ever more annoyed
at the refusal of the barber to engage in a serious discussion of the issues.
Instead, the barber repeatedly refers to Darmon as "Mother Hubbard"
and dismisses him as an effete, long-winded "nigger-lover." Waxing lyrical
over Hawkson's demagoguery, the barber so irritates Rayber that the professor eventually mutters, despairingly, "you ever heard about reasoning?"
Yet when Rayber does try to persuade the barber of Darmon's virtues he
finds it impossible to convey his reasons in a pithy fashion, and the story
ends with him storming out of the barber's shop with lather dripping from
his face.[1]

Sixty years after "The Barber" was written, echoes of Rayber's exas-
peration at the futility of trying to overcome emotional prejudice using
rational argument can still be heard in liberal and progressive discussions
of southern politics. The apparent paradox of the South having become
a conservative Republican stronghold after the racial desegregation,

economic modernization, and expansion of education of the post–World War II years has been especially galling for liberals in this regard, for it was these same forces that were supposed to allow the region's repressed liberalism to flourish. Perhaps no group would be more disappointed at this outcome than Loyalist Democrats, who, after all, had championed education and modernization as the way to loosen the grip of social traditionalism on southern politics. To explain this disappointment, many on the left have therefore found themselves coming to the same conclusion as Rayber: the white South is close-minded and culturally conservative, and white southerners consistently vote against their own socioeconomic interests to feed emotional prejudices.

Such a view seemed to be born out during the 2008 presidential election. While four of the eleven southern states did follow the national trend toward greater white support for Barack Obama than for John Kerry, only Virginia (39 percent) and Florida (42 percent) came close to matching Obama's national level of white support (43 percent). In three southern states—Mississippi, Alabama, and Louisiana—Obama actually lost ground with white voters relative to Kerry, registering an anemic 11 percent, 10 percent, and 14 percent support, respectively.[2] While one therefore imagines that liberals today conclude arguments over southern politics without suffering quite the same loss of dignity as Rayber, they did not appear to have any more success in winning them in 2008 than the professor did in 1946.

Given this seemingly inexplicable Republican dominance in the South and the GOP's reliance on disproportionate white support, the white backlash narrative still has a powerful appeal as an explanatory force, not just historically but also psychologically. Historically, it fits as an explanation at the aggregate level for why a party that had overwhelming support from white southerners only a few generations ago now struggles to break 40 percent white support in any southern state. Psychologically, if the failure of liberal Democrats to win office in the South is down to an intractable racism that has drowned out reasoned appeals on other social and economic issues, then this absolves the Democratic Party of any blame for the situation. Instead, the blame can be placed either on racially unreconstructed white southern voters or on sinister Republican operatives who have succeeded in manipulating an ignorant electorate's emotional fears in a way that Democrats are powerless to resist. The attitude toward white southern voters among liberal scholars and pundits has therefore frequently been one of either "screw them" or "pity them," but there is little disagreement that it is not liberalism itself that is responsible for the current conservative advantage in southern politics. The most recent scholarly manifestation of this, though written in a far more nuanced tone than either of the above epithets, can be found in Glenn Feldman's essays at the start and end of his edited collection on race and the South, *Before Brown*.[3] In the world of political commentary, one of the most in-depth and recent expositions of the white backlash critique of southern politics appeared in Thomas Schaller's *Whistling Past Dixie*.[4]

Schaller's book, which has justifiably been the subject of a good deal of debate and attention, illustrates just how pervasive the white backlash narrative remains to discussions of southern politics. Almost every tenet of the white backlash narrative appears at some point in *Whistling Past Dixie*. Schaller opens his account of the South's partisan transformation with Lyndon Johnson's pessimistic prediction of the impact of the 1964 Civil Rights Act on southern politics.[5] The narrative then proceeds through various Republican candidates deploying the southern strategy to convert white Democrats to their cause by deploying racially coded rhetoric about "states' rights" and running racially charged TV ads such as that featuring black felon Willie Horton in 1988.[6] Carter's victory in 1976 was a "rude, post-Watergate interruption of the emerging Republican hegemony." The embodiment of southern Republicanism was North Carolina's race-baiting U.S. senator Jesse Helms.[7] Schaller also puts forward some other explanations for the Democrats' weaknesses in the South, including the relatively low levels of education in the region, the strength of fundamentalist Christianity, lower unionization rates, and a greater proportion of rural voters than is found elsewhere in America. Nonetheless, Schaller's overall verdict is clear: the Democrats have lost the South because of a backlash against racial liberalism from the region's white voters, and there is not much they can do about it. Schaller's recommendation to the Democrats is therefore to ignore most of the old Confederacy, just as he advised Barack Obama to do in a 2008 *New York Times* opinion piece suggesting that Obama "write off" Georgia and North Carolina and focus his attention elsewhere.[8]

Whether or not writing off the South is good political strategy for the Democratic Party is not an issue that a work of history can resolve. Schaller may be correct that the party should focus on other parts of the country, although as Obama won in North Carolina and came within five points of John McCain in Georgia, arguably neither state was as much of a lost cause as Schaller suggested. However, the fact that Schaller's analysis, like so much of what has been written on southern politics, is based on too straightforward an understanding of the impact of civil rights on the South is a problem that historians can address, and indeed is one of the primary aims of this book.

Contra the white backlash narrative, civil rights did not destroy the Democratic Party in the South. Instead, accommodating the civil rights movement turned out to be smart politics for southern Democrats, while relying on the white backlash to win elections was a risky undertaking. That it was smart politics does not mean it was the result of a carefully thought out long-term strategy. Far from it—neither Loyalist Democrats nor their New South successors welcomed having to deal with racially divisive issues, and neither had much interest in advocating racial change. Instead, they responded to racial issues in an ad hoc fashion, often scrambling to find a politically viable position to take. In Georgia's case, whether it was James Carmichael trying not to get into a fight over the white primary in 1946, Hamilton Lokey trying to preserve the public school system in 1959, or Charles Weltner trying to hedge over the Civil Rights Act of 1964, Loyalist Democrats consistently found themselves pressured by the civil rights movement to address racial questions they would rather avoid. In each case, they fell back on the rhetoric of progressive color blindness, which gave them the political space to accept a certain level of racial change without committing them to promoting any more change than was already inevitable.

If Loyalists were to be persuaded to support racial change, they had to be convinced either that it truly *was* inevitable or that the price of resistance in terms of economic growth and social stability was too high. Accordingly, Georgia's civil rights activists spent the first few decades after World War II alternately pressuring and cajoling Loyalists to acquiesce in changes to the racial order as if trying to coax a shy teenager onto the dance floor at a middle school mixer. With their potential electoral support as a carrot, and their potential to keep the state's racial divisions firmly in the public eye through federal court rulings and direct-action protests as a stick, civil rights activists and black political leaders were able to box Loyalists into a corner on multiple occasions. The amount of leverage black Georgians had over Loyalists was rarely enough to secure the kinds of change that the more assertive civil rights activists hoped for. In almost every case, the ultimate compromise was at best half a loaf, but by applying pressure to what they correctly identified as a fissure in southern white opinion, black Georgians were a crucial catalyst in the transformation of both the racial order and the Democratic Party.

After the federal civil rights legislation of the mid-1960s, the equation changed once more. Appealing to black voters for support was no longer something that had to be done in hotel service elevators, two-party politics was replacing the one-party system, and with desegregation now the law of the land there was no longer an electoral imperative for Georgia's white politicians to demonstrate their fealty to the Jim Crow system. And yet even in this changed environment, New South Democrats continued to find it politically useful to speak of race in terms of progressive color blindness. It allowed them to paint Republicans pursuing the southern strategy as racial extremists; it enabled them to build biracial coalitions at election time; and it allowed them to present themselves as progress-orientated statesmen. In short, despite the different political and racial contexts of the 1940s and 1970s, progressive color blindness retained an appeal for New South Democrats similar to that which it had held for Loyalists.

The continuing appeal of progressive color blindness enabled Georgia's Democrats to accept the scale of change that the South experienced at minimal political cost. Even though the racial positions of 1970s New South Democrats were substantially more progressive in policy terms than those of 1940s Loyalists, the basic mentality behind their rhetoric remained the same. Ellis Arnall could use progressive color blindness to justify accepting the end of the white primary in 1946 while pledging his general support for segregation, but Jimmy Carter could also make use of it in 1976 to describe desegregation as the best thing to happen to the postwar South while pledging his opposition to "forced busing." It may have appeared that Carter was espousing a different attitude on race than Arnall, but really, their rationales were fundamentally the same: each was defending the racial order as it stood while also supporting acceptance of a recent change to that order they had not publicly advocated.

From a political perspective, progressive color blindness was a great success for the Democratic Party in Georgia and in most of the South. The biracial coalition the New South Democrats were able to build delivered them majorities in southern congressional and statewide offices until the mid-1990s. This in turn helped ensure Democratic control of Congress over that same time period. Indeed, it is possible to argue that by at least one measure, far from being a burden for the Democratic Party since 1964, the South has actually been a net plus. True, only two Democratic presidential candidates have outpolled their Republican opponents in the South since then (Carter in 1976 and Clinton in 1996); and yet if in every single election between 1968 and 1996 the Democrats had won every single southern state carried by the Republicans, it would not have changed the result of any one of them. Not until the elections of 2000 and 2004 did a failure to prevent southern states voting Republican cost the Democrats a presidential race. At the congressional level, by contrast, majorities in the southern House delegation helped keep Democratic Speakers in office until 1995, while the party also held on to at least eleven (50 percent) of the region's U.S. senators throughout the same period, even when Republicans held overall control of the chamber from 1981 to 1987.

But electoral success was not the only reason that Loyalists and New South Democrats could feel satisfied with the political situation in Georgia by the 1970s. They could also take heart from the steady growth of activist government in the South over the postwar years. It is not possible to do justice to all the developments in social and economic policy after 1946 in just a few pages, but even by looking at only a few indicators of the way in which the state governments' roles changed between the 1940s and the 1970s, the overall trend is clear: just as Loyalists had hoped would happen, state governments were becoming much more involved in the economy and were investing far more heavily in education and other social programs. In Georgia, total dollar spending by the state government rose from $115 million in 1942 to $5.2 billion by 1977.[9] This amounted to a twelvefold increase in real terms. By comparison, real terms spending by state governments across the nation increased only by a factor of eight. In per capita terms (measured in 1942 dollars), Georgia's government increased the amount it spent from $35.91 to $277.96 over the same period. Compared to the rest of the United States, Georgia went from spending 60.5 percent of the national per capita average in 1942 to 80.1 percent of the average by 1977.

The largest share of the increase in state government spending went on the Loyalists' main priority: education. In real terms, per capita spending on education in Georgia rose from $11.70 in 1942 to $102.38 in 1977, an 875 percent increase. The overall increase nationwide during this time was 661 percent (from $19.31 to $127.75 per capita). As with overall state expenditure, Georgia closed the gap on per capita education spending in the rest of the nation and did so by a similar margin: from spending approximately 60 percent of the national average in 1942, Georgia was spending just over 80 percent by 1977. Georgia was not an exceptional case in this regard. Across the eleven states of the old Confederacy, real terms per capita spending on education compared to the national average rose from 67.5 percent in 1942 to 85.6 percent by 1977.

True, Georgia and the South were still playing catch-up relative to the level of activism of state governments in the rest of the nation; and true, a good chunk of the additional money was coming from the federal government (the share of Georgia's expenditure that came from federal funds rose from 10.1 percent in 1942 to 24.2 percent in 1977). Yet notwithstanding these qualifications, the overall trend of government activism was moving in just the direction Loyalists in the 1940s had hoped for. For instance, although state spending in the South remained lower than the national average, this was at least in part a function of the disparity in per capita *income* between southern and nonsouthern states. Georgia's per capita personal income was 85.6 percent of the U.S. national average in 1977 (the South as a whole was at 85.2 percent). As such, the 80.1 percent of the national average Georgia spent on education was only marginally less than what one might have expected, given the lower tax base. The South as a whole, which spent 85.6 percent of the national average on education, was actually spending a fraction more on education than its level of per capita income would have suggested.

As for the federal government's increased provision of funds, this, too, was fully in line with Loyalist thinking in the 1940s. Ellis Arnall had specifically advocated it in *The Shore Dimly Seen*, and it remained a part of the Loyalist platform throughout the postwar years, so that when Jimmy Carter called for providing more federal money for education in 1976, he was simply reflecting a policy position that had been part of Loyalist and New South Democrat thinking for a generation.[10]

Furthermore, even with the extra federal funding, Georgia and other southern states were also increasing the amount of revenue they were raising from their own citizens—another sign of a more activist government. In real terms, Georgia's per capita revenue increased from $40.11 in 1942 to $302.48 in 1977. Of that revenue, the amount provided by taxes levied within the state rose in real terms from $31.18 to $164.80 per capita. Much of this increase came from a mixture of direct taxes (on income and property) and indirect taxes (on sales), but a sizable chunk was also raised by the introduction of fees and charges for state services. This helps explain why the relative share of its revenue that Georgia raised through taxes fell from 86 percent to 71 percent, even as the overall state tax burden relative to personal income rose from 5.5 percent in 1942 to 10.2 percent in 1977. Georgia was in line with a general trend across the South, where the tax burden increased from 6.4 percent to 10.1 percent of personal income. Across the United States over the same period, the tax burden rose from 7 percent to 11.6 percent. It therefore remained true that both Georgia and the South in general had lower rates of taxation and spending—that is, less activist state governments—than the nation as a whole. However, it was also true that both Georgia and the southern states had substantially increased the amount they raised and spent in the postwar years, often at a faster rate than the nation as a whole, and with a significantly lower tax base to start with.

In two other major areas of social spending—health care and welfare— southern states in the postwar years also began to commit more resources. Measured in real terms, Georgia went from spending $2.32 per capita on health care in 1942 to $45.43 per capita in 1977. Relative to the national average, Georgia was committing barely half as much (52.6 percent) as the national outlay in 1942, but by 1977, despite the gap in personal income, it was spending over 50 percent more than nonsouthern states (whose per capita average in 1977 was $28.64 in 1942 dollars). The situation in Georgia was replicated across the South as a whole, which went from spending 53.7 percent to 109 percent of the national per capita average on health care during the same period.

By contrast, welfare spending paints a different picture. Unlike in health care, southern states in the 1970s were devoting far less of their resources to welfare programs than other states across the nation. Real terms spending on welfare did increase by a factor of 8.2 in the South, compared to 4.7 in the rest of the nation from 1942 to 1977; however, this was largely due to an exceptionally high rate of increase in southern welfare spending up to 1957. At that point, despite a per capita income level that was only 70.4 percent of the national average, southern states were spending 103.7 percent of the national average on public welfare. By 1977, when the South's per capita income was up to 85.2 percent of the national average, welfare spending was down to just 64.3 percent of the rate across the United States. From 1972 to 1977, there was a real terms decline in the amount of per capita spending on welfare in the South, from $24.80 to $24.40, while the national rate rose from $39.50 to $42.90. Georgia was marginally above the southern average in 1977 ($27.60 per capita), but even here the state devoted just 9.9 percent of its expenditures to public welfare programs, compared to a national average of 12.6 percent.

Both health care and welfare spending are tricky indicators to use for measuring government activism, the latter especially so. Economic booms and recessions will cause welfare spending to fall and rise respectively, even if there is no underlying change in government policy or political support for welfare programs. Nonetheless, despite these inevitable ambiguities, even from this brief overview of some of the changes in government activism during the postwar years, it is possible to see both why Loyalists could be pleased at the changing role of government in the South and why those of a more liberal persuasion would be frustrated at the scale of that change.

Georgia and the South as a whole had seen government become more activist and progressive over time, yet in most areas of importance to liberals, southern states were still spending less and taxing more regressively than the rest of the nation. For instance, southern states used income taxes—the favored progressive form of taxation—to raise 9.3 percent of their revenues in 1977 compared to 5.2 percent in 1942. This was a definite shift in a more progressive direction, but by 1977, nonsouthern states were raising 15.6 percent of their revenue from income taxes. By contrast, southern states relied on sales taxes—the favored regressive form of taxation—to raise 29.7 percent of their revenues in 1977, compared to 23.5 percent in the nation as a whole. Similar trends were evident in most areas of social spending—southern states were investing far more than they had ever done, but (with the exception of health care spending) were still investing less than nonsouthern states.

As such, it makes sense that many liberals—then and now—would have liked southern states to be focusing not just on economic growth and education but also to be doing more to address economic justice. This is precisely what several historians have critiqued about the priorities of the New South, such as with James Cobb's verdict that it represented a "conservative capitalist's dream come true."[11] Others have similarly criticized the New South Democrats and their like-minded allies in the national Democratic Party for, in Bruce Miroff's words, jettisoning "concerns about corporate power and economic inequality," and instead, "embracing economic growth as the panacea that would established shared prosperity amid social harmony."[12]

As a complaint about misplaced values or priorities, this is a perfectly valid line of criticism—however, it should be kept in mind that ever since the 1940s, southern Loyalists and New South Democrats had been convinced that the "panacea" of economic growth would indeed bring about prosperity and social harmony. The proactive pursuit of social justice or racial equality had never been a Loyalist priority. In other words, the frequently told narrative of a "lost" liberal South whose 1940s idealism was crushed by the white backlash overlooks the fact that the basic agenda of many of those who were the "great liberal hopes" of the 1940s was precisely the kind of growth-centered policies that dominated the New South. The New South may not have been what the left wing of the national Democratic Party was hoping for, but much of the change in the South after the 1940s was the kind of change called for by Ellis Arnall in *The Shore Dimly Seen* and by Calvin Kytle and James MacKay in *Who Runs Georgia?*

A further sign of the lasting influence of Loyalists and New South Democrats on Georgia's politics was the basic continuity of the electoral coalition they had built up by the 1970s, a coalition that proved both potent and durable. A strong presence in urban areas and sufficient support from rural and small-town voters offset the Republican presence in the suburbs. Faced with this New South coalition, Republicanism growth in Georgia was initially stymied at the state level. The southern strategy, when tried, was generally ineffective, and attempts to implement it helped ensure the Republican Party actually regressed in Georgia during the 1970s. Over the course of the 1980s, Republicans became more adept at utilizing a suburban strategy that relied on conservative color blindness, which also embraced the end of Jim Crow but implied that subsequent attempts to bring about structural reform in race relations were benefiting undeserving minorities at the expense of deserving whites in a "racist" fashion of which Martin Luther King Jr. would not approve.[13] While New South Democrats generally used progressive color blindness as part of an effort to win over black voters, the effectiveness of New South Republican conservative color blindness was to persuade suburban white voters that voting Republican did not mean voting for a racist.

At first, presidential Republican candidates were markedly more successful in attracting votes in Georgia than statewide Republicans, but by the early 1990s the two had converged. For most of that decade, the

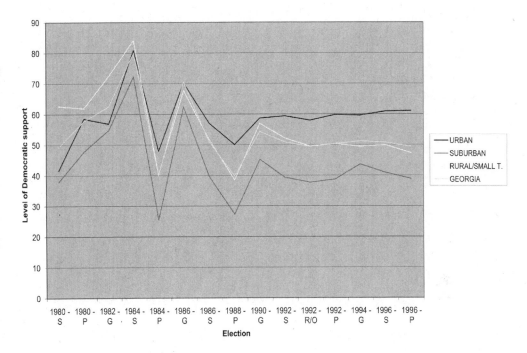

Figure 17. Democratic support by county demographic, 1980–1996.

balance of party politics in Georgia was on a knife-edge, but it was a balance whose roots were still in the same basic partisan divide as had existed since 1970. This can be seen by considering the voting trends in Georgia after 1980. Figure 17 tracks the level of Democratic support received among urban, suburban, and rural/small-town counties in Georgia from 1980 to 1996.[14] Two trends are immediately noticeable. First, Republicanism in Georgia was still based in the suburbs. In every statewide election from 1980 to 1996, the suburbs were the weakest portion of the state for the Democratic candidate. Any time a Democrat broke 40 percent of the suburban vote, he or she would carry the state, but even 40 percent was tough to hit during this period, especially in the 1990s. Second, the shift in relative support for the Democrats among rural/small-town and urban areas is apparent. As the 1980s and 1990s unfolded, urban areas became the number one source of Democratic votes, and rural/small-town counties became number two. Nonetheless, as late as 1996 Democrats were able to split or win the rural/small-town vote while they still trailed by around 20 percent in the suburbs.

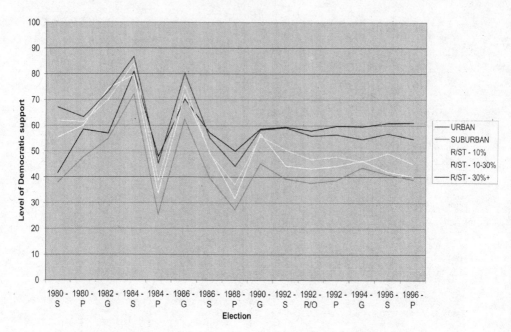

Figure 18. Democratic support by county demographic and racial composition of rural/small-town counties, 1980–1996.

Even this relative decline in the rural/small-town vote followed a gradual, consistent pattern over time. Figure 18 shows the period 1980–1996 with rural/small-town counties broken down into those with a black population of less than 10 percent, those with a black population between 10 percent and 30 percent, and those with a black population of more than 30 percent. All three showed a general decline in the number of votes for Democrats over this time period, though Democrats consistently performed best in counties with populations over 10 percent black. In none of these categories, however, did any Democrat perform worse than in the suburbs in any election during this time. What also becomes apparent from considering trends across these fifteen contests is the "leveling out" that occurred in the 1990s. In the six senatorial, gubernatorial, and presidential contests from 1992 to 1996, Democrats polled from 58.0 to 61.1 percent of the urban vote, 47.3 to 52.1 percent of the rural/small-town vote, 37.7 to 43.6 percent of the suburban vote, and 49.4 to 51.1 percent of the two-party vote across the state.

Republican strength in Georgia in the 1990s remained a suburban phenomenon, as it had been in the 1970s and indeed as it had been since the

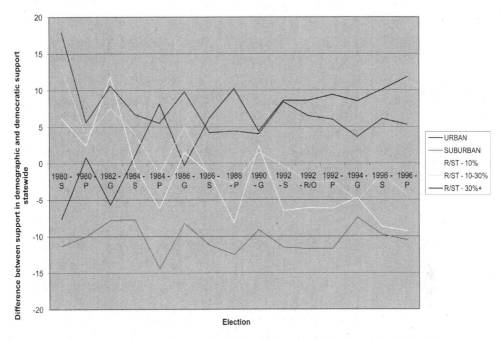

Figure 19. Relative Democratic support in Georgia by county demographic, 1980–1996.

1950s. Over the course of the 1980s and 1990s, the GOP was able to eat away at Democratic support in heavily white rural/small-town counties, so that by 1996 GOP support there was nearly as high as in the suburbs. However, this was a slow, gradual process, and the counties with a black population of less than 10 percent were the smallest of the rural/small-town counties in terms of number of votes cast. The largest, those with a black population of 30 percent or more, continued to lean Democratic. Figure 19 illustrates this by measuring the discrepancy between the Democratic vote statewide and the Democratic vote in the various types of counties from 1980 to 1996. While the relative position of urban and rural/small-town support did change, both the pattern within the rural/small-town counties and the consistent "underperforming" in the suburbs is apparent.

In short, in the New South party system in Georgia, urban areas, the core of the Loyalist faction from the 1940s onward, remained central to the New South Democrats after the 1970s. Similarly, the suburbs, the original base of the GOP, remained the base of Georgia Republicanism into the 1990s. The former base of the Regular Democrats—rural and small-town Georgia—occupied the middle ground between the two. Of that middle ground, the whitest counties—which had also been the most pro-Republican in the 1950s—began to approach suburban levels of Republican support by the 1990s. While a general trend in favor of the Republicans is therefore evident, none of this suggests a sharp break to the Republican Party as a result of the white backlash: first, because of the time lag involved; second, because of the considerable continuity between the Republican coalition of the 1990s and the 1950s; and third, because those parts of the state that in the mid-1990s were the most Republican, suburbs and white rural counties, had been the least enthusiastic about supporting white backlash politics during the postwar years.

None of this is to imply that there was no such thing as the white backlash, or that race had only a minor role to play in the changes undergone by southern and American politics since 1945. Clearly, the fact that over 85 percent of white Mississippians voted for John McCain in 2008 and over 95 percent of black Mississippians voted for Barack Obama shows that the racial dimension of southern politics cannot be ignored. Similarly, there is no question that support for desegregation cost the Democratic Party some support from white southerners, just as there is no doubt that several southern Republicans have been able to tap into racial prejudices to gain support for other economically and socially conservative positions. However, the white backlash narrative's suggestion that Republicans now dominate the South *because* the Democrats supported civil rights, or that the New South is *only* a socially and economically conservative, or even reactionary, creation is inaccurate. The white backlash, important as it was, was more ambiguous than that. Georgia's Democrats were able to adjust to the civil rights movement as successfully as could reasonably be expected—more successfully, at least for one generation, than southern Republicans.

To put it another way, it is undoubtedly the case today that Democrats fare worse among southern white voters than they do among white voters in general. This does not mean, however, that resentment at the Democrats' support for civil rights made it so. As the continued resilience of Democrats at the state level in the South has shown, adopting the national party's attitude on race did not mean inevitable electoral defeat at the hands of a southern strategy Republican. In fact, Republicans pursuing the southern strategy were central to the continued Democratic strength in the New South. As such, it would be worthwhile to consider other explanations that might shed light on the white South's current dispropor-tionate fondness (relative to whites across the nation) for the Republican Party rather than rely on the most morally straightforward explanation of the backlash against the civil rights movement.

The impact of the Vietnam War has yet to be fully examined; the ex-traordinarily high levels of Republican support among upper-income white southerners (70 to 75 percent for those making over $50,000 a year in Georgia in the 2008 federal elections, compared to 56 percent nation-wide) and college-educated white southerners (69 to 73 percent in Geor-gia in 2008, compared to 51 percent nationwide) is not easily explained by the white backlash; the fusion between evangelical Christianity and the Republican Party that took place in the late 1970s has clearly had a par-ticularly strong influence on the South (89 percent of white evangelicals backed John McCain in Georgia, where they made up 37 percent of all voters, while nationwide, 74 percent voted Republican, where they made up 26 percent of all voters); the particular resonance of rhetoric about "toughness" and anti-elitism (in a cultural and intellectual sense) among white southern voters, and what this reveals about the role of gender, es-pecially masculinity, and class in southern political culture, deserves more scrutiny, especially for the period since the large-scale Republican mobi-lization of new voters in the South in the mid-1990s; and the politics of abortion, of gay rights, and of immigration reform could also help explain the current popularity of Republicanism among white southerners.

All of these factors can, and many do, intersect with racial concerns; but they cannot simply be subsumed into the category of "race" or attrib-uted to a white backlash against desegregation. To pick one example, there may indeed be parallels between the way rhetoric about abortion and gay rights is used to prime voters' cultural concerns over their economic ones and the way that race was used in similar fashion by Regular Democrats in the 1950s. However, given that there is no logical reason why black southerners should have different views on abortion than white southern-ers, and that, if anything, there are suggestions that black voters are often *more* conservative on gay rights than white voters, it is clearly not a direct continuation of the backlash against the civil rights movement.[15] To re-turn to a topic discussed in chapter 7, it may very well be that the essential themes of the attacks by today's southern Republicans on liberalism and the Democratic Party—weakness, moral permissiveness, fecklessness, ef-feteness—echo those of the southern opponents of civil rights, but the issues about which these charges are made are very different from what they were fifty years ago.

The central problem for Democrats in the South at the moment is therefore not "getting right on race." It is that too many white southerners look at the party's candidates and decide "he or she is not one of us." Race may indeed play into this assessment, but so do white southerners' views on religion, economics, gender, sexual morality, cultural values, and national defense. In the end, the biggest hurdle Democrats need to overcome in the South is not that they supported civil rights. Rather, it is the exact same one that was holding back Darmon's appeal in "The Barber," for despite Rayber's anger and frustration at the barber's persistent belittling of Darmon as weak and ineffective, Rayber was also angry at Darmon for allowing himself to be portrayed in this way: "He wished to Hell 'Mother Hubbard' weren't so accurate. He wished to Hell Darmon spit tobacco juice."[16] In the New South, spitting tobacco juice is no longer a requirement for winning elections. For a candidate to be perceived as a "Mother Hubbard," however, regardless of his or her position on civil rights, can be as great a political liability in the South of today as it was in the South of 1946.

Notes

Abbreviations

DNC Papers   Democratic National Committee Papers, Lyndon B. Johnson Library, University of Texas, Austin

GDF Records   Georgia Democratic Forum Records, Georgia State University, Atlanta

GGDP   Georgia Government Documentation Project, Georgia State University, Atlanta

GPHC   Georgia Political Heritage Collection, University of West Georgia, Carrollton

HOPE Papers   Help Our Public Education Papers, Atlanta History Center, Atlanta

LBJL   Lyndon B. Johnson Presidential Library, University of Texas, Austin

Introduction: "Out of the Shadows"

Epigraph source: Mann, *Walls of Jericho*, 18.

1. This version of Johnson's comment, reportedly made to Bill Moyers, appeared in Califano, *Triumph and Tragedy of Lyndon Johnson*, 55. It has since appeared, with occasional variations, in many biographies of Johnson and in contemporary political journalism on the South.

2. Jarding and Sanders, *Foxes in the Henhouse*, 115.

3. Important works that emphasize this perspective include Phillips, *Emerging Republican Majority*; Lamis, *Two-Party South*; Edsall and Edsall, *Chain Reaction*; Sylvia, "Presidential Decision Making"; Carter, *From George Wallace to Newt Gingrich*; Black, "Newest Southern Politics"; Black and Black, *Rise of Southern Republicans*.

4. Kruse, *White Flight*, 231.

5. Sokol, *There Goes My Everything*, 237.

6. Donna Brazile, "Roundtable: Decisive Moments," *This Week with George Stephanopoulos*, November 2, 2008.

7. "Road to 270: Georgia," November 2, 2008.

8. Todd and Gawiser, *How Barack Obama Won*, 173. This particular quote was Todd's description of Arkansas. Variations on this statement appeared in the opening segments of the descriptions of most southern states.

9. Radosh, *Divided They Fell*, 2.

10. Sullivan, *Days of Hope*; Daniel, *Lost Revolutions*.

11. Feldman, "Prologue," in Feldman, *Before Brown*, 4.

12. Feldman, "Epilogue," in Feldman, *Before Brown*, 274.

13. This was the phrase used by Harry Truman's aide Clark Clifford in a memo on political strategy for the 1948 election. The memo is discussed in several places, including in Bartley, *New South*, 78. The original memo is dated November 19, 1947, and is in the Clifford Papers.

14. The "Solid South" was the name given to the region for the period approximately 1890–1960—it referred to the fact that the South was so "solidly" Democratic that there was little point in Republicans even campaigning there.

15. Two particularly important examples of this liberal critique of the New South are Bartley, *New South*, and Schulman, *From Cotton Belt to Sunbelt*.

16. The term "progressive" has been widely contested, and I do not want to simplify the complexities of the debates surrounding the term by using it without a full discussion of its various meanings here. For the purposes of this narrative, I am deploying the term to mean, in race relations, a greater willingness to support the principle of racial equality and, in terms of the role of government, a greater willingness to use government power to regulate economic growth and guarantee a certain level of social welfare.

17. Lassiter, "Suburban Origins," 550. The issue is also discussed in more depth by Lassiter in *Silent Majority*, 1–18, passim.

18. Shafer and Johnston, *End of Southern Exceptionalism*, 182.

19. Examples of the post-1960s studies are Rae, *Southern Democrats*; Berard, *Southern Democrats*; and Hood, Kidd, and Morris, "Of Byrd and Bumpers." Examples of national party histories of the Democrats are Martin, *Civil Rights*; Parmet, *Democrats*; Witcover, *Party of the People*; and Rutland, *Democrats*.

20. Frederickson, *Dixiecrat Revolt*.

21. Miroff, *Liberals' Moment*.

22. White House Tapes, July 7, 1965.

23. Cover page, "New Day A' Coming in the South" and "Four Men for the New Season," *Time*, May 31, 1971.

24. Shipp, "Carter Is Sworn In," *Atlanta Constitution*, January 13, 1971.

25. The term "Loyalist" was not widely used as a collective term by these Democrats to describe themselves until the 1960s. However, throughout the postwar years, this faction of the Democratic Party regularly spoke of the need for "loyalty" to the national party and contrasted their own willingness to be loyal with the repeated threats of a party bolt by their opponents. As such, I am using the term to describe this faction collectively from the 1940s to the 1970s.

26. See, for example, Kruse, *White Flight*; Lassiter, "Suburban Origins"; Kousser, *Colorblind Injustice*; and Eastland, *Ending Affirmative Action*.

27. A good summary of the conservative intellectuals and politicians who deploy color-blind rhetoric can be found in Cose, *Colorblind*, xi–xv, 180–181.

28. This passage of King's speech is directly cited as a reason to oppose affirmative

action by Eastland in *Ending Affirmative Action*, 21. Cose also cites several conservative politicians referring to this King quote in *Colorblind*, xi–xxvii, 179–213.

29. See, for example, King's 1967 presidential address to the Southern Christian Leadership Conference, "Where Do We Go from Here?" in Washington, *Testament of Hope*, 245–252.

30. Cose, *Colorblind*, 180; Kousser, *Colorblind Injustice*, 467; Lassiter, *Silent Majority*, 1.

31. This complaint would apply to both white and black political leaders; supporters of progressive color blindness would be similarly critical of Jesse Helms and Jesse Jackson.

32. There is no way that in the days of Jim Crow, color blindness could have been used as an argument to *preserve* the existing racial status quo in the way that Kousser argues it does now. However, with all now agreed that the death of Jim Crow should be celebrated, it is no longer "subversive" to argue against legalized segregation.

33. These two developments are the central argument for the racial and economic liberalization of southern Democrats put forward in Hood, Kidd, and Morris, "Of Byrd and Bumpers," 465–487.

34. For a fuller discussion of how liberals and conservatives deployed the rhetoric of "color blindness" during the debate over the King Holiday, and indeed in continuing discussions over the legacy of the civil rights movement in general, see Kuryla, "Integration of the American Mind," 194–199, passim.

35. I am defining the "Deep South" as comprising Alabama, Georgia, Louisiana, Mississippi, and South Carolina. The "Rim South" consisted of Arkansas, Florida, North Carolina, Tennessee, Texas, and Virginia.

Chapter 1. Competing Visions for Postwar Georgia: 1946

Epigraph source: Guthman and Allen, *RFK*, 228.

1. Clifford, Memo to President Truman, November 19, 1947, Clifford Papers.

2. See, for example, Miller, "Generational Changes," 333–352; Sylvia, "Presidential Decision Making," 405; Hood, Kidd, and Morris, "Re-Introduction of the Elephas Maximus," 68–101; Niven, *Politics of Injustice*, 127.

3. Black, "Newest Southern Politics," 592.

4. Kirby, "Black and White in the Rural South," 442.

5. LaPalombara, *Politics within Nations*, 502.

6. Well-known examples of this behavior would include antislavery Whigs and Democrats, the Populists, the Reform Party, and, most important for the 1940s South, the states' rights Democrats ("Dixiecrats").

7. Kousser, *Shaping of Southern Politics*.

8. Williamson, *Rage for Order*; Loewen, *Sundown Towns*.

9. Cobb, *Selling of the South*, 3.

10. Wright, *Old South, New South*, 203.

11. See, for example, Schulman, *From Cotton Belt to Sunbelt*; Kirby, *Rural Worlds Lost*; Fite, *Cotton Fields No More*; Daniel, *Breaking the Land*; Cobb, *Selling of the South*; and Wright, *Old South, New South*.

12. Kirby, *Rural Worlds Lost*, 65–66; Fite, *Cotton Fields No More*, 157.

13. Cobb, *Selling of the South*, 27.

14. Bartley, *New South*, 143.

15. It must be noted that the U.S. Census definition of "urban" changed significantly in 1950 and in 1960 in ways that counted areas previously considered "rural" as "urban." Both these changes meant that the overall rate of increase would have been less had 1950 or 1960 definitions been used in 1920. Nonetheless, the increase was clearly substantial, even allowing for this discrepancy as to its precise scope. For more on the changing definition of "urban," see *Geographic Areas Reference Manual*, chapter 12.

16. All figures are derived from U.S. Census data laid out in Dodd, *Historical Statistics*.

17. Wright, *Old South, New South*, 236.

18. LaPalombara, *Politics within Nations*, 500.

19. The so-called white primary was a further insurance policy, additional to the general disfranchisement measures, for keeping black voters out of the political process. State Democratic parties could openly disallow African Americans taking part in the primary and not violate the Fifteenth Amendment (prior to 1944) by claiming that the Democratic Party was a private, rather than a state, organization.

20. Bartley and Graham, *Southern Politics*, 25–26.

21. African Americans, even with 20 percent registration, could of course still easily be outvoted by the region's whites, so greater black registration did *not* mean an inevitable end to the idea of white supremacy. However, those African American voters would be highly unlikely to permanently align with a party advocating white supremacy and so would create pressure for a second party to emerge. Of course, this picture was further complicated by the pull of a racially progressive national Democratic Party and the distaste for a racially conservative regional one.

22. Brooks, *Defining the Peace*, 10 (first quotation), 5 (second quotation).

23. Luebke, *Tar Heel Politics*, viii.

24. Luebke, *Tar Heel Politics*, 20.

25. Luebke, *Tar Heel Politics*, 22.

26. Luebke, *Tar Heel Politics*, 21; Bartley, *New South*, 31–34.

27. Key, *Southern Politics*, 108.

28. Tuck, *Beyond Atlanta*, 18 (on Talmadge and *Mein Kampf*); Logue and Dorgan, *Oratory of Southern Demagogues*, 94 (Talmadge quotation).

29. In 1948, Georgia cast 418,844 votes in the presidential election; 135,915 of these came from the six counties comprising the specified cities—32.5 percent of the total. Figures taken from Scammon and McGillivray, *America at the Polls*, 158–160.

30. In other words, using the same 8:30:121 split in county classification, the first group had 6, the second 4, and the last 2 "unit votes" each.

31. Logue and Dorgan, *Oratory of Southern Demagogues*, 84.

32. Landry, "Ike Party Gains Held Negative by Democrat," *Macon Telegraph and News*, April 25, 1954.

33. James S. Peters to Herman E. Talmadge, August 20, 1953, Talmadge Papers.

34. O'Brien, "Georgia's Response to *Brown*," 243–244.

35. James S. Peters to John J. Flynt, December 22, 1960, Vandiver Papers.

36. Frederickson, *Dixiecrat Revolt*, 130.

37. Speech by Charles J. Bloch to the Associated Industries of Georgia, March 27, 1959, Russell Papers.

38. Letter from Charles Bloch sent to unnamed newspaper, forwarded by Bloch to Richard Russell, September 14, 1959, Russell Papers.

39. "Let's Stop the Retreat," Memo from the States' Rights Council, undated, likely 1959–1960, Vandiver Papers.

40. Kytle and MacKay, *Who Runs Georgia?* 18.

41. Luebke, *Tar Heel Politics*, 23.

42. Luebke, *Tar Heel Politics*, 23.

43. Brooks, *Defining the Peace*, 115.

44. Brooks, *Defining the Peace*, 38–107.

45. Kytle and MacKay, *Who Runs Georgia?*

46. Chappell, "Lost Decade of Civil Rights," 38.

47. Arnall, *Shore Dimly Seen*.

48. Arnall took the title from the opening line of the second verse of "The Star Spangled Banner": "On the shore dimly seen, thro' the mists of the deep."

49. Arnall, *Shore Dimly Seen*, 24, 79–80, 91.

50. Arnall, *Shore Dimly Seen*, 226.

51. Arnall, *Shore Dimly Seen*, 266.

52. Arnall, *Shore Dimly Seen*, 40.

53. Arnall, *Shore Dimly Seen*, 34.

54. Arnall, *Shore Dimly Seen*, 263.

55. Arnall, *Shore Dimly Seen*, 267.

56. Arnall, *Shore Dimly Seen*, 271.

57. Arnall, *Shore Dimly Seen*, 101.

58. Arnall, *Shore Dimly Seen*, 93–94.

59. Kytle and MacKay, *Who Runs Georgia?* 25, 43.

60. Kytle and MacKay, *Who Runs Georgia?* 25.

61. Kytle and MacKay, *Who Runs Georgia?* 20.

62. Kytle and MacKay, *Who Runs Georgia?* 74 (emphasis added).

63. Key, *Southern Politics*, 5.

64. For a more thorough description of the manner in which black politics changed in the early 1970s after the death of Jim Crow, see Chappell, "Lost Decade of Civil Rights."

65. Jacob Henderson, Interview, June 8, 1989, GGDP.

66. Robert Flanagan, Interview, November 10, 1988, GGDP.

67. Martin, *William Berry Hartsfield*, 46–49, 87.

68. Chappell, *Inside Agitators*, xxv.

69. Tuck, *Beyond Atlanta*, 24–25, 44.

70. Tuck, *Beyond Atlanta*, 50–54.

71. Tuck, *Beyond Atlanta*, 25.

72. Tuck, *Beyond Atlanta*, 41.

73. Martin, *William Berry Hartsfield*, 50.

74. Ben Brown, Interview, October 15, 23, and 31, 1996, GGDP.

75. Tuck, *Beyond Atlanta*, 97.

76. Osgood Williams, Interview, May 12, 1988, GGDP.

77. Eugene Patterson, "A. T. Walden: A Great Southerner," Clipping, *Atlanta Constitution*, [July 1965], Hamilton Papers.

78. Tuck, *Beyond Atlanta*, 48.

79. Tuck, *Beyond Atlanta*, 49.

80. Wesley W. Law, Interview, November 15 and 16, 1990, GGDP.

81. Bartley, *Creation of Modern Georgia*, 186.

82. Bartley, *Creation of Modern Georgia*, 189.

83. Figures calculated from *1977 Census of Governments: Historical Statistics on Government Finances and Employment*. The relevant tables are on 12, 30–31, and 83.

84. Figures taken from *1977 Census of Governments*, tables as in note 82 above.

85. Spritzer, *Belle of Ashby Street*, 107.

Chapter 2. Politics in Georgia before *Brown*: 1946–1954

Epigraph source: Spritzer, *Belle of Ashby Street*, 83.

1. Spritzer, *Belle of Ashby Street*, 68.

2. Spritzer, *Belle of Ashby Street*, 56–57.

3. Spritzer, *Belle of Ashby Street*, 66.

4. Spritzer, *Belle of Ashby Street*, 60.

5. Spritzer, *Belle of Ashby Street*, 71.

6. Spritzer, *Belle of Ashby Street*, 60.

7. Helen Bullard, Interview, July 25, 1977, GGDP.

8. Henderson, Interview.

9. Clarence Bacote, Interview, July 23, 1977, GGDP.

10. Bacote, Interview.

11. Spritzer, *Belle of Ashby Street*, 29.

12. Frances Pauley, Interview, April 11, 1988, GGDP.

13. Hamilton Lokey and Muriel Lokey, Interview, January 26, 1989, GGDP.

14. Spritzer, *Belle of Ashby Street*, 83.

15. Cox, "In His Own Words," 17–18. For a fuller discussion of Arnall's term as governor, with further examples of his modernizing beliefs, see Henderson, *Politics of Change*.

16. Arnall, *Shore Dimly Seen*, 53.

17. Anderson, *Wild Man*, 218; Novotny, *Georgia Rising*, 132.

18. Anderson, *Wild Man*, 218.

19. Anderson, *Wild Man*, 223.

20. Novotny, *Georgia Rising*, 132–135.

21. Novotny, *Georgia Rising*, 137.

22. Novotny, *Georgia Rising*, 171.

23. Anderson, *Wild Man*, 232.

24. Osgood Williams, Interview, May 12, 1988, GGDP.

25. Novotny, *Georgia Rising*, 141.

26. Spritzer, *Belle of Ashby Street*, 97–98.

27. Spritzer, *Belle of Ashby Street*, 99–100.

28. The lengths that Davis's supporters went to in order to force the primary to be

decided by county-unit rules is too intricate to go in to at length here, but has been comprehensively detailed in Spritzer, *Belle of Ashby Street*, chapters 5–8.

29. Spritzer, *Belle of Ashby Street*, 118.

30. Spritzer, *Belle of Ashby Street*, 97.

31. Campaign leaflet, Davis Papers.

32. Spritzer, *Belle of Ashby Street*, 100.

33. Anderson, *Wild Man*, 220–222.

34. Anderson, *Wild Man*, 222, 229; Novotny, *Georgia Rising*, 130; Kruse, *White Flight*, 24.

35. Anderson, *Wild Man*, 230.

36. The regional divisions are taken from the definitions offered by Bartley in *From Thurmond to Wallace*, 13–19.

37. All calculations for the 1946 primary have been made using voting returns taken from the *Georgia Official Register*, 490–493. Calculations are based only on the votes received by the two major candidates. There were several other candidates, most prominently former governor E. D. Rivers, who attracted around 10 percent of the overall votes. The demographic information is taken from U.S. Census Bureau, *Sixteenth Census of the United States: 1940*, Vol. 2, *Characteristics of the Population, Part 2: Florida to Iowa*, Georgia Table 21, 216–225; and the *Seventeenth Census of the United States: 1950*, Vol. 2, *Characteristics of the Population, Part 2: Georgia*, Table 5, 9–11, and Table 12, 37–38. For each demographic calculation, Georgia's counties were divided in a 40:79:40 ratio, so that, for example, the "largest" counties refers to the 40 with the highest populations, and the "smallest" to the 40 with the lowest populations, and the remaining 79 are considered "midsize." Obviously, many of the counties in the various demographic categories overlapped (that is, those with high incomes were also often large counties with high median years of education completed, and so forth); however, it is still useful to reference these different categories just to emphasize the different demographics that the Loyalist and Regular factions appealed to.

38. Burner, *Politics of Provincialism*.

39. For all but one of the southern states that went for Hoover in 1928, this was the first occasion they had deserted the Democratic ticket since 1876; the only exception was Tennessee, which had also voted for Republican Warren G. Harding in 1920.

40. Patterson, *Congressional Conservatism*, 21–30.

41. Frederickson, *Dixiecrat Revolt*, 184.

42. Frederickson, *Dixiecrat Revolt*, 163.

43. Frederickson, *Dixiecrat Revolt*, 162.

44. The statewide contests referred to here include all contested gubernatorial primaries from 1946 to 1962, all statewide referenda from 1946 to 1954, and all presidential elections from 1948 to 1960.

45. Henderson, Interview; Tuck, *Beyond Atlanta*, 88–89.

46. "Why Eisenhower Should Be Elected President of the U.S.," *Atlanta Daily World*, October 12, 1952.

47. Arthur Powell Sr. to James C. Davis, August 14, 1946, Davis Papers.

48. *Georgia Official and Statistical Register, 1951–52*, 470–474.

49. This was effectively what Mankin had tried to do after being "counted out" in 1946, and when she ran for a second time in 1948; a candidate who lost because of county-unit rules but was ahead in the popular vote could clearly present a claim to the electorate that he or she was a "legitimate" contender and not just a spoiler suffering from a case of sour grapes.

50. *Georgia Official and Statistical Register, 1951–52*, 575–579.

51. "Your Stake in the County-unit Amendment" (1952), Pauley Papers.

52. Williams, Interview.

53. "We Take Our Stand," Athens League of Women Voters Papers.

54. "Vote Against Amendment No. 1," Athens League of Women Voters Papers.

55. Bullard, Interview.

56. "Abram in Congress Race Opposes Unit System," *Atlanta Constitution*, May 11, 1954; "Abram Charges Davis with Last-Minute Smear," *Atlanta Constitution*, September 5, 1954.

57. Charles Weltner, Interview, July 9 and 17, 1986, GGDP.

58. James MacKay, Interview, March 18, 1986; Williams, Interview; Everett G. Millican, Interview, July 30, 1977, GGDP.

59. *Georgia Official and Statistical Register, 1951–52*, 470–474, 575–579.

60. The presidential election of 1952 undoubtedly boosted turnout that November, but it is still indicative of the importance voters attached to the issue that so many of them cast ballots on the question of county-unit voting.

61. Bernd, "Study of Primary Elections," 233.

62. Pauley, Interview; Paid Political Advertisement, Clipping, Walden Papers.

63. Statement by A. T. Walden on the County-unit Amendment, September 21, 1952, Hamilton Papers.

64. Tuck, *Beyond Atlanta*, 76.

65. John H. Calhoun to A. T. Walden, October 26, 1957, Walden Papers.

66. Sherrill, *Gothic Politics*, 62.

67. John Calhoun, "Report of Executive Secretary to ANVL," September 23, 1949, Walden Papers; Tuck, *Beyond Atlanta*, 89.

68. Calhoun, "Report of Executive Secretary to ANVL."

69. William Randall Sr. and William Randall Jr., Interview, February 4, 1989, GGDP.

70. Tuck, *Beyond Atlanta*, 95.

71. Claudius Turner to A. T. Walden, April 2, 1948, Hamilton Papers.

72. A. T. Walden to Claudius Turner, May 15, 1948, Hamilton Papers.

73. Press release from the Democratic National Committee, October 4, 1952, Walden Papers.

74. *Georgia Plain Dealer*, October 20, 1952, Walden Papers.

75. "Desirability of a Two-Party System," *Georgia Plain Dealer*, October 20, 1952, Walden Papers.

76. A. T. Walden to the *Atlanta Journal*, August 4, 1952, Walden Papers.

77. Halberstam, *Fifties*, 421.

78. O'Brien, "Georgia's Response to *Brown*," 78–95.

79. O'Brien, "Georgia's Response to *Brown*," 132.

80. O'Brien, "Georgia's Response to *Brown*," 92–95; Henderson, *Ernest Vandiver*, 25.

81. Pajari, "Herman Talmadge," 83–86.

82. "Gowen Tags His Plan for Schools 'Legal,'" *Atlanta Constitution*, June 3, 1954; "Hand and Thompson Lash Out at Griffin as 'Creating Strife,'" *Atlanta Constitution*, June 18, 1954.

83. "Gowen, Griffin Clash with Linder on Separate Schools," *Atlanta Constitution*, July 9, 1954.

84. "Linder Repeats Proposal for Control of NAACP," *Atlanta Constitution*, August 25, 1954.

85. Calculations for the 1954 primary are based on figures from the *Georgia Official and Statistical Register, 1953–54*, 620.

86. *Georgia Official and Statistical Register, 1953–54*, 688–692.

Chapter 3. Contesting Massive Resistance: 1954–1962

Epigraph source: Lokey and Lokey, Interview.

1. "The Southern Manifesto," *Congressional Record*, vol. 102, 1956.

2. The three senators who did not sign were Al Gore and Estes Kefauver of Tennessee and Lyndon Johnson of Texas. All three had national presidential ambitions (as well as moral scruples over the language of the Manifesto) that would have been fatally damaged by signing it. In the House, seventeen out of twenty-one Texan congressmen (including Speaker Sam Rayburn, who lobbied other members of his state delegation to withhold their signatures) did not sign; three Democrats from North Carolina and one each from Florida and Tennessee also refused. The Manifesto was also not signed by the two Republican congressmen from east Tennessee. For more details on the fate of those who refused, see Badger, "Southerners Who Refused to Sign."

3. Black, *Southern Governors*, 198; Black dates the period of political dominance of massive resistors as being 1957 to 1965.

4. Badger, "Southerners Who Refused to Sign," 517–519.

5. Bartley, *Rise of Massive Resistance*, 141.

6. Richard Russell to Ross Sharpe, April 7, 1959, Russell Papers.

7. "Cook Urges Laws to Oust State NAACP," *Atlanta Constitution*, August 7, 1956; Galphin, "NAACP Yields Records," *Atlanta Constitution*, December 15, 1956.

8. Galphin, "Cook Drafts 3 Counters to NAACP," *Atlanta Constitution*, January 19, 1957.

9. "Georgia Slaps NAACP with 11-Year Tax Levy," *Atlanta Constitution*, June 22, 1957.

10. "200 Integration Plaintiffs Here Let Suit Die on Vine," *Atlanta Constitution*, May 18, 1956.

11. Bates, "Ward Drops University Entry Fight," *Atlanta Constitution*, June 6, 1957.

12. Tuck, *Beyond Atlanta*, 79.

13. Tuck, *Beyond Atlanta*, 84–85.

14. O'Brien, "Georgia's Response to *Brown*," 167–169; Bates, "More Power to Fight Integration," *Atlanta Constitution*, January 24, 1957.

15. Henderson, *Ernest Vandiver*, 95.

16. In this 1964 movie, the Soviets reveal that they have created a "Doomsday Device"

that will automatically detonate multiple nuclear blasts and thereby make Earth unin-
habitable if any attack is launched against the USSR. As the device cannot be overridden
once it is in place, it is, as Dr. Strangelove explains, the perfect deterrent against any
attack. Eliminating the need for any further action by any individual makes it an utterly
credible threat.

17. "Cook Would Make Enforcing Integration a Capital Crime," *Atlanta Constitution*,
April 26, 1956.

18. Dubay, "Marvin Griffin," 106–107.

19. O'Brien, "Georgia's Response to *Brown*," 55.

20. O'Brien, "Georgia's Response to *Brown*," 243–244.

21. Tuck, *Beyond Atlanta*, 74.

22. Tuck, *Beyond Atlanta*, 84–87.

23. O'Brien, "Georgia's Response to *Brown*," 139.

24. Luther Alverson to A. T. Walden, August 15, 1956; M. R. "Randy" Dodd to A. T.
Walden, August 27, 1956, both in Walden Papers.

25. John Calhoun, "Report on Candidates, August 1961," Walden Papers.

26. Robert Thompson, Interview, June 5, 1989, GGDP.

27. "Revised Report of Committee on Objectives," February 13, 1954, Walden Papers.

28. A. T. Walden to William Hartsfield, July 25, 1955, Walden Papers.

29. Tuck, *Beyond Atlanta*, 92.

30. Galphin, "School Segregation May Be Tested Here," *Atlanta Constitution*, December 31, 1957; Wells, "City Pledges Defense in Negro Suits," *Atlanta Constitution*, January
13, 1958.

31. "U.S. Refuses to Void Negroes' School Suit," *Atlanta Constitution*, May 20, 1958;
O'Brien, "Georgia's Response to *Brown*," 233–234.

32. O'Brien, "Georgia's Response to *Brown*," 223.

33. Henderson, Interview.

34. Alfred "Tup" Holmes to A. T. Walden, September 6, 1961, Walden Papers.

35. Lokey, *Low Key Life*, 183.

36. Lokey, *Low Key Life*, 183–93.

37. Lokey and Lokey, Interview.

38. O'Brien, "Georgia's Response to *Brown*," 150–153.

39. Millican, Interview.

40. Lokey and Lokey, Interview.

41. Lokey, *Low Key Life*, 197.

42. "Rep. MacKay Urges Local Control," *Atlanta Constitution*, November 17, 1958;
Gaines, "Smith Vows Bill on School Option," *Atlanta Constitution*, November 19, 1958;
"Lokey Backs Whitman's School Stand," *Atlanta Constitution*, November 22, 1958.

43. Lokey, *Low Key Life*.

44. This summary of white suburban attitudes is based on the extensive descriptions
of these mind-sets given in Lassiter, *Silent Majority*, and Kruse, *White Flight*.

45. Nan Pendergrast, Interview, June 24, 1992, GGDP.

46. Pendergrast, Interview.

47. "Moye, LeCraw Petitions Are Circulated," *Atlanta Constitution*, August 26, 1954.

48. "GOPs Say 5th District to Elect Moye," *Atlanta Constitution*, October 9, 1954.

49. Charlie Yates to Judge Gunby, October 12, 1954; Copy of letter from Moye campaign organizer Randolph Thrower and unsigned memo to James C. Davis, October 28, 1954, all in Davis Papers.

50. "GOPs Say 5th District to Elect Moye."

51. "GOP Candidate Moye Opposes Amendment," *Atlanta Constitution*, October 16, 1954.

52. Results for the 1954 amendment are based on the returns listed in the *Georgia Official and Statistical Register, 1953–54*, 688–92.

53. Riley, "Unit Rule, Davis Hit by Thrower," *Atlanta Constitution*, October 4, 1956; Handwritten notes of speech by Thrower given in Avondale, Georgia, October 29, 1956, Davis Papers.

54. "GOP Selects Thrower to Face Davis," *Atlanta Constitution*, September 10, 1958.

55. "GOPs Here May Have Missed Out," *Atlanta Constitution*, September 24, 1958.

56. Lokey and Lokey, Interview; Pendergrast, Interview.

57. Technically, there were General Assembly elections scheduled for November 1960, but the strength of local incumbency, added to the malapportionment favoring areas supportive of massive resistance, made this far less plausible than a gubernatorial victory, even with the county-unit system in place. Not only that, but even November 1960 was too long to wait to begin to mobilize public opinion—the showdown over massive resistance was by then only weeks away. Prevailing in that showdown required campaigning long before then.

58. Chappell, *Inside Agitators*, xxv.

59. Text of Address to HOPE Rally, March 4, 1959, Pauley Papers.

60. HOPE, Official Statement, December 5, 1959, Pauley Papers.

61. Lokey and Lokey, Interview.

62. Speech by Hamilton Lokey to Georgia League of Women Voters, Savannah, April 7, 1959, HOPE Papers.

63. Pendergrast, Interview.

64. O'Brien, "Georgia's Response to *Brown*," 227.

65. Lokey and Lokey, Interview.

66. Lassiter, *Silent Majority*, 61–62.

67. Brady, *Black Monday*, 45.

68. Nasstrom, *Everybody's Grandmother*, 56.

69. Lassiter, *Silent Majority*, 77.

70. Pendergrast, Interview.

71. Mertz, "Mind Changing Time All Over Georgia," 52.

72. Nasstrom, *Everybody's Grandmother*, 55.

73. O'Brien, "Georgia's Response to *Brown*," 251–257.

74. Kruse, *White Flight*, 134–141.

75. O'Brien, "Georgia's Response to *Brown*," 273.

76. Griffin Bell, Interview, September 24, 1997, GPHC.

77. An example of Bloch's view can be found in a private letter he wrote to Ralph McGill in which he promised that "the Federal Government may someday enjoin the

operation of segregated schools in Georgia. *It can never compel Georgia to operate integrated schools—never, never*" [emphasis in original letter]. Charles Bloch to Ralph McGill, December 12, 1958, HOPE Papers. Roy Harris made several public statements to similar effect; see, for example, his editorial in the *Augusta Courier* of November 9, 1959, a clipping of which is in the HOPE Papers.

78. Henderson, *Ernest Vandiver*, 140–142.

79. Henderson, *Ernest Vandiver*, 133.

80. Cook, "Carl Sanders," 179.

Chapter 4. "A Truly Democratic Party": 1962–1966

Epigraph source: Erwin Mitchell, speech to DeKalb County Democrats, February 19, 1961, Williams Papers.

1. J. B. Fuqua to Mrs. James E. Duffell, December 27, 1962, Williams Papers.

2. Jones, "Atlanta Politics," 22.

3. Tuck, *Beyond Atlanta*, 110–112.

4. Kruse, *White Flight*, 183.

5. Jones, "Atlanta Politics," 89–95.

6. Kruse, *White Flight*, 192; Tuck, *Beyond Atlanta*, 120–121; Jones, "Atlanta Politics," 42.

7. Bartley, *From Thurmond to Wallace*, 30, 33.

8. *Georgia Official and Statistical Register, 1959–60*, 867.

9. Henderson, *Ernest Vandiver*, 122–23.

10. Wannamaker, "Charles Longstreet Weltner," 100.

11. Wannamaker, "Charles Longstreet Weltner," 102–103.

12. Charles Weltner to Richard Russell, August 10, 1960, Russell Papers.

13. Scammon, McGillivary, and Cook, *America at the Polls*, 247–249; Calhoun, "Significant Aspects," 88.

14. John M. Bailey, "Remarks at Fulton County Democratic Club Dinner," May 18, 1965, DNC Papers.

15. Wannamaker, "Charles Longstreet Weltner," 204, 248; Weltner, Interview, GGDP; Charles Weltner, Interview, May 16, 1991, GPHC.

16. Wannamaker, "Charles Longstreet Weltner," 38–53 (Philip Weltner quote on 53).

17. Weltner, Interview, GGDP; Weltner, Interview, GPHC.

18. Wannamaker, "Charles Longstreet Weltner," 57; Weltner, Interview, GPHC.

19. Wannamaker, "Charles Longstreet Weltner," 98–99.

20. Weltner, Interview, GPHC.

21. Wannamaker, "Charles Longstreet Weltner," 110.

22. "Davis Tied to the Past," *Atlanta Constitution*, August 11, 1962; "Rep. Davis Views Belong in Nineteenth Century," *Atlanta Constitution*, August 30, 1962; "Weltner Rips Davis," *Atlanta Constitution*, August 10, 1962.

23. "He Helped 5th District, Davis Says," *Atlanta Constitution*, August 7, 1962.

24. Wannamaker, "Charles Longstreet Weltner," 118–120.

25. Weltner, Interview, GPHC.

26. "Weltner Hits Back at O'Callaghan Jab," *Atlanta Constitution*, October 11, 1962.

27. "It Isn't Over," *Atlanta Constitution*, October 17, 1962.

28. "It Isn't Over"; "Weltner, O'Callaghan Get Tough in the Final Stretch," *Atlanta Constitution*, October 29, 1962.

29. "O'Callaghan Trades Jabs with Weltner," *Atlanta Constitution*, October 12, 1962.

30. Wannamaker, "Charles Longstreet Weltner," 127; "2 Congress Rivals Battle to the Wire," *Atlanta Constitution*, November 6, 1962 (Weltner quote).

31. "O'Callaghan Denies Weltner Charges," *Atlanta Constitution*, October 31, 1962.

32. Wannamaker, "Charles Longstreet Weltner," 150.

33. Weltner, Interview, GPHC.

34. Wannamaker, "Charles Longstreet Weltner," 147, 155.

35. Wannamaker, "Charles Longstreet Weltner," 172.

36. Wannamaker, "Charles Longstreet Weltner," 166–167.

37. Weltner, Interview, GGDP.

38. Black and Black, *Rise of Southern Republicans*, 174–201.

39. Wannamaker, "Charles Longstreet Weltner," 204, 218–228, 241–244.

40. Wannamaker, "Charles Longstreet Weltner," 249.

41. Weltner, Interview, GGDP.

42. Weltner, Interview, GGDP.

43. Wannamaker, "Charles Longstreet Weltner," 187.

44. Weltner, Interview, GPHC.

45. Untitled/undated newspaper clipping, "DeKalb County Democrats: Minutes, Clippings, Proposals," Williams Papers.

46. "Statement of Purpose for DeKalb County Democrats," October 10, 1961, Williams Papers.

47. "Statement to Election Laws Study Committee by DeKalb County Democrats," July 13, 1961, Williams Papers.

48. Mitchell, "Speech to DeKalb County Democrats."

49. "Reapportion by Jan. 1," *Atlanta Constitution*, September 6, 1962; "Senate Votes 54-Seat Plan," *Atlanta Constitution*, October 2, 1962.

50. Murphy, "Georgia GOPs Pave Way to Prestige," *Atlanta Constitution*, October 8, 1962; "16 in GOP Senate Race as Time Runs Out," *Atlanta Constitution*, October 12, 1962; List of Georgia GOP candidates, *Atlanta Constitution*, October 13, 1962.

51. "Negro Democrat Wins," *Atlanta Constitution*, November 7, 1962.

52. Melba Williams to J. B. Fuqua, October 1962, "DeKalb Democrats Correspondence," Williams Papers.

53. J. B. Fuqua to Mrs. James E. Duffell, December 27, 1962, Williams Papers.

54. Melba Williams to J. B. Fuqua, May 14, 1963, Williams Papers.

55. J. B. Fuqua to Melba Williams, July 17, 1963, Williams Papers.

56. Some of these Republican moderates, Alderman Rodney Mims Cook himself for one, had a sincere moral belief in the rightness of ending Jim Crow, and it would be unfair to dismiss their appeals for black support solely in pragmatic terms; however, the belief that racial strife would hamper economic progress was common to both sincere and opportunistic Republican moderates by the early 1960s.

57. Memo from Fulton County Planning Committee, January 1961, Cook Papers.

58. Recommendations of the Planning Committee Concerning the Public Schools, 1961–1962, Cook Papers.

59. *Operation Breakthrough*, Fulton County Republicans, 1963, Cook Papers.

60. "The Militant Mood of the Georgia Republicans," clipping from *Atlanta Magazine*, February 1963, Cook Papers.

61. Proposed Resolution for the Georgia Republican Party, July 12, 1963, Cook Papers.

62. Kelsey D. Howington to Democratic County Officials in DeKalb County, August 1963, Williams Papers.

63. Melba Williams to Charles Weltner, August 25, 1963, Williams Papers.

64. Melba Williams to J. B. Fuqua, August 26, 1963, Williams Papers.

65. J. B. Fuqua to Melba Williams, October 27, 1963, Williams Papers.

66. J. B. Fuqua to Melba Williams and Carl Sanders to Melba Williams, January 9 and 11, 1964, both in Williams Papers.

67. Press release from the Democratic Party of DeKalb County, July 1966, Williams Papers.

68. Kenneth O'Donnell to Kelsey D. Howington, June 15, 1964; Lyndon B. Johnson to Liona Levatan, June 17, 1964, both in White House Central Files.

69. James MacKay, Speech to the DeKalb County Convention, July 16, 1966, Williams Papers.

70. Mrs. Charles J. Alford to Kelsey Howington, July 11, 1966, Williams Papers.

71. George H. Carley to Kelsey Howington, July 18, 1966, Williams Papers.

72. A special round of General Assembly elections was held in 1965 when the state house was also reapportioned. The new apportionments benefited both local parties in Fulton and DeKalb counties, with the former's delegation going from three Democrats elected to the House in 1962 to nineteen Democrats and five Republicans in 1965; in DeKalb, the figure went from three Democrats in 1962 to eight Democrats and four Republicans in 1965.

73. Shafer and Johnston, *End of Southern Exceptionalism*, 47–50.

74. http://www.dekalbdems.org/.

75. Brown, Interview.

76. Tuck, *Beyond Atlanta*, 193. Tuck also notes that it was not long after this appearance, where Talmadge promised to support black appointments and causes, that he began kissing black babies on the campaign trail.

77. Jack Turner to Louis Martin (DNC vice-chair), November 19, 1966, White House Central Files.

78. Herman Talmadge to John Bailey, November 21, 1966, White House Central Files. Exactly what Talmadge meant by Booker being a "neutral" organizer is not entirely clear—he certainly did not mean it in a partisan sense, as the rest of his letter is clearly about organizing Democratic votes. It is possible he meant someone who was not openly affiliated with the civil rights movement.

79. Cook, *Carl Sanders*.

80. Henderson, *Ernest Vandiver*, 133.

81. "Griffin, Sanders Hold Giant Rallies," *Atlanta Constitution*, August 16, 1962.

82. "Negro Democrat Wins."

83. Untitled *New York Times* clipping, February 12, 1963, New York Times Research Collection.

84. Watters, "Senator Johnson's Role Is Lonely & Troubled," *Atlanta Journal*, February 12, 1963, New York Times Research Collection.

85. J. B. Fuqua to Jack Valenti, December 9, 1963, White House Central Files.

86. Spritzer and Bergmark, *Grace Towns Hamilton*, 167–168.

87. Ralph McGill to Lyndon Johnson, May 21, 1965, White House Central Files.

88. Spritzer and Bergmark, *Grace Towns Hamilton*, 159; for details of the visits to the White House, see the White House Names File for "Johnson, Leroy" and "Hamilton, Grace Towns," LBJL.

89. Brown, Interview.

90. "Georgia House Dispute," *Congressional Quarterly*, January 14, 1966, 46.

91. For a discussion on the various civil rights campaigns in Georgia at this time and the response of the state government and local law enforcement, see Tuck, *Beyond Atlanta*, chapters 4–6.

92. Simpson, "Loyalist Democrats," 33.

93. Lyndon Johnson and Carl Sanders, July 24, 1964, White House Tapes. It is important to note that in this and other phone conversations, Johnson knew he was being recorded, whereas Carl Sanders (as far as we know) did not; it is always possible that Johnson was speaking for posterity rather than offering his full thoughts, but he was nonetheless trying to convince Sanders to do what he (Johnson) wanted, so at the very least the actions he wants Sanders to carry out are likely genuinely desired by the White House, even if the motives Johnson gives for them may not necessarily be the true ones.

94. Lyndon Johnson and Carl Sanders, August 1, 1964, White House Tapes.

95. Lyndon Johnson and Carl Sanders, August 17, 1964, White House Tapes.

96. Lyndon Johnson and Carl Sanders, August 25, 1964, White House Tapes.

97. Lyndon Johnson and Carl Sanders, August 25, 1964, White House Tapes.

98. J. B. Fuqua to Jack Valenti, July 6, 1964, White Central Files.

99. Lyndon Johnson and Carl Sanders, August 29, 1964, White House Tapes.

100. Julian Webb to Lyndon Johnson, October 5, 1964, White House Central Files.

101. Lawrence O'Brien, Memo to Lyndon Johnson, September 24, 1964, White House Central Files.

102. Douglass Cater, Memo to Lyndon Johnson, October 16, 1964, White House Central Files.

103. Ellis Arnall to Lyndon Johnson, November 4, 1964, White House Central Files.

104. Ernest Vandiver to Jack Valenti, November 1964, White House Central Files.

105. H. M. Conway to Lyndon Johnson, November 13, 1964, White House Central Files.

106. Walter McDonald to Lyndon Johnson, November 12, 1964, White House Central Files.

107. Carl Sanders and Lyndon Johnson, May 23, 1966, White House Tapes.

108. Cook, "Carl Sanders," 179–182.

109. The 1970 election campaign will be discussed more fully in chapter 6, but the

personal nature of the Carter-Sanders campaign is well covered in Sanders, *Mighty Peculiar Elections*, 146–169.

110. Carl Sanders and Lyndon Johnson, July 1, 1966, White House Tapes.

Chapter 5. "The Damndest Mess": 1966

Epigraph source: Lee White, Memo to Paul Popple, January 28, 1966, "Maddox, Lester," White House Names Files.

1. Lester Maddox to Lyndon Johnson, June 26, 1964, "Maddox, Lester," White House Names Files.

2. Tuck, *Beyond Atlanta*, 194; Bartley, *From Thurmond to Wallace*, 67–68; Sherrill, *Gothic Politics*, 133; Henderson, "1966 Gubernatorial Election," 5; Kruse, *White Flight*, 233.

3. This was the cautionary reply allegedly given by British prime minister Harold Macmillan when an overeager Conservative Party aide rhetorically asked what could possibly derail Macmillan's seeming certain reelection in 1959.

4. Lyndon Johnson and Richard Russell, June 2, 1966, White House Tapes.

5. Henderson, "1966 Gubernatorial Election," 52.

6. Henderson, "1966 Gubernatorial Election," 52. To diehard "massive resisteors" such as Lester Maddox and former Speaker of the General Assembly Roy Harris, Vandiver was still a sellout little better than either Carl Sanders or Ellis Arnall—but to the bulk of Regular Democrats, Vandiver was an eminently acceptable choice.

7. Walter McDonald to Jimmy Carter, February 21, 1965, Williams Papers.

8. Undated, untitled newspaper clipping, Williams Papers.

9. Examples of this included a change to "Rule 10" of the state party that would allow the governor to dismiss party officials suspected of disloyalty, a move that alarmed Melba Williams of the DeKalb County Democrats, who argued that Loyalist organizations should not fear a gubernatorial veto over their appointments. Undated, untitled newspaper clipping, Williams Papers.

10. "Ellis Arnall, the Orator and Happy Warrior," *Atlanta Constitution*, July 27, 1966.

11. Lyndon Johnson and Carl Sanders, May 23, 1966, White House Tapes.

12. A. J. Strickland III to Bill Jordan, October 1, 1966, Russell Papers.

13. Tyson, "Talmadge's Bandwagon for Governor Rolls On," *Atlanta Constitution*, May 19, 1966.

14. Lyndon Johnson and Carl Sanders, May 23, 1966, White House Tapes.

15. Henderson, "1966 Gubernatorial Election," 67.

16. The "kingmakers'" explanation is offered by Sherrill, *Gothic Politics*, 70; the fear of failure suggestion is put forward by Henderson, "1966 Gubernatorial Election," 67–68. Of course, these reasons are not necessarily mutually exclusive—but there is evident disagreement over Talmadge's *primary* reason for dropping out.

17. This section is based on a nonstatistical survey of the letters, telegrams, and postcards that Talmadge left in his papers at the Richard Russell Library. At a minimum, according to the estimate offered by an Atlanta journalist, there were several thousand messages received over the two days during which the possibility of his candidacy was

discussed. Tyson, "[Talmadge] Has Made No Decision," *Atlanta Constitution*, May 21, 1966.

18. Tyson, "State GOP Blocked, Say Democrats," *Atlanta Constitution*, May 20, 1966.

19. Cortez Lamb, Chairman, Catoosa County Democratic Executive Committee, to Herman Talmadge, May 19, 1966, Talmadge Papers.

20. Joe Frank Harris to Herman Talmadge, May 18, 1966; Frank Twitty to Herman Talmadge, May 18, 1966, both in Talmadge Papers.

21. Hamilton Lokey to Herman Talmadge, May 19, 1966; Robert M. Clark Jr. to Herman Talmadge, May 18, 1966, both in Talmadge Papers.

22. Walter Davis to Herman Talmadge, May 19, 1966, Talmadge Papers.

23. K. T. Mayfield, telegram to Herman Talmadge, May 19, 1966; Rose Johnson, telegram to Herman Talmadge, May 18, 1966; "Six Registered Voters," telegram to Herman Talmadge, May 19, 1966, all in Talmadge Papers.

24. Frank M. Scarlett to Herman Talmadge, May 20, 1966, Talmadge Papers.

25. Hopkins, "Talmadge? He's Just in a Mess," *Atlanta Constitution*, May 23, 1966; Tyson, "Talmadge Case: The Way It Was," *Atlanta Constitution*, May 24, 1966.

26. Henderson, "1966 Gubernatorial Election," 169.

27. See, for example, Bourne, *Jimmy Carter*; Morris, *Jimmy Carter*; or Lasky, *Jimmy Carter*.

28. Bourne, *Jimmy Carter*, 105.

29. Travis B. Stewart to Jimmy Carter, December 17, 1964, Carter Papers.

30. Jimmy Carter to Leroy Johnson, March 22, 1965, Carter Papers.

31. Jimmy Carter to Herman Talmadge, March 28, 1966, Carter Papers.

32. Jimmy Carter to Will Wallace, November 3, 1965, Carter Papers.

33. Jimmy Carter to Edward Kennedy, November 3, 1965, Carter Papers.

34. Bourne, *Jimmy Carter*, 158.

35. Henderson, "1966 Gubernatorial Election," 156.

36. All calculations for the 1966 primary results are taken from the official voting returns by county listed in the *Georgia Official and Statistical Register, 1965–66*, 1736–1738. The demographic information comes from the *Nineteenth Census of Population: 1970*, Vol. 1, *Characteristics of the Population, Part 12: Georgia*, Table 16, 53–54, Table 43, 232–233, and Table 44, 234–235.

37. Maddox received 185,672 votes to Carter's 164,562; a switch of 10,556 ballots from Maddox to Carter—just 1.4 percent of all ballots cast—would have put Carter in second place.

38. Bass and DeVries, *Transformation of Southern Politics*, provides good summaries of the situation in Virginia (349–351), South Carolina (255, 259–260), and Arkansas (91–93); Earl Black, in *Southern Governors*, gives an overview of the campaigns and candidates in Tennessee (194–196) and Florida (226–230, 272–273).

39. John Criswell to Marvin Watson, September 15, 1966, White House Central Files.

40. Hopkins, "Arnall Says Real Issue Is Peace or Ax-Handles," *Atlanta Constitution*, September 21, 1966 (first and third quotations); Hopkins, "Maddox Preaching Fear, Extremism, Arnall Says," September 22, 1966, *Atlanta Constitution*, (second, fourth, and

fifth quotations); "Arnall Cites Need of Party Platform," *Atlanta Constitution*, September 24, 1966 (sixth quotation).

41. Riner, "Maddox Offers a Prayer for 'Frustrated' Arnall," *Atlanta Constitution*, September 22, 1966 (first quotation); Hopkins, "Arnall Says Real Issue Is Peace or Ax-Handles" (second and third quotations); Riner, "Maddox Accuses Arnall of Extremes," *Atlanta Constitution*, September 24, 1966 (fourth quotation); Maddox campaign ad, *Atlanta Constitution*, September 27, 1966.

42. In 1954, with a five-man field, north Georgia gave the two Loyalist candidates combined 2.7 percent less of the vote than they received across the state.

43. Calculations for the 1966 runoffs are taken from the official voting returns by county listed in the *Georgia Official and Statistical Register, 1965–66*, 1777–1779. Demographic information is taken from the tables in the U.S. Census Report of 1970 listed in note 36 above.

44. Henderson, "1966 Gubernatorial Election," 181. Having an open primary meant that any registered voter in the state could take part, regardless of party affiliation. In the old days of the one-party South, this had been perfectly rational, as there was no opposition party to speak of. The view among Loyalists that there had been Republicans voting in the 1966 Democratic primaries led to a rule change, which took effect by 1970, that voters would have to register their party preference and choose in which of the two parties' primaries they wanted to cast their ballot.

45. Galphin, *Riddle of Lester Maddox*, 115; Henderson, "1966 Gubernatorial Election," 187–188.

46. It is of course also theoretically possible that these were different people—that is, that tens of thousands of those who had supported Maddox in the runoff simply stayed at home in November, while tens of thousands of Republican voters who had not taken part in the Democratic primary voted for Callaway; this is, however, extremely unlikely in reality—those who vote in primaries tend to vote in general elections as well.

47. Henderson, "1966 Gubernatorial Election," 178.

48. Brown, "No. 2 Race Is Bitter to Last," *Atlanta Constitution*, September 28, 1966.

49. "Geer, Smith Agree on Top 2 Needs," *Atlanta Constitution*, September 19, 1966.

50. Galphin, *Riddle of Lester Maddox*, 135.

51. As was the case in many states, Georgia provided a space on its ballot papers where one could write in the name of a candidate other than those listed on the ballot. Should someone whose name is "written in" achieve more votes than any designated candidate, he or she would win the election.

52. Penetration Research, Ltd., "A Survey of the Political Climate in Georgia, October 1966," Vandiver Papers.

53. Galphin, *Riddle of Lester Maddox*, 137; Henderson, "1966 Gubernatorial Election," 203.

54. Frederickson, *Dixiecrat Revolt*, 163.

55. "Memorandum No. 1," October 5, 1966; Address by John Sibley to DFC, October 24, 1966; Pre-Election Statement by Robert Heard at a DFC Meeting, November 5, 1966, all in Vandiver Papers.

56. Galphin, *Riddle of Lester Maddox*, 124–125.

57. "Smith Wins Poll on Write-In Candidates," *Atlanta Constitution*, October 5, 1966; Galphin, *Riddle of Lester Maddox*, 125–126.

58. Al Kehrer, Memo to WIG Members, "Georgia Independent Democratic Caucus," October 6, 1966; John B. Morris, "Letter to a Fellow Georgian," October 7, 1966, both in Morris Papers; "1,000-Member Union Unit Endorses Arnall Write-In," *Atlanta Constitution*, November 4, 1966.

59. Galphin, *Riddle of Lester Maddox*, 124.

60. Carl Sanders to John Morris, October 13, 1966, Morris Papers.

61. Ellis Arnall to John B. Morris, October 21, 1966, Morris Papers.

62. Galphin, *Riddle of Lester Maddox*, 126–127.

63. All calculations for the 1966 general election and comparisons with the 1964 presidential election in Georgia are taken from voting returns listed in, respectively, the *Georgia Official and Statistical Register, 1965–66*, 1786–1788, and Scammon, McGillivray, and Cook, *America at the Polls*, 244–246. The demographic information is taken from the tables in the U.S. Census report of 1970 listed in note 36 above.

64. That the Republican Party faced such a dilemma was a further reflection of the impact that uncertainty about an electorate's preferences can have on partisan political strategy. With the demographic changes (in-migration and the rise in black voter population) taking place in the southern electorate during the 1960s and the transition to two-party politics, neither party could be quite sure where the "median voter" it needed to appeal to was located; as such, the back-and-forth in the Republican Party over which political strategy to follow during the 1960s and 1970s was in part a perfectly understandable (even rational) response to the uncertainty of the political situation. This issue is considered in more theoretical detail in Grose and Yoshinaka, "Ideological Hedging in Uncertain Times."

65. In reality, the total was probably substantially higher. More than 18,000 votes for Arnall in Fulton County were discounted because they had not been transmitted to the Georgia Assembly in the "proper" envelope. Likewise, all ballots spelling Arnall's name as "Arnold," "Arnell," or "Armdell" (and many other variations) were dismissed, which included several thousand more; see Galphin, *Riddle of Lester Maddox*, 165–166.

66. Bartley, *New South*, 392.

Chapter 6. The Loyalist Backlash: 1966–1971

Epigraph source: John B. Morris, "Testimony Before the Credentials Committee, Chicago," August 21, 1968, Morris Papers.

1. Roberts, "Will the Real Maddox Please Stand Up?" *New York Times*, January 15, 1967.

2. Roberts, "Will the Real Maddox Please Stand Up?"

3. See in particular Lassiter, *Silent Majority*, 251–275; and Sanders, *Mighty Peculiar Elections*, 170–175.

4. Galphin, *Riddle of Lester Maddox*.

5. Lee White, Memo to Paul Popple, January 28, 1966, "Maddox, Lester," White House Name Files.

6. Galphin, *Riddle of Lester Maddox*, 168.

7. Henry H. Wilson, Memo to Marvin Watson, January 13, 1967, White House Central Files.

8. Farris Bryant, Memo to Lyndon Johnson, February 27, 1967, White House Central Files.

9. Hubert Humphrey, Memo to Lyndon Johnson, April 17, 1967, White House Central Files.

10. Galphin, *Riddle of Lester Maddox*, 213–214.

11. Galphin, *Riddle of Lester Maddox*, 203–204.

12. John Morris to John M. Bailey, April 9, 1967, Morris Papers.

13. John Morris to Richard Russell, Herman Talmadge, and Lester Maddox, April 9, 1967, Morris Papers.

14. William Trotter to John Morris, April 18, 1967, and reply from Morris, May 3, 1967, Morris Papers.

15. John Morris to John M. Bailey, Carl Sanders, Ellis Arnall, and George T. Smith, May 16, 1967, Morris Papers.

16. John Morris to Robert Kennedy, April 20, 1967, Morris Papers.

17. John Morris to Joe Sports, April 13, 1967, Morris Papers.

18. Tyson, "Maddox Blasts Loyal Democrats," *Atlanta Constitution*, July 12, 1967.

19. Robert Griffith, "The Georgia Challenge: New Politics and Old," Clarke County McCarthy for President Collection.

20. "Gray Repeats '68 Backing of Slate as Maddox Jeers," *Atlanta Constitution*, November 21, 1967; "Demo Official Denies Maddox, Gray Rift," *Atlanta Journal*, November 28, 1967; "Maddox Fears Loss in Support for Johnson," *Atlanta Journal*, November 29, 1967.

21. "G. T. Smith Urges National Party Support," *Atlanta Journal*, December 1, 1967.

22. "Gray to Bar Non-Democrats in the Primary," *Atlanta Constitution*, May 22, 1968.

23. John B. Morris to John Bailey, December 12, 1967; Morris to Bailey, January 2, 1968, February 13, 1968; E. T. Kehrer to John Bailey, January 30, 1968; John Bailey to John B. Morris, March 5, 1968, all in Morris Papers.

24. John B. Morris to Governor Richard J. Hughes, January 15, 1968, Morris Papers.

25. Phinizy Spalding, Open letter to Governor Hughes, July 24, 1968, Clarke County McCarthy for President Collection; John B. Morris, Telegram to Governor Hughes, July 27, 1968, Morris Papers.

26. Letter from the Office of Governor Hughes to Phinizy Spalding, August 9, 1968, Clarke County McCarthy for President Collection.

27. John Morris to Governor Hughes, January 15, 1968; E. T. Kehrer to John Bailey, January 30, 1968, both in Morris Papers; Open letter from Phinizy Spalding, July 24, 1968, Clarke County McCarthy for President Collection.

28. For more on the Loyalists' organizing efforts in Mississippi, see Simpson, "Loyalist Democrats," 51–79.

29. John B. Morris to Dr. John Cashin, February 13, 1968, Morris Papers.

30. Claude Ramsey to John B. Morris, February 19, 1968, Morris Papers.

31. Governor Hughes to State Democratic Chairmen, Morris Papers.

32. John B. Morris, "Draft Position Paper on Maddox Delegation," June 18, 1968, Morris Papers.

33. See, for example, "Two-Man Consensus," *Atlanta Constitution,* July 5, 1968; "Maddox Choice Ignores Party Faithful," *Macon Telegraph,* July 6, 1968; "Georgia Democratic Party 1968," Morris Papers.

34. John B. Morris to GDF Members, July 9, 1968; John B. Morris to John Bailey, July 9, 1968, both in Morris Papers.

35. E. T. Kehrer to Robert W. Griffith, June 14, 1968; Robert W. Griffith to Maurice Rosenblatt, July 7, 1968, both in Clarke County McCarthy for President Collection.

36. Griffith, "Georgia Challenge."

37. Ralph B. Draughan to McCarthy Supporters, August 6, 1968, Clarke County McCarthy for President Collection.

38. John B. Morris, "Testimony to the Credentials Committee," August 21, 1968, Morris Papers.

39. Julian Bond, "Testimony to the Credentials Committee," August 21, 1968, Morris Papers.

40. John B. Morris, "A Summary of Factors," Morris Papers.

41. Robert Griffith to John B. Morris, September 1, 1968, Morris Papers.

42. All calculations for the 1968 presidential election are taken from the voting returns in the *Georgia Official and Statistical Register 1967–68,* 1651–67. Information for the demographic categorization comes from the *Eighteenth Census of the United States: 1960* and the *Nineteenth Census of the United States: 1970* as explained in note 36 in chapter 5.

43. The loss in Fannin County was surprising in that the GOP had won the seat in 1966, and Nixon carried the county with 59 percent of the vote in 1968—his highest proportion of the vote in any Georgia county.

44. Rev. John Gregg, "Seeking a New Day for Cobb County Democrats," June 16, 1969, Morris Papers; "Democrats Score Party in Georgia," *New York Times,* June 17, 1969.

45. "Hearing in Atlanta," *Louisville Courier-Journal,* February 22, 1970.

46. E. T. Kehrer to James Gray, May 11, 1970; GDF Press Release, May 28, 1970, both in New York Times Research Collection.

47. Shipp and Nesmith, "Maddox Sees Disaster If Can't Run," *Atlanta Constitution,* January 27, 1970; "Carter Would Invite Wallace to Georgia," *Atlanta Constitution,* August 26, 1970.

48. "Campaign of Issues Sought by Sanders," *Atlanta Constitution,* June 4, 1970; Shipp, "Democrats Push On, Pledging Fairness—Sanders," *Atlanta Constitution,* September 3, 1970.

49. Shipp, "Surge of Candidates," *Atlanta Constitution,* June 4, 1970.

50. Sanders, *Mighty Peculiar Elections,* 150.

51. Shipp, "Carter Extols Maddox," *Atlanta Constitution,* October 27, 1970.

52. Nesmith, "Candidates Rap Protests," *Atlanta Constitution,* January 13, 1970.

53. Stephens, "Carter Announces, Raps Sanders," *Atlanta Constitution,* April 4, 1970.

54. Riner and Shipp, "Carter: Aid Retarded; Sanders: Battle Drugs," *Atlanta Constitution,* September 2, 1970.

55. Seddon, "Increase Sales Tax for Schools—Carter," *Atlanta Constitution,* July 28, 1970; Shipp, "Carter Vows to Halt Crime in Atlanta," *Atlanta Constitution,* August 6,

1970; "Carter Pledges Quality Schools," *Atlanta Constitution*, August 19, 1970; Riner and Shipp, "Carter: Aid Retarded"; Shipp, "Carter Extols Maddox."

56. Shipp, "Sanders' Day at Statesboro," *Atlanta Constitution*, August 8, 1970.

57. "Governor Candidates Debate Desegregation," *Atlanta Constitution*, August 4, 1970.

58. All calculations for the 1970 Democratic runoff results are taken from the official voting returns by county listed in the *Georgia Official and Statistical Register, 1969–70*, 1658–1660. The demographic information comes from the *Nineteenth Census of Population: 1970*, Vol. 1: *Characteristics of the Population, Part 12: Georgia*, Table 16, 53–54, Table 43, 232–233, and Table 44, 234–235.

59. Ball, "Survey Shows Bentley Holds Lead over Suit," *Atlanta Constitution*, April 26, 1970.

60. Shipp, "Seems as if It's Bentley v. Bus," *Atlanta Constitution*, August 18, 1970.

61. Stephens, "GOP Hopefuls State Positions on Schools," *Atlanta Constitution*, August 28, 1970; Stephens and Adamson, "Bentley Launches Stop-Busing Drive," *Atlanta Constitution*, September 2, 1970.

62. Stephens, "GOP Hopefuls State Positions on Schools."

63. "Hal Suit May Enter Gubernatorial Race," *Atlanta Constitution*, January 6, 1970.

64. Shipp, "Bentley Troubled by Own Party," *Atlanta Constitution*, February 18, 1970; Bowler, "Pressure in GOP Charged," *Atlanta Constitution*, March 21, 1970; "G. Paul Jones to Campaign for Hal Suit," *Atlanta Constitution*, August 9, 1970.

65. Riner, "Suit Backs 3-Day Wait on Purchase of Guns," *Atlanta Constitution*, August 12, 1970; Riner and Stepp, "Hal Suit Lays Religion Smear to 2 GOPs," *Atlanta Constitution*, August 14, 1970; "Nine Questions for Carter, Suit," *Atlanta Constitution*, November 1, 1970.

66. All calculations for the 1970 Republican primary are taken from the official voting returns by county listed in the *Georgia Official and Statistical Register, 1969–70*, 1669–1671. The demographic information comes from the same tables as in note 58 above.

67. Shipp, "School Desegregation Has Failed, Suit Says," *Atlanta Constitution*, October 21, 1970.

68. "Suit Politics in Atlanta, Thomasville," *Atlanta Constitution*, October 8, 1970.

69. Shipp, "Carter Asks Reform at Macon Convention," *Atlanta Constitution*, October 7, 1970.

70. Merrill, "Young Says Carter Can Unite Demos," *Atlanta Constitution*, October 4, 1970.

71. All calculations for the 1970 gubernatorial general election are taken from the official voting returns by county listed in the *Georgia Official and Statistical Register, 1969–70*, 1752–1753. The demographic information comes from the same tables as in note 58 above.

72. Stephens, "Miller Raps Foe on Funds," *Atlanta Constitution*, September 15, 1970.

73. Shipp, "Carter Is Sworn In."

74. Shipp, "Carter's Pledge to End Bias Shows Times Have Changed," *Atlanta Constitution*, January 13, 1971.

Chapter 7. The New South in State and Nation: 1971–1976

Epigraph source: Jimmy Carter, Third Presidential Debate, October 22, 1976, quoted in *Presidential Campaign, 1976*, Vol. 3, 140–141.

1. See, for example, the discussion of the 1976 result from writers sympathetic to and critical of Carter, including Rae, *Southern Democrats*, 55–56; Bourne, *Jimmy Carter*, 270; Black and Black, *Rise of Southern Republicans*, 213; Carter, *From George Wallace to Newt Gingrich*, 54; Barone, *Our Country*, 558, 596.

2. Lassiter, *Silent Majority*, 270.

3. Wheeler, *Jimmy Who?* 80–81.

4. Wheeler, *Jimmy Who?* 184; Bourne, *Jimmy Carter*, 213.

5. Rohrer, "Georgia Sues on Schools," *Atlanta Constitution*, April 28, 1971.

6. Hurt, "Thompson Hits Nixon on Housing," *Atlanta Constitution*, June 16, 1971; Riner, "GOP's Shaw Raps Romney," *Atlanta Constitution*, June 19, 1971.

7. Hurt, "Thompson Stresses Busing and Job Quotas," *Atlanta Constitution*, September 2, 1971.

8. Shipp, "Wallace Urges Busing Battle by Governors," *Atlanta Constitution*, September 14, 1971.

9. Shipp, "Dixie Wooed for '72 Race," *Atlanta Constitution*, March 8, 1971.

10. Riner, "Democratic Leader Woos Georgia," *Atlanta Constitution*, March 18, 1971; Shipp, "Four Southern Governors Call for End to Politics of Fear," *Atlanta Constitution*, May 1, 1971.

11. Shipp, "Wallace Denies He's Losing Dixie Support," *Atlanta Constitution*, May 20, 1971.

12. Carter, *Politics of Rage*, 417–418.

13. Shipp, "Help Select Nominee, Carter Asks Wallace," *Atlanta Constitution*, May 21, 1971.

14. Shipp, "Wallace Can Hurt Nixon—Carter," *Atlanta Constitution*, August 4, 1971; Shipp, "Governors Cool," *Atlanta Constitution*, November 9, 1971.

15. Shipp, "Wallace Vote in '72 Termed Act of Futility," *Atlanta Constitution*, October 20, 1971.

16. Shipp, "Governors Cool."

17. Fliess, "Carter Avoids Nod to Wallace," *Atlanta Constitution*, June 18, 1972.

18. E. T. Kehrer to Jimmy Carter and David Gambrell, October 7, 1970, GDF Records.

19. James Moore and E. T. Kehrer to David Gambrell, October 30, 1970; James Moore to Laurence O'Brien, December 8, 1970; James Moore to David Gambrell, December 18, 1970, all in GDF Records.

20. Boswell, "Governor Asks Party to Change Old System," *Atlanta Constitution*, July 11, 1971.

21. Shipp, "Democrats Must Elect Delegates," *Atlanta Constitution*, November 20, 1971.

22. Boswell, "Georgia Democrats," *Atlanta Constitution*, November 28, 1971.

23. Shipp, "You've Got to be a Racist to Win?" *Atlanta Constitution*, January 7, 1971.

24. Nesmith, "Georgia Works out Accord," *Atlanta Constitution*, July 10, 1972.

25. "King Holiday Bill Includes Russell," *Atlanta Constitution*, February 16, 1971.

26. "City to Honor Dr. King," *Atlanta Constitution*, January 14, 1973.

27. Bourne, *Jimmy Carter*, 251.

28. Hurt, "Thompson Decides He'll Go for the Senate," *Atlanta Constitution*, January 27, 1972.

29. Cuff, "Thompson Urges Statewide Boycott," *Atlanta Constitution*, February 16, 1972.

30. The comparison with North Carolina is more ambiguous: Jesse Helms was technically less senior in terms of political experience than Congressman Galifianakis, but his status as a well-known and controversial media personality in the state meant that Helms was arguably the "bigger name" in the contest.

31. Fort, "Thompson Top Spender," *Atlanta Constitution*, October 25, 1972.

32. The major exceptions to this were the contacts in many of the state's counties that Nunn had built up through his connections with fellow Democrats in the General Assembly.

33. Nordan, "Fletcher Thompson Denies Using Racist Digs," *Atlanta Constitution*, September 10, 1972.

34. Fort, "Nunn Vows a Calm Drive," *Atlanta Constitution*, September 15, 1972.

35. Fort, "Nunn-Wallace Visit Fake," *Atlanta Constitution*, September 30, 1972.

36. Fort, "Nunn Receives Backing," *Atlanta Constitution*, October 21, 1972.

37. For these calculations, as with the rest of the chapter, "suburban Atlanta" is being counted as Cobb, Clayton, Cherokee, DeKalb, Douglas, Fayette, and Gwinnett counties—the seven counties referenced in the above paragraph.

38. All calculations for the 1972 senatorial election are taken from the official voting returns by county listed in the *Georgia Official and Statistical Register, 1971–72*, 1840–1841. The demographic information comes from the *Nineteenth Census of Population: 1970*, Vol. 1, *Characteristics of the Population, Part 12: Georgia*, Table 43, 232–233, and Table 44, 234–235; and the *Twentieth Census of the United States: 1980. General Population Characteristics: Georgia*, Table 14 and *General Social and Economic Characteristics: Georgia*, Tables 56, 57, and 175.

39. Hamilton Jordan, Memo to Jimmy Carter, November 4, 1972, Carter Papers.

40. Raines, "Racial Attitudes Affect Campaign," *Atlanta Constitution*, July 21, 1974.

41. This image that Busbee sought to promote is well described in Main and Gryski, "George Busbee," 261–278.

42. Porter and Head, "Maddox Opens His Campaign," *Atlanta Constitution*, June 16, 1974.

43. Raines, "Maddox Opens Runoff Race," *Atlanta Constitution*, August 15, 1974.

44. Main and Gryski, "George Busbee," 276.

45. Raines, "Busbee Attacks 2 Rivals," *Atlanta Constitution*, June 7, 1974.

46. Brown, Interview.

47. "Busbee Gets Key Black, Union Help," *Atlanta Constitution*, August 1, 1974.

48. Short, *Everything Is Pickrick*, 147.

49. "Carter Raps Maddox Defeat of Park Land," *Atlanta Constitution*, June 28, 1974; "Carter Hits Lt-Gov. Post," *Atlanta Constitution*, June 28, 1974; "Maddox Mis-Used Patrol," *Atlanta Constitution*, July 26, 1974.

50. Granum, "Carter Calls Maddox Vote 'Poor Showing,'" *Atlanta Constitution*, August 16, 1974.

51. Short, *Everything Is Pickrick*, 145–146.

52. All calculations for the 1974 Democratic runoff are taken from the official voting returns by county listed in the *Georgia Official and Statistical Register, 1973–74*, 1819–1822. The demographic information comes from the same tables as listed in note 38 above.

53. Tuck, *Beyond Atlanta*, 214–215.

54. The four are George Busbee (1975–1983), Joe Frank Harris (1983–1991), Zell Miller (1991–1999), and Sonny Purdue (2003-); the fact that each of these ran for election *as an incumbent* was no doubt also significant—something that had not been possible for serving governors from 1950 to 1974.

55. Bartley, "Moderation in Maddox Country?" 348.

56. Raines, "The Last Hurrah," *Atlanta Constitution*, September 4, 1974.

57. Morrison, "Lester's Fans Still Cheer," *Atlanta Constitution*, September 4, 1974.

58. A notable exception was Larry McDonald, an extremely conservative Democrat who represented Georgia in the U.S. House from 1975 to 1983.

59. Raines, "The Difference: Busbee's Strategy, Style," *Atlanta Constitution*, August 15, 1974.

60. "Thompson Predicts Victory," *Atlanta Constitution*, October 30, 1974.

61. Berman, "Shaw Should Quit—Ronnie," *Atlanta Constitution*, September 6, 1974.

62. Hopkins, "Thompson Not Invited by Ford," *Atlanta Constitution*, September 25, 1974.

63. "Ronnie Ups Security: Blasts Busbee Backing," *Atlanta Constitution*, October 12, 1974.

64. Granum, "Savage Blasts Miller's Support of Race Quotas," *Atlanta Constitution*, October 29, 1974.

65. All calculations for the 1974 elections are taken from the official voting returns by county listed in the *Georgia Official and Statistical Register, 1973–74*, 1898–1900. The demographic information comes from the same tables as listed in note 38 above.

66. Hathorn, "Frustration of Opportunity," 48.

67. Martin, *Civil Rights*, 243.

68. "2,500 Hear Wallace at Calley Rally," *Atlanta Constitution*, April 3, 1971.

69. Woods, "Macon Mayor Urges Calley Medal of Honor," *Atlanta Constitution*, April 11, 1971.

70. Gambrell had been appointed to the U.S. Senate by Jimmy Carter upon the death of Richard Russell in February 1971.

71. Shipp, "Vandiver Attacks Gambrell," *Atlanta Constitution*, June 11, 1971.

72. Shipp, "Carter Move Hits Muskie, McGovern," *Atlanta Constitution*, June 22, 1971.

73. Carter, *Politics of Rage*, 327.

74. "Wallace Puts Defense at Top of '72 Issues," *Atlanta Constitution*, December 7, 1971.

75. Stewart, "Nunn Fires 'Hypocrisy' Charge," *Atlanta Constitution*, July 15, 1972.

76. Cason, "Vandiver Likens Gambrell to McGovern," *Atlanta Constitution*, June 30, 1972.

77. "Gambrell Raps McGovern," *Atlanta Constitution*, July 6, 1972.

78. Hurt, "Senate Votes Strong Ban on Busing," *Atlanta Constitution*, February 26, 1972; "Nunn Raps Gambrell's Busing Vote," *Atlanta Constitution*, May 26, 1972.

79. "Party Too Far Left, Gambrell Warns," *Atlanta Constitution*, February 18, 1972.

80. Fort, "Carter Won't Campaign for McGovern," *Atlanta Constitution*, July 15, 1972.

81. Fort, "Miller Puts Stress on State Races," *Atlanta Constitution*, July 28, 1972.

82. Miroff, *Liberals' Moment*, 177.

83. Miroff, *Liberals' Moment*, 77.

84. Miroff, *Liberals' Moment*, 198.

85. Taylor, "Jane a 'Puppet'—Thompson," *Atlanta Constitution*, July 27, 1972.

86. "Thompson Predicts Victory," *Atlanta Constitution*, October 30, 1974.

87. Berard, *Southern Democrats*.

88. This was the phrase deployed as an analytical framework throughout Scammon and Wattenberg, *Real Majority*.

89. Arnall, "Foreword," in Spritzer, *Belle of Ashby Street*, x.

90. Hamilton Jordan, Memo to Jimmy Carter, November 4, 1972, Carter Papers.

91. Hamilton Jordan, Memo to Jimmy Carter, "The Future of George Wallace," Carter Papers.

92. "The Campaign: Candidate Carter—I Apologize," *Time*, April 19, 1976.

93. Jimmy Carter, "Speech at the Georgia Human Relations Council," July 25, 1974, Carter Papers.

94. Jimmy Carter, "Speech at the Equal Opportunity Employment Council," September 6, 1974, Carter Papers.

95. Press release, "Jimmy Carter Supports Voting Rights Extension," July 24, 1975, Carter Papers.

96. *Presidential Campaign, 1976*, Vol. 1, Part I, "Formal Announcement, December 1974," 4; *Presidential Campaign, 1976*, Vol. 1, Part I, Jimmy Carter, "Interview with Encore & American News," April 1976, 136.

97. Jimmy Carter, Position paper for 1976 presidential campaign on "School Busing," *Presidential Campaign, 1976*, Vol. 1, Part I, 610–611.

98. Carter, Position paper for 1976 presidential campaign on "School Busing," 610–611.

99. Stu Eizenstat, Memo to Jimmy Carter, "Minority Affairs Coordinator & Labor Coordinator," Carter Papers.

100. Barone, *Our Country*, 590.

101. *Presidential Campaign, 1976*, Vol. 1, Part I, "Formal Announcement, December 1974," 8; *Presidential Campaign, 1976*, Vol. 1, Part I, National Press Club Speech, February 1973, 34; *Presidential Campaign, 1976*, Vol. 1, Part I, National Education Association Question & Answer Session, June 1976, 251–252; *Presidential Campaign, 1976*, Vol. 1, Part I, "Advisory Session, Domestic/Education Policies, August 1976," 379.

102. *Presidential Campaign, 1976*, Vol. 1, Part I, "Business Week Interview—May 1976," 158.

103. Barone, *Our Country*, 552.

104. *Presidential Campaign, 1976*, Vol. 1, Part I, "National Issues Conference, November 1975," 81.

105. *Presidential Campaign, 1976*, Vol. 1, Part I, "Address to the American Legion, August 1976," 511.

106. *Presidential Campaign 1976*, Vol. 1, Part I, "Letter to National Abortion Rights League, February 1976," 92–93.

107. *Presidential Campaign, 1976*, Vol. 1, Part I, "Position Paper—Guns & Hunting," 594.

108. *Presidential Campaign, 1976*, Vol. 1, Part I, "Statement on the American Family, August 1976," 462.

109. The correlation within Georgia has been calculated in depth in Walton, *Native Son Presidential Candidate*. Walton charts the correlation of support over Carter's whole career, arguing that even in 1966, Carter was building a New South coalition. Walton also demonstrates the extraordinary vote-gathering ability of Carter among black voters in Georgia thanks to his close connection with the King family.

110. All of the remaining calculations in this chapter based on the 1976 and 1980 presidential elections involve taking U.S. Census data from the tables listed in note 38 above. In all eleven state volumes from 1970 and 1980, the table numbers correspond to those for Georgia. The listing of results by county has been taken from the various listings for each state for 1976 and 1980 in Scammon, McGillivary, and Cook, *America at the Polls*.

111. Shafer and Johnston, *End of Southern Exceptionalism*, 167–169.

Conclusion

Epigraph source: O'Connor, "The Barber," in O'Connor, *Complete Stories*, 21.

1. O'Connor, "Barber," 15–25.

2. These figures are taken from the national and state exit polls for the 2004 and 2008 presidential elections, which can be found at http://www.cnn.com/ELECTION/2004/pages/results/president/ and http://www.cnn.com/ELECTION/2008/results/polls/#val=USP00p1.

3. Feldman, "Prologue" and "Epilogue," in Feldman, *Before* Brown.

4. Schaller, *Whistling Past Dixie*.

5. Schaller, *Whistling Past Dixie*, 21–22.

6. Schaller, *Whistling Past Dixie*, 35–47.

7. Schaller, *Whistling Past Dixie*, 77, 86.

8. Schaller, "Why Obama Will Be the Latest Democrat to Lose in Dixie," *New York Times*, July 1, 2008.

9. All of the following statistics are compiled from figures found in several tables in two publications. Rather than repeatedly list all the tables used for each individual statistic, I note here that all the numbers for the years 1942 to 1957 are taken from *State and Local Government Special Studies*, 12–13, 21–34, 41; those for 1957 to 1977 are from the *1977 Census of Governments: Historical Statistics on Government Finances and Employment*, 31–36, 73–119, 148–149.

10. Arnall, *Shore Dimly Seen*, 32–34.

11. Arnall, *Shore Dimly Seen*, 87; Cobb, "Sunbelt South," 39.

12. Miroff, *Liberals' Moment*, 123.

13. See Lassiter, "Suburban Origins."

14. All the subsequent calculations for Georgia during this time are based on voting figures reported in the *Georgia Official and Statistical Register, 1979–80* and *1981–82* and volumes 16–23 (1985–1997) of Scammon, *America Votes*. The categorization of counties is based on the information presented in the *Twenty-first Census of the United States: 1990,* Vol. 1, *General Population Characteristics: Georgia,* and Vol. 2, *General Social and Economic Characteristics: Georgia.* Counties were separated into those containing more than 50,000 residents and those with fewer than 50,000. Of those with more than 50,000, counties that included one of Georgia's eight metropolitan centers were considered "urban," and those that were immediately contiguous to one of those centers were considered "suburban." All remaining counties were classified as small-town/rural, and were then subdivided further into those with a black population of less than 10 percent, between 10 percent and 30 percent, and more than 30 percent.

15. See, for example, the exit polls from the 2008 vote on Proposition 8 in California, where white voters supported gay marriage 51 to 49 percent but black voters voted against gay marriage by 70 to 30 percent: http://www.cnn.com/ELECTION/2008/results/polls/#val=CAI01p1.

16. O'Connor, "Barber," 21.

Bibliography

Primary Sources

Athens League of Women Voters. Official Papers. Richard Russell Library, University of Georgia, Athens.

Atlanta Constitution, Atlanta Journal-Constitution. 1956–1974.

Atlanta Daily World. 1952.

Bacote, Clarence. Interview. July 23, 1977. Box G-1. Georgia Government Documentation Project, Special Collections, Georgia State University, Atlanta.

Bell, Griffin. Interview. September 24, 1997. Georgia Political Heritage Collection, University of West Georgia, Carrollton.

Brown, Ben. Interview. October 15, 23, and 31, 1996. Box E-3. Georgia Government Documentation Project, Special Collections, Georgia State University, Atlanta.

Bullard, Helen. Interview. July 25, 1977. Box G-1. Georgia Government Documentation Project, Special Collections, Georgia State University, Atlanta.

Carter, Jimmy. Pre-Presidential Papers. Jimmy Carter Presidential Library, Atlanta.

1977 Census of Governments: Historical Statistics on Government Finances and Employment. Washington, D.C.: U.S. Department of Commerce/Bureau of the Census, 1978.

Clarke County McCarthy for President Collection. Richard Russell Library, University of Georgia, Athens.

Clifford, Clark. Political Papers. Harry S. Truman Library, Independence, Missouri.

CNN Exit Polls. 2004 and 2008 presidential election and Proposition 8 in California. http://www.cnn.com/ELECTION/2004/pages/results/president/; http://www.cnn.com/ELECTION/2008/results/polls/#val=USP00p1; http://www.cnn.com/ELECTION/2008/results/polls/#val=CAI01p1.

Congressional Record. Vol. 102. Washington, D.C.: Government Printing Office, 1956.

Cook, Rodney M. Papers. Richard Russell Library, University of Georgia, Athens.

Davis, James C. Papers. Manuscripts and Rare Books Library, Emory University, Atlanta.

DNC [Democratic National Committee] Papers. Lyndon B. Johnson Library, University of Texas, Austin.

Dodd, Donald B., ed. *Historical Statistics of the United States, 1790–1990.* Westport, Conn.: Greenwood Press, 1993.

Flanagan, Robert. Interview. November 10, 1988. Box E-1. Georgia Government Documentation Project, Special Collections, Georgia State University, Atlanta.

Geographic Areas Reference Manual. Washington, D.C.: U.S. Bureau of the Census, 1994.

Georgia Democratic Forum Records. Southern Labor Archives, Georgia State University, Atlanta.

Georgia Official and Statistical Register, 1951–52 through 1995–96. Atlanta: Georgia Department of Archives and History, 1952–1996.

Georgia Official Register, 1945–1950. Atlanta: Georgia Department of Archives and History, 1950.

Guthman, Edwin O., and C. Richard Allen, eds. *RFK: Collected Speeches.* New York: Viking Press, 1993.

Hamilton, Grace Towns. Papers. MSS 597. Kenan Research Center, Atlanta History Center, Atlanta.

Henderson, Jacob. Interview. June 8, 1989. Box E-1. Georgia Government Documentation Project, Special Collections, Georgia State University, Atlanta.

HOPE Collection. MSS 427. Kenan Research Center, Atlanta History Center, Atlanta.

Law, Wesley W. Interview. November 15 and 16, 1990. Box E-2. Georgia Government Documentation Project, Special Collections, Georgia State University, Atlanta.

Lokey, Hamilton, and Muriel Lokey. Interview. January 26, 1989. Box B-6. Georgia Government Documentation Project, Special Collections, Georgia State University.

Louisville-Courier Journal. 1970.

MacKay, James. Interview. March 18, 1986. Box B-6. Georgia Government Documentation Project, Special Collections, Georgia State University, Atlanta.

Millican, Everett G. Interview. July 30, 1977. Box G-1. Georgia Government Documentation Project, Special Collections, Georgia State University, Atlanta.

Morris, John B. Papers. Richard Russell Library, University of Georgia, Athens.

New York Times. 1963–1967, 2008.

New York Times Research Collection. Richard Russell Library, University of Georgia, Athens.

Pauley, Frances F. Interview. April 11, 1988. Box B-7. Georgia Government Documentation Project, Special Collections, Georgia State University, Atlanta.

———. Papers. Manuscripts and Rare Books Library, Emory University, Atlanta.

Pendergrast, Nan. Interview. June 24, 1992. Box J-1. Georgia Government Documentation Project, Special Collections, Georgia State University, Atlanta.

The Presidential Campaign, 1976. 3 vols. Washington, D.C.: U.S. Government Printing Office, 1976.

Randall, William, Sr., and William Randall Jr. Interview. February 4, 1989. Box E-2. Georgia Government Documentation Project, Special Collections, Georgia State University, Atlanta.

"Road to 270: Georgia." November 2008. http://www.fivethirtyeight.com/2008/11/road-to-270-georgia.html.

Russell, Richard B., Jr. Papers. Richard Russell Library, University of Georgia, Athens.

Scammon, Richard M. *America Votes.* Vols. 16–23. Washington, D.C.: Congressional Quarterly Press, 1985–1997.

Scammon, Richard M., and Alice V. McGillivray. *America at the Polls, 1920–1956: A*

Handbook of American Presidential Election Statistics. Washington, D.C.: Congressional Quarterly, 1994.

Scammon, Richard M., Alice V. McGillivray, and Rhodes Cook. *America at the Polls, 1960–2004: A Handbook of American Presidential Election Statistics*. Washington, D.C.: Congressional Quarterly Press, 2005.

State and Local Government Special Studies. Washington, D.C.: U.S. Department of Commerce/Bureau of the Census, 1959.

Talmadge, Herman E. Papers. Richard Russell Library, University of Georgia, Athens.

This Week with George Stephanopoulos. November 2, 2008. "The Roundtable: Decisive Moments." http://abcnews.go.com/video/playerIndex?id=6164718.

Thompson, Robert. Interview. June 5, 1989. Box E-2. Georgia Government Documentation Project, Special Collections, Georgia State University, Atlanta.

Time Magazine. 1971, 1976.

U.S. Census Bureau. *Sixteenth Census of the United States: 1940*, Vol. 2, *Characteristics of the Population, Part 2: Florida to Iowa*. Washington, D.C.: Bureau of the Census, 1943.

———. *Seventeenth Census of the United States: 1950*, Vol. 2, *Characteristics of the Population, Part 2: Georgia*. Washington, D.C.: Bureau of the Census, 1952.

———. *Eighteenth Census of the United States: 1960*, Vol. 2, *Characteristics of the Population, Part 2: Georgia*. Washington, D.C.: Bureau of the Census, 1962.

———. *Nineteenth Census of the United States: 1970*, Vol. 1, *Characteristics of the Population, Alabama, Arkansas, Florida, Georgia, Louisiana, Mississippi, North Carolina, South Carolina, Tennessee, Texas, and Virginia*. Washington, D.C.: Bureau of the Census, 1973.

———. *Twentieth Census of the United States: 1980*, Vol. 1, *General Population Characteristics, Alabama, Arkansas, Florida, Georgia, Louisiana, Mississippi, North Carolina, South Carolina, Tennessee, Texas, and Virginia*; Vol. 2, *General Social and Economic Characteristics, Alabama, Arkansas, Florida, Georgia, Louisiana, Mississippi, North Carolina, South Carolina, Tennessee, Texas, and Virginia*. Washington, D.C.: Bureau of the Census, 1983.

———. *Twenty-first Census of the United States: 1990*, Vol. 1, *General Population Characteristics—Georgia; General Social and Economic Characteristics—Georgia*. Washington, D.C.: Bureau of the Census, 1993.

Vandiver, S. Ernest. Papers. Richard Russell Library, University of Georgia, Athens.

Walden, Austin T. Papers. MSS 614. Kenan Research Center, Atlanta History Center, Atlanta.

Washington, James M., ed. *A Testament of Hope: The Essential Writings of Martin Luther King, Jr.* San Francisco: Harper Collins, 1991.

Weltner, Charles. Interview. July 9 and 17, 1986. Box B-9. Georgia Government Documentation Project, Special Collections, Georgia State University, Atlanta.

———. Interview. May 16, 1991. Georgia Political Heritage Collection, West Georgia University, Carrollton.

White House Central Files. Lyndon B. Johnson Library, University of Texas, Austin.

White House Name Files. Lyndon B. Johnson Library, University of Texas, Austin.

White House Tapes, 1964–1966. Lyndon B. Johnson Library, University of Texas, Austin.

Williams, Melba R. Papers. Richard Russell Library, University of Georgia, Athens.

Williams, Osgood. Interview. May 12, 1988. Box B-9. Georgia Government Documentation Project, Special Collections, Georgia State University, Atlanta.

Secondary Sources

Anderson, William. *The Wild Man from Sugar Creek: The Political Career of Eugene Talmadge*. Baton Rouge: Louisiana State University, 1975.

Arnall, Ellis G. *The Shore Dimly Seen*. Philadelphia: Lippincott Press, 1946.

Badger, Tony. "Southerners Who Refused to Sign the Southern Manifesto." *Historical Journal* 42, no. 2 (1999).

Barone, Michael. *Our Country: The Shaping of America from Roosevelt to Reagan*. New York: MacMillan Press, 1990.

Bartley, Numan V. *The Rise of Massive Resistance: Race and Politics in the South during the 1950s*. Baton Rouge: Louisiana State University Press, 1969.

———. *From Thurmond to Wallace: Political Tendencies in Georgia, 1948–1968*. Baltimore: Johns Hopkins University Press, 1970.

———. "Moderation in Maddox Country?" *Georgia Historical Quarterly* 58, no. 3 (1974).

———. *The Creation of Modern Georgia*. Athens: University of Georgia Press, 1990.

———. *The New South, 1945–1980*. Baton Rouge: Louisiana State University Press, 1995.

Bartley, Numan V., and Hugh D. Graham. *Southern Politics and the Second Reconstruction*. London: Oxford University Press, 1975.

Bass, Jack, and Walter DeVries. *The Transformation of Southern Politics: Social Change and Political Consequence since 1945*. New York: Basic Books, 1976.

Berard, Stanley P. *Southern Democrats in the House of Representatives*. Norman: University of Oklahoma Press, 2001.

Bernd, Joseph L. "A Study of Primary Elections in Georgia, 1946–1954." Ph.D. diss., Duke University, 1957.

Black, Earl. *Southern Governors and Civil Rights*. Cambridge, Mass.: Harvard University Press, 1976.

———. "The Newest Southern Politics." *Journal of Politics* 60, no. 3 (1998).

Black, Earl, and Merle Black. *The Rise of Southern Republicans*. Cambridge, Mass.: Belknap Press, 2002.

Bourne, Peter G. *Jimmy Carter: A Comprehensive Biography from Plains to Post-Presidency*. New York: Scribner, 1997.

Brady, Tom P. *Black Monday*. Winona, Miss.: Association of Citizens' Councils, 1954.

Brooks, Jennifer E. *Defining the Peace: World War II Veterans, Race, and the Remaking of Southern Political Tradition*. Chapel Hill: University of North Carolina Press, 2004.

Burner, David. *The Politics of Provincialism: The Democratic Party in Transition, 1918–1932*. New York: Knopf, 1968.

Calhoun, John H. "Significant Aspects of some Negro Leaders' Contributions to the Progress of Atlanta, Georgia." MBA thesis, Atlanta University, 1968.

Califano, Joseph, Jr. *The Triumph and Tragedy of Lyndon Johnson*. New York: Simon and Schuster, 1991.

Carter, Dan T. *From George Wallace to Newt Gingrich: Race and the Conservative Counter-Revolution*. Baton Rouge: Louisiana State University Press, 1995.

——. *The Politics of Rage: George Wallace, the Origins of the New Conservatism and the Transformation of American Politics*. New York: Simon and Schuster, 1995.

Chappell, David L. *Inside Agitators: White Southerners in the Civil Rights Movement*. Baltimore: Johns Hopkins University Press, 1994.

——. "The Lost Decade of Civil Rights." *Historically Speaking* 10, no. 2 (2009).

Cobb, James C. *The Selling of the South: The Southern Crusade for Industrial Development 1930–1980*. Baton Rouge: Louisiana State University Press, 1982.

——. "The Sunbelt South: Industrialization in Regional, National and International Perspective." In *Searching for the Sunbelt: Historical Perspectives on a Region*, ed. Raymond A. Mohl. Knoxville: University of Tennessee Press, 1990.

Cook, James F. "Carl Sanders and the Politics of the Future." In *Georgia Governors in an Age of Change: From Ellis Arnall to George Busbee*, ed. Harold P. Henderson and Gary L. Roberts. Athens: University of Georgia Press, 1988.

——. *Carl Sanders: Spokesman of the New South*. Macon, Ga.: Mercer University Press, 1994.

Cose, Ellis. *Colorblind: Seeing Beyond Race in a Race-Obsessed World*. New York: Harper Collins, 1997.

Cox, George H. "In His Own Words: Ellis Arnall On Political Reform." Paper presented at the Georgia Political Science Association Conference, Savannah, Georgia, 2005. Personal copy in author's possession.

Daniel, Pete. *Breaking the Land: The Transformation of Cotton, Tobacco and Rice Cultures since 1880*. Chicago: University of Illinois Press, 1984.

——. *Lost Revolutions: The South in the 1950s*. Chapel Hill: University of North Carolina Press, 2000.

Dubay, Robert W. "Marvin Griffin and the Politics of the Stump." In *Georgia Governors in an Age of Change: From Ellis Arnall to George Busbee*, ed. Harold P. Henderson and Gary L. Roberts. Athens: University of Georgia Press, 1988.

Eastland, Terry. *Ending Affirmative Action: The Case for Colorblind Justice*. New York: Basic Books, 1997.

Edsall, Thomas, and Mary Edsall. *Chain Reaction: The Impact of Race, Rights and Taxes on American Politics*. New York: Norton Press, 1991.

Feldman, Glenn, ed. *Before Brown: Civil Rights and White Backlash in the Modern South*. Tuscaloosa: University of Alabama Press, 2004.

Fite, Gilbert C. *Cotton Fields No More*. Lexington: University of Kentucky Press, 1984.

Frederickson, Kari. *The Dixiecrat Revolt and the End of the Solid South, 1932–1968*. Chapel Hill: University of North Carolina Press, 2001.

Galphin, Bruce. *The Riddle of Lester Maddox*. Atlanta: Camelot, 1968.

"Georgia House Dispute." *Congressional Quarterly* 24, no. 2 (1966).

Grose, Christian R., and Antoine Yoshinaka. "Ideological Hedging in Uncertain Times: Maverick Representation and Voter Enfranchisement." Paper presented at the Midwest Political Science Association, Chicago, 2006. Personal copy in author's possession.

Halberstam, David. *The Fifties*. New York: Ballantine Books, 1993.

Hathorn, Billy B. "The Frustration of Opportunity: Georgia Republicans and the Election of 1966." *Atlanta History* 31, no. 4 (1987–1988).

Henderson, Harold P. "The 1966 Gubernatorial Election in Georgia." Ph.D. diss., University of Southern Mississippi, 1982.

———. *The Politics of Change in Georgia: A Political Biography of Ellis Arnall*. Athens: University of Georgia Press, 1991.

———. *Ernest Vandiver: Governor of Georgia*. Athens: University of Georgia Press, 2000.

Hood, M. V., III, Quentin Kidd, and Irwin L. Morris. "Of Byrd and Bumpers: Using Democratic Senators to Track Political Change in the South, 1960–1995." *American Journal of Political Science* 43, no. 2 (1999).

———. "The Re-Introduction of the *Elephas Maximus* into the Southern United States: The Rise of Republican State Parties, 1960–2000." *American Politics Research* 32, no. 1 (2004).

Jarding, Steve, and Dave "Mudcat" Sanders. *Foxes in the Henhouse: How the Republicans Stole the South and the Heartland and What the Democrats Must Do to Run 'Em Out*. New York: Simon and Schuster, 2006.

Jones, Stanley S. "Atlanta Politics and the Sit-In Movement, 1960–61." B.A. honors thesis, Harvard University, 1971.

Key, Valdimer O., Jr. *Southern Politics in State and Nation*. Knoxville: University of Tennessee Press, 1949.

Kirby, Jack T. "Black and White in the Rural South, 1919–1954." *Agricultural History* 58, no. 3 (1984).

———. *Rural Worlds Lost*. Baton Rouge: Louisiana State University Press, 1987.

Kousser, J. Morgan. *The Shaping of Southern Politics: Suffrage Restriction and the Establishment of the One-Party South, 1880–1910*. New Haven, Conn.: Yale University Press, 1974.

———. *Colorblind Injustice: Minority Voting Rights and the Undoing of the Second Reconstruction*. Chapel Hill: University of North Carolina Press, 1999.

Kruse, Kevin M. *White Flight: Atlanta and the Making of Modern Conservatism*. Princeton, N.J.: Princeton University Press, 2005.

Kuryla, Peter A. "The Integration of the American Mind: Intellectuals and the Creation of the Civil Rights Movement, 1944–1983." Ph.D. diss., Vanderbilt University, 2006.

Kytle, Calvin, and James MacKay. *Who Runs Georgia?* 2nd ed. Athens: University of Georgia Press, 1998.

Lamis, Alexander P. *The Two-Party South*. New York: Oxford University Press, 1984.

LaPalombara, Joseph. *Politics within Nations*. London: Prentice-Hall Books, 1974.

Lasky, Victor. *Jimmy Carter: The Man & the Myth*. New York: Marek Books, 1979.

Lassiter, Matthew D. "The Suburban Origins of 'Color-Blind' Conservatism: Middle-Class Consciousness in the Charlotte Busing Crisis." *Journal of Urban History* 30, no. 4 (2004).

———. *The Silent Majority: Suburban Politics in the Sunbelt South*. Princeton, N.J.: Princeton University Press, 2006.

Loewen, James. *Sundown Towns: A Hidden Dimension of American Racism*. New York: New Press/W. W. Norton, 2005.

Logue, Cal M., and Howard Dorgan, eds. *The Oratory of Southern Demagogues*. Baton Rouge: Louisiana State University Press, 1981.

Lokey, Hamilton. *The Low Key Life of Ham Lokey*. Athens: Agee Publishers, 1991.

Luebke, Paul. *Tar Heel Politics 2000*. Chapel Hill: University of North Carolina Press, 1998.

Main, Eleanor C., and Gerard S. Gryski. "George Busbee and the Politics of Consensus." In *Georgia Governors in an Age of Change: From Ellis Arnall to George Busbee*, ed. Harold P. Henderson and Gary L. Roberts. Athens: University of Georgia Press, 1988.

Mann, Robert. *The Walls of Jericho: Lyndon Johnson, Hubert Humphrey, Richard Russell and the Struggle for Civil Rights*. New York: Harcourt Press, 1996.

Martin, Harold. *William Berry Hartsfield: Mayor of Atlanta*. Athens: University of Georgia Press, 1978.

Martin, John Frederick. *Civil Rights and the Crisis of Liberalism: The Democratic Party, 1945–1976*. Boulder, Colo.: Westview Press, 1979.

Mertz, Paul. "Mind Changing Time All Over Georgia: HOPE, Inc. and School Desegregation, 1958–1961." *Georgia Historical Quarterly* 77, no. 1 (1993).

Miller, Warren. "Generational Changes and Party Identification." *Political Behavior* 14, no. 3 (1992).

Miroff, Bruce. *The Liberals' Moment: The McGovern Insurgency and the Identity Crisis of the Democratic Party*. Lawrence: University Press of Kansas, 2007.

Morris, Kenneth E. *Jimmy Carter: American Moralist*. Athens: University of Georgia Press, 1996.

Nasstrom, Kathryn L. *Everybody's Grandmother and Nobody's Fool: Frances Freeborn Pauley and the Struggle for Social Justice*. Ithaca, N.Y.: Cornell University Press, 2000.

Niven, David. *The Politics of Injustice: The Kennedys, the Freedom Rides and the Electoral Consequences of a Moral Compromise*. Knoxville: University of Tennessee Press, 2003.

Novotny, Patrick. *This Georgia Rising: Education, Civil Rights and the Politics of Change in Georgia in the 1940s*. Macon, Ga.: Mercer University Press, 2007.

O'Brien, Thomas V. "Georgia's Response to *Brown v. Board of Education*: The Rise & Fall of Massive Resistance, 1949–1961." Ph.D. diss., Emory University, 1992.

O'Connor, Flannery. "The Barber." In *Flannery O'Connor, The Complete Stories*. New York: Noonday Press, 1995.

Pajari, R. N. "Herman Talmadge and the Politics of Power." In *Georgia Governors in an Age of Change: From Ellis Arnall to George Busbee*, ed. Harold P. Henderson and Gary L. Roberts. Athens: University of Georgia Press, 1988.

Parmet, Herbert S. *The Democrats: The Years after FDR*. New York: Macmillan, 1975.

Patterson, James T. *Congressional Conservatism and the New Deal: The Growth of the Conservative Coalition, 1933–1939*. Lexington: University of Kentucky Press, 1967.

Phillips, Kevin. *The Emerging Republican Majority*. New Rochelle, N.Y.: Arlington House, 1969.

Radosh, Ronald. *Divided They Fell: The Demise of the Democratic Party, 1964–1996*. New York: Free Press, 1996.

Rae, Nicol C. *Southern Democrats*. New York: Oxford University Press, 1994.

Rutland, Robert. *The Democrats: From Jefferson to Clinton*. Columbia: University of Missouri Press, 1995.

Sanders, Randy M. *Mighty Peculiar Elections: The New South Gubernatorial Campaigns of 1970 and the Changing Politics of Race*. Gainesville: University Press of Florida, 2002.

Scammon, Richard, and Ben Wattenberg. *The Real Majority*. New York: Coward-Mc-Cann, 1970.

Schaller, Thomas F. *Whistling Past Dixie: How Democrats Can Win without the South*. New York: Simon and Schuster, 2006.

Schulman, Bruce J. *From Cotton Belt to Sunbelt: Federal Policy, Economic Development and the Transformation of the South, 1938–1950*. New York: Oxford University Press, 1991.

Shafer, Byron, and Richard Johnston. *The End of Southern Exceptionalism: Class, Race and Partisan Change in the Postwar South*. Princeton, N.J.: Princeton University Press, 2006.

Sherrill, Robert. *Gothic Politics in the Deep South*. New York: Ballantine Books, 1968.

Short, Bob. *Everything Is Pickrick: The Life of Lester Maddox*. Macon, Ga.: Mercer University Press, 1999.

Simpson, William M. "The Loyalist Democrats of Mississippi: Challenge to a White Majority, 1965–1972." Ph.D. diss., Mississippi State University, 1974.

Sokol, Jason. *There Goes My Everything: White Southerners in the Age of Civil Rights*. New York: Knopf, 2006.

Spritzer, Lorraine N. *The Belle of Ashby Street: Helen Douglas Mankin and Georgia Politics*. Athens: University of Georgia Press, 1982.

Spritzer, Lorraine N., and Jean B. Bergmark. *Grace Towns Hamilton and the Politics of Southern Change*. Athens: University of Georgia Press, 1997.

Sullivan, Patricia L. *Days of Hope: Race and Democracy in the New Deal Era*. Chapel Hill: University of North Carolina Press, 1996.

Sylvia, Ray D. "Presidential Decision Making in the Civil Rights Era." *Presidential Studies Quarterly* 25, no. 3 (1995).

Todd, Chuck, and Sheldon Gawiser. *How Barack Obama Won: A State-by-State Guide to the Historic 2008 Presidential Election*. New York: Vintage Books, 2009.

Tuck, Stephen G. N. *Beyond Atlanta: The Struggle for Racial Equality in Georgia, 1940–1980*. Athens: University of Georgia Press, 2001.

Walton, Hanes. *The Native Son Presidential Candidate: The Carter Vote in Georgia*. New York: Praeger Books, 1992.

Wannamaker, George N. "Charles Longstreet Weltner: A Public Life." Ph.D. diss., Georgia State University, 1999.

Wheeler, Leslie. *Jimmy Who?* New York: Barron's Woodbury, 1976.

Williamson, Joel. *The Rage for Order: Black/White Relations in the American South since Emancipation*. New York: Oxford University Press, 1986.

Witcover, Jules. *Party of the People: A History of the Democrats*. New York: Random House, 2003.

Wright, Gavin. *Old South, New South*. New York: Basic Books, 1986.

Index